REGARDING WARHOL

MARK ROSENTHAL

MARLA PRATHER

IAN ALTEVEER

REBECCA LOWERY

THE METROPOLITAN MUSEUM OF ART, NEW YORK

Distributed by Yale University Press, New Haven

REGARDING
WARHOL

SIXTY
ARTISTS

FIFTY
YEARS

This catalogue is published in conjunction with "Regarding Warhol: Sixty Artists, Fifty Years" on view at The Metropolitan Museum of Art, New York, from September 18 through December 31, 2012, and at The Andy Warhol Museum, Pittsburgh, from February 2 through April 28, 2013.

The exhibition is made possible by

Morgan Stanley

Additional support is provided by the Gail and Parker Gilbert Fund and The Daniel and Estrellita Brodsky Foundation.

The exhibition is supported by an indemnity from the Federal Council on the Arts and the Humanities.

This publication is made possible in part by the Mary and Louis S. Myers Foundation Endowment Fund.

PUBLISHED BY THE METROPOLITAN MUSEUM OF ART, NEW YORK
Mark Polizzotti, Publisher and Editor in Chief
Gwen Roginsky, Associate Publisher and General Manager of Publications
Peter Antony, Chief Production Manager
Michael Sittenfeld, Managing Editor
Robert Weisberg, Assistant Managing Editor

Edited by Elisa Urbanelli
Designed by Roy Brooks, Fold Four, Inc.
Production by Jennifer Van Dalsen
Bibliography by Penny Jones
Image Acquisitions by Jane S. Tai

Typeset in CorporateEBQ and Solex
Printed on Magno Satin and Edixion Offset
Separations by Professional Graphics, Inc., Rockford, Illinois
Printed and bound by Die Keure, Brugge, Belgium

Front cover: Andy Warhol, *Self-Portrait*, 1967 (cat. 32, detail)

Back cover: Andy Warhol, *Self-Portrait*, 1967 (cat. 33, detail)

Page 8: Andy Warhol, *Mona Lisa*, 1963 (cat. 11, detail)

Photograph credits appear on p. 304.

The Metropolitan Museum of Art
1000 Fifth Avenue
New York, New York 10028
metmuseum.org

Distributed by
Yale University Press, New Haven
yalebooks.com/art

Cataloging-in-Publication Data is available from the Library of Congress.
ISBN 978-1-58839-469-9 (hc: The Metropolitan Museum of Art)
ISBN 978-1-58839-470-5 (pbk: The Metropolitan Museum of Art)
ISBN 978-0-300-18498-3 (hc: Yale University Press)

CONTENTS

"They always say time changes things, but you actually have to change them yourself." So said Andy Warhol, whose transformative contributions to the worlds of art and media of the twentieth century and beyond are among the cultural milestones of the modern era. From the perspective of 2012, the impact of Warhol's artistic enterprise and distinctive persona on the global stage seems as relevant today as in the heyday of Pop's reign. To relate this expansive story, one not previously addressed on this scale, the curators of the exhibition "Regarding Warhol: Sixty Artists, Fifty Years" have assembled approximately 150 works across an array of media, nearly a third of which are by Warhol and the rest by a selection of leading artists. Among the artists featured in this exhibition and its even more inclusive accompanying publication are those who pay overt tribute to Warhol in their singular way, as well as those who have absorbed, transformed, or challenged his example in a more subtle fashion. The fundamental goal is to present the diversity of response to and continuing debate about the life and work of Andy Warhol.

Our special thanks go to independent curator Mark Rosenthal, who conceived this extraordinary exhibition and who has served admirably as its guest curator. He has worked in close collaboration with Met colleagues in the Department of Modern and Contemporary Art, including Marla Prather, curator, Ian Alteveer, assistant curator, and Rebecca Lowery, research assistant. Together they have created a fresh and richly textured presentation to demonstrate the broad phenomenon of the "Warhol effect." In addition to identifying the finest signature works by Warhol and relevant examples by other artists, the organizers have each contributed in essential and provocative ways to this catalogue. In his key essay, "Dialogues with Warhol," Mark Rosenthal addresses the myriad ways in which artists across several generations have interacted with Warhol. Organized, as in our galleries, into five thematic sections, the essay explores how works of art in the show speak to each other and how artists have both worked in parallel modes with Warhol's art and developed it in dynamic new directions. Marla Prather has gathered previously published commentaries on Warhol by artists in the exhibition and conducted a number of new interviews, exploring Warhol's enduring impact by directly engaging with artists represented in our show. Hardly an aspect of life has been untouched by Warhol, and the reach of his influence is too vast to represent every artist who has embraced, appropriated, or parodied his work on some level. To amplify the works in the show, Ian Alteveer has assembled a fascinating archive of the innovative and often humorous responses of contemporary artists to Warhol's legacy. Rebecca Lowery's lively timeline is less a conventional chronology than a tribute to Warhol's cultural omnipresence from 1961 to the present day. The constant challenge was to limit the seemingly endless occurrences of Warholiana within the confines of the catalogue.

Throughout the organizing process and preparation of the catalogue, the curators have relied deeply on contact with the artists in the show, as well as their studio and gallery representatives. We are sincerely indebted to those artists who offered their personal recollections and professional observations for the project. We would also like to express gratitude to our lenders, including both public institutions and private collectors in Europe and the United States, who have entrusted us with the care of their works of art. At the Met we owe a very special thanks to Eric Shiner for his wise counsel, for the support of his staff, and for the twenty-three critically important works by Warhol lent to the show.

Finally, in New York we are grateful to Morgan Stanley for its generous support of the exhibition. We also thank the Gail and Parker Gilbert Fund and The Daniel and Estrellita Brodsky Foundation. For making this catalogue possible, we owe our thanks to the Mary and Louis S. Myers Foundation Endowment Fund. Lastly, we wish to acknowledge the Federal Council on the Arts and the Humanities for granting an indemnity for this project.

Thomas P. Campbell
Director, The Metropolitan Museum of Art

Eric C. Shiner
Director, The Andy Warhol Museum

LENDERS TO THE EXHIBITION

PUBLIC COLLECTIONS

Art Gallery of Ontario, Toronto
The Art Institute of Chicago
The Baltimore Museum of Art
Museum Boijmans Van Beuningen, Rotterdam
Carnegie Museum of Art, Pittsburgh
Corcoran Gallery of Art, Washington, D.C.
Des Moines Art Center
Detroit Institute of Arts
Solomon R. Guggenheim Museum, New York
Henry Art Gallery, University of Washington, Seattle
Hirshhorn Museum and Sculpture Garden,
    Washington, D.C.
The Hood Museum of Art, Dartmouth College,
    Hanover, New Hampshire
The Menil Collection, Houston
The Metropolitan Museum of Art, New York
Museum of Contemporary Art, Chicago
Museum of Contemporary Art, San Diego
The Museum of Modern Art, New York
Nasher Sculpture Center, Dallas
National Gallery of Art, Washington, D.C.
The Nelson-Atkins Museum of Art, Kansas City
Philadelphia Museum of Art
San Francisco Museum of Modern Art
University of California, Berkeley Art Museum
    & Pacific Film Archive
Wadsworth Atheneum Museum of Art, Hartford
The Andy Warhol Museum, Pittsburgh
Whitney Museum of American Art, New York

FOUNDATIONS AND GALLERIES

The Richard Avedon Foundation
Marianne Boesky Gallery
The Broad Art Foundation
Paula Cooper Gallery
FLAG Art Foundation
Gagosian Gallery
Marian Goodman Gallery
Hauser & Wirth
The Hermes Trust
The Peter Hujar Archive
Paul Kasmin Gallery
Galerie Lelong
Galería Javier López
Luhring Augustine
The Robert Mapplethorpe Foundation
Matthew Marks Gallery

Metro Pictures
Galleria Franco Noero
Andrea Rosen Gallery
Skarstedt Gallery
Timothy Taylor Gallery
Lucien Terras, Inc.

PRIVATE COLLECTIONS

Douglas B. Andrews
Polly Apfelbaum
John Baldessari
Matthew Barney
Marianne Boesky and Liam Culman
Mary Boone
Jeffrey and Susan Brotman
The Hon. Ann and Donald Brown
Constance R. Caplan
George and Vivian Dean
Mandy and Cliff Einstein
Avram Finkelstein
The Doris and Donald Fisher Collection
Glenn and Amanda Fuhrman
Robert Gober
Nan Goldin
Hans Haacke
Audrey Irmas
Alfredo Jaar
Marc Jacobs
Deborah Kass
Rachel and Jean-Pierre Lehmann
Mugrabi Collection
Francesco Pellizzi
David and Marlene Persky
Richard Prince
Rubell Family Collection
Beth Rudin de Woody
Cindy Sherman
Gilbert and Lila Silverman
Nancy and Stanley Singer
Ströher Collection
Wolfgang Tillmans
Ryan Trecartin
Barbara Walters
Ealan and Melinda Wingate
Angela Westwater
Christopher Wool
Neda Young
David and Monica Zwirner

And those who wish to remain anonymous

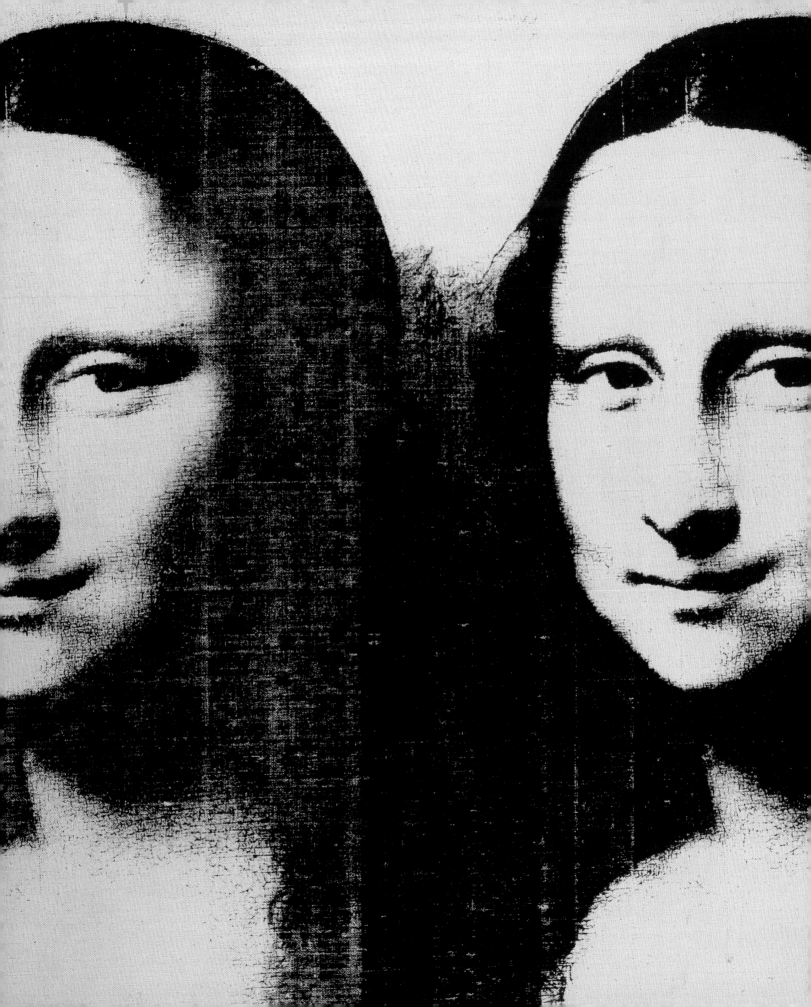

REGARDING WARHOL

DIALOGU
WITH
WARHO

From almost the start of his career, Andy Warhol cast a very broad shadow over the art world, one that covers a period of about fifty years and has had a sweeping effect on a group of far more than that number of artists from around the globe.

Among his influential pursuits, he made art the province of all manner of prosaic themes and sources; he put photography, appropriation, and serial composition at the center of his methodology; and he gave permission to do virtually anything in the name of art. By his example, the premises and practices of art-making were dramatically transformed.

Though artists were relatively quick to take note of Warhol, writers were slower to respond. Certain historians were exceptions, however, as in a 1970 monograph in which the German critic Rainer Crone declared, "He is the most important living artist in North America . . . yet almost no critical work on him [has] recognized this fact."[1] Henry Geldzahler, a curator at The Metropolitan Museum of Art and a close friend of Warhol's, predicted in 1973, "Andy's going to feed a lot of artists for a long time."[2] The American artist Jason Rhoades observed that Warhol, with others, "cut down trees and cleared territory . . . we're all living off that."[3] In other words, Warhol's personal intentions were not necessarily as significant as the liberated field left by his work. Even a political dimension was intuited among some Europeans. For example, the German painter Gerhard Richter, speaking from the Marxist perspective that typified the Continental scene, described Warhol's art as "a symptom of a cultural situation."[4]

Warhol can be seen as a crucial transitional figure in the cultural situation of the 1950s and 1960s. Though he arrived in New York poor, by the end of the 1950s he had become prosperous as an illustrator for high-end advertisers. Starting out as a wannabe in bohemia, Warhol had, unlike most of the crowd that he hoped to join, participated in the decade's economic boom. In this regard, his embrace of "business art"

can be seen as a natural development; moreover, for subsequent artists of the 1980s and after, money was rarely a divisive issue at all. Warhol's personal life, too, held an interestingly contradictory position. In a frequently repeated, if apocryphal, story, Warhol asked his friend Emile de Antonio in 1960 why Jasper Johns and Robert Rauschenberg would not accept him. De Antonio, who was a friend of the pair, said that they found Warhol "too swish."[5] This anecdote reveals much about the transition from one decade, when gay artists, including Johns and Rauschenberg, remained in the closet, to the next, when some came out. Warhol played a central role in this social shift, which was reflected in his work and that of many other artists.

Again, an anecdote told by De Antonio is instructive, specifically with regard to the increasing significance of recognizable subject matter from the 1960s forward. On visiting Warhol's studio in early 1962, De Antonio found Warhol in a quandary. Warhol showed him two paintings of Coca-Cola bottles he had just completed — one, dated 1961 (p. 12), with a loosely painted, arguably subjective or interpretive handling of the object, and the other, made at the start of 1962 (p. 12), rendered in a completely hard-edged, descriptive, even declarative fashion. Warhol wanted De Antonio to pick the better one. The very fact that Warhol was painting this subject could be laid at the feet of Johns and Rauschenberg, for their embrace of common objects proved to be a major turning point from the dominant aesthetics of abstraction that had been practiced by the likes of Jackson Pollock and Barnett Newman, members of the New York School. With their willful turn to art made from consumerist logos and everyday icons, including the American flag by Johns, starting in 1954, and the Coca-Cola bottle by Rauschenberg, in 1958, these

considered a synthesis of high and low. More to the point, high-art ideals were unequivocally jettisoned. Nevertheless, Warhol, along with others, continued the triumphal procession of American artists invading and supplanting European modernism, forging a path that was littered with banal signposts of American life — from Johns's flags to Warhol's soup cans.

What we might call the Warhol phenomenon may be best understood by reviewing a series of visual "dialogues" between his work and that of other notable artists who embraced, elaborated, mined, or wrestled with his approach. Influence, per se, is at times a given, but it is of far less interest in these juxtapositions than the sweeping perception of events and careers unfolding. In effect, Warhol's protean art would become a veritable mainstream from which many offshoots and points of view would be spawned and significant careers forged.

DAILY NEWS: FROM BANALITY TO DISASTER

Warhol found his subject matter in the most casual of ways — perusing daily newspapers and seeking suggestions from friends. His subjects were effectively "found objects" depicted as if without premeditation or predisposition. Indeed, it can be argued that John Cage, even compared to Johns and Rauschenberg, had the most pivotal and overriding effect on the young Warhol.[8] Chance was the principal strategic vehicle for both individuals, and its bounty was held in reverential regard.

In Cage's revolutionary *4'33"* of 1952, a pianist sat at his instrument with head bowed for four minutes and thirty-three seconds, and the audience was compelled to realize that the chance sounds and sights that occurred in the duration of the performance consti-tuted the work of art. This work dismissed art that was involved in traditional notions of music and beauty, as well as of compositional structure, replacing all that with a Zen demonstration of simply living attentively in the moment and celebrating its pleasures. Warhol's most overt bow to Cage could be seen in his 1964 film *Empire* (p. 26), wherein the viewer is shown the facade of the Empire State Building from a stationary point of

artists replaced the grandiloquence of New York School painters' personal expressiveness. But their art still evinced the previous generation's love of an exquisite or autograph brushstroke. Warhol's 1961 rendering of the Coke bottle reflected his roots in his predecessors' subject matter and paint handling, whereas the later depiction represented a dramatic new turn in the handling of such a theme. Without hesitation, De Antonio recommended that Warhol destroy the first, saying the second "is remarkable — it's our society, it's who we are, it's absolutely beautiful and naked."[6] Warhol took De Antonio's advice, sealing his future development; in the process he could also be said to have buried the 1950s romantic soul.

An extended discourse on so-called high- and low-art expressions is evident in Warhol's art and that of the other artists discussed here. Stuart Klawans very insightfully said that Warhol "turned art into a Brillo Box," not vice versa.[7] In other words, only to the extent that elevated aspirations were then embedded in the vernacular of everyday life might Warhol's art be view for an unmediated period of eight hours and five minutes. A building recorded in real time (though shown at a slower speed) provides the form and content of the work of art, with nothing extraneous to divert attention.[9] Like Cage, Warhol posits an unstructured world that is simply a field of experience. To grasp that Warhol, according to all accounts, tape-recorded virtually every minute of his life[10] is to be confronted with his remarkably Cage-like appreciation of unedited and chance moments. Compared to Rauschenberg, who famously explained that he worked in the gap between art and life,[11] Warhol altogether eliminated the gap.

Cage's approach had remarkably varied and long-lived ramifications,[12] including for Warhol the embrace of haphazard and prosaic subject matter, regardless of how embarrassing such material might appear in the context of art-historical tradition; witness, for example, *Dr. Scholl's Corns*, 1961 (p. 15). Warhol was, like Cage, unashamedly accepting of banal events. Put another way, events experienced in a period of time and appearances perceived on a pictorial surface were quite sufficient to be the most fundamental material of art; meanwhile, the traditional aesthetic verities held no interest. Instead, the subjects of life that could be made into art were to be glimpsed in newspapers and magazines.

To record this sort of material was to rely on the truths found in manifestations that have a time-sensitive dimension. The very essence of a daily newspaper is that it is a report of real-time, recent events, the pages of each edition in aggregate a sequence of blank slates on which the previous day's notable moments are emblazoned. Warhol took enormous pleasure in exploiting this prosaic material—newspaper headlines, photographs, and advertisements—for art purposes.[13] In this regard, he described, in 1963, his delight in the sheer prurient interest of Jean Genet's writing and the realization that "style [read 'art'] isn't really important."[14] His experience reading Genet was one more confirmation of the wisdom gained by comparing the two paintings of Coke bottles: style should be minimized and subject matter emphasized. By basing many of his early paintings on images taken from popular media, Warhol, like many of his contemporaries, dismissed traditional artistic values, with their attendant appearances and metaphors, as well as the province of high-art practice. Instead, he became a student of passing events—a chronicler of the commonplace

and banal—and of the vehicle by which such topics were recorded, the daily newspaper.

Warhol favored the tawdry New York tabloids and the *National Enquirer*, not the *New York Times*, as sources. In this choice, too, we have a blunt expression of that high/low distinction, here between the decorous *Times*, the "newspaper of record," and the rough-and-tumble *Daily News*, with its emphasis on sensationalism and celebrity. Warhol made use of images and advertisements that sold papers in working-class neighborhoods, seeing potential in the unremarkable and the momentarily interesting, as in, for example, *Dr. Scholl's Corns*. He termed his subject matter "leftovers," things thought to be "no good."[15] If he is a painter of history, as some have claimed,[16] Warhol's "histories" are reclamation projects taken from waste bins filled with discarded newspapers.

Warhol's interest in borrowed imagery, rather than personal expression, and his dispassionate painting style leave unanswered the great questions in Warhol studies: how exactly did the artist feel, and what did he think, about his subject matter? Many writers want to discount any possibility of Warhol having deeply considered feelings on this issue,[17] while some take the opposing position.[18] To this point, Warhol surely learned a key lesson from Johns and his series of American flag paintings, that is, to leave all possibilities open for interpretation. Focus on the surface appearance and avoid any suggestion of an interior life of the artist. But Warhol's choice of the *Daily News* rather than the *New York Times*, and his taste for Genet rather than, say, Hart Crane, a favorite of Johns, start to hint at his intentions.

Warhol's paintings, such as *A Boy for Meg [2]*, 1962 (p. 14), and *Ambulance Disaster*, 1963–64 (p. 16), are rooted firmly in the banality and calamity that are simultaneously endemic to American life. But whereas his deadpan presentations convey an apolitical outlook, many of the works that engage in a pictorial dialogue with Warhol evince an altogether politicized point of view. Recognizing that the newspaper is a fundamental vehicle for the vision of a specific society, other artists, too, made use of it. In *Bavarian*, 1965 (p. 17), Sigmar Polke blurred the headlines in order to leave aside anecdotal matters and emphasize national and regional identity, as indicated by the word *Bavarian* and all that it might signify within and beyond Germany. Working at a time when there were two Germanys and

Sinatra AND HIS 'Rat Pack'

TODAY: The Leader Himself (Cont'd)

WEATHER

Fog tonight. in the 60s. Tomorrow: cloudy and warm, chance of showers.

New York Post

NEW YORK, FRIDAY, NOVEMBER 3, 1961   10 Cents

LATEST STOCK PRICES
Pages 85-88

See Page 3

A BOY FOR MEG

an overwrought political environment in the wake of the recent Nazi past, Polke emerged from a hothouse atmosphere in which any indication at all of national identity was a deliberately provocative act. By simply naming a newspaper, Polke skillfully called attention to what was virtually unspeakable. In contrast, Sarah Lucas immersed the viewer in extensive and even comic details of an English tabloid vision in *Hunk of the Year*, 1990–92 (p. 17), reconstructing the vulgarity, hypersexuality, and exploitative nature of British newspapers and the interests of their readerships. With Warhol's use of the newspaper, national character, rather than the modernist vision of universality, returned to the body of concerns of contemporary artists.

A newspaper is simply one form of the media, and magazines are another. For one of her most important early works, Vija Celmins chose an event of great social import in America, the Watts riots of 1965 in Los Angeles, where she was then living. She commemorated in paint the front cover of *Time* (p. 18), as if to declare the significance of this unfolding historic drama by transposing it from a passing weekly periodical to the posterity of art. But her transposition was not entirely neutral, as she changed the color of the magazine logo and border of its design in order to merge the images and frame into a gray field.[19] A year after Warhol made a screenprint titled *Moonwalk*, 1987, which recalled

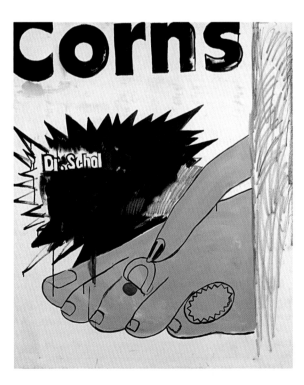

Neil Armstrong's televised walk on the moon in 1969, Vik Muniz turned to the same subject, but with a different image, in *Memory Rendering of the Man on the Moon*, 1988–90 (p. 18). The work celebrates the power of media to impact an adolescent's consciousness, for it was made from the artist's memory of a photograph in the 1973 periodical *The Best of Life*, showing the historic moment.

In 1984 Alfredo Jaar addressed his attention to a current event, the horrific Bhopal gas tragedy in India, which was at the time viewed as the worst industrial disaster in history. During the whole of Jaar's career, he has examined people living behind the facades of abundance in capitalist and colonial societies, postulating that "no difference" exists between political activism and art.[20] In *BusinessWeek Magazine Cover*, 1985 (p. 19), Jaar reconfigured the cover of the magazine's December 24, 1984, issue into a four-part composition. The image of a suffering Indian woman is made equal in prominence to that of the president of Union Carbide, whereas the headline on the unmodified cover might have the viewer believe that the principal victim of the disaster is, in fact, the company. By his manipulation, Jaar suggests the magazine is essentially a press vehicle for business and part of the facade created by capitalism.

Like Warhol, Barbara Kruger had a successful career in advertising, in her case as a graphic designer, before turning to art in 1969. In her work she has aggressively attacked consumerism in American life with a brashness that brooks no disagreement. She is particularly skilled at making use of language, sometimes at the scale of billboards, to give force to her confrontational style. In 1992 she was commissioned by magazine companies to make a series of covers (p. 20) in which she would bring to life the subjects assigned to her. Kruger took possession of the very media that she had often attacked, the media for which she had formerly worked. By contrast, Robert Gober's seizure of the media was accomplished by subterfuge. In 1992 he created false *New York Times* pages on which actual news stories were juxtaposed with fictional ones, headlines were adjusted, and images of the artist dressed as a bride were added (p. 20; see p. 90 for the bride image). With these cunning techniques,[21] Gober placed his personal life as a gay American into the larger context of the "newspaper of record," though this stratagem may be difficult to discern in the camouflage and, moreover, was hidden in an unprepossessing stack of papers on the ground, seemingly destined for the

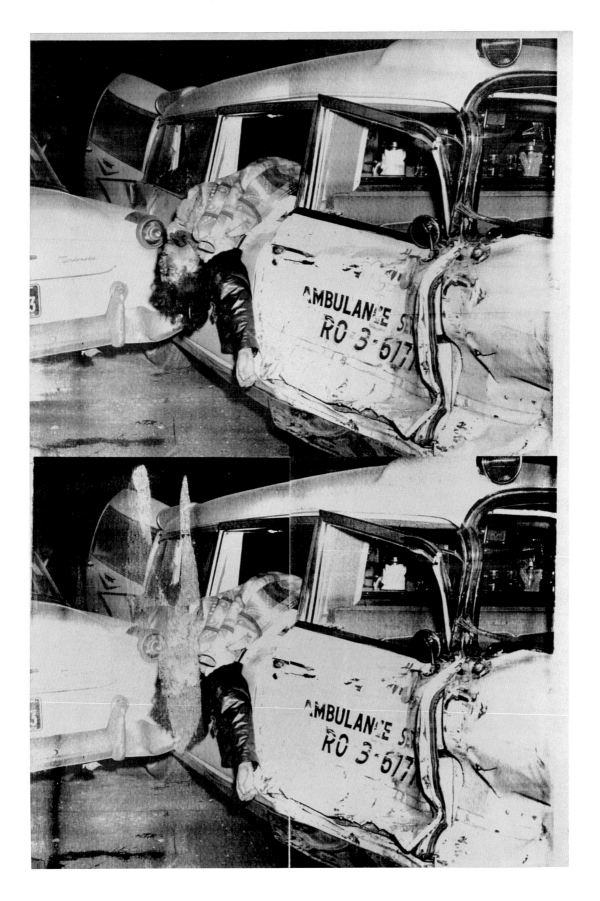

ANDY WARHOL
Ambulance Disaster, 1963–64
Silkscreen on canvas
CAT. 16

SIGMAR POLKE
Bavarian, 1965
Oil and dispersion on canvas
CAT. 126

SARAH LUCAS
Hunk of the Year, 1990–92
Four gelatin silver prints
CAT. 105

VIJA CELMINS
Time Magazine Cover, 1965
Oil on canvas
CAT. 66

VIK MUNIZ
*Memory Rendering of the Man
on the Moon*, 1988–90
Gelatin silver print
CAT. 112

ALFREDO JAAR
*BusinessWeek Magazine Cover,
December 24, 1984*, 1985
4 chromogenic prints
CAT. 88

trash. What we see in all of these works are visual artists co-opting the bully pulpit of popular media and opening new paths by which to integrate their personal views within the macrocosmic territory of newspapers, magazines, and television. In the process, they have chosen to make more popular and commonplace forms of communication the focus of the so-called fine arts.

When Hannah Arendt titled her 1963 book *Eichmann in Jerusalem: A Report on the Banality of Evil*,[22] she suggested that evil has an insidious effect partly because of its seemingly innocuous appearance. Conversely, her phrase could be turned around to become the "evil of banality." Might that rhetorical expression somehow apply to much of Warhol's subject matter, for instance, that of *Dr. Scholl's Corns, Icebox* (p. 22), *Big Campbell's Soup Can, 19¢ (Beef Noodle)* (p. 32), *Brillo Soap Pads Boxes* (p. 32, cat. 18), and the seemingly innumerable flower paintings (p. 141)? Could these works and the tedium they might arouse have unwanted, even "evil," consequences to do with the loss of attention to serious matters, or is a banal subject by Warhol simply one of his "leftovers," something, in fact, worthy of contemplation and rescue? While Warhol's intent in the case of the flower paintings may have started from a wish for mass appeal,[23] his banal subject matter was, in effect, a provocation, a means to offend the proper art world, which was attuned to the concerns expressed by high-art manifestations. With that result, banality had a dangerous connotation indeed.

Banality can have fascinating and fascinatingly varied implications, perhaps even evincing a whiff of evil when broached by other artists. Polke and Gerhard Richter helped to forge a German type of Pop art that they dubbed, at the time of a 1963 exhibition in Düsseldorf, Capitalist Realism. With the subject matter of Polke's *Plastik-Wannen (Plastic Tubs)*, 1964 (p. 23), and Richter's *Kitchen Chair* (Städtische Kunsthalle Recklinghausen) and *Toilet Paper* (private collection), both 1965,[24] the two German painters could be said to have stooped lower than Warhol, as if determined to show that banality logically ought to reach a level beneath Warhol's standard, a notion that Gober later extended with a meticulous sculpture of a bag of cat litter (p. 32). Here, arguably, is an even more mundane and pathetic stratum, one in which the aesthete is aggressively confronted and dislodged from passivity. For the truly insignificant to become notable is to challenge the presumptive powers of art,

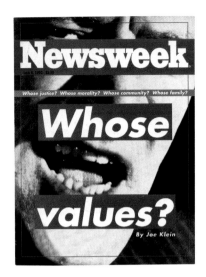

BARBARA KRUGER

CONTEMPT AND ADORATION

1987

Mixing scattered serialities with the promiscuous capabilities of the silk-screen process, Warhol crammed his images with the commodities and commotions of his time, and made them belt out a national anthem which sounded suspiciously like "Money Changes Everything." The singularity of specific icons was processed through an assembly line of fluent, varietal repetitions. But although these procedures were employed with machine-like detachment, the work, nevertheless, has the feel of a cottage industry in which the tiny mismatches and eccentric registers of the silkscreen process become as resonant as de Kooning's rapturously brushy orchestrations. From the ironic presentation of the renovation of affliction (the nose job, dance instruction, and paint-by-numbers pictures) to his portraiture, Warhol's images coalesced into a facetious cataloguing of photographic and painterly gesture: a testament to inaccessibility, to the rumor of a stainless beauty, to the constancy of glamorous expenditure.

ANDY WARHOL
Icebox, 1961
Oil, ink, and graphite on canvas
CAT. 3

SIGMAR POLKE
Plastik-Wannen (Plastic Tubs),
1964
Oil on canvas
CAT. 125

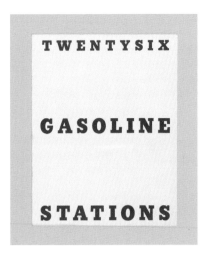

hence the issues raised in John Baldessari's *Econ-O-Wash, 14th and Highland, National City, Calif.*, 1966–68 (p. 34), and Ed Ruscha's *Twentysix Gasoline Stations*, 1962–67 (above). Just compare these potentially soporific subjects to an ostensibly charming street scene by Camille Pissarro or Gustave Caillebotte, and yet these works also demonstrate the possibility for the banal to become gripping. In Bruce Nauman's video *OFFICE EDIT I*, 2001 (p. 26), as in Warhol's *Empire*, that same potential occurs over a long period of time, during which the viewer is either beaten into submission or is rewarded for his or her attentiveness with a new kind of artistic wonder.

By virtue of banal subject matter being an assault on traditional notions of sincerity and authenticity in art, it courts the potential for farce and parody to become serious matters, as is the case with Jeff Koons. He upped the ante in this rush to intermingle sensibilities with *Ushering in Banality*, 1988 (p. 27), wherein the subject named in the title is given a reverential personification—a pig, naturally—and is attended by puttilike figures taken from Hummel ceramics. With Koons, there is unashamed exhilaration in the banal. Following the model of Warhol, he neither disdained banality nor found a political raison d'être to support it, but embraced this arena with gusto.

Some of Warhol's most celebrated excursions into banality are his uses of American logos and labels, including *Big Campbell's Soup Can, 19¢ (Beef Noodle)*; *Brillo Soap Pads Boxes*; and *Green Coca-Cola Bottles* (p. 30). Warhol loved the democratic notion that Coca-Cola was inherently egalitarian, enjoyed equally by all segments of society; for him, this was an example of the triumph of American capitalism.[25] Furthermore, he reveled in the very sight of these logos, as during his 1963 cross-country trip to Los Angeles.[26] In his usual patriotic way, Warhol pronounced:

> The most beautiful thing in Tokyo is McDonalds
> The most beautiful thing in Stockholm is McDonalds
> The most beautiful thing in Florence is McDonalds
> Peking and Moscow don't have anything beautiful yet.
> America is really The Beautiful.[27]

Warhol's reactions to logos during his trip, along with his art, are remarkably prescient in light of Susan Sontag's 1964 essay "Notes on 'Camp,'" for she speaks of an aesthetic experience of the world in which a certain camp attitude frames all observations.[28] Sincerity and tragedy play no role, nor does irony, whereas a sense of detachment is ever present.[29] In camp, banal sights are not empty but are source material for further reflection and elaboration. Warhol's narration of his road trip is replete with similar aperçus, which, at the time, he called "Pop":

> The farther west we drove, the more Pop everything looked on the highways. Suddenly we all felt like insiders because even though Pop was everywhere . . . most people still took it for granted, whereas we were dazzled by it—to us, it was the new Art. Once you "got" Pop, you could never see a

EDWARD
RUSCHA

1989

*I first met Andy Warhol in June of 1963 after Joe Goode and I
had hitchhiked to New York from L.A. We were invited by Andy to
have lunch with him and Gerard Malanga and walked to a
luncheonette on Seventy-second Street. He was wearing a pair
of British walker shoes that looked expensive and had been spotted
with little drips of paint. Gerard was the more serious of the two,
while Andy was more off in the clouds and asked if we knew any
movie stars and seemed to be content with art gossip. We walked
to his studio in an old firehouse, then to a brownstone on Lexington
Avenue where he was living. Right away, he asked Joe and me
to kneel together behind a couch and began shooting Polaroid
pictures of us. While all this was going on, a 45-rpm record player
sat on the floor of the dark living room repeatedly playing "I Will
Follow Him," by Little Peggy March, for over an hour.*

*Most artists are born to be opinionated, but he was like
no artist I had ever met because he was for everything and nothing
at the same time.*

ANDY WARHOL
Still from *Empire*, 1964
16mm film transferred to
DVD in black-and-white with
sound, 8 hr. 5 min.
CAT. 20

BRUCE NAUMAN
Still from *OFFICE EDIT I
(Fat Chance John Cage)*, 2001
Single-channel video installation
transferred to DVD with color
and sound, 51 min. 44 sec.
CAT. 117

JEFF KOONS
Ushering in Banality, 1988
Polychromed wood
CAT. 97

sign the same way again. And once you thought Pop, you could never see America the same way again.[30]

Warhol's "Pop" was about seeing the world through a certain kind of urban homosexual lens, though America, not the rest of the world, was "the place where everything was happening."[31] By the late 1960s, according to George Melly, as noted by Fabio Cleto, the terms "*camp* and *pop* . . . were interchangeable,"[32] though Warhol, no doubt, already knew this. In 1966, in discussing the then-current fad for the Batman television series, he observed that "camp was really being mass-marketed—everyone was in on the joke now."[33]

In another discussion of camp, Andrew Ross defines it as "a rediscovery of history's waste," in other words, the leftovers from a "serious high-cultural 'tradition.'"[34] Camp bestows "glamour," without irony, on this material.[35] Such descriptions are perfectly apt for Warhol's art of

the banal, but it is important to realize that the work of other artists does not always display the defining characteristics of camp. Here we can introduce a distinction between the meanings of camp and two of its historical precedents—the terms *kitsch* and *vulgar*, which Milan Kundera has conjoined as the German and French forms of the same concept, respectively. He describes kitsch as the "syrupy dregs of the great Romantic period" in Germany; further, citing Robert Musil, it is "bread dripped in perfume." Summarizing, Kundera dismissively writes that kitsch is "*supreme aesthetic evil*," and exclaims that it is "anti-modern."[36] But these dismissals are precisely the aim: for Warhol and the artists discussed here, there is an explicit rejection of what had been valued by the modernist vision, and that rejection was accomplished, in large part, by the use of banal subject matter, which Kundera, interestingly, goes so far as to characterize as "evil."

BANKSY
Napalm, 2004
Screenprint
19¹¹⁄₁₆ × 27⅝ in. (50 × 70.2 cm)

The sight of almost any animal induces exuberance in the camp/kitsch aesthetic point of view, as, for instance, in Koons's *Puppy*, 1998 (opposite). Likewise, Richter's *Kuh (Cow)*, 1964 (opposite), Polke's heron paintings of 1968–69 (for example, *Reiherbild I*, 1968, Kunstmuseum Bonn), and Warhol's *Cow Wallpaper*, 1966 (opposite), appear to be evocations of affectless wonder. And that is what Banksy exploits in *Napalm*, 2004 (above), wherein the happy-go-lucky Mickey Mouse and Ronald McDonald accompany the victim of the chemical weapon named in the title.

The camp aesthetic is also characterized by its sense of detachment and its absence of irony. These qualities are seen in Warhol's *Brillo Soap Pads Boxes*, which draws forth analogies to Jasper Johns's *Ale Cans (Painted Bronze)*, 1960 (Museum Ludwig, Cologne), and before that to Marcel Duchamp's readymades, for all are inextricably linked. Though Warhol's objects are replicas, as are Johns's, and Duchamp's are taken from life and declared to be art, we are perhaps confronted with distinctions without differences. It is the shock of the subject matter, unabashedly stated, that is the great impetus toward reflection in these works. Likewise, Koons expressed a Pop-inspired fondness for utilitarian American machines in *New Hoover Deluxe Shampoo Polishers, New Shelton Wet/ Dry 10-gallon Displaced Tripledecker*, 1981–87 (p. 31).

American sights are very much central in a variety of artists' works. In a series of paintings, drawings, and prints, Ed Ruscha imparted a glamorous aura to the Standard gas station logo set in a vast expanse of sky, as if a welcome sight on a long-distance journey across the country. However, in one version of the subject (p. 35), Ruscha's familiar gas station is inexplicably set ablaze. Staying with scenes from the American open road and its ubiquitous vehicle, Matthew Barney's

depictions of a Sinclair gas pump, 1999 (p. 34), and very large American automobiles, 2002 (p. 35), possess a palpable sense of emptiness and foreboding, as if no human being dares tread in the land of Sinclair or will be doomed by the omnipotent forces of capitalism. Similarly commenting on American capitalist society, Cady Noland contemptuously viewed the "pleasure" Americans take in "wasting things,"[37] hence many of her sculptures and installations (p. 38) include distinctly American artifacts to ensure the locale is correctly identified and the idea of aesthetic wonder is transposed into a landscape covered with refuse.

Elsewhere, too, American logos appear to be signals of outright danger. For the creators of these works, unlike Warhol, American brands are cultural and nationalistic statements, and "packaging" means concealment, not of individual personality but of mercantile intention or even designs on world monopoly. Hence, Hans Haacke repackaged the Marlboro brand into something he named *Helmsboro Country*, 1990 (p. 33). The title plays on advertisements for "Marlboro Country" while locating that place in the land of Senator Jesse Helms, Republican from North Carolina and a crucial supporter of the tobacco industry. In a passage where, normally, a warning about the dangers of smoking are shown, Haacke castigates Philip Morris, the manufacturer of Marlboro and a major funder of the arts.

Logos, which denote identity, can have an unintended and incendiary implication that is quite separate from their apparently positive reputation. For example, Tom Sachs equated a renowned French luxury fashion house, associated with elite taste, with a working-class tool, if not lowbrow violence, in *Chanel Chainsaw*, 1996 (p. 37).[38] By means of a Coca-Cola logo painted on a Neolithic Chinese vessel, 2010 (p. 37), the Chinese artist Ai Weiwei suggested a capitalist takeover of the culture of his country, hence the logo is imbued with a malevolent force.

A counterpart, even a corollary, to Warhol's preoccupation with banality is his fascination with death and disaster, powerful subjects that have the potential to be rendered banal by their ubiquity. Interviewed about his upcoming 1964 show at Sonnabend Gallery in Paris, which included works from the *Car Crash*, *Tuna Fish Disaster*, and *Electric Chair* series, Warhol explained that its focus was "death in America."[39] Indeed, looking to newspaper and media sources for inspiration, Warhol was attracted to calamitous scenes of death from early in his career.[40]

JEFF KOONS
Puppy, 1998
Glazed ceramic
CAT. 99

ANDY WARHOL
Cow Wallpaper, 1966
Screenprint
CAT. 27

GERHARD RICHTER
Kuh (*Cow*), 1964
Oil on canvas
CAT. 135

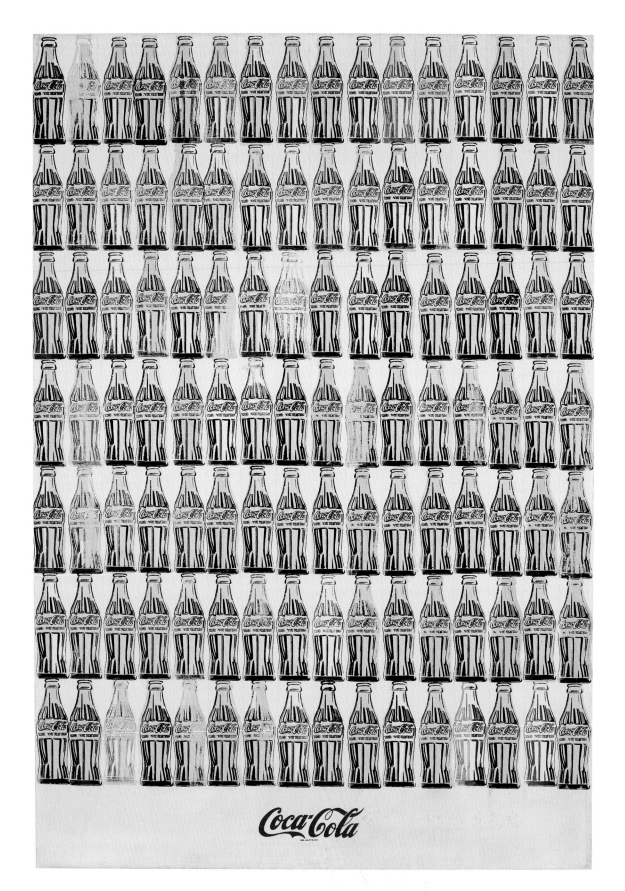

JEFF KOONS
New Hoover Deluxe Shampoo Polishers, New Shelton Wet/Dry 10-gallon Displaced Tripledecker,
1981–87
Shampoo polishers, vacuum cleaner, Plexiglas, and fluorescent tubes
CAT. 94

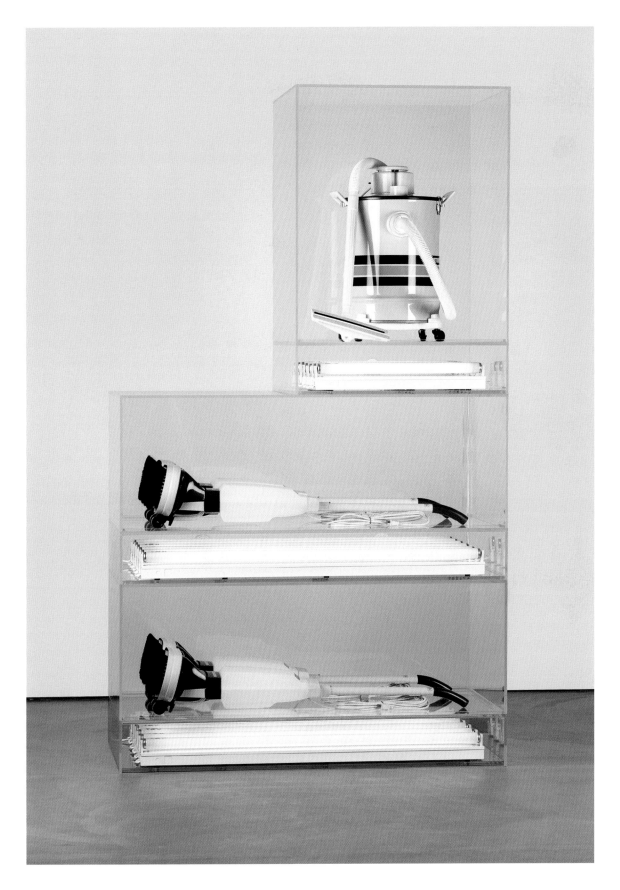

ROBERT GOBER
Cat Litter, 1989
Plaster, ink, latex paint
CAT. 71

ANDY WARHOL
*Big Campbell's Soup Can, 19¢
(Beef Noodle)*, 1962
Acrylic and graphite on canvas
CAT. 5

ANDY WARHOL
Brillo Soap Pads Box, 1964
Silkscreen and enamel on plywood
CAT. 19

HANS HAACKE
Helmsboro Country, 1990
Silkscreen and photographs on
wood, cardboard, and paper
CAT. 83

Moreover, the subject spanned a good deal of his oeuvre, culminating in the *Skull* paintings of 1977 (p. 41). As with other themes, Warhol made death *aesthetic*, meaning distant and/or beautiful.[41] In *Ambulance Disaster*, 1963–64 (p. 16), the newspaper photograph used as a source establishes a psychological distance from the subject and the serial composition serves to dilute the impact of the image, both factors leading the viewer to feel separated from the victims' pain and the tragedy of the moment. Still, there is a raw impact that is retained by the black-and-white palette of the newspaper-based works. But in many of the *Electric Chair* series, like *Orange Disaster #5*, 1963 (p. 42), the subject is painted with candy-colored hues, orange in this case, despite its ominous theme. In his treatment of death, he exhibited his usual ambivalence: the aesthetic approach belies the brute force of the

subjects and the bluntness of his words. Warhol described his films as "sociological . . . like documentaries,"[42] and he was similarly "sociological" in this statement on the topic of death:

> I'm not saying you should be happy when a person dies, but just that . . . you don't *have* to be sad about it, depending on what you think it means, and what you think about what you think it means.
>
> A person can cry or laugh . . . you have the choice![43]

Warhol seems to suggest that contemplating mortality, pathos, and tragedy are simply choices one makes. For him, death was "so ordinary," even banal perhaps, that his rendering of it, according to Robert Rosenblum, "probably tells us more truth about the realities of the

ECON-O-WASH
14 TH AND HIGHLAND
NATIONAL CITY CALIF.

EDWARD RUSCHA
Burning Gas Station, 1966
Oil on canvas
CAT. 138

MATTHEW BARNEY
Cremaster 3: 1967 Chrysler Imperial, 2002
Chromogenic print in artist's acrylic frame (shown unframed)
CAT. 63

TOM
SACHS

2004

Unless you're a real genius, like Louis Armstrong, it's hard to have a new idea and a new way of expressing it. The most the rest of us can hope for is to either tell a new story with old tools and words, or an old story with new tools and new words. Once you've solidly established your own language, you can improvise and build new ideas. The power of using brands — in my case, from fashion — and mixing it up with violent iconography lies in merging two things together to form a third. What's important to me about Pop is that using brands and other identifiable, everyday things gives you the opportunity to communicate. You're speaking a common language. I think part of the reason my work with fashion brands in the nineties really took off was because of an anxiety between the rich and everyone else. Another reason was that regardless of whether the work was critical of fashion itself, it still traded on the value of the brand. Like Prada. It's a death camp, but it's a Prada death camp.

TOM SACHS
Chanel Chainsaw, 1996
Cardboard and thermal adhesive
CAT. 140

AI WEIWEI
*Neolithic Vase with
Coca-Cola Logo*, 2010
Paint on Neolithic vase
(5000–3000 BC)
CAT. 51

CADY NOLAND

TIN FOILED

2004

Charlie Chaplin and Andy Warhol both contemplated the machine and came to the same conclusion: Its effects were dehumanizing. But where Chaplin issued a de facto warning about the mechanization of life in his art, Warhol fell madly in love with the idea. For Warhol, it was man who paled in comparison to the machine, not the other way around.

Warhol's quixotic enterprise, his impossible dream of becoming a machine, was ultimately doomed to (unmechanical) failure. He was sold short by his poor animal body: by going bald (he hid it under a big logo of a wig), getting shot (by a woman), and succumbing to a small, unnecessary death that was absurdly anti-climactic (going out like a lamb). And, despite his efforts to disappear the human, his work couldn't really be produced in his absence — other people's touch (however light) would find its way in and flub up his aesthetic.

In his quest to construct an ever-expanding, self-perpetuating assembly line, Warhol perused all conduits through which he might pump out images and information. In this, he became part of a larger machine — namely, the media machine — as a filter or screen through which notables, newsworthies, and wouldliketobes pass. He wasn't a member of the media gauntlet, as we have come to know it, because he wasn't hunting for a trophy, and he didn't seem interested in dragging the reluctant into the limelight. (He enjoyed exposing those who enjoyed being exposed.)

Editing (of behavior or material) wasn't Warhol's bailiwick. He kept his lens open and the microphone on. I relate to some post-Warholian artists, like Dara Birnbaum (her Wonder Woman work) or Gilbert & George, who zoomed out more than Warhol did — to include the spectator or media source in the frame, directing attention to the machinery that created an image rather than to the image itself.

Warhol's machine impersonation was not fated to last. He was the Tin Man in reverse. He didn't want a heart, much less his rotten gallbladder. I was shocked when I heard that he'd died. Unawares, I had internalized the myth he'd fostered that he was a thing, not a person. His death was a surreal reminder that he'd actually been alive.

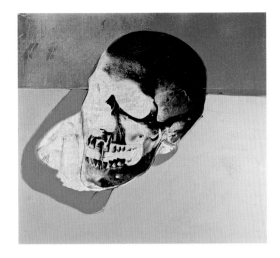

modern world than do the rhetorical passions of *Guernica*."[44] Indeed, his work treads onto the path of a "banality of evil" interpretation, whereby unimaginable pain is explicitly mooted in sensuous or dispassionate circumstances.

Notwithstanding Warhol's native subject matter and embrace of his country's way of life, he embedded within his work an implicit critique of the United States, and a significant group of artists evolved from his example to stress the darker aspects of American life. This subsequent strain of art activity either concerns the theme of death in America or implies a degree of moral outrage at immoral behaviors found in this country. Virtually the whole of Matthew Barney's oeuvre is permeated by the twinned themes of death and evil in America—witness his preoccupation with the story of the murderer Gary Gilmore in *Cremaster 2*, 1999 (p. 44), and *Cremaster 3*, 2002, for instance. Gilmore's murderous rampage in Utah, including a stop at a Sinclair station, and his subsequent execution by firing squad, which he had petitioned for, and which was the first execution after the Supreme Court reinstated the practice in 1976, epitomized an utterly American saga. Richard Prince's *Spiritual America*, 1983, takes a derisive tone toward the theme named in the title, itself borrowed from a famous photograph by Alfred Stieglitz of the hindquarters of a gelded workhorse. Prince reused—appropriated—a 1975 publicity photograph that was published the following year in *Playboy*, in which the ten-year-old Brooke Shields, with the approval of her mother, had been rouged and posed nude. By conjoining the image and title, Prince mockingly indicted the degree of spirituality to

be found in America.[45] Aiming an indictment in a different direction, Gober's wallpaper design titled *Hanging Man/Sleeping Man*, 1989 (p. 43), depicts two male personages in the great racial tragedy of this country's history.[46] In *Eat/Death*, 1972 (p. 44), Bruce Nauman emphasizes the place of language in the subject of death, in effect saying that the relationship between the two words shown on the sculpture makes for a cold, uncaring situation. In typically urgent fashion, Nauman's neon sign exhorts the viewer to pay attention. Approaching death with a different kind of urgency, Felix Gonzalez-Torres devoted his career to the victims of a scourge, mourning friends who died of AIDS. His *Untitled (Portrait of Ross in L.A.)*, 1991 (p. 45), composed of a pile of candy, forms a fascinating corollary to Nauman's suggestion to "eat," in that the candy is intended to replicate his dead lover, so that ingesting it takes on the dimension of the Christian Eucharist.

German artists, too, have similarly confronted the theme of death in their work. With a newspaper photograph and headline as his source for the image and title of *Tote* (*Dead*), 1963 (p. 48), Richter followed closely on Warhol's example. But in his use of the German word for corpse, he, like Nauman in *Eat/Death*, explored the impact of language. Polke's series of paintings depicting watchtowers, 1984–88 (p. 48), conveys an effect very similar to that of Warhol's *Electric Chairs*, the themes of each being uniquely identified with the haunted history of its country of origin. Like Warhol, Polke used color and pattern to make the paintings in this series visually pleasing, so as to partially camouflage the emotional content of the motif. Only after careful viewing does one discern the chilling sight of a watchtower that might oversee the occupants of a concentration camp, the inmates of a prison, or the residents at the eastern border of the two Germanys. As with Warhol's grisly subjects, the viewer is immediately and perhaps unwillingly turned into a voyeur, a tourist visiting a macabre scene of murder.

The history of art is replete with images of the skull, a physical reminder of human mortality. After Warhol painted images of the skull starting in 1976 (above), however, the theme assumed great currency among contemporary artists,[47] as seen in Jean-Michel Basquiat's especially powerful *Untitled (Head)*, 1981 (p. 47), which imparts the force of graffiti to the age-old subject. Basquiat often expressed mourning in his work for famous black musicians and cultural figures.

ANDY WARHOL
Orange Disaster #5, 1963
Acrylic, silkscreen, and graphite
on canvas
CAT. 12

ROBERT GOBER
Hanging Man/Sleeping Man, 1989
Screenprint
CAT. 72

MATTHEW BARNEY
Cremaster 2: The Drone's Cell, 1999
Chromogenic print in artist's
acrylic frame
CAT. 62

BRUCE NAUMAN
Eat/Death, 1972
Neon tubing, clear glass
suspension frame
CAT. 116

FELIX GONZALEZ-TORRES
Untitled (Portrait of Ross in L.A.),
1991
Multicolored candies, individually
wrapped in cellophane, with
an ideal weight of 175 pounds
CAT. 78

Mourning is not likely the aim of the Italian artist Paolo Canevari, who filmed a young man in a vacant lot in Belgrade aimlessly kicking what looks like a soccer ball but turns out to be a skull. In documentary fashion, the artist's *Bouncing Skull*, 2001, depicts the cheapness of life.

Banality, even to the point of outright vulgarity, has become an altogether new and exciting area with numerous possibilities for investigation and expression. As with some earlier works in the twentieth century that were intended as an affront and at first elicited shocked reactions—collages, for example—an art of banality has come to seem unexpectedly beautiful. And as the banal has subsumed various forms of death and disaster, it has given rise to new interpretations and renderings of tragedy that have accorded with contemporary life.

JEAN-MICHEL BASQUIAT

1986

JEAN-MICHEL BASQUIAT
Untitled (Head), 1981
Acrylic and oil stick on canvas
CAT. 64

Listening to what [Warhol] had to say was probably the most fun. Seeing how he dealt with things was the best part. He's really funny. He tells a lot of funny jokes. We worked for a year [on our collaborations]. . . .

He would start most of the paintings. He'd start one, you know, put . . . something very concrete or recognizable like a newspaper headline or a product logo and I would sort of deface it and then I would try to get him to work some more on it, you know, and then I would work more on it. I tried to get him to do at least two things. He likes to do just one hit, you know [laughs] and then have me do all the work after that. . . . We used to paint over each other's stuff all the time.

SIGMAR POLKE
Hochsitz mit Gänsen (*Watchtower
with Geese*), 1987–88
Artificial resin and acrylic on
various fabrics
CAT. 128

SIGMAR POLKE
Hochsitz II (*Watchtower II*),
1984–85
Silver, silver oxide, and resin
on canvas
CAT. 127

GERHARD RICHTER
Tote (*Dead*), 1963
Oil on canvas
39⅜ × 59 in. (100 × 150 cm)
Private collection

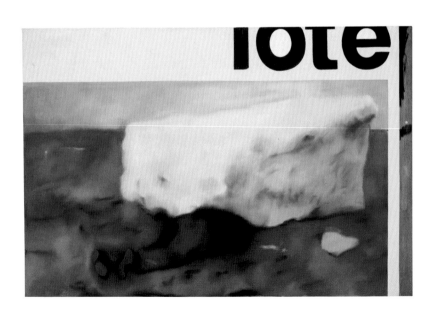

PORTRAITURE: CELEBRITY AND POWER

As the deaths and spiritual disasters of the decade of the sixties came one by one to American Kings and Queens . . . so the decade that began with Hemingway as the monarch of American arts ended with Andy Warhol as its regent.[48]

Warhol's elevation to "regent," in the words of Norman Mailer, should come as no surprise, given his stature as portraitist to the reigning, albeit mostly tabloid, royalty. He had trained for the role from childhood, when he devoted hours to reading movie magazines and writing famous people for their press photographs and autographs. Once he arrived in New York, he wanted, more than anything in life, to be part of grand parties with famous people. Given all this celebrity worship, the designation "regent" likely delighted him. Portraiture became a principal métier of Warhol's, and with this practice, according to Robert Rosenblum, he was "virtually single-handed in the early 1960s in resurrecting from near extinction that endangered species of grand-style portraiture of people important, glamorous, or notorious."[49]

Warhol's early forays into portraiture naturally emerged from the pages of the tabloids. His first portraits, in late 1961, were loosely copied from photographs in the *New York Post* showing Princess Margaret and Frank Sinatra (p. 14). About six months later, in

June–July 1962, he reproduced Eddie Fisher and Elizabeth Taylor from a photograph in the *New York Daily News* (*Daily News*, 1962, Museum für Moderne Kunst, Frankfurt am Main). Shortly thereafter, in late summer of 1962, and coincident with his adoption of the silkscreen technique, he wholeheartedly embraced the practice of portraiture, starting with teen stars Natalie Wood, Warren Beatty, and Troy Donahue (for example, *Natalie*, *Warren*, and *Troy*, all 1962, The Andy Warhol Museum, Pittsburgh). Then, like a newspaper reporter jumping on a story, he began his series on Marilyn Monroe just after her death in early August (p. 56).[50]

Warhol's interest in portraiture was not a complete anomaly at the time. Even in post–World War II New York, a milieu of ascendant abstraction, Willem de Kooning painted *Marilyn Monroe*, 1954 (Neuberger Museum of Art, Purchase College, State University of New York), and Ray Johnson rendered Elvis Presley in *Oedipus (Elvis #1)*, 1956–57 (Collection of William S. Wilson). In Britain, Peter Blake made *Sinatra Door*, 1959 (Museum Ludwig, Vienna), composed of two rows of repeated images of the singer. Also in the late 1950s, Alex Katz began his long New York career of primarily painting portraits. Those of the dancer Paul Taylor (left) and of the artist's wife, Ada (for example, *Ada, Ada*, 1959, New York University Collection, Grey Art Gallery and Study Center), have particular resonance in Warhol's practice, the former for Katz's signature use of a flat, monochrome background, and the latter for the pairing that prefigured, if not influenced, similar compositions by Warhol.[51] As usual, though, Warhol proved to be both a synthesizer of earlier art and a beacon in terms of his example to others.

Warhol said that he loved "plastic idols,"[52] a comment that applied equally to a Brillo box and an image of Troy Donahue, in that both are constructions of advertising programs to persuade viewers of their significance and appeal. Like the rendering of a consumer object, the packaging of these celebrities (their "official" images, not their actual appearance or humanity) is what interested Warhol. For that reason, he employed for his sources film stills, publicity photographs, or images taken from the media—in other words, highly artificial, "plastic" portrayals. Whether one considered Warhol's portraits to be "soulless"[53] or, as another writer opined about his subject matter in general,[54] "abandoned . . . to public gaze," they are relatively affectless renderings that are, therefore, open to interpretation. Unlike his paintings of ripped-from-the-headlines disasters,

ALEX KATZ
Paul Taylor, 1959
Oil on linen
72 × 84 in. (182.9 × 213.4 cm)
Museum Brandhorst, Munich

ANDY WARHOL
Triple Elvis, 1963
Aluminum paint and silkscreen
on canvas
CAT. 14

ANDY WARHOL
Silver Liz, 1963
Spray paint and silkscreen
on canvas
CAT. 13

Warhol's portraits often evoked earlier time periods. For example, when he turned to Marlon Brando in 1966 (p. 50), the actor's career was in a state of decline. Nevertheless, Warhol romanticized him by basing his painting on an image from Brando's prime and youth—the 1953 film *The Wild One*. Likewise, other portraits of stars were based on publicity shots from the past: among them, *Twenty Marilyns*, 1962 (p. 76); *Turquoise Marilyn*, 1964 (p. 51); *Triple Elvis*, 1963 (p. 52); and *Silver Liz*, 1963 (p. 53). In contrast, the *Jackie* series of 1964 (p. 55), which communicated the tumultuous news of the president's assassination through Jackie's gestures and expressions both before and after the shooting, was produced in the weeks following the event and is imbued with a sense of being in the moment— in this case, the flickering, fleeting moment just before the tragedy occurred. But for the paintings of Jackie made later that year, such as *Red Jackie* (p. 54), Warhol employed as his source a formal photograph taken from the cover of a 1960 book, showing the soon-to-be first lady seated in the Kennedy compound at Hyannis Port.[55] For the mid-1960s viewer, the paintings of Jackie, Liz, Marilyn, Elvis, and Marlon linked their subjects as they were known in the present to a time when they were, arguably, at the height of their careers or beauty or power. Warhol's conflation of eras creates a degree of pathos, like reading an obituary that is accompanied by a photograph from an earlier point in the subject's life. If this method borders on the hackneyed, never- theless, it is in keeping with a fan's (Warhol's) attentive view of the relative glamour and status of his idols. To further compound the meaning of Warhol's choices: he painted Marilyn just after her death, Elizabeth Taylor at a time when she was thought to be near death;[56] and Jackie for the first time just after the death of the president. This maudlin approach relates to Warhol's aforementioned interest in death in America.

Warhol's personal predilections emerge in the way he composed his portraits: the portrayals of women are limited to the head; those of men depict more of the body.[57] If the depiction of Marilyn on a Byzantine field of gold leaf (right) was the expectation of her worshipful public, then the homoerotic image of a leather-clad Marlon similarly swathed in gold paint could have been aimed at a gay audience. But Warhol had further thoughts about many of the film stars whom he depicted and the vehicles of their fame, saying contemporary American films "really didn't have much to say."[58] He soon added to the cast of flat,

timeless Hollywood icons his own "Superstars," the people who had become part of his life. In fact, he found these people equally worthy, saying, "I've never met a person I couldn't call a beauty."[59] Starting in 1964, he made "film portraits" (opposite), as he called them,[60] in the form of screen tests, during which the viewer could study the subject trying to remain stationary or fidgeting a bit for the standard three- minute duration. Captured in real, Cage-inspired time, these portraits demonstrate a completely different approach from that of the painted portraits, in keeping with Warhol's film work.

The vulnerability displayed in the Marilyn and first Jackie portraits was largely provided by the photographic sources that Warhol employed, though we, no doubt, project quite a bit of the sentiment onto them.[61] A similarly vulnerable characterization can be seen in Cindy Sherman's photograph of herself as Marilyn Monroe, 1982 (opposite), and in Elizabeth Peyton's paintings of Kurt Cobain, 1995 (p. 58). As Warhol had done with Marilyn's image, Peyton started her series on Cobain almost immediately after his suicide and made many tributes to the musician's fragile beauty. Taking a different tack, Francesco

ANDY WARHOL
Gold Marilyn Monroe, 1962
Acrylic, silkscreen ink, gold paint, and spray paint on linen
83¼ × 57 in. (211.5 × 144.8 cm)
The Museum of Modern Art, New York, Gift of Philip Johnson, 1962
(316.1962)

Vezzoli's embroidery of Liza Minnelli, 1999 (p. 58),
Jeff Koons's sculpture of Michael Jackson and his pet
chimpanzee, 1988 (p. 59), and Keith Haring's manipulated poster of Elvis Presley (p. 58) follow the stereotype of unadulterated adoration and distended glamour.

Because we continue to live in a celebrity-drenched
society, in which images of the famous and infamous
assault us at all turns, it is not surprising that artists,
following after Warhol, have made extensive and varied
use of topically interesting figures. However, rather
than express the adoration implicit in Warhol's portraits
of Marilyn and Elvis, for example, some artists take
a more nuanced approach toward their subjects and
toward the practice of portraiture. A case in point
is Cady Noland, whose series devoted to Lee Harvey
Oswald, 1989–90 (p. 60), reuses the legendary news
photo of the Kennedy assassin that was ceaselessly
peddled by the media. Noland was deeply offended by
the tabloids' deceitful "tactics" with regard to notable
people and their methods of "reducing them to photo-
objects," if not "trash,"[62] hence she turned the figure
of Oswald into a life-size image.

Gerhard Richter, whose admiration of Warhol's
portrait style is evident in *Evelyn (Blau)* (*Evelyn [Blue]*),
1964 (p. 62), was also interested in tarnished individuals,
specifically a woman named Helga Matura. His 1966
portrait of her (p. 61), however, is not immediately
recognized by a non-German audience of decades later,
and yet at the time her fame undoubtedly made just
the name, given at the bottom of the painting but
without the blurb that accompanied the newspaper
photograph that was Richter's source, identification
enough. A seemingly conventional, pretty, young woman,
Matura was, in fact, a prostitute, murdered in 1966.
However, due to the vagaries of time, she has become
not a portrait but a type of person—albeit named.

Another portrait practice, started in recent decades
by Warhol, entwines celebrity with political power.
When Warhol turned to Mao Zedong in 1972, he had
not yet devoted much attention to the subcategory
of political figures.[63] While he was avowedly apolitical,
he was ever the news hound, and he found artistic
inspiration in President Richard Nixon's meeting with
Mao on February 29, 1972, which was an extraordi-
narily important international event. He suddenly
realized the potential of the political portrait to take
a position in his pantheon of stars. According to Bob
Colacello, the longtime editor of Warhol's *Interview*
magazine and later biographer of the artist, the

ELIZABETH PEYTON
Blue Kurt, 1995
Oil on canvas
CAT. 123

FRANCESCO VEZZOLI
Liza Minnelli, 1999
Cotton embroidery on canvas
in artist's frame
CAT. 153

KEITH HARING
Elvis Presley, n.d.
Sumi ink and gold paint on poster
CAT. 84

JEFF KOONS
Michael Jackson and Bubbles, 1988
Ceramic, glaze, and paint
CAT. 96

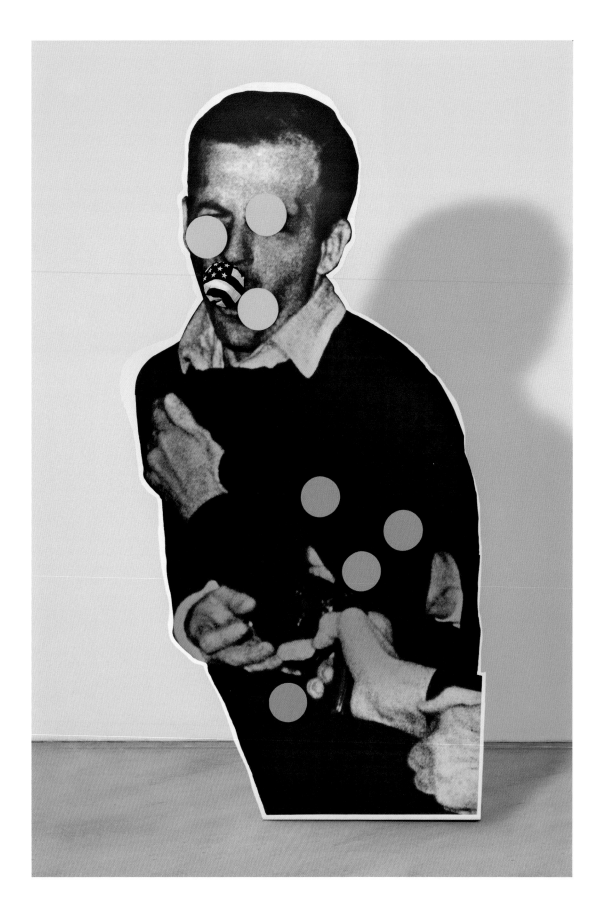

Helga Matura

GERHARD RICHTER
Evelyn (Blau) (Evelyn [Blue]), 1964
Oil on canvas in artist's frame
CAT. 134

combination of fame and political power was immediately of deep interest.[64] Warhol proceeded to paint many portraits of the Chinese leader (p. 64) based on official government images, including, as befitted Mao's stature, some of his largest canvases to date. After all, here was a "Superstar" for hundreds of millions of people.

Although a plethora of official images of Mao were made during his lifetime, independent artistic interest in the leader arose in China only after Warhol started to have a significant influence in that country, and the posthumous attention was hardly celebratory. During the early 1990s a Chinese art movement emerged known as "Political Pop" or "double kitsch," which satirically conjoined Chinese iconography and propaganda with the recently arrived advertising imagery of Western consumer culture. A key figure in this movement is Wang Guangyi, whose paintings of Mao and *Great Castigation Series: Coca-Cola*, 1993 (p. 222), are a direct response to Warhol.

Whereas Warhol's portraits of Mao take a seemingly neutral, or perhaps ambiguous, stance, there is an artistic industry involved in deconstructing or denigrating official, visionary-type portraits of famous political leaders. In Haacke's *Taking Stock (unfinished)*, 1983–84 (p. 65), an exceedingly formal portrait of Margaret Thatcher, based on a press photograph, is set within an altarpiecelike frame. The artist undercut the prime minister's image by introducing into the background numerous details relating to the advertising firm Saatchi & Saatchi, which played a major role in electing her. That Charles Saatchi was a preeminent art collector at the time only adds to this complex depiction of power.[65] In a more aggressive gesture, the artists' collective the Silence = Death Project took a familiar, seemingly noble portrait of Ronald Reagan and defaced it in *AIDSgate*, 1987 (opposite), accusing the president of having condoned AIDS, as Richard Nixon had condoned the Watergate break-in, and having hidden his role in the spread of the disease. Using a child's coloring book as source material, Glenn Ligon's disturbing *Malcolm X (small version 1) #1*, 2001 (p. 66), represents the black political activist as not fully delineated, except for the pink lips and rouged cheeks, very much like a tarted-up portrait by Warhol.[66] In this portrayal by a gay black artist, the viewer might wonder if society has similarly diminished Malcolm X and his ideals.

Images of those in political power have multiplied in the contemporary art world. Recent portraits of William J. Clinton by Chuck Close, 2006 (Collection of Ian and Annette Cumming), and Barack Obama by Shepard Fairey (p. 249) have celebratory qualities, the Clinton exuding his characteristic charisma and the Obama suggesting stately vision. However, some portraits make subtle modifications to the pretense of impassive formality in an attempt to reveal the deception or artifice of the subject's power and status. For instance, Hiroshi Sugimoto's ersatz portrait of Cuban leader Fidel Castro, 2001 (p. 67), actually a waxwork figure, is infused with the "dignity" of a "plastic idol." Rooted in an amalgam of portraits, *Louis XIV* by Jeff Koons, 1986 (p. 68), is appropriately baroque, even if it is anachronistically rendered in steel. Cindy Sherman's *Untitled #183A*, 1988–89 (p. 68), presents an artificial French aristocrat with great languorous ceremony, though her prosthetic breasts make her look grotesque. In *Marie Antoinette out for a walk at her petite Hermitage, France, 1750*, 2005 (p. 69), Karen Kilimnik demonstrates an uncomfortable continuity between spoiled women equally out of touch with the masses—

Marie Antoinette and Paris Hilton. Luc Tuymans's painting of Secretary of State Condoleezza Rice, 2005 (p. 69), based on a cropped image from an official website, diminishes the ceremony of her office by its casual horizontal composition and undermines the vision of a typical political portrait by Rice's facial expression.

It is possible to speak of a category of portraiture in which the depiction is itself banal, both in style and in the characterization of the sitter. With *The American Man (Portrait of Watson Powell)*, 1964 (p. 70), Warhol created, on commission from the founder of the American Republic Insurance Company, an image of corporate power. But this captain of Midwest business is portrayed as in a generic photographic portrait of the era, and the work is titled so as to render him a cipher. Warhol dubbed him "Mr. Nobody."[67] Relying on a snapshot rather than a studio portrait, Polke painted the German trade-union minister, Heinz Kluncker, in 1964 (p. 70). Though he was then a well-known figure, Kluncker similarly becomes a nobody in Polke's painting, owing to the casualness of the image and the vagaries of time.

Portraits of anonymous or characterless persons represent an interesting counterbalance to Warhol's celebrity preoccupation. By the early 1960s Katz had long been working the field of apparently nameless individuals. Although one example, *Passing*, 1962–63 (The Museum of Modern Art, New York), is a self-portrait, the image could stand as another "Mr. Nobody" from the era when men wore such hats. The image vaguely recalls a world of banal advertising where many such people reside. A later contribution to the practice of anonymous portraiture is Andreas Serrano's *Nomads*, 1990 (p. 71), a photographic series of highly dignified, homeless persons who are sadly banal because of their obscure identity.

Similarly banal at first sight is Haacke's *The Right to Life*, 1979 (p. 72), in which we find another "pretty young woman," unnamed but of a blond type fitting American taste. Taken from a 1970s installment in the long-standing "Breck Girl" advertising campaign for Breck shampoo,[68] the advertisement is based on the portrait of a young woman named Yvonne Schneider, according to the original ad copy, but Haacke further objectified the blond beauty by rendering her anonymous. He sabotaged the banal advertisement in order to expose the unsavory practices of the maker of the product, with the intention of revealing the dirty

SILENCE = DEATH PROJECT
AIDSgate, 1987
Lithograph
CAT. 146

HANS HAACKE
Taking Stock (unfinished),
1983–84
Acrylic on canvas with
artist's frame
CAT. 82

GLENN LIGON
Malcolm X (small version 1) #1, 2001
Paint, silkscreen, and gesso
on canvas
CAT. 103

JEFF KOONS
Louis XIV, 1986
Stainless steel
CAT. 95

CINDY SHERMAN
Untitled #183A, 1988–89
Chromogenic print
CAT. 145

KAREN KILIMNIK
Marie Antoinette out for a walk at her petite Hermitage, France, 1750, 2005
Oil on canvas
CAT. 93

LUC TUYMANS
The Secretary of State, 2005
Oil on canvas
CAT. 152

ANDY WARHOL
The American Man (Portrait of Watson Powell), 1964
Acrylic and silkscreen on canvas
CAT. 17

SIGMAR POLKE
Porträt Heinz Kluncker (Portrait of Heinz Kluncker), 1964
Dispersion and graphite on canvas
CAT. 124

laundry of American Cyanamid Corporation. His text, which replaces the original copy exclaiming the virtues of the shampoo, repeats the report that female Breck employees of "child-bearing age were exposed to toxic substances" at the corporation factory. The work's title reinvents the purpose of the image by alluding to the fight against abortion rights.

Warhol emerged as a significant portrait painter in the 1960s and amplified this activity by adding commissioned portraits, which greatly accelerated as his career continued. Starting with *Portrait of Ethel Scull 36 Times*, 1963 (Whitney Museum of American Art and The Metropolitan Museum of Art, New York), Warhol based his commissions on photo-booth snapshots; from the 1970s, he used Polaroids. In *Nan Kempner*, 1973 (right), the socialite's portrait is derived from a rather clichéd pose, with her head turned back and a slightly surprised and appealing smile on her face. Warhol's willingness to make a profusion of commissioned portraits, which had been frowned upon by virtually the entire legion of modern artists before him, did not go unnoticed. Among Warhol's contemporaries and later artists who have taken on commissioned portraiture, Alex Katz painted the well-known collector Lita Hornick in 1964 (p. 73); Robert Mapplethorpe undertook many commissions, including portraits of the famed Los Angeles collectors Eli and Edythe Broad,

1987 (p. 74); Julian Schnabel applied his signature broken-plate painting technique to the ubiquitous American television interviewer Barbara Walters, 1990 (p. 75); and Maurizio Cattelan sculpted the supermodel and collector Stephanie Seymour in a notorious work of 2003 (p. 80) that was nicknamed "Trophy Wife."[69] There is a degree of Warholian glamour among these examples that at times can verge on parody. Even when that is not the case, there is in the subject matter a sense of *Lifestyles of the Rich and Famous*. But just as the matter of *Lifestyles* so pervades our society, thus has Warhol's exaltation in the cult of celebrity and the practice of portraiture become widespread.

In the 1960s, artists themselves achieved celebrity status, a phenomenon that was certainly epitomized by Warhol, who was immensely well known from nearly the outset of his career. Although Warhol had painted a series of portraits of Rauschenberg in 1962 (for example, *Texan [Robert Rauschenberg]*, Museum Ludwig, Cologne), he did not in earnest turn his attention to depicting other artists until the mid- to late 1970s. One of the most notable was Joseph Beuys (p. 77), whom he painted on a number of occasions in 1980 and again, not surprisingly, in 1986, after the German's death. Often covered with diamond dust and sometimes on a scale rivaling the Maos, the Beuys paintings were celebratory to the point of perhaps being commemorative.

During the 1960s and 1970s, a fascinating pictorial dialogue could be witnessed among New York artists who reintroduced the practice of large-scale portraiture. These artists, with Warhol, brought portraiture

AMERICAN CYANAMID

AMERICAN CYANAMID is the parent of BRECK® Inc., maker of the shampoo which keeps the Breck Girl's hair clean, shining and beautiful.

AMERICAN CYANAMID does more for women. It knows: "We really don't run a health spa."

And therefore those of its female employees of child-bearing age who are exposed to toxic substances are now given a choice.

They can be reassigned to a possibly lower paying job within the company. They can leave if there is no opening. Or they can have themselves sterilized and stay in their old job.

Four West Virginia women chose sterilization. **AMERICAN CYANAMID...**

Where Women have a Choice

Portrait of BRECK Girl by James Donnelly. Text © by Hans Haacke. 1979.

ALEX KATZ
Lita, 1964
Oil on canvas
CAT. 90

ROBERT MAPPLETHORPE
Eli Broad, 1987
Gelatin silver print
CAT. 110

ROBERT MAPPLETHORPE
Edythe Broad, 1987
Gelatin silver print
CAT. 109

JULIAN SCHNABEL
Barbara Walters, 1990
Oil, plates, and Bondo on
wood panel
CAT. 141

ANDY WARHOL
Diamond Dust Joseph Beuys, 1980
Silkscreen, diamond dust, and
synthetic paint on canvas
CAT. 42

ALEX KATZ
Ted Berrigan, 1967
Oil on canvas
CAT. 91

CHUCK CLOSE
Phil, 1969
Synthetic polymer on canvas
CAT. 67

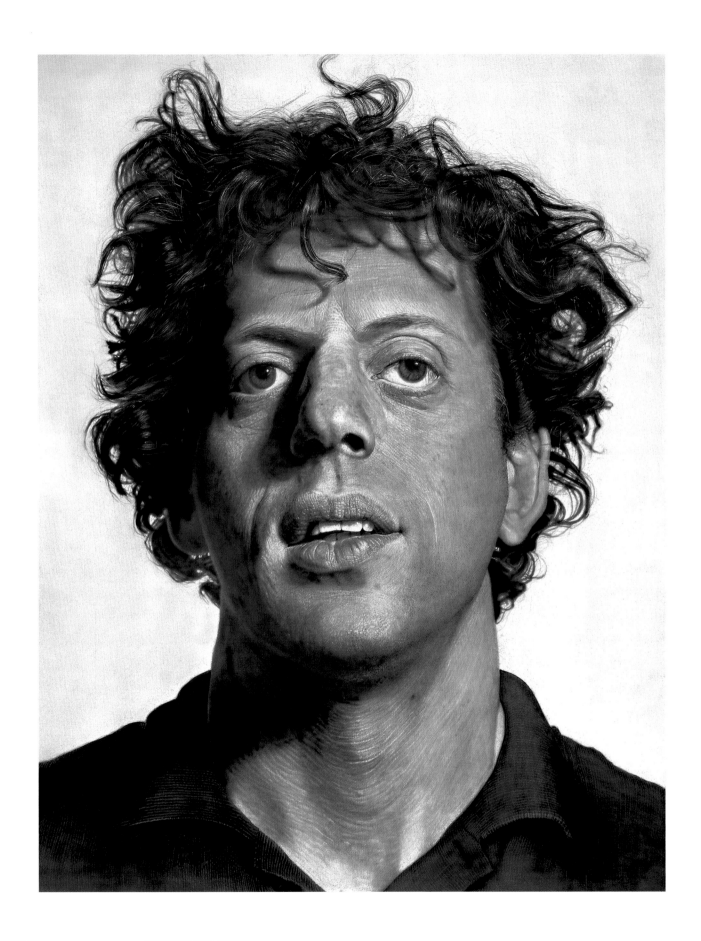

and specifically portraiture of famous artists and writers back into prominence. With a Photorealist style in works such as *Phil*, 1969 (p. 79), Chuck Close demonstrated a degree of characterization, of the composer Philip Glass, more typical of the historic portrait tradition. By contrast, Katz's stylizations, with their flat backgrounds, large scale, and generalized portrayals — as in, for example, his portrait of the poet Ted Berrigan, 1967 (p. 78) — form a different genre of portraiture at this time. Richard Avedon's insightful photographic portraits, such as that of the writer Truman Capote, 1974 (cats. 56–57), always place the sitter against an expansive blank background, which lends them a psychological impact similar to works by Close. Later artists have continued the portraiture trend. In an apparent nod to Warhol, Wolfgang Tillmans's *John Waters*, 1996 (p. 82), includes a pillow embroidered by the filmmaker's mother with an image of an electric chair.

MAURIZIO CATTELAN
Stephanie, 2003
Colored pigment, wax, synthetic hair, glass, metal
CAT. 65

MAURIZIO CATTELAN

ARMY OF ONE

2004

For me, with Warhol, it was never really about paintings or films or other artworks. It was always about him, his hair, his look. And it was about the fact that you can't really divide his work by media or style: He had developed a system, or perhaps just an attitude — a wig, a costume, a mask — that hid as much as it revealed. Or maybe we should call it a system, since he managed to build a language in which every expression, sentence, and gesture seemed to fit and to make sense. In the end, that's what we call style: the ability to lay your hands on things and make them your own. Whether Warhol was making paintings, films, posters, or Polaroids, he was making Warhols. You knew that every time he did anything he was adding a new brick to his world.

I don't even remember where I first saw his work: Warhol is so much everywhere that you can't really say when you first encountered him. Before you ever see a real Warhol you've most likely already experienced this attitude somewhere else — in a commercial, on TV, or anywhere, really. I like his work's pervasiveness a lot. . . .

That's probably the greatest thing about Warhol: the way he penetrated and summarized our world, to the point that distinguishing between him and our everyday life is basically impossible, and in any case useless. . . .

Warhol's work is not about a specific decade or style; it's about being contemporary, being now. And there's so much work, and there are so many different forms of expression — paintings, portraits, music, films, performances, studios, Polaroids, tapes — that you can always find something that's both pure Warhol and perfectly timed for your present moment.

IDENTITIES: GAY, CAMOUFLAGED, AND HYBRID

Warhol is second to none in the pantheon of twentieth-century American queer heroes.[70]

As Rrose Sélavy, Duchamp faced the camera in drag for a photograph by Man Ray, c. 1920–21 (p. 86), modifying his very identity and establishing an artistic alter ego. Subsequent artists were not quick to follow Duchamp's daring lead in transforming their own personas.[71] Although it was 1980 before Warhol depicted himself in drag, his 1960s films of transvestites ushered in an era of camp aesthetics, cross-dressing, camouflaging strategies, and identity manipulation in the visual arts. The evolution of Warhol's approach to self-portrayal was complicated. Most often, he played a coy game of hide-and-seek, as when posing for the photographer Duane Michals in 1958 (p. 86). Following the example of a drawing of himself, c. 1953 (The Andy Warhol Museum, Pittsburgh), he covered his face with his hands. From the 1960s, Warhol approached the theme of identity manipulation through the double or multiple image, as in the *Before and After* paintings (p. 84). The cosmetic-surgery advertisement on which the series is based shows the same person with two profiles, ostensibly ugly and beautiful, and echoes Warhol's sense that his own appearance needed improvement — his nose and skin, for example, which he had altered with rhinoplasty and frequent facial treatments.[72] The device of showing two versions of the same person, as well as a shadowy visage, appears in his double self-portraits, 1967 (p. 85). This depiction accords with the self-portrayal Warhol later created for his book *The Philosophy of Andy Warhol (From A to B and Back Again)* (1975), wherein he possesses a "perfected otherness . . . the shadowy . . . magical presence."[73] Although he stated that people should not seek a deeper understanding of him than is found in the surface appearance of his work,[74] this quote suggests the existence of a more profound psychological depth. This "shadowy" side of his personality may be said to stand at an opposite pole from Warhol's interest in tabloid subject matter and banality, where "magical presences" are not usually found. Elsewhere in that same description, Warhol says of himself: "the glamour rooted in despair."[75] Perhaps he only wanted to show his critics a degree of empathy not usually accorded him; at any rate, he posited in this description public and private dimensions, in other words, two sides to himself.

In two works of 1978, Warhol elaborated on his 1967 approach to self-portraiture. In one, three heads are superimposed (p. 87), and in the other, shadows envelop multiple self-images. Just before his death, in 1986, he painted himself wearing a fright wig and covered by a camouflage pattern (p. 87). As a group, these works demonstrate Warhol's desire to be his own subject instead of standing behind the camera, as when directing his films. Nevertheless, the portrayals alter, conceal, or multiply him, as if Warhol (his self, personality, or soul) requires protection or needs to be masked from the world.[76] In all cases, he wears a wig to hide his baldness and is, no doubt, covered in makeup as well.

In 1981, Warhol took a series of Polaroids of himself in drag (p. 87). Emboldened, he presented himself similarly attired for a photography session with Christopher Makos (p. 87). While Warhol's sexual interests and proclivities had been ostensibly masked or camouflaged in his paintings of the 1960s, they were completely on display in his first films of 1963–68.[77] Indeed, gay and transvestite subject matter is the overriding substance of these works, in which cross-dressers often feature prominently. In reconstructing events of 1967 in *POPism*, published in 1980, Warhol quite uncharacteristically ranted about attacks on the gay lifestyle. While defending his friends, he was surely including himself and his entire circle. Specifically, he wrote that drag queens are "sexual radicals," not "depressing losers."[78] As the 1960s was an era of Marxist criticism, his use of the description *radical* places his own films in a fascinating context. The transvestites not only depict their lives but also become politicized — protagonists in a societal struggle.[79]

Transvestism is, naturally, a perfect vehicle to show multiple aspects of a person, at least in terms of gender, as well as to hint at hidden dimensions beneath appearances. Warhol was not the first to make films of transvestites; recall Jack Smith, in particular. Whereas Smith's films exhibit a highly stylized, at times grandiose, theatricality, Warhol's show an everyday milieu. For Smith, dialogue is almost invariably absent; Warhol's dialogues require close attention. Both artists' films effectively mock formulaic Hollywood

ANDY WARHOL
Self-Portrait, 1967
Acrylic and silkscreen on canvas
CAT. 32

ANDY WARHOL
Self-Portrait, 1967
Acrylic and silkscreen on canvas
CAT. 33

movies, with Warhol's having an improvisatory air and a strong sense that the actors are absolutely playing themselves. His films possess a degree of authenticity and humor that is riveting—even charming on occasion. Although they did not attract a large general public, except for *The Chelsea Girls*, 1966, they did garner a significant audience of gays and cinephiles. Moreover, they made a strong impact on other artists.

By the early 1970s, cross-dressing, gender-bending, and androgyny had become part of mainstream culture, with "sexual radicals" to be seen especially in the realms of fashion and music. These individuals helped to make ubiquitous the camp aesthetics of "artifice" and "decadence."[80] Many artists since then have addressed transvestism and androgyny in their work, whether depicting friends, exploring them-selves and their characters, or enacting performative displays (pp. 89–92 bottom, 98 bottom). Some artists examine the codes of sexual identity, as in Prince's *(Untitled) Self-Portrait*, 1980. He starts with the Ur-male detail of the tie, slightly askew, no doubt, because the wearer's eye makeup and lipstick turn that male symbol into an accessory for an androgynous being.

In addition to transvestism and issues of gender identity, overt desire is yet another aspect of an emphasis on gay subject matter that has come to the fore in part through Warhol's example. Warhol expressed great pleasure in pornography and enjoyed, for example, drawing and taking pictures of visitors' penises.[81] He drew male nudes throughout the 1950s and painted the same subject in various works of 1977, including *Torso from Behind* (p. 93). In 1978, Warhol made a silkscreen series of explicit images titled *Sex Parts*. Many of his films are saturated with the sense of impending or just fulfilled sexual activity, or of constant tantalizing flirtation. *Lonesome Cowboys*, 1968 (p. 101), co-opts the Western movie, but Warhol's substitution of gay protagonists calls into question the authenticity of that macho identity while taking possession of it. Another frequent subject in Warhol's films is that of the gay hustler or pinup boy who is constantly being ogled, as in *My Hustler*, 1965, and *Bike Boy*, 1967–68. Perhaps Warhol's exploration of this subject led the film director John Schlesinger to adapt a 1965 novel by James Leo Herlihy into his celebrated 1969 film *Midnight Cowboy*; subsequently, the German filmmaker Rainer Werner Fassbinder

MAN RAY
Rrose Sélavy (Marcel Duchamp),
ca. 1920–21
Gelatin silver print
9 × 7³⁄₁₆ in. (22.9 × 18.3 cm)
Philadelphia Museum of Art,
The Samuel S. White 3rd
and Vera White Collection, 1957
(1957-49-1)

DUANE MICHALS
Andy Warhol, 1958
Gelatin silver
print
9¼ × 14 in. (23.5 × 35.6 cm)
Carnegie Museum of Art,
Pittsburgh, The Henry L.
Hillman Fund (2002.33.1)

ANDY WARHOL
Self-Portrait (in Drag), 1981
Polaroid print
3¹¹⁄₁₆ × 2⅞ in. (9.4 × 7.3 cm)
Solomon R. Guggenheim Museum,
New York, Purchased with funds
contributed by the Photography
Committee (2005.68)

CHRISTOPHER MAKOS
Lady Warhol, 1981, printed 2012
Gelatin silver print
CAT. 106

ANDY WARHOL
Self-Portrait, 1978
Acrylic and silkscreen ink on canvas
40 × 40 in. (101.6 × 101.6 cm)
The Andy Warhol Museum,
Pittsburgh, Founding Collection,
Contribution the Andy Warhol
Foundation for the Visual Arts, Inc.
(1998.1.806)

ANDY WARHOL
Self-Portrait, 1986
Acrylic and silkscreen on canvas
CAT. 50

focused on hustlers in films such as *Fox and His Friends*, 1975. The theme of the cowboy has an extravagant encore in Takashi Murakami's *My Lonesome Cowboy*, 1998 (p. 97), wherein the figure appears in an exultant, ejaculating, lasso-wielding pose.

The subject of the male gaze as expressed by gay men was the basis of many of Warhol's films of the 1960s, but it was only hinted at in his paintings, as in images of the macho Elvis (p. 52), the leather-clad Marlon (p. 50), and Jean-Michel Basquiat in an X-ray view (p. 94). Desire is implied by the title of his *Most Wanted Men* series, 1964 (p. 92).[82] In contrast, David Hockney's contemporaneous *Boy about to Take a Shower*, 1964 (p. 95), is more overt in its depiction of what engages the gaze of the unseen gay painter, as is Mapplethorpe's *Bill Joulis*, 1977 (p. 96). For adoration of buttocks, Gober showed an unabashed "I hear music" ardor in *Untitled*, 1990 (p. 93). He identified the source of the juxtaposition of music and a man's body as being an image by Hieronymus Bosch but said that the combination has other associations as well. It was his "image of beauty and . . . a song to be sung to the image of a man, or it was the expression of music emanating or humming from inside a man's body."[83]

Gay and lesbian love is a recurring theme for contemporary artists, from Gilbert & George to John Currin. The latter exhibits enormous pleasure in voyeuristic situations, such as that depicted in *Kissers*, 2006 (p. 98), in which he, a straight male, watches female sexuality in action. Gilbert & George have made themselves and their lives together, seen here in *Queer*, 1977 (p. 99), as well as lustful gazes toward young men, almost the entire subject matter of their work. Their photographic oeuvre is ripe with a sense of a gay English milieu. Likewise, as if taking a documentary or sociological approach, Nan Goldin (p. 96) and Catherine Opie fill their works with their circles of gay friends. Because these groups pervade the artists' imagery, an alternate universe to the heterosexual mainstream effectively becomes predominant, as was seen in Warhol's films. Opie's work is replete with the environment of American life, but in contrast to her usual forthrightness, *Dyke*, 1992 (p. 100), is fascinatingly ambiguous. The identity of the subject, who is seen from behind and without many conventional markers of gender, is indicated primarily by the word tattooed on her neck. Is this a comment about being labeled by society or is she defiantly branding herself, or both?

Cindy Sherman is certainly the most prominent artist to assume a range of female stereotypes and identities—and occasionally male ones, too. The fluidity between her self and another characterization or gender, as in her 1980 collaboration with Prince (p. 100), makes the theme of double identity Sherman's signature aesthetic strategy. Her oeuvre may be considered part self-analysis, part extravagant performative practice, and part extraordinary display of the possibilities of femininity. As a tabula rasa, Sherman has adopted what has been termed a constant "vacant and numb" facial expression.[84] But that look may have a practical application; settings, poses, hairstyles, and clothes, rather than physiognomy, define the depicted stereotype, as seen in her *Film Stills* series (p. 109). All the while, Sherman is a cipher—perhaps another kind of "plastic idol"—on which an identity can be tried.

A number of other women artists have explored the theme of identity in recent years. The French artist ORLAN has undergone numerous plastic surgeries, during and after which she photographed herself (p. 101), in an ambitious endeavor to contemplate the implications of physical appearance. She also considered the potential of genetic hybridization by picturing herself with physical masks and other alterations. Almost rivaling Cindy Sherman and ORLAN for sheer variety is the Japanese artist Mariko Mori, who has transformed herself, variously, into a teenage sexpot, a robot, and a bearer of both Eastern and Western characteristics at once.

Artists have at times compiled personalities in a veritable cascade of possibilities. A Jewish lesbian, Deborah Kass dazzlingly multiplies identities in *Double Ghost Yentl (My Elvis)*, 1997 (p. 102), creating an image of herself inhabiting her own version of Warhol's portrait of Barbra Streisand, the latter in Kass's painting in the role of Yentl—all based on Warhol's *Double Elvis*. (It should be added that Yentl, in the film of that name, disguised herself as a boy in order to attend school at the yeshiva!)

The recent films of Ryan Trecartin represent a delirious expression of the sensibility of transgression (p. 103). If Warhol's films often have a halting, improvisational quality, Trecartin's are scripted and manic. The casts of both are outrageously uninhibited, but Trecartin's exhibit Dionysian excess. They consist almost entirely of transvestites, gays, and lesbians who share a permissive sensibility that delights in all

RICHARD AVEDON
John Martin, Les Ballets Trockadero de Monte Carlo, New York, March 15, 1975, 1975
Gelatin silver print
CAT. 58

ROBERT GOBER
Untitled, 1992–93
Gelatin silver print
CAT. 75

NAN GOLDIN
Ivy with Marilyn, Boston, 1973
Gelatin silver print
CAT. 76

DOUGLAS GORDON
Self-Portrait as Kurt Cobain,
as Andy Warhol, as Myra Hindley,
as Marilyn Monroe, 1996
Chromogenic print
CAT. 79

PETER HUJAR
Ethyl Eichelberger as Medea, 1979
Gelatin silver print
CAT. 87

ANDY WARHOL
Most Wanted Men No. 2,
John Victor G., 1964
Silkscreen on linen
CAT. 23

ROBERT MAPPLETHORPE
Self Portrait, 1980
Gelatin silver print
CAT. 108

ANDY WARHOL
Torso from Behind, 1977
Acrylic and silkscreen on linen
CAT. 39

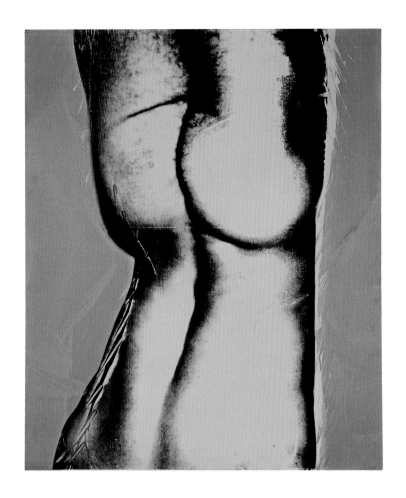

ROBERT GOBER
Untitled, 1990
Beeswax, wood, oil paint,
and human hair
CAT. 73

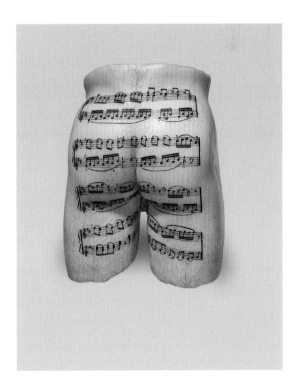

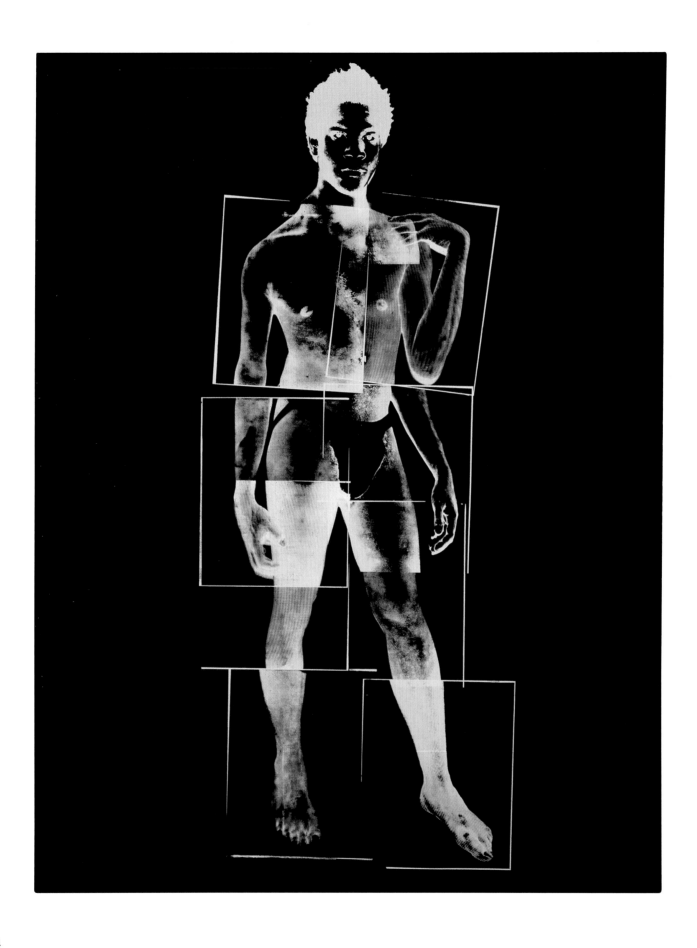

ANDY WARHOL
Jean-Michel Basquiat, 1984
Acrylic and silkscreen on canvas
CAT. 49

DAVID HOCKNEY
Boy about to Take a Shower, 1964
Oil on canvas
CAT. 86

NAN GOLDIN
French Chris on the Convertible,
NYC, 1979
Silver dye bleach print
CAT. 77

ROBERT MAPPLETHORPE
Bill Joulis, 1977
Gelatin silver print
CAT. 107

manner of crossover possibilities. In this atmosphere, the hybrid identity becomes ubiquitous. While Warhol's groups always appear to be hermetically sealed within disheveled rooms, Trecartin's are often shown out in a "straight" world, as represented by the presence of some nerdy boys, an utterly soulless mall or city-scape, or advertising slogans. It is an American world that is the foil for these characters, the same implicitly repressive sphere that can be detected in the art of Barney, Gober, and Nauman.

Finally, while sexuality and sexual politics, as well as gender identification, are rich sources of artistic interpretation, nationality and cultural traditions offer fertile territory, too, in which to explore the matter of authentic identity. Born in 1945, Anselm Kiefer spent much of his early career pondering what it meant to be a German, notwithstanding his own life experience. To locate the Nazi residing within, as it were, in 1969 he

adopted that identity by photographing himself in military garb and giving the Nazi salute. His attempt to "try on" another persona, even an abhorrent one, represents a fascinating play on self-image and on the possibility of manipulating one's given station in life. Identity is also the central subject matter for Yinka Shonibare, a native of Nigeria who has spent his adult life in Great Britain. His examination of the history of Dutch export to the African market has shown that the relationship between Europe and Africa is far more complex than is usually recognized.

Together, the works discussed in this section may be seen in political terms as confronting the conventional world, not just in its banal appearances but also in all of its underlying presumptions. In the process of using art to expand their ideas about themselves and their potential, these artists have pushed society in new directions.

JOHN CURRIN
Kissers, 2006
Oil on canvas
CAT. 68

KALUP LINZY
Still from *Conversations wit de Churun V: As da Art World Might Turn*, 2006
Digital video in color with sound, 12 min. 10 sec.
CAT. 104

CATHERINE OPIE
Dyke, 1992
Silver dye bleach print
CAT. 120

**RICHARD PRINCE
AND CINDY SHERMAN**
*Untitled (Richard Prince and
Cindy Sherman)*, 1980
Two chromogenic prints
CAT. 132

ANDY WARHOL
Stills from *Lonesome Cowboys*, 1968
35mm film transferred to DVD
in color with sound, 1 hr. 49 min.
CAT. 36

ORLAN
Seventh Surgery-Performance,
titled *Omniprésence, New York*,
1993
Silver dye bleach print
43⁵⁄₁₆ × 65 in. (110 × 165 cm)
Stux Gallery, New York

DEBORAH KASS
Double Ghost Yentl (My Elvis),
1997
Silkscreen and acrylic on canvas
CAT. 89

CONSUMING IMAGES: PHOTOGRAPHY, APPROPRIATION, ABSTRACTION, AND SERIALITY

Given Warhol's democratic tendencies, he granted equal stature to all of his images regardless of their sources, from popular culture to art history. His only requirement, it seemed, was that a subject be ubiquitous, not esoteric. Warhol's approach might be termed "promiscuous," owing to both his

willingness to accept all possibilities (and suggestions and people, as was demonstrated in his life) and his indiscriminate predilection for "leftovers," as he called his subject matter. Warhol was consumed by this material, excited by the impact of an image, and transfixed by the glut of pictures available to him. In this regard, one recalls the enthusiasms Warhol expressed during his road trip across America; his reactions exemplified what Jean Baudrillard later called "an 'esthetic' hallucination of reality."[85] Warhol's image bank became a sourcebook from which were created, in Baudrillard's terms, simulations of life, and the French philosopher described the effect of simulation being perfectly played out by Warhol.[86] With simulation, reality was effectively "confused by its own image,"[87] a concept that led presciently from Warhol to reality television.

Along with being consumed by images, Warhol thoroughly consumed, as in devoured, them.[88] Not surprisingly, then, photography took center stage in Warhol's art. He must have thought, in an image-laden world, reality could better be pondered and manipulated with a camera than with oil paint. It was as if the photograph provided proof of the veracity of his investigation. It certainly served him well in the goal of chronicling events and people of the day. Furthermore, through the technique of the photo silkscreen, Warhol literally used the photograph to create an image on the surface of the canvas.[89]

Indeed, Warhol's photo-silkscreen method effectively collapsed sacred notions about the hierarchy among media and the revered nature of painting. His practice colonized photography and, in the process, reinvigorated and reinvented the painting medium.[90] His takeover was physical, in that the photograph was not simply a source for a painting but was taken whole and applied to the canvas surface. Yes, Warhol still enjoyed streaks of paint and color—which were applied before or during the silkscreen process, or resulted by accident, or served as a base hue for the silkscreen— but clearly the photo-based image became the foundation of his art.

Painting was not simply flat because that was its natural evolution, as argued by the American critic Clement Greenberg; instead, photo-based painting made the case that the medium was flat because that was its banal character. *Baseball*, 1962 (p. 104), was one of the first of Warhol's silkscreen paintings and was, not surprisingly, based on a newspaper photograph. (Warhol's choice of subject—America's national

pastime — accorded with his predilection for the ubiquitous.) Some of Warhol's contemporaries also began to derive imagery from photographs in the early 1960s, though they did not employ the photo-silkscreen technique. In 1964, the same year Warhol filmed *Empire*, Richter made *Administrative Building* (below), creating a painting in which the image, obviously borrowed from a photograph, is blurred. The subject would appear to be as humdrum as possible — an undistinguished piece of architecture, casually photographed as if from a moving car.[91] Richard Artschwager, who had been making photo-based paintings for as long as Warhol, employed a well-known architectural site in *Rockefeller Center IV*, 1974 (p. 107). Like Richter, he practiced a form of blurring, in his case through his signature support of Celotex, a type of floorboard used for insulation. Photorealism, which emerged in the mid-1960s, was a different but related approach that more literally sought to emulate the look of a snapshot photograph with paint. Robert Bechtle, like many of the style's practitioners, based his work on the most nondescript and banal of images (p. 109). In each of these examples, the artist established, in different ways, a rapprochement or dialogue between painting and photography, while emphasizing that a painting is what is being contemplated.

In tandem with the development of painters using photography was the emergence of photographers as central to the whole of contemporary art, starting in the late 1960s and early 1970s. John Baldessari began his artistic life as a painter before turning to photo-based works in the late 1960s (p. 34) and, later, using filmic sources, as in his *Man and Woman with Bridge* (p. 108). His art came to have an enormous influence on both painters and photographers, as was the case of Cindy Sherman. She is Warhol's equal in being consumed by and a consumer of images from film to art history to advertising, her range of sources seemingly boundless.

If reality were better pondered with photography, photography could be plundered as well. Warhol's co-opting of it helped to inaugurate an era of appropriation — the seizure and duplication of imagery from commercial sources, existing works of art, and film; his *Cagney*, 1962 (p. 119), derived from a movie still, is an early example. In this art-about-art endeavor, the authenticity of the original is effectively neutered, questioned, or altered. The artist asks whether the original might or might not still sustain its aesthetic power in an age of reproduction.[92] This question had been posed quite brazenly by Duchamp, who performed

RICHARD ARTSCHWAGER

1989

Everybody has their own Warhol. For me he was a model of diligence. The job was, first, to fill in all the space between the works of art. He became more thorough and ingenious as time went on (as the remaining spaces actually became fewer). First he filled in some space by making art on commission (commercial art); then by making more than just one by employing assistants and copying devices; and then by making sub-versions by using different colors and/or sizes.

It still wasn't full, so then he invited some friends and strangers to stand in the gaps, with himself filling in the remaining one, appearing to have been there all the time.

Others have struggled, dabbled, speculated, but he did it so thoroughly that the whole enterprise is thrown open to question. And there you are.

JOHN BALDESSARI
Man and Woman with Bridge, 1984
Gelatin silver prints
CAT. 61

ANDY WARHOL
Mona Lisa, 1963
Acrylic and silkscreen on canvas
CAT. 11

BANKSY
Installation view of *Mona Lisa* on a
street in London, 2001

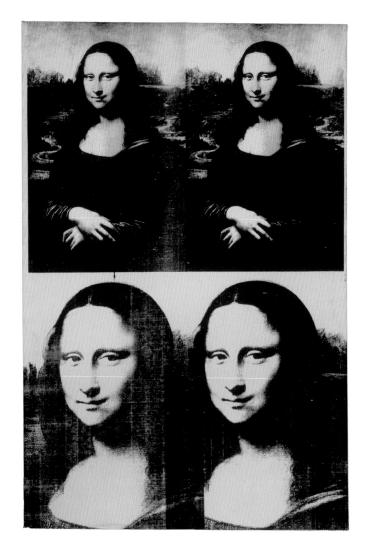

CINDY SHERMAN
Untitled Film Still #3, 1977
Gelatin silver print
CAT. 142

CINDY SHERMAN
Untitled Film Still #21, 1978
Gelatin silver print
CAT. 143

an act of vandalism toward an icon by putting a mustache on a reproduction of the Mona Lisa to create *LHOOQ* (original 1919, private collection). A hackneyed cliché in the corpus of art history perhaps, the painting was, nonetheless, an enormous attraction when it came to the Metropolitan Museum in 1963. Ever on the alert for topics of popular interest, Warhol took his turn at it that same year in his *Mona Lisa* (opposite). He eliminated Leonardo's coloration, cropped the composition, streaked the visage, and multiplied the image, all of which diminished the magical essence of the original.

Warhol went further in "murdering the original," as Baudrillard termed the process,[93] when he compromised the Christ figure from Leonardo's celebrated *Last Supper* by juxtaposing the logos of General Electric and Dove soap, along with a 59¢ price label, in his own *Last Supper*, 1986 (The Museum of Modern Art, New York). Warhol's 1984 series of appropriations of Edvard Munch's painting *The Scream* (p. 113) is a particularly startling sight, for this restatement effectively turned an iconic representation of exaggerated emotion into an example of what Rainer Crone called, regarding another work, "*prefabricated* visual content,"[94] a transformation that has been endlessly repeated by all of the toys based on the same painting. The fact that the museums that own the various versions of *The Scream* have licensed numerous appropriations of the image suggests that art about art is now mimicked by commercial cannibalizations of art—perhaps another example of Warhol's wide-ranging impact.

Subsequent practitioners of appropriation, likewise, have mined the teeming image bank of our culture, compiled from art history, advertising, the media, and social history. Embedded in this practice is a degree of investigation about the content of the chosen image

ROBERT BECHTLE
'61 Pontiac, 1968–69
Oil on canvas
59¾ × 84¼ in. (151.8 × 214 cm)
Whitney Museum of American Art, New York, Purchase, with funds from the Richard and Dorothy Rogers Fund (70.16)

and its historical background. With *The Liberation of Aunt Jemima*, 1972 (p. 112), Betye Saar made fascinating use and reuse of a vexed historical sign. Three versions of a black woman appear: the background is composed of the image from Aunt Jemima maple syrup; the second is a kind of Mammy doll holding a white baby; the third is a large woman wielding a broom and a shotgun. By the juxtaposition, the image of Aunt Jemima is appropriated and liberated. In Saar's hands, the technique of appropriation assumes a cultural dimension well beyond the art world. The appropriated image, like the individual in drag, is a transformation of an "original" in which a hybrid state is created; in these situations, it becomes difficult to ever look in the same way at the "original."

In 1980, Prince began appropriating Marlboro cigarette advertisements (p. 112), which had been employed in a campaign to persuade men to abandon nonfiltered cigarettes for filtered ones. In effect, men were being told it was the height of masculinity to smoke a type of cigarette that had largely been the

RICHARD PRINCE

GUNS AND POSES

2004

I came to New York City in 1974. In New York City in 1974 Andy Warhol was the fastest gun in town. In 1990 I wrote on a painting, ANDY WARHOL WAS A FUCKING ASSHOLE AND SO WERE ALL HIS FUCKHEAD FRIENDS AND I'M GLAD HE DIED. When I wrote it I was thinking about the movie The Gunfighter, *starring Gregory Peck. Later that year I was asked, "Is it Mr. Prince versus Mr. Warhol, or is it Richard loves Andy?" I answered the question the same way the clown did when asked, "I heard you just married a two-headed lady — is she pretty?" He said, "Well, yes and no."*

The noes: Andy wore a silver wig, and I shave what little hair I have. Andy did a lot of self-portraits and loved to have his picture taken; I've done only one self-portrait and can't stand the way I look, especially in photographs. Andy went out all night, and I go to bed around 7:30. Andy liked to surround himself with celebrities; I'm a loner and have no friends. Andy made movies, and I watch movies. Andy collaborated a lot, and I have a fear of grouping. Andy liked to go out with Bianca Jagger; I once met Bianca Jagger at a party, and she made me nervous. Andy wrote books, and I collect books. Andy had lots of assistants, and I work alone. Andy had scars on his stomach and torso; I have a scar on my head. Andy liked to take Polaroids; I've never had a Polaroid come out the way it's supposed to. Andy didn't swim — something about the bathing suit — I swim a mile a day and don't wear a bathing suit. Andy was an A-student; my marks were mostly D-plus, C-minus. I'm a recovering heterosexual; Andy was O'Sexual. Andy was a good photographer; I'm the worst photographer in the world. Andy's paintings were industrious and mechanical; my paintings are about working up a routine, going on the road, and crossing into Laos.

Andy wore a blazer and tie, a white shirt, and dungarees and loafers, while I wear cargo pants, sneakers, and a T-shirt that says, "I just heard from Bill Bailey. He isn't coming home." Andy hired a private nurse when he went to the hospital to get his gallbladder out; the nurse fell asleep, and he choked to death on his own fluids. I paint nurses. Andy published a magazine, and I buy every magazine on the newsstand, bring them home, jump up and down on them, and tear them apart. Andy used to let other people answer questions for him; I make things up, shovel the shit, and pretend to know more than I do. Andy once appeared on an episode of The Love Boat; when I was five I was a guest on The Howdy Doody Show. Andy lived with his mother; I once asked my mother to please pass the salt, and it came out "You bitch, you ruined my life." Andy produced a rock band called the Velvet Underground . . . I'm so far underground that I get the bends. Andy liked the television show Hollywood Squares; I just pitched a TV-game-show idea to CBS called "Who Gives a Shit?" Andy was shot in the stomach by the feminist playwright Valerie Solanas, and I was stabbed in the arm by my first wife. Andy had an opening at the ICA Philadelphia in 1964, and so many people came that there was a line around the block; I had a show at the Daniel Weinberg Gallery in Los Angeles in the '80s, and three people showed up.

The yesses: Andy and I have the same birthday, August 6, and we used to go to the same dentist. I remember running into him in the waiting room. I didn't shoot him; I said, "Hi, I'm Richard." He said, "Hi, I'm Andy." And we shook hands.

RICHARD PRINCE
Untitled (Cowboy), 1989
Chromogenic print
CAT. 130

BETYE SAAR
The Liberation of Aunt Jemima, 1972
Mixed media
CAT. 139

Claude Monet, among others. Going one step further in *Action Photo II (after Hans Namuth)*, 1997 (p. 115), Muniz duplicated a famous photograph by Hans Namuth of Pollock painting, thereby showing the multiple strata from the actual act of painting to the observation and recording of the act to the canvas original to a copy. The English renegade artist Banksy has demonstrated that there exists an iconography of the appropriated image: following Duchamp and Warhol, he painted the figure of the Mona Lisa as a terrorist (p. 108).

The seemingly endless appropriation of the image of Andy Warhol, as well as his works, is a kind of playful revenge on the original appropriator, but at the same time is a celebration of the practice and its potential (see "The Warhol Effect: A Visual Archive" in this volume). With Kelley Walker's *Black Star Press* series, 2004 (p. 116), the documentary photographs of the Birmingham race riot are given one more round of appropriation following on Warhol's usage of the subject in his *Race Riot*, series of 1963–64 (for example, *Little Race Riot* 1964, The Menil Collection, Houston), only here the black and white participants in the picture are distinguished by the overlay of silkscreened splotches of dark and white chocolate.

Though not the progenitor of art about abstract art,[95] Warhol was a crucial innovator in exploring the premises and appearances of abstraction. The first manifestation of the abstract painter's practice that Warhol addressed was the monochrome panel. With regard to this archetype of abstraction, Warhol claimed to admire the work of Ellsworth Kelly.[96] Nevertheless, he rejected the underlying tenets of abstraction and conceived new applications for the monochrome, which he termed a "blank." For example, in 1963, in describing the possibility of making pornographic pictures, he conceived an approach involving glow-in-the-dark paint: "They will look blank; when you turn on the black lights, then you see them. . . . If a cop came in, you could just flick out the lights."[97] Therefore, the blank held something important and personal to him but was kept secret from the casual observer, someone not in on the joke. In 1964, when ordered to remove his *Most Wanted Men* silkscreens on Masonite from the walls of a building at the New York World's Fair, Warhol chose, instead, to cover them with his signature silver paint,[98] thus, to create blank or monochrome paintings. We see in his critiques of abstraction that Warhol was, once more, attacking an ostensibly "pure" identity, with the goal of rendering a hybrid state.

province of women. Prince was exploring an area that was full of false nostalgia for and self-identification with a lifestyle few American men had ever actually experienced, except through the ads themselves, cowboy movies, historical documentary photographs, and the genre of Western art. He may have been inspired, as well, by Warhol's *Lonesome Cowboys*, which addresses the he-man stereotype.

For some artists, art itself is both the source of a work and the subject of a commentary. Louise Lawler is concerned with how an artwork is seen within the context of private and public displays, where it has a more complicated existence than being simply a revered masterpiece isolated on a wall or reproduced in a book. In her photograph *Pollock and Tureen, Arranged by Mr. and Mrs. Burton Tremaine, Connecticut*, 1984 (p. 114), she shows a fragment (not even a conventional, carefully selected detail) of a painting by Jackson Pollock above a whole frontal view of a tureen, as if to further reduce the potential for exalted dignity that the painting might otherwise possess.

Compromising the notion of an original masterpiece, Vik Muniz has built his career on creating replications of renowned pictures by Vincent van Gogh and

KELLEY WALKER
Black Star Press: Black Star,
Black Press, Star, 2004
Silkscreened chocolate and
digital print on canvas
CAT. 154

KELLEY WALKER

2004

Coming to New York in the mid-'90s, I became aware of the difference between artists: Jeff Wall was cautious, Warhol was trouble. Warhol's work seemed much more intuitive, which I liked because of its direct expression, often in the form of a failed self-negation coupled with violence. Since then, I have become conscious that, however informed, by working intuitively Warhol found in Pop his conception of a functional antagonist, a one-character avant-garde, and a duplicity achieved through a language of marketing. Warhol's direct self-promotion and soliciting — offering the prize of a glamorous dinner with the cover star of that month's Interview to someone who commissioned a multi-panel portrait, for example — point to a significant reason he achieved such success as an antagonist. Through his use of commercial strategies, Warhol honestly questioned the hegemony that had come about through the avant-garde's activity of self-maintenance. I see a similar noncynical approach in later artists such as Cady Noland. In my recent work, I attempt to continue the dialogue between a contemplative history of display and the strategies of appeal inherited from Pop. Instead of presenting objects on a pole, I silk-screened white, dark, and milk chocolate onto canvas digitally printed with a 1960s black-and-white news photo (not unlike the ones Warhol used) of a race riot in the South.

ANDY WARHOL
Shadows, 1978
Acrylic on linen
CAT. 41

ANDY WARHOL
Triple Silver Disaster, 1963
Silver paint and silkscreen
on canvas
CAT. 15

JOHN BALDESSARI
A Two-Dimensional Surface . . . , 1967
Acrylic on canvas
CAT. 60

A TWO-DIMENSIONAL SURFACE WITHOUT ANY ARTICULATION IS A DEAD EXPERIENCE

ANDY WARHOL
Cagney, 1962
Screenprint
CAT. 7

Thus we might consider Warhol's many "blanks," seen either as a large empty section of a painting or as a second panel of a diptych. *Triple Silver Disaster*, 1963 (p. 118), is composed of a trio of electric chairs juxtaposed with a field of silver, the impact of which is to suggest to the viewer a very dramatic, even archetypal, division.[99] That Warhol's blank gray field may not be nearly as visceral in content as an image of human destruction is to posit perceptions about the viewer's perspective and about art in general. Of course, the abstract painter would disagree and assert that the contrast is between the ineffable and the prosaic. On one hand, a "blank" by Warhol might appear as little more than an irreverent farce that has to do with the artistic pretentions of the abstract artist.[100] On the other hand, it may be that the blank holds within itself Warhol's personal interests, which are shown in this way because the artist fears exposure. Later in his career, he further tested the limits of representation with his *Shadows* series (p. 118), in which the paintings obliterate their titular imagery to such an extent that they approach complete abstraction.

Warhol continued to explore non-representational painting with the *Oxidation* series, 1978 (opposite), which was made by men urinating onto canvases that were prepared with metallic copper paint, creating the ultimate derisive parody about abstract gestural painting, as practiced by artists such as Pollock and Willem de Kooning, and any pretentions to seriousness it may possess. One type of "drip" painting was, thereby, replaced by another. For the *Rorschach* (right) and *Camouflage* series, 1984 and 1986 respectively, Warhol created variations on the blanks, using patterns that contain or imply the possibility of an image lurking somewhere, a possibility that is more or less inconceivable in a flat monochrome. In effect, art history, in this case the history of abstract painting, became a "dead . . . language" for him,[101] simply a subsection in his extensive warehouse of images, to be drawn upon as needed.

Warhol's playful attitude with respect to abstraction was echoed by a number of artists, including Nam June Paik, who placed a Barnett Newman–style vertical streak on a static-filled television screen and titled the work *Zen for TV*, 1963–78 (p. 122). Paik effectively questioned the notion that spiritual values are encapsulated in abstract formal strategies and used the television set as a vehicle to show the vernacular world triumphing over the sphere of abstraction.

ANDY WARHOL
Rorschach, 1984
Acrylic on canvas
158 × 110 in. (401 × 279.4 cm)
The Baltimore Museum of Art:
Purchase with funds provided
by Laura R. Burrows-Jackson,
Baltimore; and partial gift of
The Andy Warhol Foundation for
the Visual Arts, Inc. (1994.34)

Baldessari's *A Two-Dimensional Surface*, 1967 (p. 119), is a pointed send-up of the monochrome, for no abstract artist would want to see words on the surface of a field of white paint, let alone these words. Baldessari's satire was duplicated by Prince, who began locating jokes on monochrome surfaces in 1985 (p. 122). Allan McCollum took that revered abstract image, the monochrome that first appeared in Kazimir Malevich's 1915 *Black Square* (State Russian Museum, Saint Petersburg), and multiplied it so as to reduce its elevated status. In a swarm of them (p. 130), any one is like a Campbell's Soup can—infinitely repeatable, modular, and denuded of its grand ambitions.

Warhol's "most profound insights" included "repetition" and "what repetition does," according to David Hockney, who explained that repetition is founded in ornamentalism and renders everything "decorative."[102] By repetition, one understands that the grid is the prototypical Warhol composition. In the mid-1950s, Jasper Johns began making grid compositions that held either numerical or alphabetical sequences. Grid formats proliferated in the Minimalism of the next decades, for instance, in works by the painter Agnes Martin and the sculptor Donald Judd.

ANDY WARHOL
Oxidation Painting, 1978
Urine and metallic pigment in
acrylic on canvas
CAT. 40

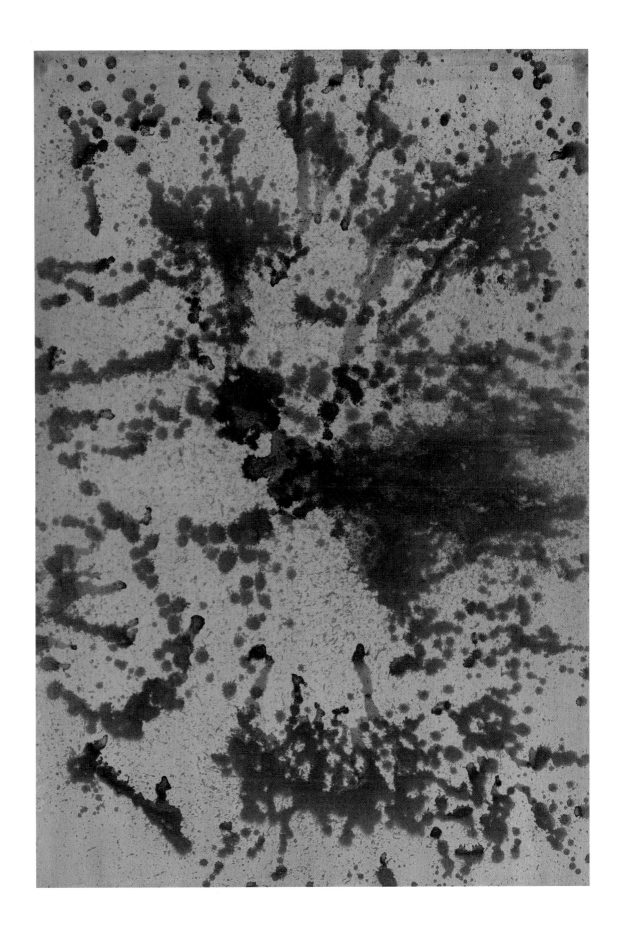

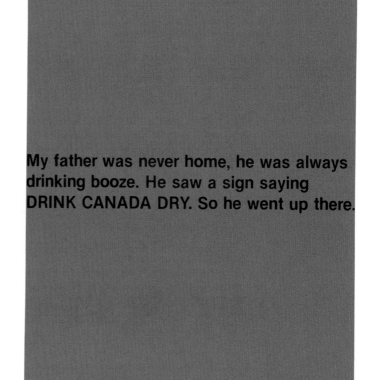

My father was never home, he was always drinking booze. He saw a sign saying DRINK CANADA DRY. So he went up there.

NAM JUNE PAIK
Zen for TV, 1963–75
Altered television set
CAT. 121

NAM JUNE PAIK
Zen for TV, 1963–78
Altered television set
CAT. 122

RICHARD PRINCE
Drink Canada Dry, 1989
Acrylic and silkscreen on canvas
CAT. 129

CHRISTOPHER WOOL
Untitled, 1988
Alkyd and Flashe on aluminum
CAT. 155

124

GILBERT & GEORGE
Red Morning Drowned, 1977
Gelatin silver prints with hand
coloring
CAT. 70

ANSELM KIEFER
Wege (*Ways of Worldly Wisdom*),
1978
Woodcut with acrylic paint and
shellac, mounted to canvas
CAT. 92

DAMIEN HIRST
Eight Over Eight, 1997–98
Glass, faced particleboard,
wood, plastic, aluminum, and
pharmaceutical packaging
CAT. 85

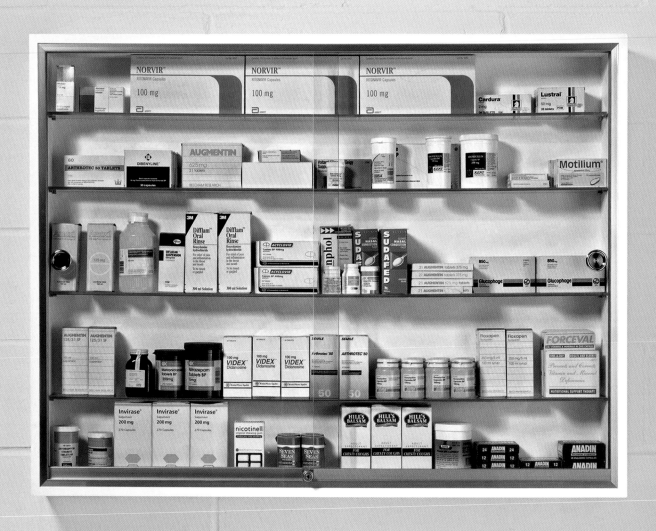

ANDREAS GURSKY
Prada I, 1996
Chromogenic print mounted to
Plexiglas in artist's frame
CAT. 80

In sculptors' hands, grids were usually composed of identical, machine-made objects. Generally speaking, Warhol's grids consist of a pattern of similar, but not identical, units placed within a fairly rigid framework, or of units that make up a serial composition. And, of course, Warhol's grids contain recognizable imagery.

By rendering the recognizable image "decorative" in a serial or grid presentation, as was pointed out by Hockney, Warhol effectively diminished the impact of people who would otherwise be considered iconic figures, such as Jackie Kennedy (p. 55) and Marilyn Monroe (p. 76). Warhol began with a conceptual framework: that repetition speaks to an industrial society in which the individual object is largely replaced by machine-made, infinite numbers of the same thing. Evidence of this condition could be found in films of assembly lines ceaselessly producing widgets and newsreels of newspapers coming off printing presses. Warhol was involved with this kind of activity in his art practice; in 1963, he famously sent a large roll of repeated silkscreens of Elvis Presley to the Los Angeles art dealer Irving Blum and instructed him to simply divide the roll into single, double, and triple Elvis paintings. Here was a conceptual-art gesture in the spirit of Sol LeWitt, in which the idea for a series

of works of art is carried out not by the artist but by his or her designate, as was also the case in Warhol's *Oxidation* series, wherein men were instructed to urinate on prepared canvases. Instead of lamenting the loss of individuality, Warhol celebrated mass production.

With *Marilyn Monroe's Lips* (pp. 124–25) as a starting point, one might trace a line to Gilbert & George's syncopated grid (p. 126), Andreas Gursky's found pattern of shoes (p. 129), and Damien Hirst's array of pill bottles in a medicine cabinet (p. 128). Whereas Gilbert & George use a grid to organize related personal images, Gursky and Hirst explicitly locate their studies in seriality within the likely setting of a consumerist or commodity-infused environment. Using history as his theme, Kiefer placed thumbnail sketches of famous Germans — more portraits of the powerful — within a grid composition (p. 127). Warhol's exploration of serial imagery very quickly evolved into his wallpaper compositions, in which the image was identical (p. 29). The same technique is seen in the paintings of Christopher Wool (p. 123), among others. Although Wool's works do not have overt subject matter, he composes what might be imagined as infinitely repeatable, flat patterns. As Hockney predicted, the grid and repetition have had tremendous viability among all manner of artists.

NO BOUNDARIES: BUSINESS, COLLABORATION, AND SPECTACLE

The year 1966 proved to be a turning point in Warhol's career. Ever on the lookout for new arenas in which to work, on February 10, he placed the following advertisement in the *Village Voice*: "I'll endorse with my name any of the following: clothing, AC-DC, cigarettes, small tapes, sound equipment, ROCK 'N' ROLL RECORDS, anything, film, and film equipment, Food, Helium, Whips. MONEY!! love and kisses ANDY WARHOL. EL 5-9941." At about the same time, he began producing performances by the Velvet Underground and the group's vocal collaborator, Nico, culminating in April with a monthlong engagement at a former Polish dance hall on Saint Mark's Place in New York. Titled *The Exploding Plastic Inevitable*, the group's performances occurred against a backdrop of Warhol's films, on which he projected variously colored gelatin slides from the lighting booth. That same month, Warhol opened a show at the Leo Castelli Gallery in New York, for which he covered the walls of one gallery

with his new *Cow Wallpaper* (p. 29) and floated helium balloons, called *Silver Clouds* (or "Pillows") (p. 134), in the second gallery. At that moment, he even thought that *Silver Clouds* might "mark the end of my art career,"[103] for he had chosen not to exhibit paintings at all. During the remainder of 1966 he toured with the Velvet Underground and made a number of films, including his magnum opus *The Chelsea Girls*, which garnered a much larger audience and more critical attention than his earlier films had. *Newsweek* grandly termed it "the *Iliad* of the underground."[104]

Due to all the attention he was receiving, Warhol reported, with satisfaction, that he was "reaching . . . different types of people. . . . It was fun to see the Museum of Modern Art people next to the teeny-boppers next to amphetamine queens next to the fashion editors. We all knew something revolutionary was happening . . . barrier[s were] being broken."[105] Those barriers were not only creative but also social. Warhol's Factory was both a studio where painting and filmmaking coexisted and a salon where the demimonde mingled with notables from various spheres, as captured by Avedon in a 1969 photograph (pp. 132–33). About the 1970s New York social scene, Diana Vreeland said Warhol "ran the city."[106] He was synonymous with the celebrity-driven club scene, too, especially at Studio 54, which he frequented with a variegated entourage. Carlo McCormick described the club world as an intersection where "all modes of cultural production were in the same room sharing the same space,"[107] a development that had incubated in Warhol's activities of the 1960s and flourished in the hybrid social atmosphere of the 1970s. And no vehicle better encapsulated the mixing of art, fashion, music, and celebrity than the popular-culture magazine *Interview*, which Warhol founded in 1969 (left).

The Argentine painter Guillermo Kuitca once said that the hybridity of Warhol's art practice "reaches a level that has no boundaries."[108] That had been the case from near the beginning of Warhol's mature career. Not satisfied with pure painting, much less the mandates given by the recent history of the medium, he had integrated the look and practice of photography into this medium. Equally radical was his attitude toward artistic style, as was suggested in his statement about reading Jean Genet and being struck by his lack of awareness of style. Here is Warhol in 1963 on the subject of working not in one mode but in many: "I think that's what's going to happen, that's going to be

RICHARD AVEDON

Andy Warhol and members of the Factory: Paul Morrissey, director; Joe Dallesandro, actor; Candy Darling, actor; Eric Emerson, actor; Jay Johnson, actor; Tom Hompertz, actor; Gerard Malanga, poet; Viva, actress; Paul Morrissey; Taylor Mead, actor; Brigid Polk, actress; Joe Dallesandro; Andy Warhol, artist, New York, October 30, 1969, 1969
Printed September 1975
Gelatin silver print

CAT. 55

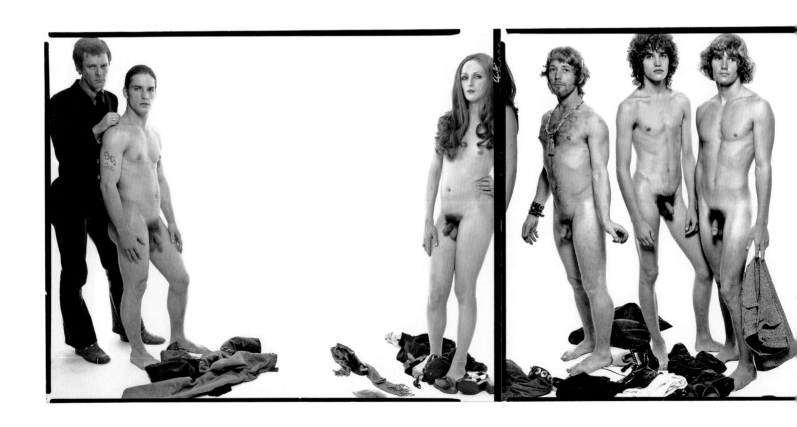

ANDY WARHOL
Silver Clouds, 1966
Metalized polyester film
with helium
CAT. 31

the whole new scene."[109] If we consider the work of Richter and Polke in Germany, Hirst in England, Murakami in Japan, and Koons, Nauman, and Prince in America, among many others, that "scene" has been with us ever since. Artists no longer take an oath to an artistic style and instead exhibit a remarkably freewheeling, promiscuous attitude toward style, medium, technical proficiency, the use of assistants, authorship, and other conventions familiar from history. Seemingly, there are no longer any virtues at all.

Within a decade of Warhol's 1963 observation about allegiance to style, he had added a dazzling array of activities to his own portfolio. The aforementioned wallpaper was hardly a novel invention in the decorative arts, but its appearance on the walls of a contemporary art gallery in 1966 was certainly a spectacle; five years later, Sol LeWitt made his first wall drawings,[110] continuing the endeavor of flat painting that had consumed so many painters of the 1960s. In the sphere of graphic design, Warhol continued to design record covers,[111] notably those for *The Velvet Underground &*

Nico, 1967, on which appeared an image of a banana that could literally be peeled, and for the Rolling Stones' *Sticky Fingers*, 1970, on which was a zipper that could be undone. Beyond producing the Velvet Underground, Warhol is thought of as integral to the development of punk, glam rock, and new wave, having influenced bands and musicians such as the New York Dolls, David Bowie, Blondie, and the Talking Heads, among many others. And he launched *Interview*, whereupon came the "mainstreaming of the Warhol sensibility"[112] into many vehicles, including *People* magazine, which began in 1974, and *Bunte*, published in Germany from 1975.

In his mentoring role to young artists such as Basquiat and Keith Haring, with both of whom he collaborated on series of works, Warhol helped lay the groundwork for the emergence of graffiti or street art as a legitimate art-world genre.[113] His example in embracing the low end of the high/low dichotomy, appropriating from any and all sources, especially vernacular ones, and adhering to populist, not elitist, ideals were all qualities that appealed to this burgeoning movement, where the preferred venue for exhibition was the streets rather than art galleries. Warhol's importance might have also been as a role model: the lower-class, gay outsider having scaled the walls of the establishment.

The Factory, once it had been entirely covered with silver foil and paint in 1963 by Warhol's assistant Billy Name, had a kind of shabby yet glitzy fabulousness, a quality that was seen repeatedly in Warhol's endeavors and embraced by others. That would have been the ambiance at the *Exploding Plastic Inevitable* shows and at the Castelli Gallery in 1966, when *Silver Clouds* created a carnival-type atmosphere. Other artists captured this quality in ways small and large. For instance, Cory Arcangel's *Super Mario Clouds v2k3*, 2003 (below), is a direct reference to *Silver Clouds*. Day-Glo paint in Haring's hands went a long way toward creating something fun, as did the silver tape covering a motley group of chairs in Rob Pruitt's 2010 installation at the Gavin Brown Gallery in New York. Warhol had brought a disco ball to the shows on Saint Mark's Place, thereby enhancing the fabulously raucous atmosphere. Subsequently, sensational chandeliers have become another method by which artists create spectacles.[114] If Warhol fashioned an American-style look of tawdry glamour, other artists have developed similar appearances from within their own cultures. In a 2008 exhibition at Gagosian Gallery in New York, Piotr Uklański concocted an unlikely image of Polish gold glam (p. 136). Similarly, Fahrad Moshiri evokes a milieu of Iranian gilded glitz in some of her works, and Murakami creates Japanese-style extravaganzas (p. 136). These expressions of shallow fabulousness may be said to allude to or encompass the sleazy banality that underlies Warhol's sensibility. In other words, banality, fabulousness, and sleaze all go together in the oeuvre of Warhol.

A kind of low-budget grandeur can be ascribed to Warhol's many paintings of flowers from the mid-1960s, which panoramically covered the walls, as if Monet's *Water Lilies*, at the Castelli Gallery in 1964 and were hung in almost suffocating profusion at the Sonnabend Gallery in Paris in 1965 (p. 136). Reinforcing the prefabricated history of these works, the image of which was appropriated, are Warhol's 1963 *Do-It-Yourself* series of paintings, which demonstrate that a perfectly satisfactory picture of a revered subject can be made through a crude exercise, or by adding Day-Glo paint from a bottle, as he had done for many of the 1964 paintings. In all, Warhol's flower paintings have a kind of false exquisiteness in comparison to any flowers from life. Likewise, works incorporating flowers by Murakami (p. 139), Koons (p. 140), and Polly Apfelbaum (p. 140) lend the subject a kind of unnatural glitz and a three-dimensional presence.

CORY ARCANGEL
Super Mario Clouds v2k3, 2003
Hacked Super Mario game
cartridge, Nintendo gaming
system, projector
CAT. 53

According to Simon Doonan, creative ambassador of Barneys New York, Warhol is "the patron saint of retail"[115] whose greatest ability was in marketing. Still, Warhol's 1966 advertisement in the *Village Voice* would appear to be a relatively farcical attempt by "the patron saint" to generate new income, especially given his early life in New York as a very successful commercial artist. But Warhol never stopped demonstrating his credo "good business is the best art,"[116] and he experimented with new ventures throughout his life. He designed the occasional advertisement, tried his hand at acting and producing television programs, and posed for product endorsements. Warhol's portrait business thrived from the 1970s on, and like the manager of a car dealership he bullied his assistants to generate new customers.[117] Along with the selling of "Warhols," he routinely made multiple examples of similar images, all the better to produce income. This activity was different from creating a single painting composed of a serial image but was certainly related to it by virtue of the mechanical silkscreen process involved in the making. Indeed, the relationship between the two genres of work is clearly quite close.

With the *Flowers*, 1964–68 (p. 141 and lower right), and *Dollar Sign* paintings, 1981 (p. 142), it would appear that Warhol was particularly shameless in selling his autograph. However, this did not deter other artists from copying him: witness Koons's *Puppy* multiple (p. 29), Hirst's *Spot* painting series,[118] or Murakami's *Flower* paintings. In 1986, Haring opened his Pop Shop on Lafayette Street in SoHo (opposite), as he, too, became an entrepreneur. Other artists have taken a less wide-eyed look at the relationship of art and money, for example, Barbara Kruger, who has made a critique of that relationship the focus of her art.[119]

Having called his studio the "Factory" (and later, the "Office"), Warhol signaled the degree to which he was running a business. Although it might be thought that the term *factory* was a subterfuge, with its blue-collar association, it is difficult not to take the name at face value, given the quantity of works that were produced there.[120] Through these activities, Warhol demonstrated his favorite crossover, that between the seemingly contradictory fields of art and business—another American hybrid that has since burgeoned in the international art world. All the while, the conventional image of the avant-garde artist was being recast as well.

PIOTR UKLAŃSKI
Installation at Gagosian Gallery, New York, 2008

TAKASHI MURAKAMI
Installation at the Museum of Contemporary Art, Los Angeles, 2007

ANDY WARHOL
Flowers exhibition at Galerie Ileana Sonnabend, Paris, May 1965

As early as 1965, at least, Warhol's fame was already enormous, such that his first retrospective, at the Institute of Contemporary Art in Philadelphia, saw an unimagined mob at the doors. In order to further his renown and encourage sales, Warhol, by the 1970s, had essentially branded himself. This process had a surprising outcome; the photographer Jeff Wall has said that Warhol gave permission for artists to embrace fame.[121] In this regard, Warhol was probably attracted to Joseph Beuys because of his extraordinary European renown, recognizing in him a kindred spirit—another avant-garde artist who did not shy away from fame and commercialism and who fabricated a persona to further his specific ambitions. Earlier, Salvador Dalí, another Warhol favorite, had completely embraced celebrity. Many artists in recent years have engaged with this aspect of art-world success, no doubt in part because their generation so adores social media, where notoriety and self-promotion are prevalent.

Warhol's oft-cited statement that "In the future everybody will be famous for fifteen minutes"[122] continues to be enormously appealing to anyone who worships celebrity and believes in the democratic notion that we are all deserving of media attention.[123] Indeed, he has proven to be remarkably prescient. The viewer of a Warhol film has the sense of watching actual people, in seemingly real time, enacting dramas that had genuine meaning for them. In this regard, Warhol's films are the direct forerunner for all forms of reality television and film. After Warhol, the next and most visible instance was the television program *An American Family*, 1973, which had a direct link to Warhol because one of the family members, Lance Loud, had been an admirer of and pen pal with Warhol from an earlier date. As if an intentionally sanitized version of a Warhol film, at least at first, this series followed the lives of what appeared to be a normal family. In a twist that befits the reality-television genre, after the program came to an end on television Lance moved to New York and wrote a column for Warhol's *Interview*.

•

Warhol's impact has been undoubtedly far-reaching, with his work and activity allowing new and diverse options to emerge in the field of contemporary art. In viewing the works assembled here, it appears that artists have not generally "fought" Warhol, as if his

TAKASHI MURAKAMI

ON THE LEVEL

2004

TAKASHI MURAKAMI
Kaikai Kiki, 2001
Acrylic on canvas over panel
CAT. 114

The first time I ever saw a Warhol was about twenty-five years ago. It was at an import bookstore in Tokyo, on the cover of Interview *magazine. A full ten years passed before I finally got the chance to see his work up close in galleries and museums. Just recently, I selected one of Warhol's "Camouflage" paintings for an artist's-choice exhibition at Marianne Boesky Gallery in New York. I chose this work because it represents the culmination of Pop, completely eliminating narrative and emotion, i.e., the conventional elements in the history of painting. As someone who is always looking to what lies beyond Pop, I feel that a work such as this that stands at its pinnacle represents, for me, a kind of starting point.*

Warhol laid the foundations for an art world where artists such as myself and Yoshitomo Nara, armed with contemporary Japanese culture, or even those already at its center, such as Jeff Koons and Damien Hirst, are able to climb free and unrestrained up and down the societal ladder. I have named this unique characteristic "superflat," as a catchphrase of a theory that I hope will succeed Pop.

Warhol often remarked that differences between "high" and "low" were disappearing. Perhaps at the beginning of his career the differences between high and low in American society were great. Of course, I can superficially understand these differences, but I cannot grasp them on an essential level, because I am Japanese and I was never in the U.S. during that period.

POLLY APFELBAUM
Pink Crush, 2007
Dye on synthetic velvet
CAT. 52

JEFF KOONS
Wall Relief with Bird, 1991
Polychromed wood
CAT. 98

ANDY WARHOL
Flowers, 1964
Acrylic and silkscreen on canvas
CAT. 21

ANDY WARHOL
Flowers, 1964
Acrylic and silkscreen on canvas
CAT. 22

ANDY WARHOL
Flowers, 1967–68
Acrylic and silkscreen on canvas
CAT. 34

ANDY WARHOL
Flowers, 1967–68
Acrylic and silkscreen on canvas
CAT. 35

ANDY WARHOL
Dollar Sign, 1981
Acrylic and silkscreen on canvas
CAT. 44

ANDY WARHOL
Dollar Sign, 1981
Acrylic and silkscreen on canvas
CAT. 45

ANDY WARHOL
Dollar Sign, 1981
Acrylic and silkscreen on canvas
CAT. 46

ANDY WARHOL
Dollar Sign, 1981
Acrylic and silkscreen on canvas
CAT. 48

ANDY WARHOL
Dollar Sign, 1981
Acrylic and silkscreen on canvas
CAT. 43

ANDY WARHOL
Dollar Sign, 1981
Acrylic and silkscreen on canvas
CAT. 47

example were suffocating.[124] Instead, they have interacted with his example, explicitly borrowing devices and ideas that they then developed following their own inclinations.

In Warhol and the artists discussed here, we see the genesis and substance of what is generally thought of as Postmodernism.[125] The central attitude of this way of thinking can be variously encapsulated, as in the title of Miles Davis's 1957 album *Birth of the Cool*; Gustave Flaubert's formulation that "depersonalization is a sign of power";[126] and Oscar Wilde's aphorism "To be really modern, one should have no soul."[127] If these ideas suggest that Warhol and the sensibility he helped engender are somehow amoral or evil, it is certainly true that for a long time he was considered so. And he was feared as well, especially as he became an international brand name that had recognition well beyond the art world. But another way to understand Warhol is as a revolutionary who, applying these attitudes along with his camp sensibility, enforced a radical rejection of any orthodoxies concerning modern art—its qualities and aspirations. Conversely, he encouraged the embrace of all possibilities that did not formerly exist in modernism; with this came a virtually shameless desire to live in the cultural moment. His cool attitude brought endless possibilities for uninhibited cross-fertilization and hybrid creations. To put it in a context that was the focus of endless debate, yes, painting was dead, so now anything was possible—including painting. If Warhol's art spelled an end to the "healing power" of modernist art,[128] and if he is the "patron saint of marketing,"[129] and if he belongs "in the pantheon of . . . queer heroes,"[130] then there begins to emerge a portrait of Warhol as a Renaissance man in the era of Postmodernism.

Having dispatched modernist art's claims to spirituality and universalism in one fell swoop, Warhol left a no-holds-barred atmosphere in the art world. By the 1970s the New York art world had become home to a multiplicity of wildly different, concurrent trends, including multimedia phenomena, installation art, performance art, representational art, and identity-focused work. With these trends came a general loosening of the hegemony of recent and past art history, as well as a willingness in America to seriously review the art of Europe, and, eventually, a desire in Europe and America to look more intently at art coming from beyond their borders. In effect, many people who

had been disenfranchised from the art capitals have become enfranchised, and the artist has been remarkably liberated to take advantage of new directions.

Is Warhol still as relevant as he has been over the past decades? In 1989, one writer observed with dismay that the contemporary art world had yet to escape his impact.[131] Almost twenty years later, in 2007, Mark Stevens, with what may have been a degree of bitter fear, wrote that Warhol would continue to "be with us" until artists abandon his values. At that point, Stevens thought, an art historian would write a text called "The Age of Warhol."[132] A recent situation perhaps updates us on Stevens's outlook: in June 2011, a retrospective exhibition of the work of the then thirty-year-old Ryan Trecartin opened at P.S. 1 in New York. In almost every way, Trecartin's riotous films appear to be the genealogical successors to Warhol's. The Trecartin films establish an uninhibited world that is completely counter to the everyday popular dramas of television and film; this realm, like Warhol's, is inhabited by a freaky and outrageous troupe of transsexual, gay, and transvestite actors. It is enlightening to see the responses to Trecartin's body of work. He has been hailed as "bound for greatness,"[133] and as "the most consequential artist to have emerged since the nineteen-eighties, he is . . . the magus of the Internet century."[134] It will require another half century to issue meaningful judgments about Warhol, but there can be no doubt that artists make art history and they still draw sustenance from him.

Warhol's fame is seemingly without end, a fact that will continue to place him near the center of much thinking about art and culture. His name is routinely applied to headlines even when the substance of an article has little or nothing to do with him, or to first-paragraph stage setting, as if knowledge of Warhol and what he stands for is instantly and universally understood.[135] He is also credited with large social changes well beyond art: the title of Elizabeth Currid's 2007 book *The Warhol Economy: How Fashion, Art, and Music Drive New York City* gives him credit for the nature of the city's economy.[136] The other side of fame, of course, is condemnation. In a 2009 article by Jonathan Jones titled "How Art Killed Our Culture," Warhol's soup cans are reproduced to signify our plunge into degradation. The writer concludes, "We're Warhol's ugly brood. . . . The modern world has screwed itself and art led the way."[137] Thus will Warhol's legacy continue to be argued.

NTERVIEWS
WITH
ARTISTS

INTERVIEW WITH
POLLY APFELBAUM

JANUARY 23, 2012

MARLA PRATHER: Your work *Pink Crush* is from 2007 (p. 140), but you have long worked with floral themes in various media and forms, with works such as the crepe-paper *Wall Flowers* series, 1990, or the fabric piece, *Fine Flowers in the Valley*, 1992–93 (collection of the artist). And in 1989 you made *Daisy Chain* (collection of the artist), consisting of a group of wooden forms installed on the floor. The shapes are borrowed directly from Warhol's 1968 screenprint *SAS Passenger Ticket* (p. 169), which he made on the occasion of his trip to Stockholm for an exhibition. What drew you to the so-called dingbat icons—the clover, flower, or starburst forms used by graphic designers—and, specifically, to Warhol's use of them?

POLLY APFELBAUM: I studied printmaking at art school, so the prints were initially my main point of reference for Warhol's work. I probably saw that image very early, before I came to New York in the late 1970s. "The Daisy Chain" was also the title of a show that I did at the Loughelton Gallery in New York in 1989. There were a lot of different pieces in the exhibition, which was like a group show by one person. *Daisy Chain* was the key to the show; it functioned as a map or a chart that opened up the show to a lot of different stories. Dingbats are arbitrary and ambiguous—suggestive and general, geometric but signlike at the same time. They were used ornamentally, by old-school hand printers, as punctuation or decoration. They are abstract signs. They don't have specific meaning and they are not part of the text. I think it's important that what Warhol does (and

what I took from that image) was not a single dingbat, which would have been just decorative, but the whole catalogue, the array of dingbats at different scales.

Daisy Chain is one of a series of wood floor pieces that I was working on at the time. They were fabricated by a patternmaker. That trade has now entirely disappeared, but it used to be an integral part of any machine shop, even in the automobile industry. I found a working patternmaker (since retired) in Pennsylvania, and I would supply him with drawings but leave the actual construction up to him. He would make these forms out of scrap wood because, in a traditional pattern, it doesn't matter what it's made of—it's just the form to make a mold. This process allowed me to investigate and reconstruct the forms at the same time. It was a way into the world of three-dimensional form through drawing and working in two dimensions, which was where I came from.

MP: In the following year, 1990, you made *A Pocket Full of Posies*, thirteen flowers cut out of flat steel and arranged in a circle on the floor. The steel forms obviously refer to Carl Andre, but the blossom forms immediately call to mind the series of flower paintings Warhol began to make in 1964. Your work has been described as a feminist response to the forms and, ultimately, the materials of Minimalism. Is it fair to say that Warhol's imagery provided a crucial example in this regard?

PA: In 1994 I was in a show at the Museum of Modern Art called "Sense and Sensibility," curated by Lynn Zelevansky, which took up this theme of feminist responses to Minimalism. So it's clearly there in the work, but for me it's not the only reading of the work. I'm a feminist, but not a programmatic artist in the sense of having a feminist agenda in my work. So it's not what I had in mind when I was making the work. I think it's more that I make work out of my experience and I make work out of the visual and artistic culture I inhabit. And Andre and Warhol are very much part of that culture, but so are Lynda Benglis and Eva Hesse.

I also resist the other implication of this reading, which is to ascribe a specifically male point of view to Minimalism. It just seems a bit obvious to see steel as male, fabric as feminine. And as far as *A Pocket Full of Posies* is concerned, it was the first outdoor piece I had ever made, and in part it was just a case of having a material that worked outdoors. The forms were literally taken from a Warhol print. I don't think I had in mind an act of appropriation, perhaps because for him, too, they were found forms. It's that character above all that interests me — the idea of a found form that has some broader legibility and cultural significance.

MP: I believe it was in the same year, 1990, that you shifted to soft materials, paper and fabric, and continued to work largely on the floor. What prompted this change in media?

PA: The major shift was away from the hardness of found (or fabricated) objects, although some of those were soft, too. The floor and the serial aspect continued, and what I added to that was an element of chance, by giving up control through both the staining — which can be only loosely controlled — and the fluidity of the support: sheets, stretched velvet, etc. I loved the malleability of the fabric, that it was never the same twice. The informality was also important to me. It seemed very irreverent to just throw something down on the floor. I like to say that gravity is my best friend. The fabric takes on the form of whatever it's draped over, and I love this yielding quality of the material.

At the same time, the process aspect was still important. When someone else fabricates the work,

there is a kind of mechanical, impersonal aspect to it, which I like. Although it sounds counterintuitive — because the process of staining and cutting was repetitive and somewhat mechanical — with the fabric work I was able to foreground that process aspect, but now under my own control. I was interested in touch and mark-making, not as a personal touch but as the record of process.

I also wanted to get back to a more explicit use of color, which, like the dingbats, can be suggestive and emotionally rich without specific meanings or associations. As to what prompted the shift, I think one thing was a sense that I had a lot of things going on in the work at the time, maybe some of them contradictory, and I wanted to clarify and focus. Unifying everything through the use of the fabric was one way of doing that. There could still be a lot of variation, but the techniques and the material would tie it all together.

MP: *Pink Crush* is made up of hundreds of unconnected, overlapping pieces of synthetic velvet. Can you talk about the qualities, practical and symbolic, of this particular material that appeal to you?

PA: That's an easy one. I love the cheapness, the lowness of the material; it's almost tacky. It comes in a lot of colors (I have not left the found object behind in that sense). It's bright and loud. It is 100 percent artificial. It didn't exist twenty years ago. Being in New York, I can take advantage of the fashion and theater industries — they produce things like this, which were never intended for art-making. It's also always changing. It's made in lots, and I buy remnants so I can rarely get exactly the same fabric or color twice. I like the idea that these are the leftovers of the fashion industry.

Practically speaking, the way the fabric takes the dye is fundamental. When I first started experimenting with dye, the way it bleeds out to create a kind of halo was a real discovery. It appears almost as a double line. And the optical properties are very important, too. The fabric has a flat nap. That means it is perceived completely differently from different angles, that it's very sensitive to light conditions. This makes it almost alive. Depending on your vantage point, it looks different. As you move, activating your perception, it changes. I call it cheap magic.

MP: A work like *Daisy Chain* was fabricated, but I gather you now make all of your own works. Are there no Factory-like operations in your studio?

PA: I am a factory of one. Even though the work is very repetitive and time consuming, I don't like to work with assistants. Never have. I actually enjoy the machinelike repetition involved in doing this work. I don't think of it in a craft sense, but that idea of embedded time, that the piece is like a record of the time spent making it, is important in the work. There is another simple reason that I don't use assistants, which is that I don't plan the works in advance. The ideas and patterns emerge out of the process itself, and I need to be there to steer the process. Doing and thinking are integrated. I know each shape; these are like my brushstrokes.

MP: When and why did the Warholian floral motif make a comeback in your work? As you know, Warhol made *Flower* paintings on several scales and arranged the smaller works in allover grid patterns on the wall. Was this serial aspect part of their appeal?

PA: For a show in 2003 at the Massachusetts College of Art I did a large installation called *Cartoon Garden*. Part of that invitation was the amazing opportunity to work with the large-scale Polaroid camera up in Cambridge. The flowers were drawn on the fabric first and then photographed. For me, the flowers, which originate with Warhol, are not about sentimentality. I think instead of graffiti, doodles, asterisks, etc. The work is about iconic mark-making—the flowers are diagrammatic, almost automatic, and not representational—and it depends on accumulation.

I am a factory of one. . . .
I actually enjoy the
machinelike repetition
involved in doing this work.

The clusters of marks layer and accumulate to make a kind of urban landscape. Around that same time, I was also invited to participate in the Valencia Biennale, which had as its theme "Vacant Lots." I don't usually do outdoor installations. My idea was to draw on the walls of vacant sites, and I wanted something iconic, recognizable. The narrative dimension came back because of the drawing. I took the drawings from *A Pocket Full of Posies*, which were originally based on Warhol, and transferred them to the walls with luminescent paint so they would glow in the dark. A year later, I created *Flags of Revolt and Defiance*, a series of flower flags that evolved from those same drawings, which were shown at the 2004 Lodz Biennale. So, in some sense, I never really left the flower behind. Also, in 2004 I was in a show called "Flowers Observed, Flowers Transformed," at The Andy Warhol Museum in Pittsburgh, and in 2008 a show called "Flower Power: A Subversive Botanical," at the New Mexico Museum of Art in Santa Fe.

And absolutely, as it is for Warhol, the serial aspect is very important to me. It's much less about the motif itself than about the repetition of the motif and the abstract, serial character that it takes on through repetition. By using an entire sheet of dingbats, a catalogue of all possible dingbats of interest to me, it becomes about more than the flowerlike character of any individual sign. It's about the structure of the chart and the order of the signs. In fact, I think this is true of all of my work; the flower may be there as a motif, but it's the serial nature of the flower repeated many times that is significant. In *Wall Flowers*, for example, there are more than five hundred individual flowers that together make a target, not a flower.

It's also important to say that my large-scale installations are often based on combinatory systems and rules for the organization of the colors. For example, in *Ice* [1998, Whitney Museum of American Art, New York] I used all 104 colors of the Sennelier dyes sequentially in a series of fixed combinations. Giving myself over to rules, to the logic of a serial system (even if it's maybe a completely illogical system), has been part of this work for a while now.

MP: Improvisation is clearly essential to your working method. *Pink Crush* is made on-site by you each time it is installed. Many of your previous floor works have fluid or seemingly unfixed boundaries. As you have said, "The assemblage of pieces moves through the space like an organic growth—mold or lily pads—like stones in a stream, like liquid spills." *Pink Crush*, however, has the fixed dimensions of a large square, which approximates the format of painting, and you have described your floor compositions as "fallen paintings." One could invoke many traditions of art composed on the ground, from Navajo sand painting to the paintings of Jackson Pollock or the poured latex works of Lynda Benglis. In 1962 Warhol made the radical *Dance Diagram* works that can be installed horizontally. Even the *Oxidation* or so-called piss paintings (also very improvisational) began essentially as floor pieces. And, as you know, Warhol based his *Flower* paintings on reproductions in the magazine *Modern Photography.* The viewer is essentially looking down at flowers in the grass, so his original source image was, in fact, horizontally oriented. How much did these factors enter into your own floor-based works?

PA: The scale is more important to me than the shift from the vertical to the horizontal. As I moved into more installation-based work, it was this sense of taking over a room and having the viewer inhabit the space of the piece that attracted me to the floor. That said, you can't get away from the history of the horizontal. I think it was Lynda Benglis who first talked about "fallen paintings," and, of course, her work is a major influence. I also recently reread Leo Steinberg's essay on the "flatbed picture plane." I remain very attracted to the idea that these works are collections, accumulations of things, on a horizontal surface—that's one way to think about the piss paintings! You can collect anything on a flat surface. I think that's where the improvisational comes in, this sense that you can drop anything on a flat surface and it stays there. It's a great organizing device. That basic insight of the Steinberg essay, that the work no longer alludes to some sort of vertical window onto the world, remains important to me: the very simple idea of operating by a process of accumulation on a horizontal receptor surface, whether it is dyed fabric on the floor or the Plasticine works I am making now that sit on tabletops.

MP: You have described *Pink Crush* as a drawing. It seems to consist of different types of drawing. First there are the drawn images of the flowers themselves, then there are the forms cut around the flowers, *à la* Matisse. Can you talk about the nature of drawing in your work?

PA: In the color/line dichotomy I was always on the side of color, and my point of reference was painting more than drawing. But beginning with a piece called *Single Gun Theory* [2001, FRAC, Nord-Pas-de-Calais] that I made for a show at Frith Street in London ["Drawings," 2001], curated by Rose Lord, I started to draw more consciously with the dye. It was the first time that the work was contextualized as drawing as opposed to painting. This piece was much more linear, and following it I decided to accentuate that idea, limiting myself to just the black dye and activating the hand more.

In this work, cutting is about drawing, which speaks directly to the Matisse cutouts. It's just another way of defining an edge. The edges in the work are always marked and controlled in several ways: the shifting edge of the stain (which makes a shadow line, a double line), the sharper edge of the cut fabric itself, and the layering of pieces that accumulate edges. So it extends these previous concerns, but there is also a new emphasis on mark-making, the arc of the hand, the liquidity of the stain, and the weight of the line. Actually, these qualities also make the work somewhat more sculptural, in that it is physical and object based. And earlier, you mentioned that *Pink Crush* forms a square. For me, that was more about the format of a sheet of paper than the shape of a canvas, because I was thinking of drawing.

MP: You have said that you prefer to work outside of "defined disciplinary limits." A work such as *Pink Crush* inhabits an ambivalent place between painting, drawing, and sculpture. Why is this quality important to you?

PA: I like very much what the critic Lane Relyea said about my work: "Apfelbaum's art is both painting and sculpture, and perhaps photography and fashion and formless material process as well. It is all these things—wildly so, and wildly not

Pop is absolutely fundamental to me. It's so much a part of the work that maybe I am no longer conscious of it.

so."[1] Thinking back, one reason this is important to me has to do with personal history. I arrived in New York at the end of the 1970s, and I loved the energy of the art world at that time. It was all about alternative practices, experimentation, installation—open and speculative. I liked that sense of not having to fit into a defined disciplinary category, that all was available. Especially important models were some of the women working at that time: Ree Morton, for example. And I didn't study sculpture or painting specifically. Rather than thinking about particular problems within painting or sculpture, I followed certain ideas through, and where they ended up was where they ended up. I am very happy to be contextualized sometimes as a painter and sometimes as a sculptor or an installation artist. The work is chameleonlike in that it is conceptually open, too—sometimes Pop, sometimes abstract, mostly both. For me, the motivation in the work is inclusive, not exclusive. However, I like to have these categories to push back on. I am not so comfortable in a "postmedium" world. The specificity of the history of painting, sculpture, or installation is always there for me as a reference. A friend once called me a "painter with problems." Maybe that's a good description, but in that sense I am also a sculptor with problems, an installation artist with problems.

MP: Despite the fact that the fabric is one color, *Pink Crush* exerts a remarkably rich chromatic punch, with almost kinetically optical properties. Can you talk about your color choices? Was Warhol's use of Day-Glo colors and fluorescent paints a model for you?

PA: Absolutely, but it's more a question of light than color. This is one of the effects of a large-scale installation. There is a reflected light that transforms the space; it gets picked up by the walls and is visible beyond the limits of the piece. Although the piece is on the floor, it fills the space. For me, that's what makes it sculptural. It may seem like a stretch, but I think of this work in relation to artists such as Robert Irwin or Dan Flavin as much as to Warhol's painterly colors.

MP: Like Warhol, you enthusiastically embrace popular culture, from your cartoonish, graffitilike imagery, to your interest in commercial imagery and logos, to the cartoon references in your titles. Now that you are no longer making flower pieces, is Pop still an important touchstone for you?

PA: Yes, Pop is absolutely fundamental to me. It's so much a part of the work that maybe I am no longer conscious of it. But, to me, it means less as a specific reference to art history or forms in the work than as a kind of openness to the world, a sense that artworks don't exist in a separate domain apart from popular culture, mass media, commercial logos, cartoons, etc. The installation I did in Ireland, for example, was based on an album cover from Stax Records [*Stax*, Carlow Visual Center for Contemporary Art, Carlow, Ireland, September 25, 2009–January 16, 2010]. The sequined fabric that I have been using references Las Vegas showgirls; an older piece, *Blossom* [2000, The Museum of Modern Art, New York], was inspired by the cartoons of Chuck Jones and the Powerpuff Girls. None of these references actually exist in the work as a specific image, but they are all important to me as background and inspiration. For me, this background is just part of the world today, and I think we have to be generous and accepting of that reality as it is given to us, not push back or reject it for some sort of abstract ideal. Libby Lumpkin has written that I have "one foot in the 'conceptual' world and the other in the world itself."[2] I am happy with that description.

INTERVIEW WITH
JOHN BALDESSARI

JANUARY 6, 2012

MARLA PRATHER: When Calvin Tomkins wrote his fine profile of you for the *New Yorker*, in October 2010, he said, "Andy Warhol's shadow hangs heavy over the international art world, but not in L.A., where the most relevant artist of the moment is John Baldessari." I won't put you on the spot, as to whether you agree with his assessment of your paramount relevance, though he has a point. But it does seem that Warhol made less of an immediate and long-term impact in California than in New York and Europe. I wonder if you agree with that, and if so, why do you think that is?

JOHN BALDESSARI: I think I agree. The dominant mode at that time was probably artists from the Ferus Gallery, Light and Space work, or people working in plastic. And I don't see how Andy's aesthetic and those aesthetics could converge.

MP: As you no doubt know, Warhol's first solo show was at the Ferus Gallery, in 1962. It included the *32 Campbell's Soup Cans* (The Museum of Modern Art, New York).

JB: Yes, and that show really influenced me a lot. I don't know if I knew anything about him prior to that. I did do a lot of reading, so maybe I did. The *Campbell's Soup Can* paintings were all lined up, as I remember, on a shelf, one after another. And my reaction was, "Wait, you can't do this!" I remember the only time I had had that reaction before was when I was looking at Yves Klein's all-blue paintings. And I thought, "Well, somebody did it, and you should think about it." But, in a way,

it made sense to me because Sol LeWitt had influenced me a lot, and John Cage, Duchamp. I guess the subtext of saying "you can't do this" was that it looked like a lot of work by untrained artists, as if somebody decided that they were going to paint something, and they looked around and said, "Oh, I'll paint a soup can." They don't know a lot about the history of art, and there you have it; you have a soup can. But put it in a different context— that was new to me.

MP: In 1963 Warhol showed the *Liz* and *Elvis* paintings at the Ferus Gallery, and that's when he made his famous cross-country trip with friends. He said of the experience, "The further west we drove, the more Pop everything looked." Around that time, you were still painting on fragments of billboards, but you were also making prescient works, like the grid of photographs titled *The Backs of All the Trucks Passed While Driving from Los Angeles to Santa Barbara, California, Sunday, January 20, 1963* (p. 170). These were the kinds of trucks that Warhol was passing as he headed west. A work like this has an uncanny affinity with Warhol's grids of coffee labels and movie stars, and even with similar automobile subjects, such as his *Optical Car Crashes* of the same period. You mention Sol LeWitt, who used grids and serial forms but not until a bit later. Was there at that moment any relationship to Warhol?

JB: I had this sort of war within, trying to bring photography into the realm of art or art into the realm of photography—which, of course, was not unique to me. And to deal with that I was using

billboard material because, in essence, these portions of billboards were nothing but large photographs. So I painted on them and left some parts exposed, some not exposed. Some I didn't paint on at all.

I knew about Warhol's silkscreen and Bob Rauschenberg's silkscreen. I said, "I don't want to do that, because then I'm going to get tossed into that camp." But somehow, I wanted to have the photograph on canvas because that canvas would signal that it was art. About that time, I discovered this photographic emulsion that one could use, and that solved my problem.

MP: You're just a few years younger than Warhol would have been, had he not died in 1987. How well did you know him?

JB: I can't say that I knew him. He was showing with Ileana [Sonnabend] and Leo [Castelli], and I was showing with Ileana; and they were, as you know, joined at the hip. Anyway, I'd see him quite often and we'd talk—but he wasn't very talkative, so I can't say that I knew him.

MP: You've said that you feel in Warhol a kindred spirit because of his use of photography. He renounced painting for a time to make films; and you renounced painting quite ceremoniously, in 1968, to make photo-based work. You're certainly a dedicated cineaste. In fact, you've said that the most important artist of the twentieth century wasn't Warhol or Duchamp but the French filmmaker Jean-Luc Godard. I wonder if Warhol's films were of any interest to you.

JB: Yes. He and his gang were in San Diego at that time, and they did a showing of *The Chelsea Girls*.

I had this sort of war within, trying to bring photography into the realm of art or art into the realm of photography.

And I liked that it had three screens going at once. But I saw it as something that Godard would do. I think that the Warhol film that impressed me the most was *Empire*. And, of course, his portraits of people, the screen tests, were very much like *Empire* (p. 26), except they didn't go on as long.

MP: Going back to your early paintings, one of my favorites is *Art Lesson*, from 1964 (private collection), which is a monochrome painting with imagery from an appropriated source, an advertisement for a how-to manual on art. It could easily be shown in this exhibition alongside an early Warhol, the hand-painted *Icebox*, from 1961 (p. 22), which uses the image of an open, fully stocked refrigerator that he took from a newspaper advertisement.

JB: They're destroyed now, but I was making blow-ups using an opaque projector and the covers of Bible tracts—for example, there is some guy floundering in the water and being thrown a life preserver, and the tract says, "Have you accepted Jesus?" When I saw Warhol was doing something similar, I said, "Well, you know, nobody's unique."

MP: In terms of your use of an appropriated source in *Art Lesson* and his appropriated source in *Icebox*, do you see the acts of appropriation as different in any way?

JB: I don't know if I can say that. I look around and say, "Why can't *that* be art?" I was constantly moved by this question, and I still am moved by it. We seem to have this tendency to put things into two baskets. And I said, "Why can't everything be in one basket?" I just liked the looks of stuff around me; it did look like art to me.

MP: So it wasn't so much about the content of the appropriated image in *Art Lesson*.

JB: Not for me. But I must say, about those Bible tract works—I had a strong religious background. I think I was taking a poke at that. But that's the only case where content might've mattered.

MP: Your two works in the exhibition are both from the late sixties—*Econ-O-Wash, 14th and Highland, National City, Calif.*, from 1966–68 (p. 34), and a text painting

I look around and say, "Why can't that _be art?_" I was constantly moved by this question, and I still am moved by it.

called *A Two-Dimensional Surface without Any Articulation Is a Dead Experience*, from 1967 (p. 119). *Econ-O-Wash* is included in the first section of the exhibition, called "Daily News," which is about banality in many manifestations. It includes works by a number of artists, including Warhol, who, like you, combined image and text. But you didn't lift your image from the daily news; you supplied the photograph yourself. Yet you've said you wanted the quality of a fuzzy newspaper image. Why was that?

JB: I was trying to get away from the idea of the photograph as something beautiful and exquisite, with good paper quality and print quality, that sort of thing.

MP: The other work, *A Two-Dimensional Surface*, was hand painted, though not by you. It was outsourced to a professional sign painter. You've said you see language as the equivalent of an image. And the painting makes me think of late works by Warhol, small works that he made in 1985–86. In them he used all text or text and image, such as in *Have Gun Will Shoot* (The Andy Warhol Museum, Pittsburgh), which features an image of a handgun and hand-lettered text. They're all lifted from available sources. But what strikes me about them is that they begin to look like early Baldessaris. Certainly by that time your view of the world had begun to affect other artists. I wonder if you've ever looked at Warhol, especially later Warhol, and perhaps seen some of your own impact on his work.

JB: [laughs] Oh, now that would be interesting! [The curator] Nora Halpern said she was at the Warhol Museum when they were unpacking, very carefully, all of the *Time Capsules* that Warhol deposited stuff in. And in one box, he had saved an announcement of mine. I was so pleased!

MP: He was looking at everything, all the time.

JB: That's why he's a good artist.

MP: In 1968, Warhol covered the facade of the Moderna Museet in Stockholm with cow wallpaper during the run of his retrospective exhibition. You've also used wallpaper in a number of situations. For example, you covered the facade of the main pavilion at the 2009 Venice Biennale with a photographic paper depicting palm trees and the Pacific Ocean. And you, like Warhol, step comfortably outside of conventional contexts for art. Was he any kind of inspiration in that regard?

JB: No, but I thought it was a great idea. I loved just making something banal even more banal. Somebody that really impressed me, but you don't hear about him too much anymore, is William Anastasi. At Virginia Dwan's gallery [in New York] he did a photo blowup of the wall on which the photograph of the wall was on ["Six Sites, Images of the Wall on the Wall," 1966]. It was the same size. I thought, "Wow, that's great." I had the greatest response I could give to any artist: I wish I had done it.

MP: In the profile in the *New Yorker*, you said that you hadn't thought about Warhol in forty years. But it seems like he's been on your mind lately. We were just talking about art on a facade. And, in what seemed like an homage to Andy's great statement, "In the future, everyone will be world famous for fifteen minutes," last summer you designed a work called *Your Name in Lights*, on the marquee for the front of the Stedelijk Museum in Amsterdam, a work that had premiered at the 2011 Sydney Festival in Australia. Could you describe that work and how it came about?

JB: I was invited to Sydney by John Kaldor [Kaldor Public Art Projects], and he'd shown me around various sites. The first idea I had was to use the vacant area along the dock, near the bridge, where the pope gave his address. It was slated to be a park. I had an idea to have two-dimensional cutouts of people, and if you wanted to be included, you'd give money for the production cost of having a cutout of your silhouette mounted. There was going to be a row of thousands of these along the dock. I got that idea because of photographs I'd seen in Sydney of food lines of the dockworkers. I wanted to replicate that. Behind it all was

some sort of democratic process in my mind. Anyway, Sydney decided to move up the date for making the area into a park, so we couldn't do it. Still thinking along the same lines, I said, "Well, I'll just make it more conceptual. I don't have to have anything physical. I'll just have people's names instead of their cutouts."

That's how I got there. And yes, it seems very Warholesque. It's partially Warhol one step further. I think I called it something like "entry-level celebrity," using the idea that you could have your name in lights. And certainly, it was redolent of Warhol's phrase "famous for fifteen minutes."

MP: Except in this case, you could sign up online and for fifteen seconds your name flashed on an enormous electronic billboard.

JB: I also had in mind all these studies about the average length of time anybody gives to a painting in a museum. I think the last I heard it was an average of seven seconds. In my mind, people's attention span keeps going down. Because of technology, our being bombarded with information, the intervals get shorter and shorter.

MP: And the length of time one remains a celebrity gets shorter and shorter as well. Do you blame Warhol at all for our current obsession with fame and celebrity?

JB: I don't blame him because I think it's always been in the world, in various manifestations. He certainly comes out of Dalí, walking down the street with a lobster on a leash. And Jeff Koons comes out of Dalí, too. But you can trace Dalí going back, too. People like attention.

MP: Last year, you made a series of paintings based on Campbell's Soup cans, which at the same time invoke other artists you admire, such as Henri Matisse and Sol LeWitt. Could you talk about how that body of work came about?

JB: I think it was just a shift in my work. I had been appropriating found photography wherever I could find it, and a lot of it comes from movie stills, but not always. I decided that I would just continue appropriating photography, but it would be photography of things in art history.

So I wouldn't be appropriating the art itself; I would be appropriating photographs of that art. It's a fine distinction, but it was important in my mind. And then I was just playing a giant art-history test for people. I began to move things around, where people weren't so sure what they were seeing. That could be interesting for me and maybe for them. Could I change Dalí to look like Duchamp, let's say? On and on, making these shifts to make people uncertain of what they were seeing. And so you would have to have some knowledge of art history. I guess I was getting really sick of people having trophy art. Oh, that's a Warhol, that's a Richter, and so on. You can say about the work, "Well, wait a minute; maybe that's not a Richter. Maybe that's not a Warhol."

MP: I have one last question about this mantle of influence. You are a figure to whom the word *influential* is constantly attached, as an artist, a teacher, a role model. I could imagine down the road a show called "Regarding Baldessari."

JB: Good lord! Okay, let me laugh, but go ahead.

MP: The importance of being a model to younger artists—I know it matters to you. Do you think in the end that Warhol was a critical model for younger artists?

JB: Yes, I think so. I don't know if he intended it, but he certainly is. And I do have this ethical idea of art, which is that you have to give back. You just can't take all the time. That informs me a lot. I think art is a conversation and you should say something that somebody responds to, and keep the conversation going. You just don't want to say the same thing over and over and over again.

MP: That's great, because this exhibition is about dialogue and conversation between works of art and between artists and generations, and not all moving in one direction but moving back and forth.

JB: Also, because I'm working with art history right now, I remember this great thing that De Kooning said, that a masterpiece is something that informs the present. He's exactly right. If it doesn't speak to you, then it's dead.

INTERVIEW WITH
VIJA
CELMINS

AUGUST 3, 2011

MARLA PRATHER: What is your level of comfort being included in an exhibition that is centrally about the phenomenon of Warhol?

VIJA CELMINS: First of all, when I started out, I wanted to be an abstract painter. I've always liked that kind of painting best. But in the early 1960s, I was caught up in the fact that things were imploding in the art world. People were doing objects and people were going to representation. They were using images. And I found myself sort of backed into a corner, making gestures. I came to the feeling that the work I was doing meant nothing to me, that it was about somebody else's life, somebody else's paintings. I don't know whether Andy Warhol was so much an influence, but, in retrospect, I can see that he just exploded like the bomb, and that his influence must've been everywhere. But my own interest in the object came from a couple of different areas.

One of them was Giorgio Morandi, whose work I saw really early, when I was still in art school in Indiana [John Herron Institute, Indianapolis]. I was amazed that something so small could be so powerful. When I began to make decisions about throwing away the work that I had been doing in school—throwing it away mentally— I also collapsed my paintings from big to small, first to actual size. For instance, a painting of a TV is an actual-size TV, like all of the objects. And then I started painting the little clippings that I had been collecting, subjects that were more about my past than about the current times.

In the early sixties, we were crazed with all the war images that came on TV and having antiwar protests. I was a child in Germany during the last six months of World War II. There was a lot of bombing and a lot of destruction. I don't know whether cause and effect are so clear always, because, when you're doing art, everything funnels into your work. But when I think back on it, one of the reasons that I started choosing the war images at that time was to make a connection, somehow, with another part of myself that was more than just looking at the objects that I had been painting. The other artist that I really connected to, emotionally, was Jasper Johns, who depicted objects that had a bit more touch to them.

Now, I did see that first show that Andy Warhol had ["Andy Warhol: Campbell's Soup Cans," Ferus Gallery, Los Angeles, 1962] because I was in Los Angeles at the time, getting a degree at UCLA. It was something that came from New York and was really hip. But I thought it was a commercial world, which I was not interested in. I didn't come from commercial art. I could never print or make straight edges. I couldn't handle that sort of decorative look. Ed Ruscha could print. But I was always a more bungling artist, unfortunately, a sincere paint lover. I had no overview then at all, no irony, no distance from my work. I also did not know much about American culture, which was so much a part of Warhol's work.

Andy Warhol brought a kind of excitement to the art world, even though there wasn't that much

excitement in L.A. There was a little bit. I sometimes think, when I look back on it, that I had one
foot in European painting and one foot in American
painting, you know? Maybe I'm still like that.
I tend to be very paint oriented, with the history
of painting looming over me.

I did one painting, which is a little Warhol-ish,
of a Shasta can—it was sitting on a table, which
was sort of Morandi-ish, but it had "Shasta" crook-
edly painted on it. In L.A., there were other artists
who were doing paintings with writing on them.
Obviously, Ed Ruscha, John Baldessari, and Wallace
Berman. There was a guy named Phillip Hefferton
who was making paintings of money. So those
things were in the air. Andy Warhol was painting
words, as was Roy Lichtenstein. I also liked Johns's
use of text.

MP: But there is a point when you are painting three-
dimensional, quotidian objects in your world, and then
there's a shift.

**VC: It occurred when I got through with the things
in my rather empty studio. Then, since I'd been
collecting clippings, I started painting them.**

MP: Warhol was a maniacal collector of clippings and
images. He went to the picture collection at the New
York Public Library. He culled material from magazines
and newspapers.

**VC: I did not know that. But I wonder if he
collected things from old Europe, just for nostalgia's sake, like I did? I, of course, collected images**

that were gray paintings already, images of past
disasters. I realized, about twenty years later,
that Gerhard Richter also collected some of these
same war images. He must have found some
of the same World War II books. There weren't
so many around in the 1960s.

I began to love the grays. First I drew. Because
I'd been doing objects, I drew some of the clippings as objects with torn edges. And then I
thought that was a little thin, so I decided just to
paint the photographs. The look was like still life,
but they were airplanes and war machinery,
distanced, flattened already. I could concentrate
on finding the right form in the painting.

I began to think a little bit more about the
whole painting, instead of just making the marks.
What Andy Warhol introduced was this kind of
detachment, which I also picked up on. I was
becoming more of a conceptual artist, which was
sort of Warhol-like. I was aiming for a cooler
image, a more abstract image.

MP: You have talked about how you don't reproduce an
image, you redescribe it.

**VC: Yes, I thought I was like a scribe. I was going
over the surface like a little ant, redescribing
through my body, my intelligence, my eyes, my
hands. Remaking the image, leaving my traces,
bringing it into another space and another context.**

MP: So in *T.V.*, 1964 (p. 169), this is your television,
and you have placed onto your television a found image
of an airplane diving, crashing. You said at one point
that you were especially moved by the image of the
plane falling out of the sky.

**VC: Yes, I liked the idea of airplanes falling and
spiraling down.**

MP: And how did *Time Magazine Cover*, 1965 (p. 18),
come about?

**VC: I was at a party in Hollywood in August 1965,
and we looked out and there was Watts burning.
There was fire and smoke coming up, all this
violence right there. I got the issue of *Time* magazine and painted the cover right away. I just
couldn't make the surround red. I tried it red;**

*Andy Warhol brought a kind of
excitement to the art world,
even though there wasn't that
much excitement in L.A.*

I was at a party in Hollywood in August 1965, and we looked out and there was Watts burning. . . . I got the issue of Time magazine and painted the cover right away.

kind of commercial, silkscreened way. The image is totally removed and kind of made into a design. I saw it as a silkscreen. I never saw them as violent images first. I saw the commercialness of his methods more. Some of his early works are handsome, with a kind of gritty, earthy graininess. I also liked the objects, like the Brillo boxes, which must have inspired me though I have never admitted it. My work was also becoming cooler and more restrained.

MP: But what about *Burning Man* of 1966 [private collection, New York]? A painting that isn't gray. It has brilliant color.

VC: Well, I thought I could maybe try a little color, but I didn't like it.

MP: It is a kind of anomaly.

VC: Oh, yeah. It was too real. I thought, "I can do this so fast." And that was the cause for not going on with it in some perverse way. I saw the work again about six months ago, forty-four years after I painted it. It looked good.

MP: It was a color image, a color photograph?

VC: It was a printed color image I found in a magazine. I've tried a couple of colored images of photographs, but I didn't feel that they had that certain emotional tone that I was trying to find in my work. A short time later I gave up painting. I thought my painting was too "nice" and it had all this space that I couldn't control. I dropped down to one tool, a pencil. For fifteen years I pushed a pencil because it was more of a material, and the material became more of a player. And I totally dropped making singular images with a background.

MP: One can't imagine two more different practices, Warhol's and yours. He worked quickly, in a factory situation, collaboratively.

VC: I never liked to work quickly. I hated that five-minute pose in art-school figure-drawing class. Probably Warhol had to work quickly for his commercial work. And he had other people

took it out. The printing is a little wacko, as you can see. But I liked doing the grays, and this was a beautiful set of grays. There was this car fallen over, and I love cars. And, of course, it had people in despair and burning and running, which all seemed to speak to me and seemed very topical.

Later I realized that Warhol had done car crashes. I may have seen them in art magazines. Around 1968, I stopped dealing with that kind of imagery. After I had made the series of war things and the *Time* cover, I actually felt that subject matter was too much for painting to hold. I decided that I would spread out the image on the surface where it really belonged. I kept the image in little pieces, so it would relate in and out with the two-dimensional plane.

I saw the Andy Warhol retrospective at the Pasadena Museum of California Art in 1970 ["Andy Warhol"]. I remember I saw an Agnes Martin show there, too—she is someone I like now but didn't understand then. I was a young artist from Indiana. I was in my own world. I didn't really realize what was important and what wasn't. Everything was coming in and going out, but through me.

Warhol made work into posters and into flat things that were quite elegant. I was thinking, "God, this guy really has a good eye." The paintings are very cool, they're elegant, they're flat in a making his work. So many people now do that. I rejected that because I had a hard time working with anybody at all. I still use my hand to make a slightly undulating space, just to keep a bit of me in there.

I thought of these images that I worked with as something dead that I was looking at. So I brought them alive by redescribing them. Actually, I was more into the making, and the little traces of me that might remain after I had applied the rigorous set of rules that I made for myself and for the work. Andy was much more of an idea person, and he inspired other people to do all this work for him.

While I was still living in L.A. I found a book written by Andy Warhol [*The Philosophy of Andy Warhol (From A to B and Back Again)*, 1975]. His parents were immigrants. And where were they from, Czechoslovakia? I thought, "Hey, now, here's this guy finding his way and really making it." It was sort of inspirational. And he was really smart and funny, too, very smart about thinking about art. I had some sympathy for it.

Now it seems somebody is still making more of his paintings in some factory somewhere. Every time, you think, is this a new artist? No, it's just Andy Warhol, but there are another forty paintings up for auction.

At any rate, one has to admit his influence. And I should mention his slow, real-time films, which I really liked. He became such a phenomenon. That may have been a little destructive, at the end there—or a little before the end, actually. When everyone glommed on and made him into a famous figure. I guess it continues now because so many people have invested in him.

MP: I asked how you would measure your comfort level in being included in this show. Now, after our conversation, do you have any final thoughts?

VC: I don't know. I'm feeling sort of generous now toward Andy Warhol. He brought so many people to the art world. Maybe I'm coming around—50 percent, okay?

MP: I'll take that.

INTERVIEW WITH
CHUCK CLOSE

AUGUST 18, 2011

MARLA PRATHER: You moved permanently to New York in 1967, a tumultuous time and a very heady time in the art world. When you arrived here, what was your sense of what Warhol meant? Within your generation, how much did he matter at that point?

CHUCK CLOSE: My first experiences were really when I was in graduate school at Yale, from '62 to '64, when I would come to New York. I remember going to the Stable Gallery and seeing the Heinz Ketchup and Brillo boxes. It was a mind blower. It just looked like a storeroom for a supermarket. Later, in 1965–66, I taught at Amherst [University of Massachusetts] for two years, but I came down to New York all the time. One of my students was Roberta Bernstein and another was Debbie Wye.[1] They were the young sorority girls in the department, and they were Warhol groupies. We'd go to *The Exploding Plastic Inevitable* at the Dom. I actually got a chance to play with all of Andy's equipment—you know, the strobes and projections. It was great. The Velvet Underground was there, Lou Reed. I saw all the movies. I was there every night for *Empire*.

So I was pretty deeply immersed in his world. I was also beginning to work from photographs while I was at Amherst. It was sort of transitional work. I started *Big Nude* [1967, destroyed] in color. I decided I couldn't do a color painting from a black-and-white photograph, so I dumped it, came to New York, and did the twenty-two-foot-long black-and-white nude [Shirley Collection, Seattle]. Then I started my first portrait (p. 171).

But Andy and Alex Katz—and to a certain extent, Philip Pearlstein, who, of course, was Andy's friend—were really important to me. Figuration was being held captive by a very reactionary group of people who insisted on painting from life. I was the Antichrist for working from photographs. I got spit on. I was giving a lecture, and people from the Figurative Art Alliance actually threw beer cans at me.

In 1971 Pearlstein wrote a long piece for the *Times* that said, "I get my highs from using my eyes," which was very critical of anybody, Andy included, who used the worthless photograph. I didn't know about Gerhard Richter, I didn't know about the other people on the West Coast. I did get to know Malcolm Morley, who was at the School of Visual Arts with me. And then I also discovered Richard Artschwager, who was working from photographs and working in black and white. He was important for me, as well. But the thing that interested me was that Andy, Alex, Artschwager, and Pearlstein, these guys were trying to make a truly modernist form of figuration, as opposed to the so-called realists, who wanted to breathe new life into what I thought was shopworn nineteenth-century notions of figuration. And Andy was so successful at it that the so-called eyeball realists didn't even see him as a figurative artist. They claimed De Kooning as a figurative artist but would not take Warhol. And they certainly didn't consider him important to them, which is kind of amazing to me. But, for me, my painting heroes kicked open the door for an intelligent, forward-looking, modernist form of figuration and portraiture.

When I was at Yale, I bought a Lichtenstein print out of his very first show. I remember it was ten dollars unsigned and twenty dollars signed, so I sprung for the signed version. I still have it. I was attacked by Richard Serra and Brice Marden and everybody at Yale for embracing this alien cult that embraced popular culture—because they were still trying to breathe new life into Abstract Expressionism. If you can actually believe it, huge arguments would take place as to who was capable of picking up the fallen lance of Abstract Expressionism and carrying it forward. There were long debates, but nobody was interested in work that drove a stake into the heart of Abstract Expressionism. When Frank Stella came to speak at Yale, Serra called him a fake and a fraud and walked out of the lecture. Robert Rauschenberg came up and said, "The place reeks of Matisse." So I was certainly flirting with the work of the devil, in a sense, by embracing this stuff. And I just loved it from the beginning.

MP: What was your impression of Warhol?

CC: Well, my wife loved him. He would not talk. But if we were at dinner together, he would spend the whole night chatting animatedly with Leslie. I don't know what it was. Maybe the fact that she didn't care about art made it less threatening. But he was not flippant with her. He'd talk about his mother and his dogs.

Figuration was being held captive by a very reactionary group of people who insisted on painting from life. I was the Antichrist for working from photographs. I got spit on.

In 1985, when Sidney and Frances Lewis had a new wing designed for their collection at the Virginia Museum of Fine Arts in Richmond, they chartered a 727 from New York for the opening. They peopled the plane with virtually every artist in New York, every curator, every art historian, every critic. And I remember how, for the 1964 New York World's Fair, Madame Tussauds flew all of their "people" over from London seated in passenger seats, so they wouldn't have to pack their heads in excelsior. There was a photograph looking down the center aisle, and Hitler is sitting next to Betty Grable sitting next to Charlie Chaplin. It's the most surreal photograph. But the Lewises' planeload was like that. People who were not necessarily friends were sitting next to one another. I had Andy on one side and Philip Pearlstein on the other. I looked around the plane and I said out loud to both of them, "Wow, you know, if this plane went down, it would pretty much wipe out the art world in one fell swoop." And Philip, without losing a beat, said, "Yeah, and the *Daily News* would say, 'Andy Warhol and Others Die in a Plane Crash.'" We were clearly all the "and others." That meant Jasper Johns and Rauschenberg were "and others." It was true. Andy hated being upstaged by anyone. He was shot in 1968 about thirty-two hours before Robert Kennedy was shot. And he felt that he got knocked off the front page by having someone more famous than him shot near the same day!

MP: Didn't he want to paint you, or vice versa?

CC: Actually, Andy and I were sitting next to each other at some museum opening dinner in 1987. We had always talked about painting each other's portraits. And he said, "Ah, I've got to go to New York Hospital. I have to go through this lousy operation for my gallbladder. As soon as I get out, you know, we'll take photographs and—" And I said, "Of course." But, I said, "Wait a minute, you get your Instamatic camera, snap a picture, make a silkscreen, and produce a painting in one squeegee stroke. And I'm going to be there for three or four months." I said, "I'd like to paint your portrait. But I'm not going to give it to you." Had we traded portraits I think we both would have come out well, financially speaking. [Warhol died in the hospital following the surgery.]

MP: Yet there are so many parallels between your work and Warhol's: the basis in photography, the use of the grid. He reproduced images from one matrix in the way that you have done with portraits over so many years—for example, *Phil* (p. 79). Obviously, a different kind of matrix, but this idea of repetition and—

CC: And recycling an image. When he recycled, it always seemed to go somewhere else. I always thought that Andy recycled in a really inventive way. I mean, I'm a dyed-in-the-wool formalist, and I don't think that Andy would've ever admitted the importance of the formal aspects of his work, you know? But he was a great formalist. And a great colorist. And prior to the point when he stopped painting and started making movies, I thought there was a certain amount of recycling that really extended what was already there, that pushed it somewhere else. To a certain extent, when he went back to painting and did endless commissioned portraits not everything added to what already had been done, to put it rather bluntly. But I thought we shared a kind of kinship in an interest in running permutations.

MP: Among painters there's a wide diversity of opinion about how good a painter Warhol was. It ranges from those who think he was a great commercial artist and a great graphic designer, not a painter, to those who argue that he was a great painter and a great colorist.

CC: I think he was a great painter. He was a lousy graphic designer. The shoe ads, they're very Ben Shahn–like and very gimmicky, I think. And I guess you could talk about the nose job [*Before and After 1*, p. 84] or *Superman* [Gunter Sachs; see p. 250], which were first in Bonwit Teller's windows in 1961, as being graphic design. But they were paintings.

They reminded me, in a way, of when I was behind the Iron Curtain and I saw Soviet-era painters who had to paint things for the government. Sometimes they would save the paint and make their own work. And sometimes they'd try and find a way to make the work that they had to make interesting. And I think Andy took the commission to do the windows and thought, "They're going to pay me to make paintings. And I'm going to make some paintings." Otherwise, he could've done them on cardboard or on foam core, something that was going to be thrown away. But he didn't. He made works on stretched canvas, as real paintings.

MP: David Hockney said that Andy's portraits aren't really about any kind of psychological penetration, but they're really about his social life.

CC: Well, people say the same thing about mine, that there's no psychology there, that there's no information about who the sitter is, that there's no emotion, that they're cold and mechanical. I just think that's a lot of bullshit, you know? You don't necessarily want to crank it up for some heightened emotional appeal or heighten its psychological impact. You don't want to draw arrows and say, "Read this image this way."

MP: And Warhol was deeply involved in the stage directing of the sitters. The Polaroid photograph could be taken at a cocktail party or at a formalized sitting in the studio.

CC: Or first in a photo booth. Ethel Scull, all the quarters he asked her to bring.

> *People say the same thing about [my portraits], that there's no psychology there, that there's no information about who the sitter is, that there's no emotion, that they're cold and mechanical. I just think that's a lot of bullshit, you know?*

*[Warhol] enjoyed constructing
a situation in which certain things
happened that were outside
of his control. He was probably the
greatest voyeur who ever lived.*

MP: But he could enlist a professional makeup artist, direct what clothing the sitters were wearing, what angle they were sitting at, and ultimately he selected from the multiple images, so there was actually a considerable amount of control.

CC: Plus, he knew that he was going to take a photograph that would be reduced to a flat, high-contrast pattern, that the silkscreen itself would carry only a certain amount of information and the rest would be filled in with color. Think about how you make recognizable imagery with the least amount of marks. Tom Wesselmann painted two nipples and a pube to energize a flat, pink shape and make it into a figure, when it's just the placement of a couple symbols. That's what Warhol did with lips and eyes that floated, reducing the amount of information that's carried by the silkscreen to things that are highly modified by what else happens in that area. But big areas of undifferentiated color were charged by these highly symbolic areas and would make them warp into something. A cheek would be ahead of a chin, and yet it's all one big, flat area of color. Those are formal, painterly concerns.

I could make a case for him using Paul Cézanne or any one of a number of artists that we really don't normally think of as being important for him. He played the role of a naïve person, but he was an immensely sophisticated person. I remember I got an invitation for the night Studio 54 opened. I said, "Oh, what's this?" And I threw it in the wastebasket. And that was the best night ever to be there, right? So Andy always knew where to be. But he wasn't necessarily a generous art-world citizen. I don't think he did a lot of things to help other artists. He was very much looking out for number one. But, of course, his foundation has done a great deal to help emerging artists or overlooked older artists.

He could be generous to individual artists. He was very generous to me and always said that he admired what I did. He didn't understand how I had the patience to do what I did. But the idea that everybody made his work for him is not true. He was down there pulling the squeegee. What he did do was leave some decisions to other people, like when he printed all of the Elvises on one long strip of silver-coated canvas and he left it to Irving Blum to decide where to cut it up. This laissez-faire attitude sort of defies his formal stuff. It's also part of Neo-Dada. He was certainly aware of what Rauschenberg was doing with John Cage and Merce Cunningham, the role chance played. That was a really modernist notion of the moment. It wasn't that he didn't care; rather, I think he was interested to see how it worked out. He gave things over to accident and to chance. Certainly, he loved it in his films, he loved it essentially in the happenings and the performance stuff. And he enjoyed constructing a situation in which certain things happened that were outside of his control. He was probably the greatest voyeur who ever lived. He could construct a situation in which people would do everything he'd tell them, including committing suicide. And he had no control over it. He was simply a voyeur who gave up responsibility. But here he is, a passionate collector of everything from cookie jars to nineteenth-century paintings. This is not somebody uninterested in what his paintings look like or unaware of how he fits into art history. He's a very complicated guy, and he's dealt with in a very simplistic way. Nuance and subtlety were interesting to him. I really liked and respected him a lot.

MP: What about the idea of others giving Warhol ideas?

CC: I never bought it. Henry Geldzahler and others liked to portray Andy as an empty vessel into which they could pour whatever they wanted. They were all fellow travelers. I mean, they were hangers-on. I think they were floating ideas.

I just had lunch in Rome with Joe Hellman. And Joe, you know, takes credit for virtually everything. I'm sure he was very important. But it promotes the idea of this passive, empty vessel that other people would fill up with their ideas.

MP: Well, Warhol, of course, contributed to that.

CC: Absolutely. But I think the fact is that he was a good problem solver—and that's enough to be an artist. It can be someone else's problem, but if you come up with your own unique solution, and if you have a personal vision, it doesn't matter if you're solving someone else's problem. He put his own indelible stamp on what he was doing.

He wasn't sure if he was a Conceptual artist or not. Conceptual art came along and it was a threat, on some level, to him. So he'd pee on some metallic paint and get it to oxidize. Or he'd get someone to pee, because he rarely did anything like that himself. Forays into things like that, even then, he managed to make his own. He was more than a little aware of the way history was moving on, and he didn't want it to move on without him. His work with Jean-Michel Basquiat was an almost desperate attempt to keep current, to hip it up, by attaching himself to someone who was on the cutting edge.

I wonder what he'd be doing now, had he not died. You know, death is a great career move. And Andy painted people for whom death was a great career move, like Elvis and Marilyn. This is a guy who was not unaware of how those things played out in someone's career.

MP: Would you talk about *Phil*, your painting in the show? It's hard to think of a contemporary portrait, apart from one by Warhol, as iconic and instantly knowable as either *Phil* or your early *Big Self-Portrait*.

CC: I ran into somebody who had that image of me, with a cigarette in my mouth, tattooed on his body. I took a photograph of it. That was carrying it a little far, I think. But yes, I was driven to do those by Andy. I had to paint anonymous people because Andy owned famous people. I wanted them to be seen as portraits. In fact, I didn't call them portraits, I called them heads. I wanted to approach people in the way Giorgio Morandi

painted bottles or Cézanne painted apples. And I just picked my friends because nobody had any idea who they were. Then they turn out to be Richard Serra and Phil Glass and all those people, and they sort of screwed up my idea of anonymous people. But I was definitely trying to move as far away as possible from what Andy was doing with his superstars.

First of all, Phil was a close personal friend—that's the same reason I paint anybody. Or I paint an artist whose work I really respect and with whom I think my work has a dialogue. Phil was Richard Serra's only paid employee. Richard was smart enough to not have any sculptors work for him. So his crew was me, Phil, Steve Reich (a composer), Rudy Wurlitzer (a novelist), Bob Fiore (a filmmaker), Michael Snow (a filmmaker), and Spalding Gray (a writer). We'd go to the Towers Cafeteria, which is where the Odeon is now in TriBeCa, and we'd all sit around and work on the back of napkins. You know, because it was fun to play with those ideas.

Phil was a plumber—he plumbed two of my lofts—and a cab driver. Right after he did *Einstein on the Beach*, he went back to driving a cab. That was not a Met production. We had to rent the Metropolitan Opera. Christophe de Menil put up the money, and a bunch of artists sold works in order to rent the Met for that night.

Anyhow, after that a woman, a kind of patrician lady, got in the backseat of his cab and said, "Young man, do you know you have the same name as a very famous composer?" He never told her that it was him. But *Phil* was a very compelling image, and infinitely recyclable. I'm still using that same 1968 photograph today. You know, it's been nearly forty-five years. Those images are iconic. And I'm not sure why that happens. I'm glad it happens. But if you were to take Warhol, you'd say Marilyn, you'd say Elvis, you'd say soup cans, Brillo boxes, electric chairs. He had a lot of iconic images. Car crashes. Not all were commercially successful. He couldn't sell a car crash to save his life. They still don't do very well at auction. And yet they're painted in this benign, decorative way.

MP: Speaking more of portraits, you did that wonderful show at MoMA in 1991 ["Artist's Choice: Chuck Close,

Head-On/The Modern Portrait," Museum of Modern Art, New York].

CC: I'd gotten out of the hospital in the spring of 1989. And Agnes Gund [who became president of MoMA in 1991], Kirk Varnedoe [curator of painting and sculpture at MoMA], and the collectors Bob and Anna Marie Shapiro, who had visited me a great deal in the hospital, conspired to buy the first painting I did after I got out. It was of Elizabeth Murray. God love them, they really wanted to broadcast to the world that I was still alive and I was working. Kirk's idea was to give me the "Artist's Choice" exhibition in 1991 to show that I was intellectually still with it. It was a very successful show because it was so unlikely. Nobody knew the Modern even had portraits, and I found so many of them and then hung them cheek by jowl. Never in the history of the world had Duchamp hung next to Paul Cadmus.

MP: It reminds me of Warhol's "Raid the Icebox" exhibition, his eccentric selection and installation of objects from the Museum of Art at the Rhode Island School of Design [April 13–June 30, 1970; see p. 257]. There were so many works across many media. Was there a Warhol in your group?

CC: Yes, there was a four-part self-portrait. I learned two things in my attempt at curating. As an artist, I would think of shows and curate them in my mind. And, of course, I could borrow anything from any museum or any collection, anywhere in the world. And then I realized that curators deal only with the art of the possible, even within your own institution.

I was disappointed with the pieces in the Modern I couldn't lay my hands on. The other thing I learned was that, by placing the works on shelves and overlapping the mats and frames, any two things you put together have a relationship that seems important. And if you take away the white wall between the pieces, which erases from your memory bank what you just saw and allows you to see them separately, and then bring them together, you say, "Oh, wow, look how this looks with that." I saw them in the basement that way. I'd just be looking at two things, and they'd start to inform each other. And it was the first show ever in the history of the Museum of Modern Art that had things from more than one department. Kirk gave me a passport, which would allow me to travel freely from department to department. I spent twenty-four eight-hour days looking at the collection. It was one of the great experiences of my life.

MP: Artists can break rules or set new rules. But how do they deal with the consequences of the influence they exert?

CC: Well, my gallery, Bykert Gallery, was on East 81st Street, between Madison and Park, conveniently located across the street from Campbell's funeral home. My shows would get the spillover from the Abstract Expressionist funerals. I was having a show when Mark Rothko's funeral took place, and Philip Guston, Al Held, and Jack Tworkov came to see it. That's when I put my arm around Al Held and said, "I couldn't have done this without you." And he said, "You can't hang this shit on me."

JANUARY 17, 2012

When I came to New York in 1976 Warhol was there and working. I didn't know him but I'd see him around, and one day I had the honor of handing him an invoice. I had a job for a company that made artist's stretchers, and I built and delivered all of the stretchers for the *Shadow* paintings that were first shown at Heiner Friedrich's gallery on West Broadway. Was I influenced by them? No, I couldn't have cared less. Warhol wasn't Warhol to me back then, and from the lofty perch of youth I looked down on his ongoing celebrity portraits and on how he hawked an image of himself that was more nincompoop than inspired.

I think it was the films that first affected me, *Trash* and *Heat*. But were they made by Paul Morrissey or Warhol? Morrissey, I think. It wasn't until I visited The Menil Collection for the first time, in 1988, and saw two synergistic shows side by side that I truly began to get it. Both him and the Menil. The shows were "Andy Warhol: Death and Disasters" and "Winslow Homer's Images of Blacks: The Civil War and Reconstruction Years." So you ask if the body-part sculptures that I began making around 1989 were influenced by the *Disaster* paintings. I honestly don't know. Influence is murky water. Weegee maybe, or fragments of antiquities, or real life.

About the gay thing, I always felt that the general acceptance of Warhol was based on the perception, accurate or not, that he was asexual. That he was gay but that he didn't have sex,

and that this perception was axiomatic to his acceptance.

My appreciation of him and his work is always evolving. You ask about his portraits of genitals, did I know them. Were any of them in the big show at the Museum of Modern Art in 1989? I certainly don't remember them there. They existed more as a rumor then, at least for me. I do remember reading *The Philosophy of Andy Warhol (From A to B and Back Again)* and the truly crummy apartment that I read it in, so that was 1978 or 1979, shortly after it was written. I enjoyed it, like I enjoy John Waters's writing; both are silly and deep. But did it influence me? In a perverse way, it may have encouraged my reluctance to speak publicly about my own work, never trusting I could be that clever.

About six months ago, I bought on eBay the boxed set of catalogues from the auction that was held after Warhol's death, of his many possessions and collections. Astounding in a variety of ways. Who collects that many dull watches and why? Alongside a brilliant collection of contemporary art, the quantities of boring and second-rate stuff confused me.

And what about the foundation that he left, which enriches so many institutions and artists and initiatives? Can I say, write, accept that generosity, paradoxical as that sounds given his celebrity hunger and über-consumerism, might be his true real influence and goad?

INTERVIEW WITH
HANS HAACKE

MARCH 11, 2012

MARLA PRATHER: Did you and Warhol ever cross paths?

HANS HAACKE: No, we never met. We lived in separate bubbles of the New York art scene.

MP: You and Warhol have both taken on world leaders as subject matter. At first glance *Taking Stock (unfinished)*, 1983–84 (p. 65), appears to be a send-up of an official state (or royal) portrait of Prime Minister Margaret Thatcher, but there is a great deal more going on. It is a multipronged indictment of Thatcher and Charles Saatchi as art collector, patron, and advertising executive, whose firm ran the ad campaigns for three of Thatcher's campaigns. This must be a very rare instance of a work of portraiture instigating such an immediate reaction in the real world. When the work was first shown in your exhibition at Tate in 1984, Saatchi resigned from Tate's support group, the Patrons of New Art, and from the board of the Whitechapel Art Gallery. Given that the theme of the work was so tied to a moment in time and to the museum where it was exhibited, do you think it is perceived differently at another institution, nearly thirty years after its creation, or is that of any consequence to you?

HH: Of course, it is received very differently today. It doesn't ruffle feathers anymore, neither in London nor in New York. In 2000, it was even included in an exhibition with the title "Painting the Century: 101 Portrait Masterpieces 1900–2000" at London's National Portrait Gallery. Similarly, the Tate Gallery's acquisition of a work by Carl Andre would not cause a national uproar in the UK anymore, as it did in 1976. After a lapse of time and in a different context, reactions do change, no matter where and when and what may have been the cause of rumblings in the beginning. Obviously, this rule is not peculiar to the art world. It governs the entire social arena.

MP: The title of your 1986 exhibition at The New Museum in New York was "Hans Haacke: Unfinished Business." Why is this work "unfinished" and why did you place the work in the elaborate Victorian frame?

HH: In 1983, Margaret Thatcher was the unchallenged CEO of the UK. It would have been presumptuous to draw the bottom line on her reign then. Since she claimed to revive "Victorian values" and graciously accepted comparison with Queen Victoria, I sought inspiration from Pre-Raphaelite frames in the Tate Gallery's nineteenth-century painting collection.

One aspect of *Taking Stock* is still quite "unfinished": the role of the Saatchi brothers. Maurice Saatchi has been elevated to the House of Lords and, as a former cochairman of the party, he is still involved with Tory politics. His younger brother Charles has gone into business with the auction house Phillips de Pury, which is now under the control of the Mercury group, the largest luxury retailer in Russia. They hold forth in the former Duke of York's headquarters in London's Chelsea district, advertised as the "Saatchi Gallery." During the 2011 Christmas season, Charles railed in the *Guardian* against "Eurotrashy, hedgefundy, Hamptonites." Full of contempt for such folks, he asked: "Do any of these people actually enjoy looking at art? Or do they simply enjoy having easily recognised, big-brand-name pictures, bought ostentatiously in auction rooms at eye-catching prices, to decorate their several homes, floating and otherwise, in an instant demonstration of drop-dead coolth and wealth? Their pleasure is to be found in having their lovely friends measuring the weight of their baubles, and being awestruck."[1] I wonder what prompted this outburst.

MP: I wonder as well. I can't help but ask. Have you seen or will you see the new movie about Thatcher, *The Iron Lady*?

HH: No, I haven't.

MP: *Taking Stock (unfinished)* will be installed within the vicinity of one of Warhol's many depictions of *Mao*, 1973 (p. 64), in a section titled "Portraiture: Celebrity and Power." Warhol undertook his enormous series of Mao Zedong in 1972 (based, like yours of Margaret Thatcher, on an official portrait) because Mao, Warhol read in *Life* magazine, was the most famous person in the world. And obviously the trip by Nixon (whom Warhol vilified in his 1972 "Vote McGovern" poster, p. 172) to China played a role. The differing responses to the Maos are not unlike the often contradictory readings of Warhol himself. When a group of Mao drawings were shown in London at the Mayor Gallery, one critic called Warhol a "truly revolutionary artist whose work is an absolute condemnation of American capitalist society."[2] On the other hand, Henry Geldzahler said, "The irony that is obvious and front-row center in these

images is the fact that they are produced cheaply to be sold dearly by an artist in the capitalistic capital of the world."[3] Where do you come down on this issue?

HH: If my memory is correct, in the early 1970s Mao enjoyed the status of a Pop icon, a bit like Che Guevara. What may have mattered to Warhol was probably not so much a presumed anti-capitalist attitude but rather, as you say, that Mao was the most famous person in the world. Warhol cashed in on the celebrity cult—and became a celebrity himself. Peter Ludwig and other wealthy Pop art collectors of the period certainly did not feel challenged. I know little about Warhol's actual politics. He was not associated with the politically engaged artists I hung out with.

MP: Speaking of the relationship between art and commerce, and between institutions and their patrons, the Metropolitan has not escaped your scrutiny. You made a work called *MetroMobiltan* in 1985 (Musée National d'Art Moderne, Centre Georges Pompidou, Paris), which took aim at one of the museum's corporate sponsors, Mobil Corporation, and was shown that year at New York's John Weber Gallery. But you had made works critical of Mobil before this and the company tried to prevent you from using their logo. Do you deem a work more successful, or more effective, when it provokes direct results from the entity it targets?

HH: No. That's not how I rank my stuff. A year before *MetroMobiltan*, Mobil scared the Tate Gallery into withdrawing my exhibition catalogue by claiming the reproduction of several Mobil-related works violated their rights. A contributing factor may have been that, just before installing my show at the Tate, a Mobil-sponsored exhibition closed in adjoining galleries. I was lucky to get pro bono assistance from a prominent New York law firm. One of its partners explained to the Tate's counsel that U.S. law provides for a "fair comment" exception to copyright and trademark protections. Only then was the catalogue released again.

MP: In 2010 the Met acquired its first and only work by you, *Thank You, Paine Webber*, 1979 (p. 172), and it was

Due to the current economic crisis, Thank You, Paine Webber has gained an unexpected – and I might add unfortunate – topicality.

included in an exhibition at the museum, "After the Gold Rush: Contemporary Photographs from the Collection," in 2011. In the words of the curator, the work is so "pertinent to the recent economic downturn that it seems it could have been made yesterday." Another writer has suggested that your "lifelong commitment to unveiling the dark side of art patronage is more relevant now than ever."[4] Given that corporate sponsorship for cultural institutions has diminished considerably since the 1980s, do you think the situation has changed at all? And do you think your cause of "unveiling" has been taken up sufficiently, if at all, by younger artists?

HH: Due to the current economic crisis, *Thank You, Paine Webber* has gained an unexpected—and I might add unfortunate—topicality. This is an example for the not uncommon phenomenon that things of the past occasionally attract new attention and take on new meanings. It runs counter to what we accepted earlier as a given. No longer is *Thank You, Paine Webber* of 1979 just a quaint historic relic. It has a renewed capacity to affect the public discourse.

Now to your question: in 1975, a Mobil public-relations officer explained that art sponsorship serves the company as a "goodwill umbrella." He was not alone in recognizing the potential for a positive image transfer from having the corporate logo on posters for blockbuster museum exhibitions. But, as a consequence of the present crisis, PR people have reason to doubt whether this strategy still yields the desired result. It may even undermine their attempts to ward off public criticism of corporate conduct. This is how I interpret the end, after fifteen years, of Deutsche Bank's association with the Guggenheim in Berlin. Currently, the bank, together with others, is under critical scrutiny, in Germany as in the U.S., over suspected complicity in causing the crisis.

MP: On the issue of artistic censorship, two of the most notorious incidents in New York history involve your work and Warhol's. You had an entire exhibition canceled at the Guggenheim Museum in 1971 when the director deemed certain works "inappropriate" for display. Just seven years before, Warhol's contribution to the New York World's Fair, *Thirteen Most Wanted Men*, designed for the facade of Philip Johnson's New York

State Pavilion, was judged inappropriate by fair officials and, with the artist's permission, was painted over. Do you feel a kinship with Warhol in this regard?

HH: Apparently, we have this in common.

MP: Though Pop has not necessarily been a frequent touchstone for you, *Helmsboro Country*, 1990 (p. 33), has a strong graphic presence that has striking formal affinities with works such as Warhol's *Brillo Soap Pads Box* (p. 32), though your work is, of course, unique. And your giant cigarettes wrapped in the Bill of Rights also call to mind Claes Oldenburg's oversized objects with movable parts. You even used, like Warhol, a silkscreen technique on the wooden support. Is this a case of homage, or rather what has been described as "subversive imitation" or an "ironic sideswipe"? Or was the manipulation of the product and the logo simply the most appropriate imagery to make your trenchant point about Philip Morris, another former corporate sponsor of the arts, and Senator Jesse Helms of North Carolina, the archenemy of the National Endowment for the Arts, not to mention civil and gay rights, and a frequent recipient of Philip Morris campaign donations?

HH: Of course, *Helmsboro Country* quotes the trademark look of works by Andy Warhol and Claes Oldenburg. As did Marcel Duchamp, in a manner of *détournement*, I have occasionally adopted not only generally known imagery and documents but also called to mind works by other artists, including works by Duchamp, that great sociological trickster.

MP: Also in the portraiture section will be a very different kind of image, *The Right to Life*, 1979 (p. 72), which features an incandescently beautiful Breck girl, like one of Warhol's *Marilyn* tondi, in what appears to be an ad for American Cyanamid, a chemical company that, as you say, gave women a choice—to be sterilized or lose their job. You conduct an enormous amount of research to finalize your works. In an instance like this, do you continue to follow up on a particular corporation you have investigated? American Cyanamid, for example, is also the source of a Superfund site in New Jersey that was threatened in last year's Hurricane Irene.

HH: As my answers to some of your earlier questions show, I do try to keep up with news about

The "lockout" has eased somewhat in recent years. Still, there is a clear preference for works . . . [that] are not prone to offend the sensibilities of significant power brokers in art institutions.

some of the subjects of older works. American Cyanamid, however, has not stayed on my screen.

MP: Am I correct that another edition of *The Right to Life* was the first of your works to be purchased by an American museum, the Allen Memorial Art Museum at Oberlin College, in 1983? Although the rigor of your work has certainly not diminished since then, I wonder if what you once described as the "lockout" of your work from museums and collectors has significantly opened up in the last three decades.

HH: As early as 1972, the Milwaukee Art Center (today Milwaukee Art Museum) acquired a work of mine from the 1960s. But Oberlin is the first institution in this country to include in its collection a piece with a social edge. The "lockout" has eased somewhat in recent years. Still, there is a clear preference for works of the 1960s and works dealing with issues that are distant in time and/or for other reasons are not prone to offend the sensibilities of significant power brokers in art institutions. My 1986 show at The New Museum remains my most recent solo exhibition in this country. The name of Edward F. Fry, the Guggenheim curator who stood up in defense of

my censored exhibition in 1971 and, as a consequence, was fired, is hardly known today. Following their instinct, however, his younger colleagues and directors of museums of today have internalized that it is not wise to offend certain trustees and potential donors on whom they depend for the future of their programs, acquisitions, and careers. That's life. I am old enough to watch this with a degree of detached amusement.

MP: In a 1984 essay, "Museums: Managers of Consciousness," you wrote about the term *industry*, when applied to the art world: "With one stroke that term cuts through the romantic clouds that envelop the often misleading and mythical notions widely held about the production, distribution, and consumption of art. Artists, as much as galleries, museums, and journalists (not excluding art historians), hesitate to discuss the industrial aspect of their activities."[5] As you know, Warhol was very transparent about his means of production and his economic interests. An unapologetic promoter of his own art, he famously said, "Good business is the best art." Do you see him as an early example of an art-world figure willing to be open about the "industry" of art and thereby contributing to the demystification of the artistic process?

HH: I don't believe his goal was what we call "transparency" today, nor do I think he intended to demystify what artists do and how they make a living—or more than just a living. As you say, he was a master of marketing and self-promotion. He can be understood as having been the avant-garde for a number of artists who came on the scene in the 1980s—and later—for whom his dictum "Good business is the best art" has been a guiding principle. However, Warhol wearily also believed that "everyone will be famous for fifteen minutes." I will never forget what he reportedly said, I believe, after being shot by Valerie Solanas: "I thought everybody was just kidding."

ANDY WARHOL
SAS Passenger Ticket, 1968
Screenprint
26¾ × 48¾ in. (68 × 124 cm)
Moderna Museet, Stockholm

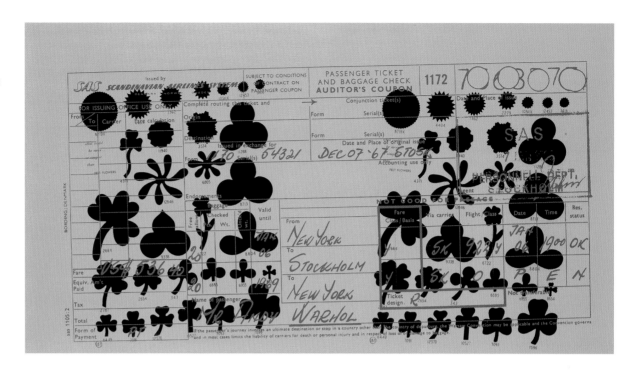

VIJA CELMINS
T.V., 1964
Oil on canvas
26¼ × 36 in. (66.7 × 91.4 cm)
Collection of Steve Tisch,
Culver City, California

CHUCK CLOSE
Big Self-Portrait, 1967–68
Acrylic on canvas
107½ × 83½ in.
(273.1 × 212.1 cm)
Walker Art Center, Minneapolis,
Art Center Acquisition Fund, 1969
(1969.16)

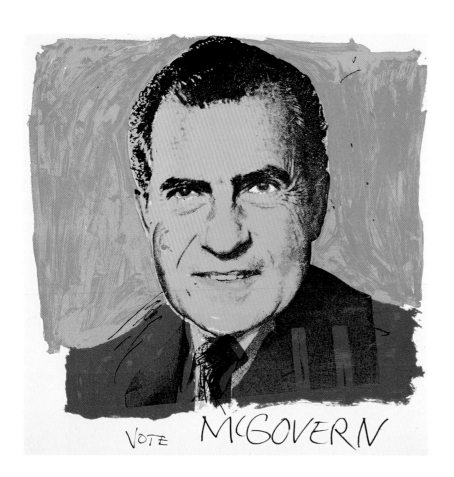

ANDY WARHOL
Vote McGovern, 1972
Screenprint
42 × 42 in. (106.7 × 106.7 cm)
Gemini G.E.L., Los Angeles

HANS HAACKE
Thank You, Paine Webber, 1979
Chromogenic prints (diptych)
42¼ × 40⅝ in.
(107.3 × 103.2 cm) each
The Metropolitan Museum
of Art, New York, Purchase,
Vital Projects Fund Inc. Gift,
through Joyce and Robert
Menschel, 2010 (2010.416a,b)

ALFREDO JAAR
BusinessWeek Magazine
Cover, December 24, 1984,
Untouched, 1985
C-print
19 × 13 in. (48.2 × 33 cm)
Collection of the artist

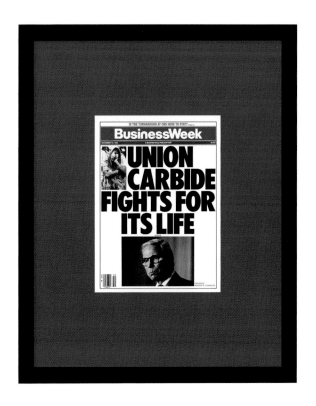

DEBORAH KASS
Red Deb, 2000
Silkscreen and acrylic on canvas
40 × 40 in. (101.6 × 101.6 cm)
Collection of the artist

ALEX KATZ
*Double Portrait with Frames
(Double Ada)*, 1960
Oil on masonite
20 × 31½ in. (50.8 × 80 cm)
Colby College Museum of Art,
Waterville, Maine, Gift of the artist

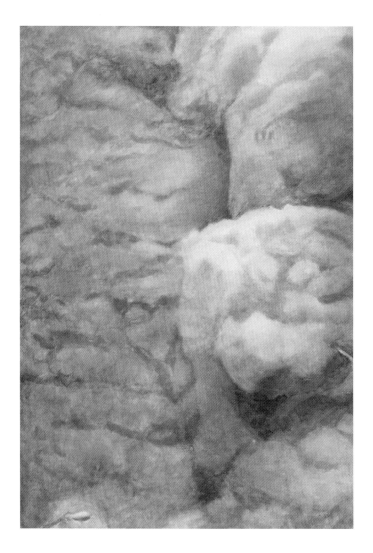

LUC TUYMANS
Demolition, 2005
Oil on canvas
65 × 44½ in. (165.1 × 113 cm)
The Museum of Modern Art,
New York, fractional and promised
gift of Leonard and Susan
Feinstein, 2006 (215.2006)

ANDY WARHOL
Julian Schnabel, 1982
Acrylic and silkscreen on linen
108 × 240 in. (274.3 × 609.6 cm)
Collection of Julian Schnabel,
New York

JULIAN SCHNABEL
Portrait of Andy Warhol, 1982
Oil on velvet
108 × 120 in. (274.3 × 304.8 cm)
Hirshhorn Museum and Sculpture
Garden, Smithsonian Institution,
Washington, D.C., Joseph H.
Hirshhorn Purchase Fund and
Regents Collections Acquisition
Program with matching funds
from the Jerome L. Green, Sidney
and Frances Lewis and Leonard
C. Yaseen Purchase Fund, 1994
(94.11)

INTERVIEW WITH
ALFREDO JAAR

JANUARY 30, 2012

MARLA PRATHER: You were born and educated in Santiago, Chile, you lived in Martinique for a time [1961–71], and, though widely traveled, you have lived in New York since 1982. You have said that you became an artist when you discovered Marcel Duchamp, but do you recall when and how you become aware of Warhol?

ALFREDO JAAR: Warhol was always part of the landscape, even before Duchamp. His work infiltrates the culture in a way that few artists have achieved.

MP: Your work has taken so many forms, from smaller, discrete examples like the one in our exhibition, to complex installations, film, and large-scale public interventions. *BusinessWeek Magazine Cover, December 24, 1984* (p. 19) consists of four stacked images, one of your many adaptations of news magazines or newspapers from around the world in a series you began in 1979 called *Press Works*. Could you describe this series and your ideas behind it?

AJ: The concept of my *Press Works* is extremely simple. It consists of displacing one image from one world, the media world, into the world of culture. By this displacement I am hoping to reveal certain realities that I see in the media representation of certain issues. I discovered that somehow, by simply changing their context, these representations become clearer, sometimes very apparent. Every representation contains an idea, a way to look at the world. The ideas, the ideology, the intent behind these representations manifest themselves in a different way in the

new context into which I insert them. I offer them as critical material for reflection and analysis within the world of culture.

MP: The original *BusinessWeek* cover (p. 173) addresses the horrific 1984 industrial disaster in Bhopal, India, and aligns images of the chairman of Union Carbide with the headline, "Union Carbide Fights for Its Life," and a detail of an Indian woman with bandaged eyes. The stacked configuration of these images in your reworked version calls to mind a number of Warhol's vertically arranged compositions, such as the *Tunafish Disaster* paintings or *Ambulance Disaster*, 1963–64 (p. 16). Setting aside subject matter and different media for a moment, was Warhol a model for you in a formal or aesthetic sense?

AJ: Warhol was a model in that he reacted to the world around him and created this displacement I was referring to. That displacement from the media world to the culture world was definitely a model that I took from Warhol. The simplicity of his gesture was important, too. He never added anything. He just repeated in a different context. But as he himself said, repetition is no repetition.

MP: Following up on the previous question, in 1971, Warhol said of his *Disaster* images, "I thought people ought to think about them: the girl who jumped off the Empire State Building, the women who ate poisoned tuna fish, the car crash victims. I wasn't sorry for them exactly, but people go on their way and they don't really care if some stranger just got killed. So I thought it would be nice for those unknowns to be thought about by people who would never normally do that."[1] In an interview from 2009 you said you have been "obsessed with the media" since childhood, and you have talked about mass media culture's desensitization to images. Many of your works, such as *BusinessWeek*, seem to implore audiences to resensitize themselves to the social and political nuances of images that, as Warhol also suggested, they could otherwise easily pass by at a newsstand or the supermarket. Nancy Princenthal aptly described your strategy as turning popular images against themselves. Warhol, of course, voraciously culled images from mass media, but, in your view, what were his motives in recontextualizing this material, and what did he achieve through its use? Do you at all see his *Disasters* as instruments of social criticism?

AJ: I always read his appropriations and displace-ments as a genuine interest in extending the visibility and meaning of these images. He was obviously fascinated by certain images and what they said about the general culture, and he wanted to amplify their outreach. These gestures were not innocent. I think he was clearly aware that all his choices could be read politically.

The concept of my Press Works *is extremely simple. It consists of displacing one image from one world, the media world, into the world of culture.*

That displacement from the media world to the culture world was definitely a model that I took from Warhol.

MP: I gather you object to being described as a "political" artist and see all art as political to some degree. In a few instances Warhol made overtly political works, such as a pro-McGovern poster in 1972 that featured a portrait of Richard Nixon (p. 172). As a result the government apparently scrutinized the artist's income more closely thereafter. He also made screenprints of Jimmy Carter in 1976–77, so one can obviously assume his inclinations were Democratic. However, he made portraits of the shah of Iran and his family, tirelessly sought wealthy subjects for his commissioned portraits, and made screenprints of "Reigning Queens." Do you see these positions as ideologically contradictory? Do they color your view of Warhol as an artist?

AJ: In my view Warhol was not "ideological" in that pure, dogmatic sense. I think he created these pictures as a reflection of their times. He felt totally free to make a picture out of these subjects and that did not mean he was endorsing them. Jean-Luc Godard said that "art is not only a reflection of reality but it is also the reality of that reflection." You can perfectly read "Reigning Queens" as a monument to kitsch.

MP: Specific Warhol references have appeared in several of your works, such as *The Final Decline and Total Collapse of the Avant-Garde*, 1979, based on a 1969 *Esquire* cover (see p. 257) and the beginning of the *Press Works* series, or *One Plus One Equals One*, 1983. In the latter installation, for example, you partially buried a reproduction of Warhol's *Marilyn* in a mound of soil to draw attention to differences between the cultures of North and South America. Could you explain why you chose that image and discuss your other direct references to Warhol?

AJ: In that particular work, I had selected Warhol's *Marilyn* as a kind of stand-in for the glamour and chic of the north in contrast to the solitude of the south that you found in the Western media. It was a convenient symbol and easy to read.

MP: *The Fire Next Time*, 1989, your site-specific installa-tion made for the lobby of the Brooklyn Museum, takes its title from a famous essay by the American writer James Baldwin and, ultimately, a spiritual. In a pile of long light boxes on the floor one saw images of civil-rights demonstrations and student uprisings from the

I have never understood those who believe that there is a separation between art and life. . . . Artists are human beings. We create models of thinking about the world. In order to act in the world, we must understand it.

1960s. You have said that your original artistic impulse often comes from real-life events, but why in the late 1980s did you turn to images of racial strife in the 1960s? Warhol's *Race Riot* images, made soon after the events in Birmingham, Alabama, in 1963, were based directly on notorious photographs from *Life* magazine, a publication you also addressed directly in the *Press Works* series. Was Warhol's work an impetus for *The Fire Next Time*?

AJ: Not really. I had moved to New York a few years before and I was still shocked at the level of racism that I discovered existed in this country. And that still exists today. I had the impression, and I was so wrong, that these demonstrations had had an effect and things had changed. In *The Fire Next Time*, I brought these images back to life to suggest that perhaps the struggle for equal rights and justice should stay alive.

MP: You have said, "The meaning of my work is the consequence of your reading of the work according to your social and cultural background." Despite the powerful imagery of a work like *The Fire Next Time*, is it fair to say that you seek a certain degree of ambiguity? Like Warhol you don't proselytize or editorialize but allow the images to speak for themselves. Do you think this is a reason behind the power of Warhol's work to still carry meaning and generate debate?

AJ: As a practicing artist during the dictatorship in Chile, I learned how to say things in a subtle way, poetically, almost in between words. I had no choice; it was a matter of survival.

In the case of Warhol, I think that he was reflecting his times and its symbols, extending the outreach of very powerful and meaningful images. In most cases, the discussion around these images existed already in the culture. He was adding his voice in a simple way without taking clear positions, almost stating known facts in his own way. And the discussion continues to this day.

MP: In later years Warhol was drawn to the powerful. You, on the other hand, are drawn to the causes of the powerless, or rather to the relationship between the powerful and the powerless. Do you make any qualitative distinctions between the early works of Warhol, tragic subjects such as the *Disasters*, and later Warhol, as many others have?

AJ: Warhol created an empire and an empire needs funds to go on. He found these funds wherever he could, sometimes in the wrong places.

MP: Are there lines of demarcation for you between private and professional life, especially given your passionate devotion to the global socioeconomic causes you bring forth in your work? Given your level of involvement in these issues, is everything about your art? Are you always working?

AJ: I have never understood those who believe that there is a separation between art and life. There is not. James Baldwin said, "Life is more important than art, that's what makes art so important." Artists are human beings. We create models of thinking about the world. In order to act in the world, we must understand it. Our life, my life, is dedicated to understanding the world so I can act in it. How can I separate that process from my work? Isn't this my work, to try to understand the world?

DEBORAH KASS

JULY 26, 2011

MARLA PRATHER: You may be a better candidate than most to put together an exhibition like this one, given your long involvement with Warhol's work. Maybe we could begin at the beginning, with your initial encounter with Warhol?

DEBORAH KASS: I started "The Warhol Project" in 1992 and I finished it, officially, with the "Debs" [a self-portrait series], in 2000 (p. 173). But my relationship with Andy started with the body of work that preceded that one, the "Art History Paintings" [1989–92], in which I referenced some of the painting canon—Paul Cézanne, Robert Motherwell, Jackson Pollock, Willem de Kooning, Warhol, and others. In that work I was talking about my exclusion from the canon because I was simply not seeing my reflection in it, particularly in the history of postwar American painting. As a teenager I prowled the galleries at MoMA [Museum of Modern Art], looking for something that might speak to my experience and not finding it. But that, by the way, didn't stop me from falling in love with Cézanne, De Kooning, Claes Oldenburg, Mark Rothko, and more.

If you look at my painting *Before and Happily Ever After*, from 1991 [collection of the artist], you can see how it led directly to my paintings of Barbra Streisand and my exclusive use of Warhol. Most importantly, the work went from being about my absence from the painting canon and beyond to becoming about imagining my presence, which my series *The Jewish Jackies* certainly did. Andy's *Before and After 1* (p. 84) might have been the first

painting I ever saw that cut close to the bone for me, literally and figuratively. It might have been the first piece of art in which I recognized myself as the subject. It was the perfect jumping-off point from which to talk about my own presence.

MP: And how did Warhol enable that in ways that other artists you had, for lack of a better term, appropriated in previous work did not?

DK: It was really simple. It was because Andy's work was so ubiquitous. By speaking in Andy's language, I could be clearer and more direct about what I wanted to say. I thought by using Warhol, images and formats that were so familiar, I'd really be able to say what I wanted to say in an accessible way.

MP: You really inhabited Warhol, co-opted Warhol. I think Robert Rosenblum said you were "reincarnating" Warhol. You embodied him in this profound and very bold way. Do you mean, by his ubiquity, that he could become a kind of neutral platform onto which you could project your own, well, desire?

DK: He's Warhol so he can't be truly neutral. But his style and substance had already passed into the vernacular in a way no other artist's had. It's hard for me to believe, but my collaboration with Andy started twenty years ago. This was before the art world had become what it is now and before Warhol was the auction star and the licensing phenomenon he is now.

MP: You went to school in Warhol's hometown.

DK: Also to Warhol's school, Carnegie Institute of Technology, Pittsburgh. When I went it was called Carnegie-Mellon University.

MP: Was that deliberate?

DK: Yes, totally deliberate.

MP: You grew up on Long Island. Do you remember seeing Warhol as a youngster?

DK: Going back to my initial encounter with Warhol as an artist, in my adolescence, around fourteen or fifteen, at the beginning of my looking at the world and trying to figure out what it meant to be an artist, Warhol was everywhere—in the *New York Times*, even on TV. He was such a presence in New York. In my family, we made up "superstar" names. My redheaded mother's was Infrared. When I first saw Warhol's *Before and After*— maybe it was in the *Times*'s "Arts and Leisure" section?—I completely freaked out. What is this? So many girls I knew had gotten nose jobs or were considering one! My mother wanted me to have one, which I resisted, thank god. Is this art? Is this bad for the Jews?

But, yes, I went to Carnegie because Andy went to Carnegie. I didn't really know other art schools. And it's not like my guidance counselor at Southside Senior High School knew anything about art schools. I didn't even know about SVA [School of Visual Arts]. If I'd known about it, I probably would've gone there. But literally, Carnegie and RISD [Rhode Island School of Design] were simply the only two art schools I knew of. I had read about Black Mountain College in books

I had picked up at the MoMA bookstore, and I tried to find it, but it was long gone by the time I was going off to college. CalArts [California Institute of the Arts] was starting that year, 1970, and had a big ad in the *Times*. But my parents wouldn't let me go to California, even though I begged. It was bad enough I was going to art school.

About twenty years ago or more my college boyfriend came to an opening of mine and asked me, "Do you still think Andy Warhol's the most important artist of the twentieth century, like you used to in school?" And I said, "Did I say that back then? Good for me!" And he gave me a Campbell's Soup can, signed by Andy.

MP: Do you still think that?

DK: Who doesn't think that?

MP: Probably lots of people!

DK: It's hard to argue with history. Not that that ever stopped me or anyone else.

MP: When did this all begin to cohere into your show "My Andy: a retrospective" [José Freire Fine Arts, New York, 1995] and, ultimately, "The Warhol Project," the museum exhibition in 1999?

DK: Well, *The Jewish Jackies* was the first series. But I didn't know that yet. I hadn't pictured a long-term project. But it did feel like a beginning. If I had left it at that, the "Barbras," it could have just seemed too cute. I needed to turn the screw and push it conceptually. Once I came up with *My Elvis*, the "Yentls," suddenly it became a body of work that was layered and complicated as well as emotional and accessible, unlike so much "theory-based" work at the time. This was really important to me. It was 1992: identity politics, recession, third-wave feminism, AIDS. Queer theory was just starting to be explored in academia. *Yentl* was released in 1982, ten years before queer theory ever hit a university. After pitching it for more than a decade, Streisand turned forty when the movie came out, and I turned forty when I made *The Jewish Jackies* series and *My Elvis* in 1992.

Andy's Before and After . . . might have been the first piece of art in which I recognized myself as the subject.

In my family, we made up "superstar" names. My redheaded mother's was Infrared.

MP: Barbra almost had a kind of virility, in the sense that she had so much power, because of her incredible voice and her beauty.

DK: Did you ever read Terry Castle? She wrote a book called *The Apparitional Lesbian*. It includes the essay "In Praise of Brigitte Fassbaender," about female opera fanatics and the female voice as power.[1] At that time there was a lot of talk about "victim" art. There is no way to perceive Barbra as any kind of victim, which is so much a part of her appeal and cultural significance. She understood her difference as glamorous and powerful. And her self-regard as a woman and as a Jew was positively radical! And inspiring. That's why those of us who felt "different" adored her.

MP: But Warhol didn't choose her.

DK: Well, that was why I chose her. My theory, and it's only a theory, was that she was too much like Andy, an outsider.

MP: Not his kind of girl.

DK: Unlike Andy's iconic women—Marilyn, Liz, and Jackie—there was nothing tragic about Streisand. In fact, quite the opposite. From the beginning of her career—and to the chagrin of Hollywood—Streisand insisted on controlling her own image, representation, and destiny. She embodied ideas of both female agency and otherness way before identity politics. Andy had a totally different agenda at that point. He was really exploring American glamour, tragedy, and values. Not particularly otherness. He was other. Much later on he did do *Ladies and Gentlemen* [1975] and *Ten Portraits of Jews of the Twentieth Century* [1980].

MP: Yes, and the latter group was shown again in 2008 at the Jewish Museum in New York. How do those images strike you now?

DK: I thought the paintings looked really good. And I'd never seen them before. I'd only seen the prints, which were never my favorites because that was the point when his work had gotten superslick. It did not have enough edge. That's how that series always seemed to me. But when I saw the paintings, I realized they were much more raw and more interesting than the prints.

MP: Back to Barbra. Where did you get the image?

DK: In the old days, before the Internet, there used to be stores that sold Hollywood memorabilia, posters, and photos. I was looking at a store that used to be on 14th Street between 7th and 8th Avenues for an image to use for a silkscreen. The still I liked was this one of Barbra's profile, very iconic, showing her "good side." It was probably shot off a TV set, so it didn't name its source. I am certain it's from *Funny Girl*. Recently it was identified as such by the art historian Michael Plante, a fellow Barbra fanatic [who organized "The Warhol Project" exhibition at Tulane University, which traveled in 1999–2001].

MP: And the "Yentl" image?

DK: Well, that's cool. It's from the laser-disc version of *Yentl*. She was a very cute boy, don't you think? It was the perfect response to Warhol's *Elvis*.

MP: So instead of a pistol-packin' Elvis, we have a Talmud-packing . . .

DK: A woman who dresses as a man in order to study sacred texts, which felt like a perfect metaphor for being a woman artist. And certainly for what I was doing, posing as Andy Warhol.

MP: And *Double Ghost Yentl (My Elvis)* of 1997 (p. 102)?

DK: I used very thinned-out ink. The double, "ghost" images had a very different resonance from that of the other "Yentls." They were apparitional, like memories of a vanished culture. I was not expecting that.

MP: Well, but what about the aspect of death in Warhol's work?

DK: I was too young to think about death. The ghosts were the first and maybe last intimation of death in "The Warhol Project."

MP: Warhol was fairly young when he was first painting ambulance disasters and electric chairs.

DK: But he was Catholic. That is a very active relationship to death and physical suffering, to put it mildly. You know, honestly, I have thought very little about death. My father died when I was twenty, too young to relate to it in terms of my own mortality. So many of my dearest friends have died. But when my mother died two years ago, it was the first time I ever imagined it would happen to me. I still can't wrap my head around death. I think it's astrological.

MP: So what came after *Yentl*?

DK: The "Chairman Mas."

MP: Featuring Gertrude Stein in lieu of Mao. I love your story of visiting the Met as a child and being struck by Picasso's great portrait of her.

DK: A very vivid memory. My first experience of what Michael Brenson called "aesthetic emotion." I don't know how the hell I got to paintings at the Met with my father. We never, ever went to art museums when I was a kid. He must have taken a wrong turn at the armor room or the Egyptian wing.

The next part of the Warhol project was "My Andy: a retrospective," shown in 1995 at José Freire Fine Arts. It was another way to extend my thinking about history, painting, feminism. And identity. I felt painting should be involved with these important conversations about identity and representation, and that there was no good reason for it not to be. The history of painting was seen as somehow off-limits to the feminist analysis of representation and power that was happening in photography at that time, the most important work being made then.

MP: Photography was never a temptation for you?

DK: Never. I always wanted to be a painter.

MP: You adapted Warhol's style, his technique, his composition. Did you have to teach yourself, then, how to make silkscreen paintings?

DK: Yes. An artist friend showed me how to make a silkscreen. And I then learned more as I went along. You know, being Andy for so long, I really, really did learn things I hadn't expected. And one of the first things I learned was how one idea can spin off so many objects. The silkscreen was the first clue. I made five Barbra paintings in one day. That was a revelation. Painting "paintings" takes a long time. Andy was just brilliant, obviously, but in ways I couldn't imagine until I started imitating him.

MP: And in *Red Deb* (p. 173) you are very effectively impersonating Andy's *Liz*.

DK: I made the "Debs" on paper first, and I tried to make them streaky and messed up. But, for some reason, they looked less like Warhols the streakier they were. It seemed like the more perfect they were the more they looked like Andy's paintings, even though I didn't think that would be the case.

MP: And that was important to you.

DK: Particularly with the "Debs."

MP: Pretty sexy.

DK: Thank you. A friend said the best thing: "When I was growing up we all wanted to be Elizabeth Taylor."

MP: And you got to be. Most of your subjects are women.

DK: Well, these are my heroes.

MP: But you are also your own subject—in the versions of *Camouflage Self-Portrait* and *Portrait of the Artist as a Young Man*, all from 1994. And you've talked about art as autobiography. You said something wonderful, that it's really the artist's job to represent oneself, after all.

DK: Well, there is that old canard: every artist's work is a self-portrait. And in the eighties and nineties, the issues of representation and identity

Some artists reflect their times and some artists change their times, you know? Andy did both.

were being interrogated in fantastically creative ways. Maybe if you see yourself writ large everywhere in the culture, this is not as pressing. If you don't, it is. And it certainly was then.

One of my questions at the time was how to make paintings that could be involved in that discussion. I showed with Sherrie Levine at Baskerville and Watson Gallery. Her work influenced me enormously, along with that of Cindy Sherman and Barbara Kruger. I love the works by Barbara Kruger: *You construct intricate rituals which allow you to touch the skin of other men* [1981, Museum of Fine Arts, Boston] and *You make history when you do business* [1982, Collection of Ealan Wingate, New York].

After the "Mas," I knew I wasn't done with Warhol. The idea of doing "My Andy: a retrospective" happened. I just kept elaborating and riffing on Andy. With my *Sandy Koufax* [1995, private collection] it could continue to be specific and autobiographical.

MP: And how is Sandy Koufax autobiographical?

DK: Well, if you grew up in New York in the sixties . . .

MP: And there was one Jewish baseball player . . .

DK: Who didn't pitch in the World Series on Yom Kippur, and then pitched a perfect game. Also Sandy Koufax is a cousin.

MP: And how did you choose the Koufax image? It's a great, expansive figure.

DK: I found it at one of those memorabilia stores. And that photo went so well with Warhol's Roger Maris [*Baseball*, 1962, p. 104]. The same thing was true of the Gertrude Stein and Alice B. Toklas images in *Let Us Now Praise Famous Women* [1994–95, private collection] and *The Family Stein*

[1994] paintings; there was a similarity with Warhol's Rauschenberg family in his *Let Us Now Praise Famous Men* series [1963]. Finding those images was really fortuitous.

After "My Andy: a retrospective" I didn't want to show any more Warhol-related work in New York because I thought it would be repetitious. But I didn't really feel that I was done with Warhol yet. The next series, one that practically begged to be made, was *America's Most Wanted* [1998], starring curators, some I had worked with, some I had not, but all of whom wanted to pose. It all became "The Warhol Project" because of the show at Tulane in 1999. We needed a title, and that was the one I came up with that covered the territory succinctly.

MP: How did it all come to an end?

DK: With the "Debs." I knew it was winding down because I didn't have any more ideas. The "Debs" were a nice exit because for the first time in a self-portrait I was not posing as an Andy self-portrait. But I was in drag again, this time as an Andy portrait of the most beautiful woman in the world, many thought, who was a Jewish lady who wasn't really a Jewish lady. It just made sense. I finished up several portrait commissions. And then I was done.

MP: Of whom?

DK: Quite a few collectors. Like *Alice Kosmin 36 Times* [1994, Collection of Alice and Marvin Kosmin]. You know, when I see Warhol's *Ethel Scull 36 Times* [1963], I think it's my painting of Alice. When I see his *Liz*, I always do a double take; I think it's me as Liz.

MP: I'm sure many of us do. So you said good-bye to Andy. Do you think his importance is more or less critical than it was when you began your Warhol project?

DK: There are the people who hate Andy Warhol, who really don't like Pop and don't like the idea of Pop. Maybe they don't like what they perceive as the values reflected in Pop. Well, some artists reflect their times and some artists change their times, you know? Andy did both.

ALEX
KATZ

OCTOBER 5, 2011

MARLA PRATHER: You were born a year before Warhol. So considering how remarkably active you are, one can imagine that Warhol could be alive and painting today. You were close contemporaries, but by 1954, you'd had your first show in New York. By 1960, you had shown at the Stable Gallery and Tanager Gallery, so you were under way as a professional artist, while Warhol was still working as a successful commercial artist. I'm wondering when you first crossed paths with him.

ALEX KATZ: It was at the time I was in art school [The Cooper Union, New York]. I was selling spot drawings to *Seventeen* magazine—that's the magazine we would go to. We were both doing the same shaky-line drawings. I had a choice to make: become an illustrator or a fine artist. And I thought it would take three years to be a successful illustrator, seven or eight years to be a painter. I really was more suited to painting.

So we both did work for the same magazine—the greatest place on the planet for a young artist to start out, and we were both accepted. The next time I met him, he asked the people at the Tanager Gallery if I'd do a portrait of him and his boyfriend for $150. I said no. Then, the next time I saw him, Red Grooms was showing his movie [*The Unwelcome Guest*, 1961] in a crummy loft on 26th Street, and Marisol came with Andy. Warhol went into movies right after that [*Sleep*, 1963].

MP: What about with Philip Pearlstein? Was there any common ground there?

AK: Yes, because the Carnegie art students all came to New York. There were other guys, Ted Repke and Joe Groll, painters, and Saul Leiter, a famous photographer at the time. And they all talked the same way, with no volume. It was very interesting. So it must've been a very good art school, the Carnegie. It produced a lot of pretty good painters.

MP: Why didn't you want to paint Warhol's portrait? He must have admired you to ask.

AK: I didn't think it was enough money. Just like that. But Fairfield Porter agreed to do it [Fairfield Porter, *Portrait of Ted Carey and Andy Warhol*, 1960, Whitney Museum of American Art, New York]. I don't know. I had a lot of social problems. I don't think I've ever gotten over them.

MP: You've talked about how 1959–60 was a turning point for you. Did you stop making the small collages in 1960?

AK: I made the collages up to '59. And when I did the figures on the flat ground, that's when people first took notice of me. The show was at the Tanager Gallery [1959]. I did the double portrait in '59 [*Ada Ada*, 1959, New York University Collection, Grey Art Gallery and Study Center]. I was the first artist to do anything like that.

MP: But there is also from 1960 the *Double Portrait with Frames (Double Ada)* (p. 174), with Ada's head placed against a flat yellow ground, which is so close to what Warhol later picked up on. Then again, a lot of painters painted portraits on flat backgrounds, from Holbein to Velázquez to Manet.

AK: Mine look different. The flat backgrounds came from two sources. One was from the classic painters, like Picasso and Rembrandt, who painted the space around the figure. They put spaces next to the figure and obliterated what was behind. Goya and Velázquez did similar things, but they did more with the field, with the color. It wasn't flat; you could look into it. But I was also coming from abstract painting. The white background in my paintings was a flat white, but it opened up, the way a Mark Rothko or Franz Kline would. That's how I got to the backgrounds.

MP: Although in this period you even made paintings with a figure within a circle or diamond on a square canvas.

AK: Right. There was a German loan show in 1951 that included a Raphael, a roundel with a Madonna in a square, and I realized it was a triangle, a circle, and a square. The figure, her position, was a triangle. Very geometric. And that led me to start fooling around with the outer borders.

MP: So that wasn't coming at all from previous abstract art, it was coming from an Italian Renaissance painter.

AK: Absolutely. But it was done with the grammar of abstract painting, at that point. My grammar's all abstract painting. The traditional painters never liked what I did.

Most figurative paintings have messages. I just wanted to deal with appearance. Rembrandt and Titian painted all these big, heavy stories. I like it empty.

MP: What was the response when these works came out?

AK: Concerning the flat background, it was violent. But Bob Rauschenberg and Jasper Johns called me up on the telephone immediately, to ask me out for dinner. Philip Guston came over. Willem de Kooning said, "Do it." All those people were very supportive. And then a lot of other people wouldn't speak to me. They were so upset by my paintings. There were also people screaming at the Sun Gallery in Provincetown, in 1959.

MP: What was the objection?

AK: They thought I was incompetent, I guess. I had a gray painting with a couple boats in it [*Provincetown*, 1959], and some guy got really upset. He thought I was trying to fool the public with a fake. I was perplexed by it, because I thought they were pleasant pictures to make people feel good. But the people who had the gallery brought my paintings there to make people scream. That was the purpose of the gallery. They were socially antagonistic. And, actually, again in Paris in 1975, people were screaming in the gallery ["Alex Katz: Recent Works," Galerie Marguérite Lamy, Paris, May 29–July 12, 1975]. The paintings were tight and had flat backgrounds, like in *Double Ada*. People were surprised. So there was a lot of hostility.

MP: There was the hostility of Hilton Kramer.

AK: He made me famous with a bad review in the Sunday *Times* in November 1965.[1] He said I used to be a good painter and I just sold out. He went on and on about how I'd sold my soul or something like that. I called my mother up and she said, "Oh, it's about time someone got interested in your work."

MP: Though he often supported your work.

AK: After that, he thought it was great.

MP: I know in one review he was uncomfortable with what he called the "emotional vacancy" of your figures.

Good artists steal, and [Warhol is] a good artist.

AK: A lot of people were. They thought it was vacant. Then forty years later, about the same paintings, someone said, "Oh, they're like Modigliani." It all changed. I think people look for messages in figurative painting, and most figurative paintings have messages. I just wanted to deal with appearance. Rembrandt and Titian painted all these big, heavy stories. I like it empty.

MP: You've said that you're more interested in appearances than personality.

AK: When you talk about narrative, it gets in the way of appearance. So appearance is the prime thing for me. If you get the appearance right, you have everything.

MP: But you have said that the flat background was the most exciting thing that happened, that you felt that you really hit it, but that you couldn't continue with it, because you'd be in a box.

AK: Right. Actually, if I'd blown up my collages, made them six foot, I would've been successful. But I'd be stuck on it, and I wanted to be able to get out, so I kept trying different things.

MP: But the flat background is something you've used periodically throughout, for example, in your recent paintings at Gavin Brown's Enterprise in New York ["Alex Katz," September 10–October 8, 2011].

AK: I went back to it, yes. The last bunch of years, I've been doing more and more flat backgrounds and less and less detail work.

MP: So you've told me what you feel Warhol borrowed from you . . .

AK: No, stole. He didn't borrow anything, it was stolen! Good artists steal, and he's a good artist. He stole the flat backgrounds, the double portraits, and the square portrait format. I'm at a party at Lita Hornick's, and she had commissioned a painting from me. And I find Warhol staring at it. I said, "Holy shit, he's going to do it again!"

MP: Your portrait of her is from 1964 (p. 73), and Warhol painted her in 1968 [*Lita Curtain Star (Lita Hornick)*, 1968, The Museum of Modern Art, New York].

AK: He got a better likeness than I did, too. But my portrait was the way she would like to be.

MP: Warhol's portrait of her contains eight images— it's the last painting he did with photo-booth snapshots. I like that she's wearing the same triple string of pearls in both paintings.

AK: She came before me with dyed bouffant hair. She had man tan or something on her skin. Her lipstick wasn't where her mouth is. She was really flashed out. And I said, "That's a great image. Let's just do it that way." Because normally, a portrait painter would say, "Take off your lipstick, so we'll see what you look like, and you'll look this way tomorrow." And I just thought—she looks like a 1956 Cadillac!

MP: She was spectacular looking.

AK: She was pretty hot. She had a nice profile. I did a great big cutout of her and her husband [*Morton and Lita Hornick*, 1971, Collection of Mr. and Mrs. Morton Hornick, New York]. But anyhow, she always loved the painting because she said that's the way she wanted to look.

MP: And she was a very accomplished person, the editor of *Kulchur* magazine. Which leads us to the poet Ted Berrigan, the subject of another portrait (p. 78). He was someone that Hornick published in *Kulchur*, and your work was reviewed there as well.

AK: She had Frank O'Hara, who was a close friend, and Leroi Jones as editors. O'Hara wrote that great review of me for *Kulchur* in summer 1962.[2] She was a terrific collector because she only wanted the best work from the artists. She didn't care about the price. It was a fantastic collection.

MP: So she asked you to do her portrait, but you didn't tend to do commissions.

AK: No, I didn't look for commissions. I think if you do enough of them, it'll ruin you because you're repeating what you've done. You're not experimenting. Now, if someone is a collector of my work, I will do a quick commission. But otherwise, I don't accept them. Warhol was courting very aggressively to do commissions. But they didn't help his art, because it's repetitive. He just cranked them out.

MP: Lita Hornick said this in her memoir: "Frank O'Hara had not come through with the cover he had promised, and I didn't dream that Frank and Andy were mortal enemies. The poets never told me any gossip. Alex Katz enlightened me when I was sitting for my portrait by him that spring."[3] So you gave her some good gossip?

AK: I must have.

MP: Because you do talk to your subjects when you're painting them.

AK: It relaxes the person and you can get some life into them. If you have them hold still, they just fall asleep, and that's like painting a potato or something, a still life. The portraits might be a little weird. The eyes might not line up in some, because they're moving a little bit. So it's a singular image, but it's sometimes from multiple positions.

MP: With Hornick's portrait, in 1964, you were very confident, obviously, about the scale. It's a five-foot painting. Were you making cartoons at that point?

AK: I was just going to start, because *The Red Smile* [1963, Whitney Museum of American Art, New York] didn't have a cartoon. It had drawing that was a little dirty, and I wanted them really clean.

MP: You make a large cartoon and then you pounce the drawing directly onto the canvas. But that's after you've made small sketches.

AK: Oh, sketches and drawings and everything. My approach is fairly pragmatic, like that of an old-fashioned painter, in a way. But I have the thing of wanting to make something as good as or better than other painters. You know?

MP: You do have a competitive spirit.

AK: Well, you actually compete for audiences. They say every artist has his audience and every audience deserves its artists. That's the other side of it.

MP: Since we're talking about Andy the thief, this is from an interview in 1963 with Gerard Malanga, recounted by Tony Scherman and David Dalton: One time, Gerard recalled, when he and Andy had just lain down the color areas on one of the portraits, and the canvas "was just these big, colorful shapes, the face and lips and eyebrows, Andy said to me, 'Oh, my paintings look like Alex Katz paintings before we silkscreen them.'"[4]

AK: Well, he knew what he was doing. It's an amazing phenomenon.

MP: That was in 1963.

AK: The illustrating world was a real hot world when he got into it. But I think it cooled off when the fine-art market took off.

MP: But do you think Warhol remained an illustrator?

AK: He was a terrific graphic artist. I mean, he couldn't paint as well as I do. And he couldn't do the things I do with paint. He couldn't do multifigure compositions. I think my paintings are really for a different audience. He could take a graphic and make it into a fourteen-foot painting, and it would be better than the work of most painters. That's extraordinary. I think he was the great graphic artist of that fifty-year period. But he couldn't paint. I once saw one of his *Rorschach* paintings next to a Franz Kline at the Whitney. It was a joke. And if you take one of his Picasso drawings and put it next to a Picasso, it's like something that should be on a napkin.

MP: He probably wouldn't disagree with you.

AK: Most likely not. He said he couldn't paint.

MP: Do you think he gets better with time, Warhol, looking back?

AK: I think he did so much work that it has to be sorted out. Some of those Campbell's Soup cans are really sensational. They look great. They buzz, the ones he painted. Throughout, there's been stuff that's interesting and stuff that isn't interesting. But I think it never gets into the heavyweight. A good painting is an experience that you carry with you the rest of your life. There are some graphic designs that come to that, but I think for the most part, they don't.

MP: Can we talk about Ted Berrigan, who was the subject of one of Warhol's *Screen Tests*?[5] Your portrait of him and Warhol's double self-portraits (p. 85) were made in the same year, 1967.

AK: It has the same pose, the hand in front of the mouth. He might've predated me on that. It's a coincidence. Ted put his hand up and I said, "Let's go for it." And it turned out to be one of the things that Warhol did. I said, "Well, it's my turn." But, basically, I don't think I stole it. I think it's a borrowed gesture.

MP: You seemed to gravitate toward writers.

AK: The poetry scene, starting in the late fifties, was much more interesting than the art-writing scene. Most of the art-writing scene, with *Artforum* and the French existential stuff, just seemed very uninteresting to me, compared with what the poets were doing. I think they were working with similar things.

MP: The real world, direct experience.

AK: Real things, concrete things, in a very sophisticated form. I felt I had a lot in common with the poets, the ones in the fifties, and that continued with the sixties group, even more so. You know, Joe Brainard and Ted. With Ted, the poems all seemed a little sentimental, but the language was amazing—the choice of words and everything. They were all on heavy drugs. It was a very lively scene. We just went to where the life was. Jazz fell down, and then there was the Puerto Rican music that was great. And then the poetry scene.

MP: You mentioned O'Hara earlier, another poet that you painted, and someone who, incidentally, recognized

Warhol's relationship to you. I ran across something he said in 1966: "Katz has found a liaison between the personal and the general, the intriguing dialog, without which, one is left with either formalism or expressionism."[6]

AK: A lot of things Frank wrote seem true now. When he wrote it, I think most people didn't think Frank was a very good art critic, but most of the stuff he said was true. He hoped I never got pushed through the mill.

MP: Yes, he said you were a "cool" painter, not easily categorized, and that you were in an "enviable position," one he hoped you could maintain in a "situation where virtually everything else has been gobbled up, if not assimilated or understood."[7] So, how were other responses to you by the late sixties, when you painted Berrigan?

AK: By the late sixties, the response to my work was beginning to fall away because Pop art took over and I was boxed out. And there was Photorealism. I was looking into an abyss. I felt that my talent was toward big things, and they were out of fashion. I said, "Let's not tighten up, let's go big." So I went big in the late sixties and through the seventies, and then it turned for me.

MP: Speaking of scale and thinking of things that you have in common with Warhol, one is an interest in mass media. You liked billboards, you've *made* billboards. And you learned from advertising, certainly.

AK: It was a new look to art, period. It was a confrontation with what was going on, right? Warhol's work is totally unsentimental and totally non-arty, which I liked. It had a nice, big style. It's almost like the style of Count Basie or Lucky Strike ads. They're just blunt and not arty, which I admired.

MP: He said, "Omit the blemishes." And there is, in your work, too, an idealization, a kind of coolness.

AK: Well, it's a style. People say everyone looks young and beautiful in my work. I say, "Look at them again." Everything's there, it's just reduced. And if a blemish is interesting, it gets in; but if it

The abstract guys always say the form is the content. To me, the styling is the most interesting thing.

isn't, it goes out. I use generalized forms. I'm working from abstract art. I don't like descriptive art, and I don't like naturalistic art. I don't think they are realistic.

MP: Thinking of Hilton Kramer's comment about emotional vacancy, it's hard to look at a painting like Berrigan's portrait and think that there is no personality there.

AK: The eyes are really accurate. You have the whole thing of this tortured guy, an artist. But a lot of people say everything's idealized. I don't know whether it is or not. I think it's highly styled.

MP: You say style is the content of your work.

AK: That's right. It is the content. The abstract guys always say the form is the content. To me, the styling is the most interesting thing. You make something that's essentially realistic, but it's highly styled.

MP: There are some other things that you do that Warhol did. You both paint flowers.

AK: I started flowers in the fifties. It was a reaction to all that kind of heavy, serious painting. And my idea was to make a flower painting knock you off the wall.

MP: What about the role of movies?

AK: Cinema was as important to me as anything. When I did the flat backgrounds, taking the image to the perimeter was traditional, but I was looking for new ways to break it up. I used to finish work and then go to a movie. I would just walk into the movie in the middle, whatever it was. I loved Westerns. They put the face on one side and the scenery on the other side. There wasn't anywhere

in old-fashioned art where you saw those images. And the size of the heads—the whole thing was just fantastic! So I was looking at movies a lot—those big, Technicolor, wide-angle things. And I really didn't care about the movie. I was just looking at the visuals. The movies were much more interesting if you walked in in the middle anyway.

MP: And what about photography?

AK: Definitely. When I started with specific portraiture in the late fifties, I was looking at the Civil War photographer Mathew Brady. His photos were like a series of images on top of images because they were exposed slowly. And that's basically what the paintings were like. And early on, in the fifties, I started using other people's photos because I liked the flatness and the nostalgia.

MP: But never taking your own and working from them—

AK: No, I never took photos in the early days. In the late nineties I started photographing on the beach. Occasionally, there would be a photograph I would like and I would set people up to pose in a real-life situation based on that photograph. I found that with the photographs I could get gestures you can't get any other way. They happen—[snaps fingers]. They don't repeat. I did it for a couple years, I got one terrific painting [*Walking on the Beach*, 2002, private collection], and then it became boring.

MP: What about other shared concerns with Warhol, such as the use of repetition and seriality? I'm thinking of not simply double portraits, but, for example, the nine-panel painting of the man in the white shirt that you did in 1996 [*Man in White Shirt*, collection of the artist], where you made nine variations on a theme. And you've done other works where you repeat a figure. Is seriality an impetus behind a work like that?

AK: Serial things just seemed interesting to me. Starting with the first *Ada Ada* in 1959, I'd try variations, and they just kept repeating.

MP: With *Ada Ada*, were you trying to make the same Ada?

AK: Well, trying to repeat it the best I could. I found it was very hard to do it, the repetitions and variations on repetitions. Some old masters do that. They pretty much have the same person running through a whole painting, seven times. It makes the painting move around. If the faces of all the people are all sort of similar, you can make it move more. The painting can be more active and not stop.

MP: Obviously, one of the points of this show is the tremendous influence that Warhol has had on subsequent generations. But you have exerted your own influence on many artists. I liked reading the press release for your show at Gavin Brown, which calls you "one of the most influential, iconic, and enduring figures in the American cultural landscape," and states "his effect is so over-arching that his presence, his style, his vision are absolutely ubiquitous."

AK: Well, it's true.

MP: So do you see your influence?

AK: It's not that important; it's not the prime thing when I'm painting. But when I was in art school, the class began to paint like me. I've always been highly concerned with style. When people asked if I was in the Whitney Biennial, I said, "Four times, but not with my paintings."

MP: So Andy wasn't the only borrower. Well, you have taught. That influences others.

AK: At Yale. And I taught at the Pratt Institute a little bit. In teaching, I pretty much tried to figure out where the person was and where he was going, and then helped him get there. I didn't tell them about truth or about what I was doing. When Robert Mangold studied with me at Yale, he was doing work like Louise Nevelson's. And so I figured right away, this guy is really hip. It was 1960 or '61. I said, "Look at Al Held." And that was his way into Minimal art. It was just one sentence, and that's all he needed. He started painting like Al Held.

And Brice Marden was painting like Franz Kline. The teachers were down on this and said, "Why don't you paint like yourself?" And I said, "Listen, Franz Kline's a great painter." It seemed to me a very intelligent way of learning about being a painter. To learn is a denial of ego. You have to throw your ego away and just learn. And then, after you learn, you have to get into your unconscious. Otherwise, you just repeat what you've learned.

MP: Who do you think taught you the most?

AK: I learned the most when I was drawing antique casts in high school. I didn't have any real talent. By the end of three years, I could draw better than most adults. And I learned all about structure and form. I learned a system, and that was the way into art. Also, I learned that with an application of energy, I could get better. I drew for three hours a day, five days a week. I did the same thing when I went to Cooper Union. I put energy into drawing and I got to be a good draftsman, much better than when I started. And I did the same with painting. I destroyed a thousand paintings. Don't worry—no loss to civilization. What I got out of that was a real skill in painting. And it was strictly an application of physical and intellectual energy.

MP: You once said that you hope that people could see the world through your eyes for a minute. What do you want us to see?

AK: This is the way the world looks and this is what a painting should be. I went to Philadelphia to look at the Cézanne show a couple of years ago. And I'm looking at all the ineptness. He can't move across a body without screwing up because of what he's doing with the paint. The system breaks down completely. So I'm thinking, "Gee, I always thought he was the greatest thing since toast," and all of a sudden I'm looking at the paintings and they're not so hot. But then, as I'm going home on the train, everything I see is a Cézanne! That's the kind of vision I'm after.

NOVEMBER 21, 2011

MARLA PRATHER: Like Warhol, you are from Pennsylvania. He was from Pittsburgh and you are from York. I find it fascinating that your first exhibit of a painting was, like Warhol's, in a store window. In your case, it was your father's furniture store in your hometown?

JEFF KOONS: My father had a furniture store and was an interior decorator. I would help him at the store. I really learned aesthetics through my dad. My parents were always very supportive. My father probably started showing my work in his showroom window when I was maybe nine or ten years old. Some of these works were placed around the local community. I guess it gave me a sense that this is something that I could do as a living. As a younger artist, I never really thought about the living part so much; you just make things because you want to participate. But maybe it helped me to have no sense of fear.

MP: Such an endorsement from your parent, displaying his son's paintings in his shop.

JK: Absolutely. My mother was also very supportive. When I was younger, she would say, "Oh, maybe you want to be an architect." She was thinking a little more on a practical side, about what to do if you like to draw. The first recollection that I have of drawing is probably about the age of three. I felt that I could do something, for the first time, better than my sister. I have one sibling. My sister's three years older, and, of course, she could do everything better than I could. She could

spell words, speak better, jump higher. There was nothing that she couldn't do better than me, other than, finally, drawing. It was the beginning of art giving me a sense of self.

MP: What were you drawing and painting?

JK: In the local newspaper, the *York Dispatch*, every Sunday they used to have a section called Cappy Dick. Cappy Dick was a ship captain. It was an art activity contest for children. There was a line drawing, and you were to cut it out, glue it on a piece of paper, color it in, and extend the drawing. I would enter this contest every week. I remember, a swordfish or something jumping out of the water that I extended and then added a boat or something. I also drew faces of relatives. I started taking lessons at seven years old, every Saturday morning.

MP: Moving ahead into your career, your Hoover floor polishers and vacuum cleaners, from the series "The New," were first shown in another window, at the New Museum at 65 Fifth Avenue, in 1980. Were you aware of how Warhol had shown paintings in Bonwit Teller's window? Was that in any way an homage? Or was it more a strategy to underscore the commercial origins of the objects?

JK: At the time, I was conscious of Andy's showroom windows, but I don't know if I made a direct association. It was just an opportunity to show the work. Yes, it was on the street; a lot of people could see it. I was excited by the sense of display. The whole work was about display.

MP: For this exhibition, the *New Hoover Deluxe Shampoo Polishers, New Shelton Wet/Dry 10-gallon Displaced Tripledecker* (p. 31) is alongside works such as Warhol's *Green Coca-Cola Bottles* (p. 30). As you know, Warhol found Coke attractive in part because, as he said, "A Coke is a Coke and no amount of money can buy you a better Coke." Is this kind of universality or democracy important to you?

JK: What I liked about the Hoover was this concept of the door-to-door salesperson, somebody knocking on your door and presenting you with something. That's really the front line of morality within a culture: sales. I was brought up to be very self-reliant. I would go door to door and sell gift-wrapping paper, bows, chocolates, and ribbons. You never know, when you knock on the door, who is going to open the door, what they're going to look like, what odors will come from the home, what the furniture's going to look like. That whole experience as a child was very important in developing a sense of acceptance, which is something that I shared with Andy.

MP: Was there a formal attraction to the vacuums? The appeal of the design? Or was it essentially something deeply psychological, as you say, lodged in your childhood?

JK: I liked that the Hoovers were anthropomorphic—they're breathing machines. I think that vacuum cleaners are also probably some of the strongest machines that you come across when you're a child. You're crawling around on the floor and all of a sudden, *rrrrrrrr*, this thing is coming across. But I think that it also is about breathing. It makes a sucking noise, it breathes.

MP: Do they have genders?

JK: I think they're both male and female. They're not functioning, they're not collecting dirt—they're just displaying their integrity of birth. Individuals have to participate to have an integrity in life. But here, the machines are able to display this integrity without acting—they are

better prepared than the individual, in a way, to survive. It plays with aspects of the eternal and an ultimate state of being.

MP: I ask about the visual or formal appeal because Duchamp said that he chose objects, readymades, with visual indifference. I wonder if you exercise visual indifference.

JK: I don't think there's visual indifference. I think that I was excited by the intensity of the cleanliness and the pure display. When I was a child I would go into my father's showroom, where there were mirrors, tables, lights, chests, and little porcelain objects. Everything would be displaying itself. I wanted to make works in which things would just display themselves.

As an artist, I came from enjoying Surrealism and Dada. It was really a routine, a way to learn how to trust in myself and develop a sense of personal vocabulary, how to articulate, to control a sensation's intensity. But after you learn to trust in yourself, you learn to look outward, and you make reference to external things. It's learning how to trust in other people and how to find acceptance and not judge others. So objects just become metaphors for people. It's a kind of objective art, you know?

MP: They are very objective, on one level. They have a cleanliness, an orderliness, a pristine sense of presentation, with the fluorescent lights that give them a marvelous otherworldly glow. But you've said that the works aren't a reconsideration of Minimalism.

JK: I love Minimalism. I remember going to Leo Castelli's gallery and Ileana Sonnabend's gallery and seeing beautiful exhibitions by Robert Morris and Donald Judd. I loved Robert Smithson's work. I was making reference to Smithson in "The New" series and also previously in the "Inflatables." But I think there's a sense of family structure in those pieces, too. There's a sense of community. There's order, there's a heightened sense of the state of being. I always enjoyed Kierkegaard and Sartre.

MP: And you've said that certain qualities in your works were designed to give the viewer a sense of economic security.

JK: That's a statement that I would've made during the "Banality" series [of 1988], when I started traveling more to Europe and seeing the way the [Catholic] church has used art. I really love the Baroque and the Rococo, but especially in institutional structures like churches, where everything in the space is gilded in gold and silver. Everything's being negotiated. You have the animate and the inanimate, and you have aspects of the eternal, through biology—flowers and animals, cows and deer—against more of an ephemeral spiritual eternity. These were the types of references that I was making in the "Banality" works, which intend you to feel like all needs are being met. When you walk outside a church, you're back in the same position you were in before you walked in.

MP: Just going back to the Hoovers for a moment, is it meaningful to you to be closely associated with a product, a design, an object? Warhol is synonymous with Campbell's Soup, and you really have become synonymous with certain images, whether it's basketballs or vacuum cleaners.

JK: Around the time of "The New" I was also thinking about how Andy was using images, like GE and other graphic, branded-type images. I was very aware that I was working with Hoover. If I was making a basketball piece, I was working with Spalding or Wilson. I took the Hoover decal and put it on the cover of *Artforum* magazine. I guess if somebody sees a Hoover, they also associate it with my work. But it was also my way of starting to look outside, to work with things and not make judgments about them, and to try to go through a process of acceptance.

The only thing that artists can do is to follow their interests. . . . When you focus on them, things become very metaphysical.

MP: You've said that the one thing that you have in common with Warhol is the readymade, a thing that exists already in the world. But can you explain a bit what draws you to a particular object? Warhol, for example, seemed to happen upon his subjects, or he sometimes took suggestions from others. I wonder if you do that, or if searching for subject matter is a very active process for you.

JK: The subject matter I work with comes to me in a very intuitive manner. Generally, the things that I'll start working on today I have already been thinking about for at least a year, a year and a half. The subject continues to present itself to me intuitively, and then I realize that it's really important enough to act on. The only thing that artists can do is to follow their interests. A lot of people think you can just construct things, that there's a way to just create art out of some type of structure. But all you have are your interests, and when you focus on them, things become very metaphysical. You start to be able to make connections to things that are vaster than your own subjective interests.

MP: You came to New York at the very end of 1976. Obviously, you would have been very aware of Warhol by that time. Did you ever cross paths with him?

JK: I ran into Andy twice, both times kind of superficially. Once was at Studio 54. I had a friend, Sue Etkin, who worked for Andy on his television program and also for the magazine [*Interview*]. Sue introduced me to Andy. Then I also ran into him in an elevator once. I would see him at openings. I wasn't shy if I really wanted to meet somebody. I called up Salvador Dalí and met him when I was seventeen, eighteen. To meet and befriend Roy Lichtenstein seemed very natural. But I never felt the desire to be part of the Factory or to go to the Factory. It didn't feel natural for me. A lot of people that have known both of us have said that we would have enjoyed each other a lot. And so I wish that I had been more aggressive in that manner. There are works that I've always loved so much. I think his *Elvis* paintings are amazing and the *Disaster* series is incredible. I shopped on 14th Street a lot for my vacuum cleaners and other supplies. So I would be near the Factory, when it was on 17th Street, and sometimes I would look

[Ushering in Banality] was kind of autobiographical. I'm ushering in banality, and it doesn't matter what people think.

up and see Andy standing in the window. But I probably felt that so many people went there and knocked on the door that I just didn't do it.

MP: Since you came to New York around that time, do you remember the Warhol portraiture show at the Whitney ["Andy Warhol: Portraits of the 70s," 1979–80]?

JK: Absolutely. But the show that really stands out in my mind is the one at Dia of the *Shadow* paintings [1978–79, Dia Art Foundation], because it had a huge influence on the community. Everybody was very excited by it. It was a beautiful installation, very minimal and very, very colorful.

MP: The "Banality" series that you presented in 1988 really seems like a remarkable departure from what preceded it. And you launched the series with a group of art-magazine ads featuring yourself in various contexts. I think Andy, who was fairly effective at manipulating mass media after all, wished that he might've thought of that himself.

JK: For the "Banality" show, Sonnabend Gallery asked if I wanted to have a catalogue or if I wanted instead to use the money for ads. I chose to use the money for ads. I thought about the different magazines and how to direct myself to each audience for that magazine. Around that time, I remember a photograph of David Bowie in *Artforum* by Greg Gorman, a celebrity photographer in Los Angeles. It looked like if you took that photograph and touched it with a hammer, it—*chhhhh*—would just shatter. So when I had the opportunity of these ads for the "Banality" show, I decided that I would design them and have Greg photograph me. I wanted to try to make images that were exciting and that could compete. I was very, very conscious about art trying to use the powers of communication, but, at the same time, to accept the moral responsibility that we have to each other and our larger community. I guess it was a response to some of the dialogue in the art world prior to this time, in the late seventies, about how, "Oh, you don't manipulate, you don't seduce. It's the object that communicates to people." It felt like there was a lack of a desire to communicate and to use the tools that we have at our disposal for actual communication.

With the image I did for *Flash Art*, with two pigs, I thought that I would call myself a pig before the viewer could so that they could only think more of me. I also liked very much the ad in *Art in America* that was like the temptations of Christ. There were a lot of plants and flowers and two bikini-clad women. One's offering me a cake, and the other one is on the ground, beside a miniature pony. It was like Christ entering Jerusalem. But instead of being on a donkey, there was this little pony, baying right at that moment. I liked that.

MP: We are including in the exhibition two works from the "Banality" series. You have said, I believe, that the source for *Ushering in Banality* (p. 27) was a postcard, an image of a boy pushing a pig.

JK: As a young artist, I was brought up with, first of all, a Duchampian vocabulary, and I enjoyed Picasso's work, Dada, the Surrealists. Collage and photomontage were very important. Then Pop art, which was about opening yourself up to the world around you, letting everything be in play. I started to respond to images, and I saw postcards and different things that I found of interest. In some way, I would make a montage of an idea and put it into a sculptural form.

Originally, I saw an image of two young boys pushing a pig, trying to get it back into some type of box. I thought, that's interesting, but I'll get rid of the second boy and I'll put two angels on the sides. And for me, it was kind of autobiographical. I'm ushering in banality, and it doesn't matter what people think. I just feel that I have good intentions here about what I'm trying to communicate to people. In a way, spiritually, it's like I have God on my side or something.

The church has used wood a lot to communicate to people that there's a sense of a continuation to life. It's considered a living material, but it's a seductive material. It has a certain sense of warmth. The carvers of *Ushering in Banality* all worked on creating polychrome sculptures for the church, so they were used to carving saints and things.

MP: *Michael Jackson and Bubbles* (p. 59) is also part of the "Banality" series. Jackson was a perfect subject for Warhol, too, a tragic celebrity who has become more so. Warhol's portrait of Jackson appeared on the cover of *Time* magazine in 1984. They supplied him with a publicity photograph. What was the source for your work?

JK: When I was doing the "Banality" series, I wanted figures that would represent a spiritual authority. I had my lawyer contact Michael Jackson's lawyers, and they informed him that I wanted to do this sculpture. I asked for different photographs, which he sent. Some were standard celebrity poses. Some were onstage, performing. I chose one where he's sitting in a yard with Bubbles. I wanted to have a contemporary Christlike figure. It's treated almost like a pietà in a Renaissance style, or like a Classical work from antiquity. It looks like the pyramids of Giza. It's got a very pyramidal shape. The way Michael's painted, in the black and the white and the gold, is also kind of Egyptian. But there is also a sense of fantasy and desire. When you were a child, didn't you want to have a chimp? I think of *Bedtime for Bonzo*.

MP: The medium is porcelain. Does the fragility of this material have anything to do with a kind of psychological fragility of the subject? And do you see Michael any differently in this work, since his death in 2009?

JK: Porcelain is a material that shrinks 19 percent when you bake it in the oven, so you can feel this tightness — it tends to be quite sexual that way. That was important in this body of work. It's a material that came from the king's kitchen. Only nobility had porcelain, but today we all can have porcelain. So again, it's communicating that there's no sense of need; you have everything.

In the "Banality" series, I was trying to tell everybody that their own history is absolutely perfect. And that in life, there's no place for judgment of the self. You have to have self-acceptance.

When I made the work I was very much in awe of Michael's powers as an entertainer. This was the time of *Thriller*, when he was doing really exciting things. I was supposed to meet him, but each time I was stood up in some way. I would receive a call, "Oh, you know, Michael wants to see the sculpture." And I'd say, "Well, I'm in Germany." "But he wants to see it. He's in New York." "But the sculpture's being made in Italy." "Oh, but can you come back and he can just meet you?" I would come back, and then there would be an excuse. "Oh, Michael is so sorry. He's in Los Angeles now. Can you come out to Los Angeles?" I went to Los Angeles, showed up at a studio where he was supposedly recording, I knocked on the door, and they said, "Michael hasn't been around here for six months." Then, I lost interest.

But when Michael started to get into problems, when his life began to fall apart, I realized that these objects don't control the world. They have a life of their own. And that's just the way I looked at it.

MP: Did he ever offer an opinion of the work?

JK: Well, I'm told that he really liked my work and was thrilled with the piece. But I never had any interaction. I regret that very much.

MP: In the portraiture section of the exhibition, which is about celebrity and power, we have included, in addition to *Michael and Bubbles*, a work from your "Statuary" series, *Louis XIV* (p. 68) from 1986. It is installed in the context of works like Hiroshi Sugimoto's image of Fidel Castro (p. 67), Warhol's *Mao* (p. 64), and Hans Haacke's image of Margaret Thatcher (p. 65). But your "Statuary" works also included Bob Hope and the inflatable rabbit. How do these objects connect in the series?

JK: When I made the "Statuary" series, I thought of it as a panoramic view of art and how art has been used. I thought of Bob Hope as art in the hands of the masses, the idea that if you give art

I don't really think of my studio as a factory. People may refer to it as a factory, but I think of it more as a studio.

to the masses, eventually it would reflect a mass ego and just become decorative. Louis XIV was at the other end of this panoramic view. If you put art in the hands of a monarch, eventually it'll reflect his ego and become decorative. The whole underlying context is that if I put art in my own hands that eventually, too, it will become decorative, reflective of my ego. But I wanted to show different ways that art has been used. The rabbit was art as fantasy. It could be anything. You could think of the *Playboy* bunny, or you could think of resurrection, of Easter. You could look at the carrot to the mouth like a masturbator or an orator making proclamations. It's so very chameleonlike.

MP: Your wall-mounted object, *Wall Relief with Bird* (p. 140), from 1991, is in the last section of the show. In 2002 you actually did a show in which your flower works were shown alongside Warhol's.

JK: That was really great. I used to make inflatable flowers, back in 1979. They were store-bought inflatables. I inflated them, put them on glass mirrors, and just let them display themselves. When I was younger, seven, eight, nine, taking lessons, I drew flowers. But there's a tension in flowers—and especially in the vases of flowers—about whether they're domesticated or undomesticated. In a vase, the flowers are cut. Even though they're a symbol, like the Garden of Eden, of life and sexuality and abundance, when you start to look at them in a philosophical way, there is actually no hope, no future. In *Wall Relief with Bird* there is a bird pollinating these large flowers. The imagery to me is about penetration. It's also about fertility and pollination, and the eternal.

A piece like *Puppy* [1992, Guggenheim Museum Bilbao], my floral sculpture, is all about hope because the flowers are growing. They're meeting their life cycle, and the viewer is conscious of this life cycle. There's a philosophical tension because it's about life and the contemplation of life.

MP: Your description of cut flowers is one of the least optimistic things I've heard you say. You mentioned that you liked Warhol's *Disaster* paintings very much, which I find so interesting. He was drawn to lugubrious subjects. But you don't seem to have any such predilection. There's no violence in your work.

JK: My 1991 sculpture *Large Vase of Flowers* [edition of 3] is about abundance. It's really referencing, like the Garden of Eden, sensual qualities and the sexuality of these flowers. They're beckoning. They're being attractive. But if you start to go in deeper, you are aware that the flowers in the vase are cut.

MP: Well, I can't think about looking at that work quite the same, once I read that you said it could be 140 assholes.

JK: It's about the sensuality of nature and people accepting sexuality. After the "Banality" work, I made the "Made in Heaven" series [1989–91]. It was about using the body as metaphor, again, for self-acceptance, the acceptance of sexuality, how we procreate, how we continue the species. It's our genes, our DNA. I believe that there are forms of communication that are biological, which are really quite profound.

MP: Then speaking of vases and flowers, what is your sense of the ideal way the *Puppy* (p. 29) should be displayed?

JK: Full of flowers. When I speak about those cut flowers, again, I'm speaking philosophically. People could plant a live flower in the back of the sculpture if they wanted. But I don't see any reason to do that. It's supposed to be cut flowers, full and abundant. It would be beautiful. I like it when there are a lot of different colors.

MP: One can draw a number of parallels between your working methods and Warhol's. You both are demon

Where I've really been inspired and impressed by Andy is in the sense of economy, of getting more out of something than is put into it.

workers, certainly. Very hands on. But he was very involved in the manual, physical making of the work, although that may not be the impression that people have. However, it was relatively simple work, silkscreen painting, compared to the sort of elaborate production methods that are involved in your very complicated work. Did the Factory and Andy's working methods provide a model for the way art could be made?

JK: I don't think that I ever consciously thought about it, because I don't really think of my studio as a factory. People may refer to it as a factory, but I think of it more as a studio. I hired my first assistant in 1986, and then I worked in Europe on my "Banality" works. I worked with companies and sought out different artisans whom I felt were best suited to make works like *Michael Jackson and Bubbles* and *Ushering in Banality*.

But I would say that where I've really been inspired and impressed by Andy is in the sense of economy, of getting more out of something than is put into it. I don't like fetishism because I think of it as a dog chasing its tail. Andy didn't do that. I think Andy's work is about acceptance. It's putting down an orange swish that blends into a violet, and then, on another canvas, putting down a turquoise that goes into a yellow, and over here a black into a red, and then screening on top. They're equal. One is not better than the other.

Aesthetic judgments are irrelevant because what's really important in life is that people are equal, that there's beauty in people, and that there's acceptance of people. The dialogue is not about objects.

INTERVIEW WITH JULIAN SCHNABEL

DECEMBER 6, 2011

MARLA PRATHER: Of all of the artists in this exhibition, apart from possibly Jean-Michel Basquiat, you presumably had the most contact with Warhol. When did you meet?

JULIAN SCHNABEL: I think I probably met him the first time around 1974. I used to see him on the street. It was amazing just to see him walking by. It was such a big deal in those days to see him. I wanted to say something, being a young artist. But I didn't. There wasn't anything really to say then. I also used to see him at Max's Kansas City. It was the last run, it closed in 1974. I met a lot of artists at that time. Richard Artschwager was one of them. I knew Larry Poons, Neil Williams, Brice Marden, David Budd, David Diao, Willem de Kooning, Richard Serra, Bob Smithson. And I saw Andy there, with Eric Emerson and Viva—different people who were at one time part of the Factory.

But we really met later, in 1979, and got to know each other better through Bruno Bischofberger. Bruno was always introducing Andy. He introduced Jean-Michel to Andy, he introduced Francesco Clemente to Andy, he introduced me to Andy. It was a way for him to meet younger artists. Andy actually saw the first plate painting before I met him. So, by that time, it was more like, "This is Julian Schnabel." "Oh, yeah, I know your work."

MP: In 1982, you painted Warhol's portrait on velvet, which is now in the collection of the Hirshhorn Museum in Washington, D.C. (p. 176). You've talked about how cooperative he was. You asked him, for example, to take his shirt off. And he was wearing what you described as this pink girdle that he had to wear.

JS: Andy liked to trade, to acquire works by other artists. So the concept was that we were going to trade a painting. He came over to the studio at 521 West 23rd Street, on the fifth floor. I had this nine-by-ten piece of velvet, and he basically stood in front of me as I painted it, just like that. He kind of looked like Peter O'Toole in *The Ruling Class*. His skin looked like it was almost sculpted, like a mask, and he was underneath it. Through that, there was a beauty and a deer-in-the-headlights look in his face. And he was very accommodating. Usually, he would never really tell you anything. But that day, when I was painting him, he started to talk about things that he didn't like. I never heard him really be critical or complain about anything. So there was a kind of intimacy that occurred.

There's a funny thing that happens when you're painting a portrait. There's a sort of parallel life that's running alongside of whatever you're saying or not saying because there's an activity going on. You're talking sometimes, but then sometimes you say, "Don't say anything for a minute," because you don't want the person's mouth to move. It's really an accumulation of movements. It's not about using some kind of mathematical aid, like a grid, or trying to keep the person in the same place all the time. So if I'm very close, the feet will be much smaller. If I get back further, it'll look more like everything's in proportion. It's an amalgam of acts and feelings that occur. I think the level of trust that's involved is something that's probably important to me.

MP: You've talked about how you establish a bond, whether you're working with an actor or a subject in a painting. Did Warhol talk about feeling under-appreciated? Not taken seriously?

JS: I think he did think that. He felt like Jasper Johns and Bob Rauschenberg were taken more seriously than he was. He had a lot of respect for them. I said, "Well, you know, you're a really good painter. You ought to spend more time painting. There are a lot of people around you and you're working on these films, but you shouldn't get distracted." It's funny that I would tell him that, given the fact that I would eventually make films, which I never thought I would do.

MP: Did he like the portrait?

JS: I think he liked it.

MP: And he made a portrait of you in exchange?

JS: A triptych. It's spectacular. I'm standing in a landscape in Amagansett. It was from a photograph that Jacqueline, my first wife, took (p. 175).

MP: It's so unlike Warhol. Maybe because the source was a photograph he didn't take. It's not a head shot. You're standing by the water. There's a kind of tenderness to it.

JS: It's different from the other portraits, where he went into a photo booth and took pictures or used the Polaroid. And the interesting thing about that painting is that he broke the figure, superimposing one screen on the other. The image became doubled. I have two belts.

MP: Just like Elvis (p. 52)!

JS: Right. Well, it's like a film sprocket. The thing is still, but it has movement at the same time. Actually, I had a choice. They sent over two *Hammer and Sickle* paintings, which I liked. But I

thought it would be great to have the portrait. I think he actually made nine panels. There are three lavender and black panels, three gold and black, and three pink and black. I have two gold and one pink. I think there are two negatives and one positive. The X-ray quality is interesting. In a sense, the portrait was related to the *Reversal* paintings [1979]. But there were a lot of things in it. There was a barbed wire fence. It reminded me of an electric chair. It had grass, because it was out in a field, which reminded me of the flower paintings. And it also had what looked like a burnt-out pillbox. It was a landscape, but it looked like a scene out of a war. It felt like a *Disaster* painting.

And, actually, I also wanted to buy a *Liz* painting. But then he went in to have his gallbladder operation and died. When we made the movie [*Basquiat*, 1996], the Warhol Foundation actually gave me the bag that Andy took with him, containing what he thought he needed at the hospital— socks and mints and perfume, different things. I gave that to David Bowie, with the wig and his jacket, to use for his character.

MP: You say that Bruno introduced everyone to each other. In your movie *Basquiat*, I love the encounter between Warhol, Basquiat, and Bischofberger in a restaurant. Basquiat is trying to sell his little paintings to Warhol, and they are negotiating the price, five dollars, ten dollars, and Warhol says, "These are great, Bruno. Maybe I'll take two. . . . Bruno, can I borrow some money?"[1]

JS: That actually took place.

MP: Back to portraiture, your work in this exhibition is the portrait of Barbara Walters, the plate painting from 1990 (p. 75). How did that come about? Your plate portraits, your portraits generally, tend to be of your friends and family.

JS: She contacted me and asked me if I'd paint a painting of her. I don't remember who organized it. She was very nice.

MP: You wrote passionately about Warhol's *Shadows*, the large series of paintings from 1978–79, when they were shown at Gagosian Gallery in 1989, at the time of

I think that there is a misconception about Andy's work, that it was vapid or superficial. There's something at the bottom of all of his work that is absolutely heartbreaking.

the Warhol retrospective at the Museum of Modern Art. And it's timely to talk about them again, since recently they've all been installed at the Hirshhorn Museum to extraordinary effect—102 paintings moving along a curved wall, abutted against one another. It's electrifying ["Andy Warhol: Shadows," September 25, 2011– January 15, 2012].

JS: I went down there to talk about the Blinky Palermo retrospective [February 24–May 15, 2011]. It is interesting that the Hirshhorn also had that show because there's a real affinity between these two artists and these two exhibitions in the colors and in metaphor and approach and attitude.

MP: When you wrote about the *Shadows*, you defended Warhol as a painter. You said, on the one hand, there's almost nothing on them. And also, "The way he used the screen as an additional brush is the printed emblem of his behavior. And his decision to select and to act without interpretation, without explanation, was the utter denial of the sentimental. No other painter has come close to this radicality of gesture and self-denial." Could you talk a bit about his radicality?

JS: I hope that you show the lavender, robin's-egg blue, and cadmium yellow skull painting [*Skull*, 1976, The Andy Warhol Museum]. It is one of the largest skull paintings and one of the most extraordinary paintings I think anybody has painted. And it's very painterly. Yes, there's the printed image on it, but like the *Shadows* it's done with a sponge mop. It's a very gestural painting, but the palette is so peculiar. The deepest value is cadmium yellow. He's really one of the great colorists.

When you start looking at the range of what Andy was doing, it's right that you have to have fifty artists in this exhibition, because the guy is a seminal figure. Look at Dan Colen or Nate Lowman or even Christopher Wool. These are people who are basically taking an aspect of Warhol's work, mining a graphic quality or a way of applying paint, and saying that they can make an abstract painting. Look at Warhol's *Camouflage* paintings. He said, "Okay, now I'm going to make a *Camouflage*, but I think I'll superimpose it on a *Last Supper* painting [*Camouflage Last Supper*, 1986, The Menil Collection, Houston], or I'll turn some of the panels upside down." Painting is thinking, and each decision is a painted one.

I think that there is a misconception about Andy's work, that it was vapid or superficial. There's something at the bottom of all of his work that is absolutely heartbreaking. Take all those *Liz* paintings in the recent show ["Andy Warhol: Liz," Gagosian Gallery, New York, September 16– October 22, 2011]. I once said that painting was a bouquet of mistakes. I was talking about my own paintings. But I could say that about his paintings. It's an accumulation of failures and idiosyncrasies that defines the virtues and the characteristics of each of these works. No matter how generic the work or how he said he liked to be like a machine, you can't get away from his personality. You can't get- away from his point of view.

Look at Roy Lichtenstein's *Popeye* [1961, private collection] next to Andy's *Popeye* [1961, private collection]. I think Andy probably thought that Roy's painting was better. He said it to me, I don't know if he meant it. Personally, I prefer Andy's painting, with its unfinished quality, the crossword puzzle. It's kind of a no-brainer why Jean-Michel and Andy worked together. Andy's early works look like Jean-Michel's paintings. There is an unfinishedness to them. There are words that are just dangling somewhere. There is paint that is just standing for paint. He had no problem leaving something like that. And he had no problem not explaining what he was doing. Sometimes I think I talk too much or explain too much. Maybe that's why I made the movie. But, obviously, he had something he wanted to express. I thought the exhibition of the *Screen Tests* at the Museum of Modern Art was riveting ["Andy

Warhol: Motion Pictures," December 19, 2010–March 21, 2011]. And really, when we look at what people are doing now, over the past twenty years, I don't know that I have seen anything that he didn't do.

One time, my mother said to him, "Andy, your paintings are so neat. Julian's paintings are so messy." And he said to my mother, "Esther, I'm trying to get mine messier."

They'd have lunch at the *Interview* offices for people who were on the cover of the magazine. My father and I walked in for some reason one afternoon, and they asked us to sit down. Andy was saying that Richard Nixon lived in Saddle River, New Jersey. And my father said, "Saddle River's in New York." And Andy said, "No, it's in New Jersey." And then my father said, "Saddle River's in New York." And then Andy said, "No, it's in New Jersey." Now, this went on for a while. And then my father says, "Saddle River's in New York." And then Andy says to him, "Oh, I didn't know that." He also said to me once, "When people start driving you crazy, just start talking about Jesus Christ and they'll leave you alone."

MP: He was a master when it came to deflecting questions.

JS: Did you know that he was on *The Merv Griffin Show* once? He didn't say anything. So Merv Griffin said to him, "If you're not going to say anything, why don't you leave?" And he got up and he walked off.

MP: In a 1966 televised interview with Alan Solomon he kept evading the questions and finally said, "Oh, you

should just tell me the words and I could just repeat them. . . . Why don't you just tell me the words and they'll just come out of my mouth."[2]

So I gather that this idea of Warhol as a kind of cipher, as an empty vessel into which others poured ideas, is not a view you share.

JS: No, I don't. But he was a good listener. I actually suggested to him once that he should make paintings of those missing children on milk cartons. I think he thought it was a good idea. I think he listened to Bruno a little too much sometimes. Bruno had a voracious appetite and total belief and very strong opinions. And so he spent a lot of time going over there and saying, "I want these," or "I want that," or "Why don't you do this?" or "You can do that."

But he made some great things. I think some of those Gropius-Bau pictures, those Albert Speer monument pictures, from 1982 are quite good.[3] I think that his work, like much great art, is really misunderstood. There are different time capsules that things fit into. Well, he was making his *Time Capsules*! But certain things, like the camouflage paintings or the fright-wig paintings, they didn't really catch on until much, much later.

People don't want a new painting until you're dead. Then, all of a sudden, everything is in the vulture's craw. And those fright-wig pictures are powerful. Obviously, it's amazing how, when somebody's dead, it just becomes all about the market. There's another reality that has nothing to do with what the paintings are about.

MP: Did you know that Warhol was deeply offended when René Ricard, the writer and poet, said that the *Shadows* were merely decorative? He describes being in a kind of rage about it. So he did really care that someone saw those works as superficial.

JS: Sure. He was a serious painter. And I was extremely happy to write about those works and actually describe the idea of not being able to *see* them. There's a great quote in the front of my book *CVJ* [1987] from William Gaddis [author of *The Recognitions*, 1955]: "Most paintings, the instant you see them, they become familiar and then it's too late." Some of the *Shadows*, those big ones that are irregular, they're so good. Just think

When we look at what people are doing now, over the past twenty years, I don't know that I have seen anything that he didn't do.

I think [Warhol is] absolutely a giant, more so now than ever. That's the great thing about making art. The guy is definitely present. You have to deal with it.

of what it is to do that. It's something that's beyond sight. I first saw them at Dia on West Broadway, and then later in a supermarket in Houston.¹

There's something about the anonymity of abstract art, of art that doesn't seem to care if you understand it or not. It's not reaching out to you, but it's there for you to come to. And the idea that somebody would make all those panels and not necessarily know where the hell they were going to go is a great act of faith.

That's really what painting is about. It has nothing to do with trying to comply with other people's expectations of who you are. Nobody really wanted those paintings. Nobody had a place to put those paintings. And he wasn't thinking about where they would fit. It really was something that he just wanted to do. I want to hit that note. I want to sing that song. You know?

So there's a split with Andy. There's the artist, on one hand, and then there's the person. The art that he made is one thing; his needs as a person—to have friends, to be cared for, because he was excited to be around certain people—are another. It made him feel good. But, when it came down to it, the decision-making process of what he called a painting was the radical thing. I saw the show of late paintings at the Brooklyn Museum ["Andy Warhol: The Last Decade," June 18–September 12, 2010]. There were some amazing things in it that really make you understand that

he was thinking about painting in a way that other people just don't ever arrive at. And that is a gift and a curse. When you're young, you want people to understand you. When you get older, you don't expect it anymore. You want to make things to surprise yourself, not to cater to other people. So you end up speaking in some language that they might not understand.

MP: Do you think Warhol is as timely now as he was in the sixties?

JS: Sure. Since 1990 there's been a lot of rehashing of stuff. I think he's absolutely a giant, more so now than ever. That's the great thing about making art. The guy is definitely present. You have to deal with it. That's what's so great. I'm directing a movie based on the 2002 book *In the Hand of Dante* by Nick Tosches. Who could judge the author, except Dante? Who will judge me? Artists have to judge themselves. I go to the Prado and look at Goya paintings and think, "Okay. Did I get it right?" You make comparisons.

It doesn't matter if the artists are dead or not; their work is alive. They're alive with you. They're communicating with you. And they know that when they're making their work. When you're a kid, you think that the idea of immortality seems pretentious and sort of sentimental. Later, you start looking at it and you really understand the beauty of stopping time and bringing people into the present of your work. So whatever the present is, once they enter into Andy's painting, they're in his present. And it happens with all great art.

MP: I like that you told someone you'd like to live the rest of your life at the Met.

JS: I should spend more time there. I think I would actually feel better if I went there more often. You know what I mean? You go stand in front of a Caravaggio painting sometime, and you think, "God, just to be able to do that." If you could do that, maybe it's not so bad, dying.

MARCH 19, 2012

MARLA PRATHER: You were born in Texas, grew up in Ohio, and entered Rhode Island School of Design in 2000. Commentators on your work have mentioned many creative inspirations for you, from Walt Disney to Cindy Sherman—but, at the same time, it's been said that you were not necessarily exposed to much fine art until you arrived at RISD. Is that the case? Do you see Cindy Sherman (who has four works in our show) as an influence?

RYAN TRECARTIN: I'm really into her work—Cindy Sherman was actually the first artist I learned about specifically through the lens of contemporary art, in my senior year of high school. I'd decided to apply to art school because it seemed like a place where people can have creative freedom and easily move between different mediums and cultural discussions. As a teen I was constructing scenes and scenarios, making costumes, sets, writing music. The end "thing" was often a photo, sculpture, or a musical composition. A teacher showed me Sherman's work, and I remember feeling a sense of agreement. I was so excited that she seemed to be using herself as a medium rather than as a vehicle for self-portraiture.

But, to be honest, contemporary art or artists alone have never been a main catalyst for me to want to make art. I've been more inspired by how language is used—in culture generally, whether in casual conversation or various forms of media—or by music, TV, dance, and movies, and especially by how responses to content are shared, organized, revised, and created. I never

think about disentangling moments from my cumulative experience of culture that may have influenced me the most. It's all stuck together, and it means more in its blended entirety than it does as a series of key experiences or authors. I don't think about references or influences as pure bits of information or inspiration. I want culture to ferment and create new meaning or articulations of otherness within the context of how memory is experienced.

MP: Do you recall when and how you first encountered the work of Andy Warhol?

RT: Before I learned of him as an artist, I think I first encountered Warhol at a Target store in Canton, Ohio, in the mid-1990s.

MP: I'm struck by the contrast between the laconic, almost static pace of some of Warhol's films (the slowest example, I suppose, being *Empire,* at eight hours plus) and the delirious, sped-up pace of your videos. Could you comment on these contrasting approaches? Does it have to do with the difference in your chosen media or rather a point you are making about our contemporary world?

RT: It's a difference in media and our contemporary world, but sometimes it's a similarity via a different equation or reasoning. I think pace and stillness are relative to one's cultural position—there is no monolithic or immutable understanding of these ideas. We read the world around us

differently now than how Warhol did. Today humanity is able to manifest ambitions of connectedness through technology (personal computers). People working today may arrive at feelings or sensibilities seemingly familiar from other times, but the context around them has changed drastically. They're ultimately dissimilar. In the same sense, one thing from the past and one from today may appear to be extremely different from each other when they're actually transpositions performing the same gesture or in the same territory. I'd say all of these scenarios happen in the work.

MP: Like Warhol, you collaborate on almost all of your productions. But, because of his passive approach to his filmmaking, Warhol has been called the anti-director. I gather that you structure your videos by very specific scripts, whether or not the result is precisely what you bargained for. This differs from the often ad hoc, unscripted nature of Warhol's early films. Can you describe your process?

RT: Today so many people have access to tools for understanding themselves as a mediated body—everyone is a production of some sort. The director/actor relationship as a concept has collapsed. It's no longer binary or hierarchical, and I see that as true not only in the process of directing a movie but also in everyday life through social networking and career hopping. I think Warhol's anti-directing was a precursor to this, or at least some sort of an intuitive foreshadowing to many current mentalities. Directing and scripting in my work happens on many overlapping levels and in many forms—and it

Today so many people have access to tools for understanding themselves as a mediated body — everyone is a production of some sort.

includes copious authors. I think of the scripts I write taking four distinct forms, which all unfold simultaneously. The most obvious one is the initial written script. The shape can change depending on the scene and the people involved. At times the script is traditional, with play-by-play, character-assigned dialogue sequences. Other times it's a list of phrases, a monologue, or a poem with no concrete delineations of characters, even if the performative space involves a group of personalities. The script can also be an agenda or a written structure, and the goals of that structure are explored based on topics and suggestions—collaborative, assignment-based translations of a phrase. The sets, props, costumes, hair, and makeup also constitute a type of script that I usually make in collaboration with Lizzie Fitch. This physical narrative space intersects with the written script during the shoot and creates an intuitive container for the performers to activate a kind of scripted improvisation, creating nuanced improvement, interpretation, and/or a revisioning within the structure of a sentence being performed. The editing, sound design, and effects processes are another phase of writing that reconsiders everything that has been captured on camera as raw supplies. Then a new script is created, and the scripting of that is watching, reading, and interacting with the movie as material.

MP: You speak often of the importance of your collaborators, and I was fascinated to read about the house in Miami you rented for some eighteen months to produce the seven-part epic *Any Ever*, 2009–10 (p. 103), to which the three videos in our exhibition belong. Do you see any parallels between this collaborative situation and Warhol's Factory, where, at least in its early day, people mingled, attended parties, and participated in the film work and even in the painting of his pictures? How do you choose the people you work with?

RT: I think what people could read as similar between where/with whom I make my work and Warhol's Factory is superficial, but there are parallels; the equation is radically different but the extended narrative is relatable. I think "the Factory" as a phrase articulates a social scene as a kind of corporation, vision, and way of living/producing/being. That can fulfill cultural labels such as movement, -ism, manifesto, collective, commune, cult, and community. I am more interested in pluralized collaborative environments that are not about a group dynamic channeled into a single vision, product, or essence—or vice versa. There's much less of a need today to distill a network or scene into a singular idea or vision, largely because of how thinking has developed in light of the Internet. People now suspend multiple and often contradictory visions of their own self with ease. We have always navigated chaos through generalizations and the creation of categories, but I think current technology has started to lessen the need for tightly controlled understandings. It's now more casually possible to be able to hold all things in flux and to allow ourselves malleability and transactional structuring because precise similarities are so easily grouped, contained, and framed via social technology. These groupings have accelerated as more people have been exploring and maintaining niche lives and articulating micro differences within them.

In effect, my collaborators and I choose each other through complementary or contrasting talents, intentions, dreams, and desires. It is much more connective than collective. It's about creating a kind of friction to spawn something other than the sum of its parts (horizontal and decentralized).

MP: You often install your videos in environments that replicate, to some extent, the sets your actors inhabit on-screen, yet you've also said that "the work is meant to have many homes: movie theatre, home theatre,

internet, computer, installation, party."[1] Why do you feel this is important?

RT: Everything I make is through collaboration, and so naturally that quality is embedded in the way it is accessed and shared as a finished product. The movies really are native to a multiplicity of situations. Different contexts bring out different aspects of the work and encourage different readings or framings—as well as different desires and ways to interact. Also, artists who are inspired by a diverse range of cultural hubs and mentalities should share with the worlds that inspire them. I don't think art is outside or higher than other aspects of culture, but it is special, since it potentially has no boundaries and can represent complete freedom.

MP: Products of mass consumption populate your videos and installations—cheap handbags, mass-produced furniture, department-store fashions—and you've said that you source them at Target or Ikea. Would you call that use of "readymades" a strategy somewhat akin to Warhol's reproductions of the objects of 1960s consumer culture—soup cans or Brillo boxes, for example?

RT: Just like a urinal can be a readymade or a silkscreened Brillo box can be a cultural reproduction, so can a theory, a personality trait, an idea, or even a proclivity toward something. I think people's brains are thinking this way naturally. Lizzie and I tend to use Ikea in particular for two main reasons: the big-box-chain aspect of the store allows us to access the mass-oriented (or mass-informed) cultural language embodied in the things they sell and with the same ease and access afforded by the Web. And second, these stores strip ideas down to their most iconic representation, allowing the object "furniture" to be cast in a way similar to the dispatching of words in a sentence. The arc of a sentence is a composite in which meaning is created out of the supplies of words. I think it is very much related to the readymade, although I think the reasons for accessing these things are different now. I'm approaching this through a more digital-influenced outlook on lifestyle and personality. The "preset" and "option" aspects of culture are more interesting

My collaborators and I choose each other through complementary or contrasting talents, intentions, dreams, and desires. It is much more connective than collective.

I don't think our current reality is lived out beyond gender or race or sexuality yet, but I think it will be — and before we know it.

than the notions of "product" and "design." I'm interested more in how ideas, sensations, vibes, and mentalities can eventually occupy the default, or preset, position in a culture, how they become a readymade—or a reproduction of one. And beyond that, I am interested in how, in a perverse way, all of these readymades can be accessed as options and then reconstituted to create collective or approachable uniques.

MP: When recently asked about the absence of masculine figures in the work, you posited that there is a masculinity there that one perhaps can't see, that you were moving toward a "kind of queerness, beyond gender or sexual orientation and toward an erasure of forms of otherness, toward their collapse."[2] In your view, are we really in a culture that is beyond gender, or does your work perhaps posit a space toward which you might wish we'd move?

RT: I think we are all currently capable of existing past static ideas or articulations of gender and sexual orientation. Not everyone consciously explores this, but the cultural tools for seeing past gendered realities are available now. We manage and mediate multiple explanations of who we are and cultivate a web of bodies or personalities daily via our computers. I don't think our current reality is lived out beyond gender or race or sexuality yet, but I think it will be—and before we know it. Functional postgender realities will most likely accompany an embrace of technology as a complete means for articulating who we are and why we choose to live and what counts as existence. The very fact that a five-year-old can comprehend queer theory even in its most abstract moments means we are in an era of implementation, when ideas and theories are becoming very real and lived. What we are on the brink of is most likely a ton more complicated and nuanced than any narrative past gender could be read.

SEPTEMBER 9, 2011

MARLA PRATHER: As someone who has organized a fair number of thematic shows of your own, I wonder how this strikes you and how you feel about being included in an exhibition largely about Warhol.

LUC TUYMANS: First of all, it took a while for me to appreciate the artwork that Andy Warhol made, basically. And the appreciation really came through for me when I saw a retrospective of his work in Paris [Centre Pompidou, 1989], where I came to the conclusion that Warhol was a very, very analytical artist—which I still believe to this day. How I came to that conclusion was to look at the importance of black in Warhol's work [in relation to] the idea of the authority of printed imagery. When something is printed, it's like it's real. And that was quite a shocking confrontation for me because, until then, I was not touched by the work in that way. Now I think he's really one of the most significant artists, so I am honored to be in a show that embraces such a broad scope of work, one that this artist helped make possible.

MP: That's very good to hear. When you were finishing up your education in Brussels and just beginning to show your work there and elsewhere in Europe, it was around the time that Warhol died, in 1987. At that point, not even necessarily for you personally, was Warhol part of the discussion? Was he considered someone one needed to think about?

LT: Absolutely, especially in the eighties. The name and fame of Warhol was fairly acclaimed. The whole idea of the Factory, the whole idea of the films—those are things we actually witnessed, so they had an inherently huge impact.

Also, looking at Warhol from the angle of Duchamp is quite interesting because, of course, Duchamp was the first to change his own gene pool by changing himself into a transvestite. There are some clear links, of course, which you can deduce. The readymade is also one of them.

As I said, the real meaning of his work came to me much later, which actually speaks well for the work, because it's not that simple to get. You could easily go into denial and say that it is commercial artwork, or that it is art but of no depth, there's no profoundness to it. However, it's the total opposite of that. It is, as I said, extremely analytical. And also, for me, there was a beautiful combination of two artists, one coming from *this* part of the world and achieving the same artistic stature as Warhol, and that is Joseph Beuys. I remember them both being interviewed. From Beuys you have this political bullshit, the [Rudolf] Steiner crap, in a very long exposé about educating the people. And then someone asked Warhol what he would do if he became president of the United States. He said—and this, I thought, was also of a very analytical nature—that he would clear the people and cars out of New York, put carpets in the street, and get on a white horse and ride naked through the streets of the city. It was a beautiful counterpoint to the long explanations of Beuys, who, to this day, I think is a great artist but a dangerous man.

MP: Speaking of artists in Europe, you recently organized the exhibition "The Reality of the Lowest Rank, A Vision of Central Europe" in the city of Bruges. And you included three artists who were born in the United States: Warhol, Alex Katz, and Paul Thek.

LT: Yes, they were included for genealogical reasons, and we also included [the photographer] Weegee, who was of Austrian origin.

MP: Did you select Warhol's posthumous portraits of his mother from 1974 specifically because of the connection to his Slovakian heritage?

LT: Yes, but also because the element of maternity plays a large role in Eastern Europe! But my idea in putting this show together was to include living artists as well as artists who are deceased—like Warhol, but also Andrzej Wroblewski, Alina Szapocznikow, and Bruno Schulz—people who could create a foundation for the new, contemporary artists. I meant to make a point, especially by quoting from Tadeuz Kantor's 1980 essay "Reality of the Lowest Rank," that if you would look at it from that perspective, you would actually enter Pop art from the rear end. And that is through Eastern European elements, which is quite interesting, I think.

MP: Why did you include Warhol's photos of shoes?

You could easily go into denial and say that [Warhol's work] is commercial artwork, or that it is art but of no depth, there's no profoundness to it. However, it's the total opposite of that. It is . . . extremely analytical.

LT: We included his photos of shoes and his Polaroid self-portraits in drag [1980] because, again, you have the genealogical element, but in this case in terms of gender. We also had Warhol's film of his mother and her "boyfriend" in the kitchen [*Mrs. Warhol*, 1966]. So those elements were played out in several combinations throughout the show. I think Warhol was present in three of the five locations of the show throughout the city.

MP: You are more likely to invoke your fellow countryman Van Eyck as an influence than certain twentieth-century predecessors. You have said that Gerhard Richter was not an influence, but that he, in a way, opened up something for you, presumably because of his use of photography. I wonder if Warhol has been a model in that sense?

LT: Strangely enough, neither of them clearly played a role in the way I put my visualization process together, or in how I decided to depart from history, or real fact, or recent history—as opposed to departing from art. Art is interesting to be admired, to be understood; but it's not something as an artist you decidedly can derive something from. That's my personal opinion, of course.

Instead of going into "isms," Richter used reality as a point of departure, as I did, as Warhol did. So maybe on an unconscious level they must have influenced me, but not directly.

In 1993, while I was in Chicago preparing my first institutional show in the United States ["Luc Tuymans: Superstition," Renaissance Society, University of Chicago, 1995], I saw a show called "Hand-Painted Pop" at the old Museum of Contemporary Art ["Hand-Painted Pop: American Art in Transition, 1955–62," 1993]. The best painting in that show was *Storm Door (1)* by Andy Warhol [1961, Daros Collection, Switzerland]. It was made, as I saw it, out of a certain urgency much more than out of a painterly pleasure. This was shocking to me because it was not like the [work of] more conceptual artists, Jasper Johns or [Roy] Lichtenstein. It was a sort of abject painting that was made out of a certain element of disgust. But nevertheless it withstood time and stood out in the entire exhibition. And I found that quite interesting.

MP: Your painting in this exhibition, from 2005, depicts Condoleezza Rice (p. 69). She was coming to Brussels, the headquarters of the European Union, and this was her first trip as secretary of state. You chose to title the work *The Secretary of State*, depersonalizing her and underscoring her official government role. How did that image come about?

LT: First of all, there was an idea to make a show, which at that time didn't yet have a title. The title ended up being "Proper" [David Zwirner, New York, 2005], which implies "improper" at the same time. In 2005, the country was in a regression, totally consumed by fear and going back to very reactionary elements. So the first thing that came to mind was Ginger Rogers and Fred Astaire. You know, the idea of ballroom dancing as a sign of escapism—because that was during the thirties and forties, a time of depression. And, of course, there is the element of denial.

So, I was browsing the Web with my wife, and by accident I found an image of the governor's ball in Texas of that year, exactly the image I wanted. A woman in an evening gown throws her head back; the guy is in a tuxedo. They are dancing on the official seal of Texas. I had my first image [*Ballroom Dancing*, 2005, San Francisco Museum of Modern Art].

Then with friends at a bar I was going through the newspaper. It was the day that Condoleezza Rice was visiting my country. And one of my best friends, Karel de Gucht, then still the minister of foreign affairs, made quite a sexist remark in the newspaper, saying, "Ms. Rice was actually a very smart woman, and not unpretty." And that's where I got the idea. Ballroom dancing, Condoleezza Rice. Not to go for the Bush administration head-on, but to go for its derivation within it.

I had the idea to portray her in a horizontal, more panoramic view—depicting just part of the face—with its resemblance to a flat-screen TV. The image is cropped in a horizontal format like a television shot, as opposed to portraits in historical painting, which tend to be vertical. It shows a media figure, but she is biting her lower lip and has a decisive frown, which are aspects pointing to the person underneath the public image. She was completely concise and totally controlled, a very cold figure. What did we know and what do we still not know about this woman? I was also suggesting the irony of the fact that Ms. Rice was not in the wrong party—because it was not the Democratic, but the Republican, party that abolished slavery. There was never an intention to point a finger or to be moralistic about it. It was much more about a question mark. What would this figure add up to?

At a preview at the David Zwirner Gallery, Thelma Golden [the director of the Studio Museum in Harlem] let out a cry when she saw the painting, and then suddenly, all the museum people were saying, "Yes, it's a great portrait, but it's Condoleezza Rice!" But Glenn Lowry [the director of the Museum of Modern Art] made a smart decision and phoned David the next day to say that MoMA would be interested in the painting, which it eventually received as a partial gift, because it should be in a public collection since she is a public figure. And if the painting were in a private collection, it would be misunderstood.

MP: You have made that point before. What is that distinction? How would it be misunderstood in a private collection?

LT: Well, it could be understood in different ways, which is great. It should have a layered meaning. To give you another example, years later—in 2010—while my touring retrospective was in Dallas ["Luc Tuymans," Dallas Museum of Art, 2010], I went to the Kimbell Museum in Fort Worth, and the director [Eric McCauley Lee] came out of his office and told me that he's so sorry that he cannot collect contemporary art because, he said, what I did with the painting of Condoleezza Rice is what Andy Warhol did for Marilyn Monroe.

MP: Although that image of Condoleezza Rice has become an iconic image; she is a personification of an era. But he was saying he would like to hang it on his wall as a tribute.

LT: As a tribute, yes, which means that it can be seen in that way as well. I had never thought of that. I had to hold my breath not to burst into laughter. But, why not? It's also true that the minute the show was installed at David Zwirner's a couple of Republican collectors made a phone call; they said they would never, ever again buy a painting of mine. One of my collectors, Lady Lynn de Rothschild, was seated next to Condoleezza Rice at a dinner, and she asked Ms. Rice if she had seen her portrait, which by then had been shown at MoMA. Ms. Rice, without turning her head, said yes. So the impact of it has been extreme.

MP: Part of its power is its ambivalence.

LT: Yes, of course. But I think that it also suggests—and this goes for Colin Powell as well—that some people accept the schism of racism in order to get somewhere in life. That's one thing.[2] In that sense, it's ambiguous, and it should be. Because I think life is ambiguous and nothing is as it seems. While at the airport on my way back home after that show, I bought the book *Condi vs. Hillary* by the Republican strategists Dick Morris and Eileen McGann.[3] The whole book was about the fact that Condi would win the 2008 presidential election because she would get there on her own merit, whereas Hillary Clinton would have been highly supported by, of course, one of the former presidents of the United States. So, you see, something was also in the air. And the funny thing is that it didn't add up to anything, eventually, which I think is even more beautiful.

MP: After you read your friend's comment about how she was a "not unpretty" woman, did you go in search of an image of the secretary of state?

LT: Exactly. The image was from a website fully dedicated to Ms. Rice. I chose one where you see a little gap between the lips, where her teeth appear, because that's the only defect she has—these slightly crooked teeth.

MP: Your show "Proper" also included the painting *Demolition* (p. 174), which was about the demolition of a building in Chicago. Yet, in the context of that show, and given its proximity to Condoleezza Rice, the assumption was that it was an image about September 11th.

LT: Yes, which is interesting, because it actually proves the element of banality, especially in the aftermath of 9/11. It takes away your vision and it deludes your vision. So it is actually a total alienation of imagery. In that sense, it's nearly an abstract painting. You could look at it as such. Only the flagpole and the lamp indicate an urban setting. And, of course, the similarity must be perceived in such a way that it could be easily part of what happened that day, as an image. But nevertheless, that image is also a nonimage.[1]

MP: Like Warhol, you have not shied away from highly charged imagery—Belgian colonialism, gas chambers. It seems that no subject is taboo for you. Of course, Warhol painted electric chairs and ambulance disasters. The assumption—and Warhol contributed to it—is that with the repetition of violent images in the mass media one eventually becomes indifferent to them. But you have said, "Violence is the only structure underlying my work."

LT: When I had my show "Luc Tuymans: Superstition" in 1995, I had a conversation with Susanne Ghez [executive director of the Renaissance Society at the University of Chicago], whom I highly admire and respect. She said, "Listen, you Europeans cannot stand the splash in the face." And I said, "Listen, violence, where I come from, doesn't have a face. It's organized. And it kills by the millions." And that's a very big difference.

Therefore, the painting *Gas Chamber* [1986, The Over Holland Collection]—which may always be my most problematic image—is a concept more than an image. It depicts a space that was deleted, in the sense that it was a sort of masked space. It was proposed as a place where you could take a shower. And it was also, therefore, very important to me not to show bodies or corpses or actual violence, but to embed the violence within the space, the space that will just be left as an anonymous space. It is space as a residue. So violence is a residue. The imagery is its consequences. And violent imagery apparently leaves more consequences than happy imagery.

Also, it is a fact that our culture, the Western one, is based upon two very violent pillars, either warfare or aggressive technology. That has enabled a very small group of people to dominate the largest part of the world. That is part of our culture. The idea is that instead of going into denial—that's where the taboo comes in—I have

It is a fact that our culture, the Western one, is based upon two very violent pillars, either warfare or aggressive technology. . . . The whole elementary idea that in order to create we must destroy is an interesting insight into the sort of culture we are a part of.

chosen to see it as part of culture and not as something that doesn't belong in culture. It is a product of it. The whole elementary idea that in order to create we must destroy is an interesting insight into the sort of culture we are a part of.

And more than going into denial, it was important to do it in a way that still goes at the issue sideways. But the gas chamber was maybe one of the most direct elements in that perception. Nevertheless, it leaves you questioning, because without the title, you would not know what it was about.

MP: With Warhol, the images are quite legible, but the use of color, the use of silkscreen, is a distancing technique.

LT: That's where the authority of print comes in. By using printed matter, combining it within the pictorial, it introduces a sense of truth within the imagery. And that's what I found interesting in Warhol's approach to how to work with an image.

MP: You were mentioning the pillars of our culture—and one could argue that another pillar of

our culture is commerce. You said something very interesting in a conversation with Ai Weiwei. In 2009, you had done an exhibition with him, "The State of Things. Brussels/Beijing" [Centre for Fine Arts, Brussels], and you were talking about how the audience for contemporary art has expanded since the 1970s, for better or worse, and one reason is because of its visibility through the medium of the art market. If contemporary art is worth that much, then maybe we ought to pay attention to it. On one level you were crediting the market with encouraging an interest. This is something that is either celebrated by supporters of Warhol or held against him by others, because he is so central to this exploding market. And, of course, Warhol was so honest and unapologetic about his own interest in business.

LT: Again, his approach to [the art market] was quite pragmatic and analytic, I have to say, far different from that of Damien Hirst, who decisively played it out until the large auction of his work, which was staged and prepared for years, during a situation when we were in a huge global financial crisis. This was a prepared coup. There is a difference between Warhol the phenomenon and Warhol the artist. I think those are two elements he wanted to play upon. To be a social phenomenon within the art world was something quite manipulated by Warhol himself, actually geared and steered by him. He was having his hand in it without actually admitting it.

The fact that Warhol was honest or not doesn't really interest me. I don't think that honesty or dishonesty is something that belongs to the art world. And especially not to an artwork. Look at August Sander. He could only get the *real* pose and the *real* situation by putting a person in a pose that is totally dishonest. That's where some kind of honesty or truthfulness to the image would appear for him.

And to dismiss Warhol because of his commercial impact is a misapprehension of the facts, because facts change. It raises a moralistic issue, which, for sure, should not exist in the world of culture.

THE
WARHOL
EFFECT

A VISUAL ARCHIVE

This visual archive, like the artful chronology that follows it, borrows its title from a short but ground-breaking essay by Simon Watney composed for a symposium at Dia Center for the Arts in 1988, the year after Warhol's death.[1] In it, Watney draws parallels between the frequently salacious coverage of Warhol's death and that of the flamboyant singer Liberace mere weeks before, as well as the subsequent auctions of their estates. Against the background of the AIDS epidemic—which killed Liberace and which, for Watney, "licenses a sadistic revenge" on the part of the media "on the body and the posthumous reputation of the dead star"—he examines Warhol's brilliant ability, as a tabloid personality as well as an artistic polyglot, to "detach himself from a traditional authorial role, to dissolve himself into an inviolable *persona*."[2] That so much attention was paid to Warhol's worldly posses-sions and his "afterlife" (to quote John Russell in the *New York Times*) is also evidence for Watney of a different kind of power.[3] Warhol—from fine artist, photographer, journalist, and filmmaker to art collector, bohemian, bon vivant, and pornographer—"lived through, and mapped out, relations of power rooted in every kind of institutionalized fantasy."[4]

The art historian and cultural theorist Douglas Crimp revisited Watney's essay ten years later, writing that it stands out from the rest of the texts in the Dia compendium as a corrective.[5] If Watney wrote at a time when the AIDS crisis put queer identity in high relief and under siege, both physically and politically, Crimp writes from the perspective of the culture wars of the 1990s, when battles raged in the academy and on gallery walls for a stake in what constituted representation and for whom and by whom it was made.[6] Warhol's impor-tance, then, for Crimp, is not merely as a traditional fine artist, but one who resists such categorization and whose "persona demands rethinking the meanings of consumption, collecting, publicity, visibility, celebrity, stardom, sexuality, identity, and selfhood."[7]

It is in this spirit, perhaps, that so many artists of the last fifty years have embraced a Warholian mode. An engagement with celebrity—whether that of a super-model, as in Banksy's (p. 229), or of a serial killer, as in Marcus Harvey's (p. 232)—is just a small part of it. Some artists instead wish to examine the structures and strictures of commodity culture—like Roy Arden in his photographs of detergent stacks at a Canadian Wal-Mart (p. 218) or Sharon Lockhart in her look into a blue-collar lunch hour (p. 225)—and some, like Fred Tomaselli in his reprisal of a painful front page (p. 234), replay the day's news. In any event, doors seem to have opened for an artistic practice that considers the political, lived-in present.

Contingent to that present is a look through film or other media at time and duration. While we include here four homages (pp. 226–27) to Warhol's film *Empire* (p. 26)—the eight-hour-long nighttime gaze at the Empire State Building—there are yet at least four more to date. Elaine Sturtevant, whose *Warhol Marilyn* (p. 215) appropri-ates an earlier Warhol diptych, made her own cinematic version of *Empire* in 1972; New York filmmaker and screenwriter Amos Poe made a poetic sequel, *Empire II*, in 2008; and the three artist collectives Reena Spaulings, Bernadette Corporation, and Claire Fontaine collaborated on *Imperio*, a film of a Mexican skyscraper, in 2007. The fourth, by avant-garde filmmaker Phil Solomon, shares something with the video-gaming world of Cory Arcangel (p. 135): his *EMPIRE*, exhibited in 2008 at the Wexner Center for the Arts at Ohio State University, is a continu-ous, high-definition projection of a close-up of the animated Empire State Building from the Sony Playstation game *Grand Theft Auto IV*.

From the beginning, artists such as Sturtevant and Richard Pettibone used Warhol's designs quite literally, reproducing them either full scale (p. 215) or in a signature small format (p. 216); but the very idea of *decoration* as Warhol used it—an allover pattern of flowers, for example, or a wallpaper print (pp. 244 and 246)—can become an incisive comment on the very condition of contemporary painting.[8] Rudolf Stingel, for example, used a dizzyingly flowered carpet in a vast train station to question notions of public and private and the status of "abstract" art (p. 243), while Jim Hodges's curtain of silk flowers recalls both the high-modernist late paintings of Claude Monet and the raft of flowers one might lay at a tomb (p. 245).

In essence, the options are endless, but exhibitions have their physical limitations. While the works reproduced here do not appear in the show itself, in myriad ways they are too innovative, too trenchant, or too much in and of the restless spirit of the "Warhol Effect" to be overlooked.

ELAINE STURTEVANT

Warhol Marilyn, 1973
Acrylic on canvas
83⅞ × 126¾ in. (213 × 322 cm)
Courtesy Sotheby's, London

Elaine Sturtevant, an American who lives and works in Paris, began to remake works by her contemporaries — Jasper Johns, Anselm Kiefer, and Andy Warhol, among others — as a conceptual practice. She does not create any work that has not been made by someone else before her, yet she insists on the status of her work as original. As the critic Bruce Hainley writes, "Copy, replica, mimesis, simulacra, fake, digital virtuality, clone — Sturtevant's work has been for more than 40 years a meditation on these concepts by decidedly not being any of them."[9]

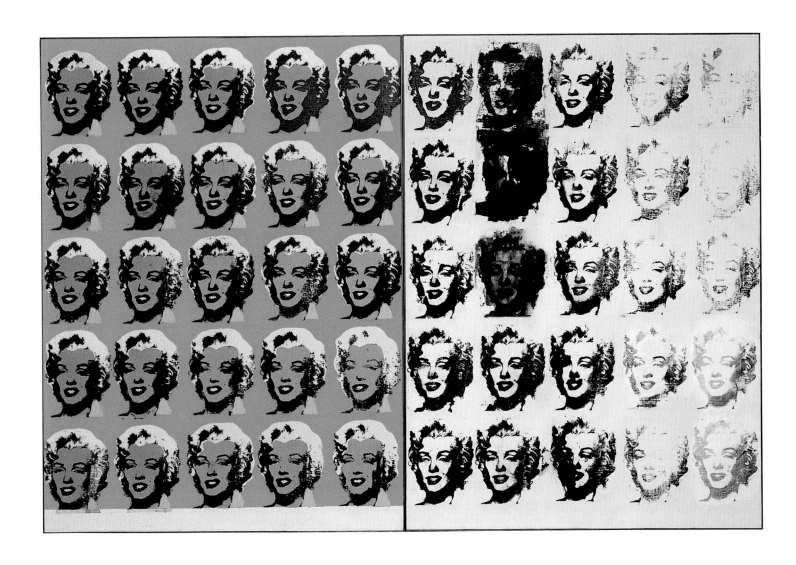

RICHARD PETTIBONE
Andy Warhol, Flowers, 1964, 1971
Acrylic and silkscreen on canvas
1⅝ × 1⅝ in. (4.2 × 4.2 cm)
Courtesy Christie's, London

LIZA LOU
Chicken Noodle Soup Can, 1990
Glass beads on plaster,
edition 9 of 250
4 × 2¾ × 2¾ in. (10.2 × 7 × 7 cm)
Courtesy Christie's, New York

Liza Lou's soup can was the first everyday object
the California artist chose to fashion at full scale
using miniature glass beads—now her signature
material. "I like the idea of slowing down Pop Art,"
she has said. "I thought about Andy Warhol a lot."[10]
Lou made an edition of the can as a way to raise
money for her ambitious *Kitchen* (1991–96), a life-
size interior of a suburban kitchen with every
surface covered with glittering beads.

THOMAS BAYRLE
Glücksklee, 1969
Installation of condensed-milk cans
Dimensions variable
Private collection, Frankfurt

ROY ARDEN
Wal-Mart Store (Tide),
Burnaby, B.C., 1996
Archival pigment print
32 × 39 in. (81.3 × 99 cm)
Courtesy the artist

The Canadian photographer Roy Arden focused
on Wal-Mart's techniques of merchandise display
for a series from the mid-1990s. Here, bright orange
boxes of Tide in seemingly endless supply are neatly
stacked in the form of a readymade minimalist
cube — a Warholian consumerist world now ever
more efficient and calculating.

MIKE BIDLO

Not Warhol (Brillo Boxes, 1964),
2005
Silkscreen and acrylic on wood
47 boxes, each 17 × 17 × 14 in.
(43.2 × 43.2 × 35.6 cm)
Lever House Art Collection,
New York

Mike Bidlo became well
known in the 1980s for
his humorous, full-scale
re-creations of Peggy
Guggenheim's 1940s town
house (*Jack the Dripper
at Peg's Place*, 1982) and
Warhol's Factory, exhibited
at P.S. 1 in Long Island
City, New York. For these
installations Bidlo made
convincing reproductions
of Jackson Pollock's drip
paintings and Warhol's
Brillo Soap Pads Boxes;
those shown here are later
versions made for a recent
exhibition at Lever House
in New York.

RIKRIT TIRAVANIJA
Installation view of *Fear Eats the Soul* at Gavin Brown's Enterprise, New York, with silver-glazed ceramic casts of a wok and a "Warhol" *Brillo Soap Pads Box*, 2011
Courtesy the artist and Gavin Brown's Enterprise, New York

Rikrit Tiravanija's 2011 installation at Gavin Brown's Enterprise included a replica of the Thai artist's 1994 exhibition at Brown's original SoHo space, where he curated a two-person exhibition in which he paired objects important to him—here a wok—with works by Warhol. In Tiravanija's melancholic recent iteration, the objects were cast in porcelain and coated with a ghostly, metallic glaze, then installed within a plywood shell that mimicked the proportions of Brown's former space.

TOM SACHS
Brillo Box, 2003
Ballpoint pen and ink on foamcore
16⅞ × 17⅜ × 14¼ in.
(43 × 44.2 × 36.2 cm)
Courtesy Sotheby's, New York

ROB PRUITT

Un Carton d'Evian Nomad, 2002
Glitter and enamel on
cardboard box
10½ × 13¾ × 10½ in.
(26.7 × 34.9 × 26.7 cm)
Courtesy Christie's, New York

Rob Pruitt's series of glitter-coated water-bottle
cartons—from Evian to Fiji to Crystal Geyser—
harks back to Warhol's *Brillo Soap Pads Boxes* in
that they play with the idea of a Duchampian
readymade now made precious. Whereas Pruitt
uses found boxes, however, Warhol's boxes were
made in the studio, replicating the assembly
line through the use of silkscreen.

WANG GUANGYI
Great Castigation Series:
Coca-Cola, 1993
Oil on canvas
78¾ × 78¾ in. (200 × 200 cm)
Collection of the artist

BANKSY
Tesco Value Tomato Soup, 2004
Oil on canvas
48⁷/₁₆ × 36¼ in. (123 × 92 cm)
Courtesy Bonham's, London

Banksy, the mysterious
street artist and provocateur,
reproduces Warhol's favorite
flavor in its thrifty British
translation. Tesco, whose
motto is "every little helps,"
began as a small grocer
in London's East End and
is now a multinational food
conglomerate with "super-
stores" in fourteen countries.

McDERMOTT & McGOUGH
Because of Him, 1966, 2008
Mirror installation, oil on wood
Dimensions variable
Courtesy Cheim & Read, New York

SHARON LOCKHART
Scott Skelton, Outside Machinist,
from the series *Lunch Break*, 2008
Chromogenic print, edition of 6
24¾ × 30¾ in. (62.9 × 78.1 cm)
Courtesy the artist and Blum & Poe,
Los Angeles

Sharon Lockhart's films and photographs explore prosaic subjects, such as a girls' gym class in Japan, children playing in the courtyards of Lodz, Poland, and — as in this project — machine workers' lunch hour at an ironworks in Maine. Her films examine the cinematic gaze through long pans, unusual vantage points, and slow tracking; like Warhol's *Empire*, *Lunch Break* was slowed down for viewing — in Lockhart's case, digitally — and lengthened from one hour to seventy-five minutes. Her photographs serve as documentation of the people and places she captures on film. Here, one of the worker's lunches is shot as if it were fine sculpture, its bright red Coca-Cola can and foil-wrapped sandwich adding spots of Pop color.

WOLFGANG STAEHLE
Empire 24/7, 1999–2004
Video stills
Dimensions variable
Courtesy the artist and
Postmasters, New York

Wolfgang Staehle, a German-born, New York–based pioneer in Web-based art, first showed his *Empire 24/7* in the exhibition "net_condition" at the Center for Art and Media in Karlsruhe, Germany, in 1999. From the Chelsea offices of his Web-art project *The Thing*, Staehle set up a camera that took still photographs of the Empire State Building every six seconds around the clock, then fed them in a constant stream to a projector in the gallery in Germany — "instant images for instant consumption," as the artist has said, in a world where "24/7" often refers to the hours of a convenience store.[11]

JONATHAN MONK
Empire (After Andy Warhol in Reverse), 2002
Installation of one Ektachrome slide projected until it deteriorates
Dimensions variable
Courtesy the artist and Casey Kaplan, New York

For the September 11–related exhibition "Dust Memories" at the Swiss Institute, New York, Jonathan Monk conceived of an elegiac tribute to Warhol's *Empire* wherein a color slide of the Empire State Building was projected until the hot light of the carousel prematurely yellowed and aged it, and it deteriorated completely.[12] The work seems to capture the melancholic side of Warhol's film while at the same time memorializing film itself — an evanescent medium that, with the advent of digital photography, is quickly headed toward obsolescence.

DOUGLAS GORDON
Bootleg (Empire), 1998
Still of a VHS video in color, no
sound, 120 min.
Courtesy the artist and
Gagosian Gallery

As Douglas Gordon once stated in an interview:
"I did a version of [Warhol's] *Empire*. . . . It is almost
like the amateur version of the auteur masterpiece—
it's very shakily done. I lived in Berlin for a while
and I went to see Warhol's [film], and I thought,
'I may never get to see this again,' so I filmed it for
an hour, went to the pub, and then came back and
filmed it for the last hour. So mine only lasts for
two hours . . . it's like 'the best of' or something.
But quite often my version is seen with his films in
exhibitions, which is kind of funny as mine is
slightly more dramatic as it is shaky and there are
shadows of people walking in front of the camera."[13]

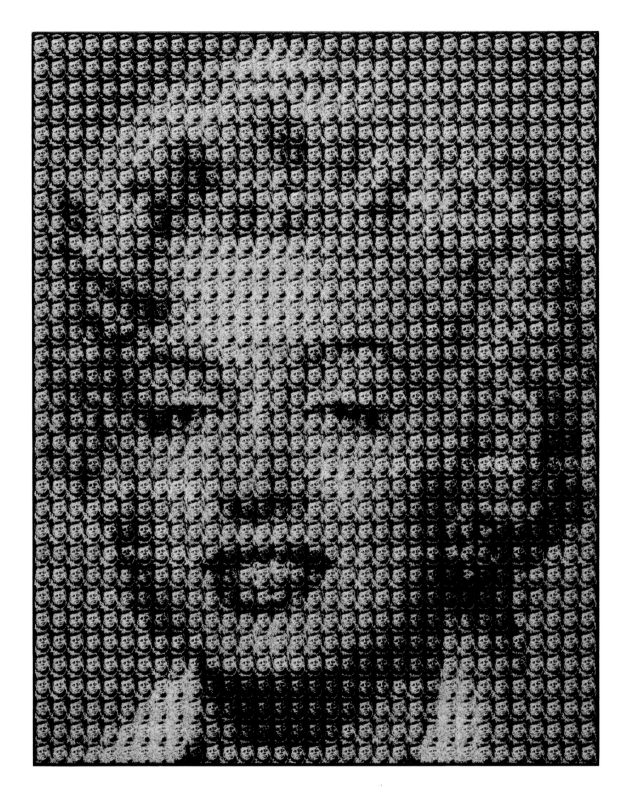

DONG-YOO KIM
*Marilyn Monroe
(John F. Kennedy)*, 2010
Oil on canvas
63¾ × 51¼ in. (162 × 130 cm)
Courtesy the artist and
Gallery Hyundai, Seoul

In Dong-Yoo Kim's paintings,
Warholian subjects such as
Marilyn Monroe and Jackie
Kennedy are rendered in
monochrome, their contours
cleverly concealing pixelated
portraits of another subject—
in this case John F. Kennedy.

BANKSY
Kate Moss, 2005
Screenprint, AP 2 of an
edition of 50
20¾ × 20¾ in. (52.8 × 52.8 cm)
Courtesy Sotheby's, London

MICKALENE THOMAS
Michelle O, 2008
Screenprint, edition 34 of 40
25 × 19½ in. (63.5 × 49.5 cm)
Courtesy the artist and Lehmann
Maupin, New York

RICHARD PHILLIPS
Most Wanted (Robert Pattinson),
2010
Oil on linen
95 × 78 in. (241.3 × 198.1 cm)
Courtesy the artist and White Cube,
London

JONATHAN MONK
Andy Warhol's Chairman Mao
Hand-Made in the People's
Republic of China, 2010
Oil on canvas
98⅜ × 140¼ in. (250 × 356 cm)
Courtesy the artist and Galeri
Nicolai Wallner, Copenhagen

Jonathan Monk's sly tributes to Warhol include
a series made after the latter's portraits of Mao
Zedong from the 1970s. Monk sends pictures
of Warhol's *Maos* to a studio of artists in China
who specialize in copying works of art. The
Chinese artists then painstakingly re-create
Warhol's silkscreened images in carefully hand-
painted oil — allowing Monk a clever take on
issues of reproducibility and originality.

MARCUS HARVEY
Myra, 1995
Acrylic on canvas
155⅞ × 126 in. (396 × 320 cm)
Private collection, New York

While Chris Ofili's painting *The Blessed Virgin Mary* (1996, Collection of David Walsh, Tasmania) caused a furor when it was exhibited as part of "Sensation: Young British Artists from the Saatchi Collection" at the Brooklyn Museum in 1999 (New York's mayor at the time, Rudy Giuliani, called it "sick stuff"),[14] Marcus Harvey's portrait of the 1960s child murderer Myra Hindley — painted on a large scale in a pattern of small children's handprints — drew protest at that exhibition's first venue, London's Royal Academy of Art, in 1997. Still so reviled was Hindley that the work was vandalized by visitors, as victims' family members and others protested outside.[15]

PIOTR UKLAŃSKI
The Nazis, 1998
Detail of an installation of 164 photographs mounted to panels, edition of 10
13¾ × 10 in. (34.9 × 25.4 cm) each
Courtesy the artist and Gagosian Gallery

Piotr Uklański's installation reproduces — in a seemingly endless array — more than one hundred actors portraying Nazis from the history of cinema, all enlarged to the same, close-to-real-life size. The result is at once humorous and scary in its look at the glamorization of horror. As Steven Heller wrote in his review of Uklański's picture book of the same title, "Being cast as a screen Nazi had certain advantages. What actor wouldn't be willing to dress up in such snappy (and very photogenic) garb for his close-up?"[16]

FRED TOMASELLI
August 31, 2005, 2011
Screenprint
14½ × 16 in. (36.8 × 40.6 cm)
Courtesy James Cohan Gallery, New York

Fred Tomaselli's *August 31, 2005* takes its title
from the date of the *New York Times* issue published
two days after Hurricane Katrina struck New
Orleans and caused the catastrophic failure of its
levee system, flooding some 80 percent of the city.
Reproducing the front page in silkscreen, Tomaselli
covered the memorable image of the flooded streets
with lines of bright color. His use of a horrifying
lead story as subject matter recalls Warhol's own
reproductions of glaring headlines.

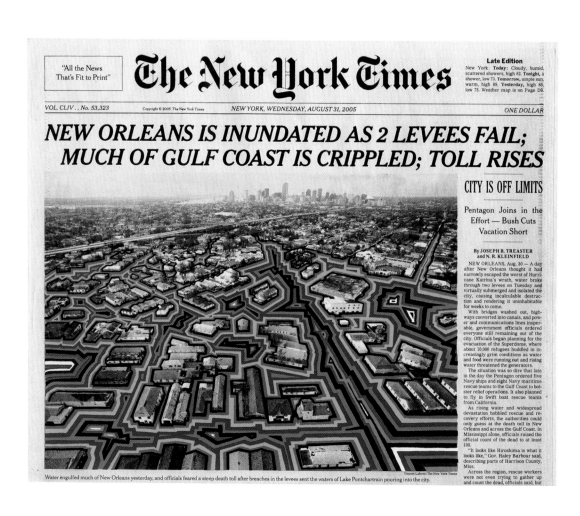

RICHARD MISRACH
Playboy #38 (Warhol), 1990
Color coupler print
37½ × 29½ in. (95.3 × 74.9 cm)
Courtesy the artist and
Fraenkel Gallery, San Francisco

Richard Misrach, known for
his elegant photographs of
desert landscapes, discovered
a makeshift shooting range
on one expedition in the
American West. There he
found a number of *Playboy*
magazines that had been
used for target practice
at the remote site. While
paging through these violent
readymades to find eerie
images to rephotograph, he
came across this page with
Warhol's ad for Vidal Sassoon
(see "Timeline," p. 267).

GUILLERMO KUITCA
Untitled (The Warhol Series),
2006
Detail of one of 63 mixed-media
works on paper
8½ × 11 in.
(21.7 × 27.9 cm) each
Courtesy the artist and Sperone
Westwater Gallery, New York

Guillermo Kuitca used a catalogue of Warhol
paintings for a series of ghostly transfers
wherein various works—here Warhol's double
self-portraits of 1967 (p. 85)—retain only
their spectral color and contour.

GAVIN TURK
*Camouflage Fright Wig Gold and
Taupe,* 2007
Silkscreen on canvas
39⅜ × 39⅜ in. (100 × 100 cm)
Courtesy the artist and Riflemaker
Contemporary Art, London

BARBARA KRUGER
Untitled (Not Cruel Enough), 1997
Silkscreen on vinyl
109 × 109 in. (276.9 × 276.9 cm)
The Museum of Contemporary Art,
Los Angeles, Gift of Vivian and
Hans Buehler

DOUGLAS GORDON
Self-Portrait of You + Me
(Elvis), 2007
Silkscreen on mirrored glass
54¾ × 39 × 3 in.
(139.1 × 99.1 × 7.6 cm)
Courtesy the artist and
Gagosian Gallery

CHRIS OFILI

Mono Rosa, 1999–2002
Oil, glitter, graphite, elephant
dung, polyester resin,
and map pins on linen
72 × 48 in. (182.9 × 121.9 cm)
Courtesy the artist and
David Zwirner, New York

Mono Rosa belongs to a
series of thirteen paintings
Chris Ofili made for an
installation, on which
he collaborated with the
architect David Adjaye,
at Tate Britain in London.
All of the paintings were
based on a 1957 drawing
by Warhol of a monkey
holding a chalice, which
reminded Ofili of various
associations, including the
Last Supper and the Hindu
god Hanuman.

RACHEL HARRISON

Installation view from *Perth Amboy*, 2001, installed at the Bard Center for Curatorial Studies, Annandale-on-Hudson, New York, 2009
Courtesy the artist and Regen Projects, Los Angeles

As part of an installation inspired by the apparition of the Virgin Mary on a pane of glass in the working-class city of Perth Amboy, New Jersey, Rachel Harrison included a labyrinth of corrugated cardboard. At its center was a file storage box on wheels that housed a thrift-store bust of Marilyn Monroe. Also included was a photograph Harrison took of her own hand "lifting the vellum sheets that protect Andy Warhol's original Marilyn Monroe reference photo." As the critic R. C. Baker wrote, "The translucent paper partially obscures the star's face (recalling Bert Stern's famous nude shots of the actress twirling a filmy veil around her body just weeks before her fatal overdose). Harrison has mounted her documentary shot on a ragged chunk of wallboard, conflating a wall of fame with ephemeral ruins."[17]

GILLIAN WEARING
Me as Warhol in Drag with Scar, 2010
Bromide print
59⅞ × 48 in. (152.1 × 121.9 cm)
Courtesy the artist; Tanya Bonakdar Gallery, New York; Maureen Paley, London; and Regen Projects, Los Angeles

JIM HODGES
Oh Great Terrain, 2002
Latex paint
Dimensions variable,
installation view
Collection of Glenn and
Amanda Fuhrman,
New York, courtesy the
FLAG Art Foundation

RUDOLF STINGEL
Plan B, 2004
Installation view of carpet
"painting" in Vanderbilt Hall,
Grand Central Terminal, New York,
July 1–July 29, 2004
Creative Time, New York

For his 2004 installation at Grand Central Station in New York, Rudolf Stingel covered the floor of the building's Vanderbilt Hall with a floral patterned carpet, "injecting a calculated dose of kitsch into this grand, Beaux-Arts structure."[18] While the carpet itself can be seen as a type of industrial readymade, the floral pattern becomes an almost dizzying reminder of the enforced separation between fine painting and mere decoration.

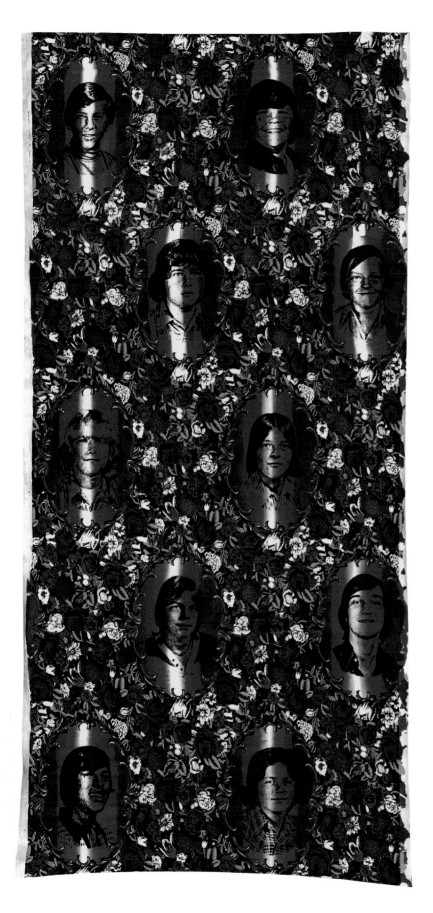

VIRGIL MARTI
Bullies, 1992–97
Fluorescent ink and rayon
flock on Tyvek
Dimensions variable
Philadelphia Museum of Art,
Gift of Marion Boulton Stroud and
the artist, 2003 (2003-39-5)

Virgil Marti's velvet floral wallpaper, while
playing with ideas of patterning and the decorative,
reproduces in cameo style all of the yearbook
portraits of his classmates who bullied him as
a child.

JIM HODGES
No Betweens, 1996
Silk, cotton, polyester, and thread
360 × 324 in. (914.4 cm × 823 cm)
San Francisco Museum of Modern
Art, Purchase through a gift of
Kimberly S. Light, 97.514

Installation view of the exhibition
"Too Much Is Not Enough,"
Kunstverein Hannover, November
25, 2006–January 28, 2007
with

JOHN ARMLEDER
Untitled, 2000
Four disco balls with motors
and spotlights
D.: 39⅜ in. (100 cm) each
and

JOHN ARMLEDER
AND SYLVIE FLEURY
Untitled, 1994
Wallpaper
Dimensions variable
Courtesy the artist and Galerie
van Gelder, Amsterdam

KELLEY WALKER

Circle in Circle, 2006
Cast chocolate with fiberglass,
motor, chain; edition of 3
D.: 24 in. (61 cm)
Courtesy the artist and Paula
Cooper Gallery, New York

Mirror balls, whose resurgence in the discos
of the 1970s may be in part related to Warhol's
use of them at the Factory and during performances
of *The Exploding Plastic Inevitable*, had their
beginnings in the speakeasies of the 1920s. Kelley
Walker's version is cast completely in chocolate,
recalling his racially tinged use of it as a silkscreen
medium in his 2004 series *Black Star Press* (p. 116).
Circle in Circle was first conceived for an installation related to the pop star Whitney Houston,
although an early exhibition that was to include
a number of balls had to do without because
the venue lacked climate control during a hot
American summer.[19]

CARY LEIBOWITZ
I Love Warhol Piss Paintings, 2007
Knit scarf
6¾ × 72 in. (17.2 × 182.9 cm)
Courtesy the artist

JONATHAN MONK
I saw Andy Warhol in my coffee cup for a second, then he vanished, 2005
Porcelain
Courtesy the artist and Galerie Yvon Lambert, New York and Paris

SHEPARD FAIREY
Barack Obama, 2008
Collage, stencil, and acrylic
on paper
69⁹⁄₁₆ × 46¼ in. (176.7 × 117.5 cm)
National Portrait Gallery,
Smithsonian Institution,
Washington, D.C.,
Gift of the Heather and
Tony Podesta Collection in
honor of Mary K. Podesta

THE WARHOL EFFECT
A TIMELINE

REBECCA LOWERY

This timeline surveys some of the most notable moments in Warhol's critical and popular fortunes during his lifetime and beyond. By no means intended as an exhaustive account of the artist's influence, this selective chronology offers a broad overview of Warhol's cultural ubiquity and suggests the impossibility of a complete telling given the singular breadth of his impact and staying power. From the art world to the world of commerce, from the physical world to the world of ideas, and from politics to popular entertainment, widespread interest in Warhol has lasted for more than fifty years and his hold on us has shown no signs of flagging.

1961

FEBRUARY Warhol purchases a Jasper Johns drawing, *Light Bulb* (1958, private collection), from the Leo Castelli Gallery for $450, which he pays in installments. This year, he also purchases six Frank Stella paintings, three Johns lithographs, an Ellsworth Kelly watercolor, a Ray Johnson collage, and a painted shirt by Jim Dine.[1]

APRIL Warhol shows his Pop paintings in New York for the first time, as part of a display in the window of the Bonwit Teller department store. The works shown are *Advertisement* (1961, Staatliche Museen zu Berlin, Nationalgalerie, Collection Marx, Berlin), *Before and After [1]* (1961, p. 84), *The Little King* (1961, private collection), *Superman* (1961, Gunter Sachs), and *Saturday's Popeye* (1961, Ludwig Forum für Internationale Kunst, Collection Ludwig). (Bonwit Teller display, 1961. Collection of The Andy Warhol Museum, Pittsburgh)

ALSO THIS YEAR Warhol is rejected by the Leo Castelli Gallery, reportedly for his artworks' similarity to those of Roy Lichtenstein, whom Castelli is already showing.[2]

1962

MAY Warhol is featured in *Time* magazine alongside Roy Lichtenstein, Wayne Thiebaud, and James Rosenquist in the first mass-media article on American Pop, despite never having shown his Pop work in a gallery. The article mentions that he is working on a series of "portraits" of Campbell's Soup cans and includes a photo of him — the only picture of an artist in the story — eating soup.[3] By November, the artist and critic John Coplans can remark that the soup cans are "now famous."[4]

Warhol pictured in "The Slice-of-Cake School," *Time*, May 11, 1962.

MAY TO JULY Twenty of Warhol's paintings are consigned to the Martha Jackson Gallery in New York. Reporting a negative reaction to his work, she cancels a planned solo exhibition for December. Jackson never exhibits them, but ten are sold and the remaining ten returned to Warhol.

JULY He has his first solo show of Pop paintings in a gallery, at the Ferus Gallery in Los Angeles, where his paintings *32 Campbell's Soup Cans* are displayed on a ledge along the wall. Though Ferus's Irving Blum advises Warhol to set a "low price level during initial exposure,"[5] a gallery down the street nevertheless counters with real soup cans, offering two for 33¢.[6] The *Los Angeles Times* is nonplussed and puts forth the antipodal interpretive possibilities that will loom over Warhol for decades to come: "This young 'artist' is either a soft-headed fool or a hard-headed charlatan."[7] Blum soon acquires the entire set.

Henry Hopkins, writing in *Artforum*, is bemused but positive overall: "To those of us who grew up during the cream-colored thirties . . . this show has peculiar significance. . . . Warhol obviously doesn't want to give us much to cling to in the way of sweet handling, preferring instead the hard commercial surface of his philosophical cronies. . . . However, based on formal arrangements, intellectual and emotional response, one finds favorites. Mine is *Onion*."[8]

BELOW OLYMPUS   By Interlandi

"Frankly, the cream of asparagus does nothing for me, but the terrifying intensity of the chicken noodle gives me a real Zen feeling . . . Besides, asparagus gives me indigestion . . .!"

The *Los Angeles Times* pokes fun at Warhol's Ferus exhibition, August 1, 1962.

SEPTEMBER The curator Walter Hopps includes Warhol in "New Painting of Common Objects" at the Pasadena Art Museum; it is the first exhibition of American Pop in a museum.

OCTOBER Warhol has four paintings in "The New Realists," a major show at New York's Sidney Janis Gallery. Critics associated with Abstract Expressionism such as Dore Ashton, Thomas Hess, and Hilton Kramer respond poorly to the show, and Warhol is often described as either a huckster or a naïf. Harold Rosenberg in the *New Yorker* discerns aggression in Warhol's banality: "Andy Warhol . . . does columns of Campbell's Soup labels in narcotic reiteration, like a joke without humor told over and over again, until it carries a hint of menace."[9] Hess derides him as a "commercial artist" for his emphasis on technique.[10] For Irving Sandler, Warhol "does not appear to satirize [mass culture's] vulgarity and idiocy but to accept its values complacently."[11]

In contrast, ironic commentary on American mass culture is precisely what some other observers discern. The *New York Times* sees Warhol as a satirist and says that the "New Realists" show "marks the entrance of artists into social criticism."[12] Another critic later writes that the "deep, dark secret of Pop art is that it is anti-popular with a vengeance."[13]

Warhol consigns six paintings and six drawings to the Ileana Sonnabend Gallery in Paris. She exhibits three of them the following May in a group show of American Pop art.

NOVEMBER Warhol has the first solo gallery show of his Pop paintings in New York, at the Stable Gallery. The show features *Marilyn* and *Elvis* paintings, among others, and sells out. Gene Swenson disagrees with the notion of Warhol as social critic ("He never uses satire"), arguing instead that Warhol "simply likes the people he paints" and that his work is "full of good will and a large natural talent."[14]

Old-guard critics tend to decry the show; for example, Dore Ashton writes, "The air of banality is suffocating."[15] In contrast, the formalist critic Michael Fried is surprisingly "moved by Warhol's beautiful, vulgar, heart-breaking icons of Marilyn Monroe." He finds Warhol to be the "most spectacular" of the Pop artists and his work to be "brilliant" technically, with "passages of fine, sharp painting," yet suggests that the contemporary nature of the subject matter may render Warhol unintelligible and thus obsolete in the future.[16]

DECEMBER The Museum of Modern Art (MoMA) accepts architect Philip Johnson's donation of *Gold Marilyn Monroe* (1962) (p. 56) to its permanent collection.

1963

JANUARY Donald Judd is unimpressed with Warhol's exhibition at the Stable Gallery. Writing in *Arts Magazine*, he notes, "It seems that the salient metaphysical question lately is 'Why does Andy Warhol paint Campbell Soup cans?' The only available answer is 'Why not?' The subject matter is a cause for both blame and excessive praise. . . . The novelty and absurdity of the repeated images of Marilyn Monroe . . . and the Coca-Cola bottles is not great."[17]

MARCH–JUNE The curator Lawrence Alloway includes Warhol in "Six Painters and the Object" at the Solomon R. Guggenheim Museum, alongside artists such as Roy Lichtenstein and James Rosenquist. The show travels to seven additional venues across the country. Reviewing the exhibition for *Vogue*, Aline Saarinen savages Warhol ("the pop-art kid" whose "face . . . you expect to see smeared with jam from an after-school sandwich"), seeing in his personal and artistic lack of affect "weak ways of seeing and feeling."[18] *Time* agrees that Warhol is childlike, stating that his work "can be excruciatingly monotonous, [and] the apparently senseless repetition does have the jangling effect of the syllabic babbling of an infant — not Dada, but dadadadadadadada."[19]

JUNE *Harper's Bazaar* runs a feature called "New Faces, New Forces, New Names in the Arts," illustrated by some of Warhol's earliest photo-booth portraits. The caption under his self-portrait labels him a "pioneer in the New Realist art."[20]

Warhol's photo-booth layout in *Harper's Bazaar*, June 1963. Warhol's layout includes his self-portrait with sunglasses and Henry Geldzahler mugging in the photo booth (center, with glasses).

JULY Warhol buys a Bolex 16-mm camera and begins making his first films: *Sleep*, *Eat*, *Blow Job*, *Haircut*, and *Kiss*.

SEPTEMBER Warhol, his assistant Gerard Malanga, Wynn Chamberlain, and Taylor Mead drive cross-country to Los Angeles for Warhol's second solo exhibition at the Ferus Gallery, featuring the Elvis Presley and Elizabeth Taylor paintings. Their arrival is celebrated with a party thrown by Dennis Hopper and attended by rising stars such as Peter Fonda and Dean Stockwell. Later, in *POPism*, Warhol recalls it as "the most exciting thing that had ever happened to me." Of the drive, he writes: "The further West we drove, the more Pop everything looked."[21] Though the show generates little critical attention, it is of great interest to artists like Larry Bell, who writes in response: "It is my opinion that Andy Warhol is an incredibly important artist; he has been able to take painting as we know it, and completely change the frame of reference of painting as we know it, and do it successfully in his own terms. These terms are also terms that we may not understand. . . . In any event, nothing can take away from it the important changes that the work itself has made in the considerations of other artists."[22]

1964

Warhol also designs the cover of the fourth issue of *C: A Journal of Poetry*, which was edited by the poet Ted Berrigan (see p. 78). The cover features Malanga posed with the esteemed poet and critic Edwin Denby, on whose work the issue was focused. It is the first known instance of Warhol having a silkscreen made from a Polaroid image. On the back cover, the men kiss, which created a minor scandal when the issue was released.[23]

The dapper Irving Blum of Los Angeles's Ferus Gallery, the first gallery to show Warhol's Pop paintings (see July 1962), wears a shirt emblazoned with a detail from the artist's *Troy Donahue* series in a full-page ad in *Artforum*, September 1963.

OCTOBER Three paintings by Warhol are included in a group show of American Pop at the Institute of Contemporary Art, London.

NOVEMBER Gene Swenson interviews Warhol in *ARTnews*. Though heavily edited, the interview demonstrates Warhol's preternatural ability to make trenchant yet impenetrable statements, which would come to define his public persona: "I think everybody should be a machine. I think everybody should like everybody."[24]

President Kennedy is assassinated in Dallas on November 22. Warhol begins his *Jackie* series shortly thereafter.

JANUARY Warhol moves with Malanga to 231 East 47th Street, which would soon become the first Factory, home to his "superstars." Warhol instructs his assistant Billy Name (Linich) to decorate it with mirrors, aluminum paint, and foil, or "silver."

Warhol exhibits his *Death and Disaster* series at Ileana Sonnabend's gallery in Paris, marking his first solo European show. The critic Alain Jouffroy writes rapturously in the catalogue, encapsulating the existentially inflected reaction to Warhol in France: "In front of these pictures we are stripped, cleansed, purified as though through contact with a natural element: the sea, fire, a glacial wind. . . . The paintings become the sacred scenes of a godless world."[25]

Sleep debuts at the Gramercy Arts Theatre. Running for four nights, it loses $382.05.[26]

APRIL *The Thirteen Most Wanted Men*, Warhol's response to a commission for the World's Fair in New York, is installed on the front of the New York State pavilion. Governor Nelson Rockefeller almost immediately orders it removed, perhaps in fear that it will offend his Italian-American constituents.[27]

On April 21, Warhol's second show at the Stable Gallery opens. He opts to fill the gallery with Brillo, Heinz, Campbell's, and Del Monte boxes. Inspired by the Brillo boxes, the philosopher Arthur C. Danto decides to develop a philosophy of art. His first essay on the subject describes the boxes as a "whole new class of artworks" that calls into question the very distinction between art and life.[28]

In *Arts Magazine*, Sidney Tillim agrees that Warhol is exploring the limits of art, but thinks there are darker implications. For him, the show is "an ideological tour de force . . . [of] essential nihilism . . . an instant of sublime but compulsive negation."[29]

Marcel Duchamp soon voices his own bid for Warhol as a conceptual artist: "If you take a Campbell's soup can and repeat it fifty times, you are not interested in the retinal image. What interests you is the concept that wants to put fifty Campbell's soup cans on a canvas."[30]

Barbara Rose advances the idea of Warhol as cipher: "I don't know if it's art, but as pure expression of the *zeitgeist* Warhol is without equal. That he draws such rancorous responses has more to do with the ugliness of the spirit of the times than it has to do with Warhol, who allows himself passively to be the instrument of its expression."[31]

MAY Campbell's product marketing manager sends Warhol several cases of tomato soup, remarking that the company admires his work and that it has "evoked a great deal of interest here . . . for obvious reasons." Warhol follows up by asking Name to see if the company will buy a group of *Campbell's Tomato Juice* boxes. The company politely declines.[32]

JULY Warhol films almost seven hours of a stationary view of the Empire State Building from an office in the Time-Life Building. The result is *Empire*, which is premiered in March 1965 and projected in slow motion to extend the footage to just over eight hours.

SUMMER Warhol wins the Independent Film Award from *Film Culture Magazine*.

SEPTEMBER At the Factory, the renegade artist Dorothy Podber, a friend of Name's, shoots a pistol at a stack of *Marilyn* paintings. The bullet goes straight through Monroe's forehead.[33]

Warhol at "The American Supermarket," an exhibition at Paul Bianchini's Upper East Side gallery. Visitors to the show buy autographed soup cans for $6 each.

1965

NOVEMBER Calvin Tomkins writes of Warhol's *Campbell's Soup* paintings in *Life*: "Repeated over and over again in numbing sequence, their effect is decidedly hostile. Warhol may, in fact, be painting the archetypal 20th Century nightmare."[34]

NOVEMBER–DECEMBER Warhol's exhibition of *Flowers* at the Leo Castelli Gallery sells out. *Newsweek* covers the opening, describing him as "the Peter Pan of the current art scene," "a legend of pop art," and "Saint Andrew."[35] For Thomas Hess, "Warhol is the brightest of Pop artists" and his achievement is to make "empty metaphysical vessels that are continually being filled with real money, which is an undeniable triumph, sociologically."[36] Photographer Patricia Caulfield later sues Warhol for using her photograph as the source for the series.

Warhol appears for the first time on a magazine cover, the December 1964 issue of *Artforum*. Rather than featuring an artwork by Warhol, however, the magazine uses a 1963 photograph of him by Dennis Hopper, suggesting Warhol's already iconic status. The image is also repeated in a grid reminiscent of Warhol's serial compositions, pointing to the emergence of a recognizably "Warholian" style.

In the same month, Warhol's reputation as a maker of stars begins to take shape with the publication of Tom Wolfe's article "The Girl of the Year," about Warhol's first superstar, Baby Jane Holzer, whom another critic called "his first major creation in the medium of Pop people."[37]

JANUARY Warhol designs the cover for *Time* magazine's January 29, 1965, issue titled "Today's Teen-Agers." *Life* notes that Warhol "is as successful these days with his movies as he was when he was painting giant Campbell's soup cans. . . . Now august museums like the Metropolitan and the Carnegie are running special screenings of his and other underground filmmakers' work." The article goes on to deem them "a droll [joke], but not very."[38]

FEBRUARY Philip Leider in *Artforum* describes "the electric influence [of] Warhol, as a personality and as an artist" and "the virtual idolatry with which [Warhol] is regarded by a younger generation of painters" and filmmakers.[39]

Underscoring the point, an eighteen-year-old John Waters responds to *Life* magazine's critique of underground cinema: "Sirs: It is bad enough when your magazine lambastes *Flaming Creatures*, Andy Warhol's films and the underground movie industry in general—BUT when you start picking on *Candy*, that is *too* much! Some people are content to read Edna Ferber and see *My Fair Lady* all their lives—but some are able to experiment and try something new. Obviously not you." The letter is signed "John S. Waters Jr., Lutherville, Md."[40]

MARCH Warhol's films (including *Henry Geldzahler* [1964], left, and Robert Indiana in *Eat* [1964], right) are the set dressing for a fashion spread in the March 19, 1965, issue of *Life*: "Underground Clothes: Bizarre Styles to Match Avant-Garde Film."

APRIL Warhol hosts the Fifty Most Beautiful party at the Factory on April 25. The varied, star-studded group of guests includes Judy Garland, Tennessee Williams, William S. Burroughs, Montgomery Clift, and Rudolf Nureyev.

MAY Warhol's exhibition of *Flowers* opens at Ileana Sonnabend's gallery in Paris. Peter Schjeldahl later writes that it is one of two experiences that inspired him to become an art critic.[41] John Ashbery reports in the *Paris Herald Tribune* that Warhol is a sensation in Paris, "causing the biggest transatlantic fuss since Oscar Wilde brought culture to Buffalo."[42] At this time, Warhol announces he's given up painting in order to focus on his films.

JUNE Warhol has by now been largely canonized as the leader of Pop. Basic Books ratifies the reputation by throwing the launch party for John Rublowsky's *Pop Art* (the first book on the subject) at Warhol's studio. Of the artists in this movement, Rublowsky writes, Warhol is in some ways "the most daring."[43] Books by Lucy Lippard (*Pop Art*) and Mario Amaya (*Pop Art and After*) follow in 1966.

Rublowsky's book is pilloried by critics. Eliot Fremont-Smith, in the *New York Times*, says, "Like pop art, 'Pop Art' is chic, banal, unanalytical, anti-critical, historically vague, repetitive, fatuous, possibly a 'put-on.'"[44] Sidney Tillim in *Artforum* calls it "secular hagiography," though he agrees with Rublowsky that Warhol stands out as "a true iconoclast."[45]

1966

The Metropolitan Museum of Art acquires its first works by Warhol, the screenprint *Birmingham Race Riot* (1964) and the painting *Mona Lisa* (1963, p. 108).

JULY Warhol's first exhibition in South America opens at the Galería Rubbers in Buenos Aires, where the following month a thirty-minute version of his *Thirteen Most Beautiful Women* is shown as part of the film festival "New American Cinema." He also exhibits at the Jerrold Morris International Gallery in Toronto, although Morris has to return *Brillo* and *Campbell's Soup* boxes to the United States without showing them when it is deemed by customs officials that they are not art and thus subject to import taxes.

AUGUST The Factory has become a place of revelry and fascination. The Sunday magazine of the *New York Herald Tribune* publishes a lengthy feature on its culture, activities, and denizens.[46]

Time magazine features Warhol and Edie Sedgwick, "the magic names" of the current social circuit, in its "Modern Living" section. The article incisively, if cynically, describes their mutually beneficial relationship: "Edie and Andy opened doors for each other — she the doors to the Park Avenue patrons of his paintings, he the doors to the world of art and the cinema where she hopes to make her way."[47]

SEPTEMBER Warhol premieres his first videotapes at a party in an unused train tunnel under the Waldorf-Astoria Hotel on September 29, having been given a Norelco video recorder by *Tape Recording* magazine to promote the company's new portable video equipment. The party takes place five days before Nam June Paik shows his video art for the first time at New York's Café Au Go Go.[48]

OCTOBER Warhol and Sedgwick arrive at his first solo museum exhibition, held at the Institute of Contemporary Art at the University of Pennsylvania, to such pandemonium that the director has to remove most of the art from the walls and devise an escape route to allow Warhol and Sedgwick to leave without being torn apart by the crowd.

FEBRUARY *Andy Warhol, Up-Tight*, a multimedia precursor to *The Exploding Plastic Inevitable* (see April 1966), has a weeklong run at the Film-Makers' Cinematheque on West 41st Street. Critics are completely bewildered, but the show is packed. The *New York Post* writes that Warhol, "king of the put-on, bring-down, nothing movie, has here thrown together some meaningless stuff well calculated to reflect not only a meaningless world but an audience so mindless that it can sit still and take it and come back for more."[49]

Warhol puts an ad in the *Village Voice* reading, "I'll endorse with my name any of the following: clothing, AC-DC, cigarettes, small tapes, sound equipment, ROCK 'N' ROLL RECORDS, anything, film, and film equipment, Food, Helium, Whips, MONEY!! love and kisses ANDY WARHOL, EL 5-9941."[50] Several people take him up on the ad.

Warhol and Edie Sedgwick, flanked by Sedgwick's collaborator Chuck Wein, demonstrate their "underground cinema" style in the *New York Times* Sunday magazine, February 13, 1966.

MARCH Barbara Feldon of *Get Smart* appears in a fashion-spread cover story by Warhol for *TV Guide*, March 5–11, 1966.

APRIL With top billing, Warhol premieres *The Exploding Plastic Inevitable* at the Open Stage, an experimental performance venue on the top floor of the social hall Polski Dom Narodowy (Polish National Home), commonly known as the "Dom," on Saint Mark's Place in New York. The multimedia show features the Velvet Underground and takes in $18,000 in its first week.[51] Warhol and the Velvet Underground take the show on the road over the summer, performing in Los Angeles, San Francisco, Chicago, Detroit, Columbus, Cleveland, Cincinnati, Philadelphia, Boston, Provincetown, and Providence.

At the Leo Castelli Gallery, Warhol shows *Cow Wallpaper* and *Silver Clouds*. For Robert Pincus-Witten in *Artforum*, the show is "an embarrassment," exposing "the hypocritical position [that art and life are one] he has suicidally forced upon himself."[52] The show travels throughout the United States, often coinciding with performances of *The Exploding Plastic Inevitable*.

AUGUST Warhol as cultural referent has taken root. *Life*, echoing Harold Rosenberg (see October 1962), likens a Paris fashion show to "Warhol's soup cans, a joke with no punch line."[53]

Warhol and Nico, dressed as Robin and Batman, respectively, team up in a shoot for the August 1966 issue of *Esquire* by photographer Frank Bez. The photos are said to epitomize the "intense and frenetic . . . Sixties whether you like it or not. But don't worry," the magazine "benevolently" announces, "because the Sixties are over."[54]

OCTOBER In the catalogue for Warhol's solo exhibition at the Institute of Contemporary Art, Boston (October 1–November 6), Alan Solomon writes, "[Warhol] is, I believe, the first art celebrity since Picasso and Dalí." He concludes with a prediction: "In a time of radical essays against modern traditions, he has made significant gestures, becoming responsible in part for the very redefinition of the role of the artist. Whether some of us like it or not, he will probably turn out to be one of the most influential artists of his generation."[55] In *Art International*, another prediction is made: "[Warhol] may well join with the forces of Mad. Ave. for money."[56]

DECEMBER *The Chelsea Girls*, which had premiered at the Film-Makers' Cinematheque in September, is the first underground film to be shown in a commercial theater, New York's Cinema Rendezvous on West 57th Street.[57] The *New York Times* sneers, "Seldom has the tedium of daily life—even life among the wicked—been documented so faithfully," yet later calls it "the masterpiece of the 'Baudelairean Cinema.'"[58] *Time* deems it a "very dirty and very dull peep show," but *Newsweek* says it is a "fascinating and significant movie event."[59] Audiences flock to the film, and it grosses more than $500,000 over its cost of $1,500 in its first two years.[60]

Warhol's films and the lifestyle they supposedly depict, now more exposed than ever with the Midtown release of *The Chelsea Girls*, also garner critical opprobrium. "It has come time," writes one commentator in the *New York Times*, "to wag a warning finger at Andy Warhol and his underground friends and tell them politely but firmly that they are pushing a reckless thing too far. . . . Heaven knows, there are more than homosexuals and dope addicts and washed-out women in this world!"[61] "There is a place for this sort of thing, and it is definitely underground," says *Time*. "Like in a sewer."[62] Similarly, a reviewer of *The Exploding Plastic Inevitable* clucks that the spectacle represents "'The Flowers of Evil' in full bloom."[63]

1967

JANUARY An essay in *Time* describes the new culture of the art world: "'Most collectors today are not just satisfied with buying art, they want to buy a piece of the artist as well,' grumbles one dissenter. 'They want to belong to the art world, go see dirty movies at night at Andy Warhol's apartment.' And Warhol in turn becomes a feature of gossip columns and a fixture at society's tables."[64] Peter Benchley (who later wrote *Jaws*) had recently made a similar observation, noting, "Pop art . . . turns both creator and collector alike into members of a new pop society. When Andy Warhol sits Ethel Scull . . . in front of an arcade photo machine and snaps away, the result may be art but it also puts Mrs. Scull on the society page."[65]

MARCH In a two-episode arc on *Batman*, the first of which is titled "Pop Goes the Joker," the Joker becomes the enfant terrible of the art world. The fright-wigged villain with his Warholian maquillage is accompanied by an overly credulous socialite named Baby Jane Towzer—a clear nod to Warhol superstar Baby Jane Holzer, who had starred in the 1964 production *Batman/Dracula* by Warhol and Jack Smith. The Joker is presented as a money-grubbing charlatan and his art described as a "hoax."[66]

After many delays, *The Velvet Underground & Nico*, the band's debut album on Verve, is released with its iconic Warhol-designed peeling banana cover. The record is heavily promoted as an Andy Warhol project.

MAY *The Chelsea Girls* premieres in Paris, after officials rule against the film's showing at the Cannes Film Festival. The artist and critic Jean-Jacques Lebel leads a walkout in the middle of the screening.[67]

JUNE Leading formalist critic Clement Greenberg mentions Warhol by name for the first time, in an essay for *Vogue* titled "Where Is the Avant-Garde?" He points out that artists like Warhol have become celebrities and argues that Pop art is merely a "Novelty art," at base "rather easy stuff, familiar and reassuring under all the ostensibly challenging novelties of staging."[68] But by this time, Pop has essentially been declared over. The art press has observed that "pop art . . . seems to have defeated itself," and the mainstream media has called Pop "past its peak."[69]

SPRING John Sandberg argues that Pop has its origins in the art of the past, drawing on both European and American sources. For Sandberg, the "same reliance on the flowing, biomorphic shape" that was present in Jackson Pollock's work also "characterizes" Warhol's.[70]

1968

This continues a thread of "traditionalist" criticism that has run concurrent with the huckster/naïf debate since at least 1963, when Irving Sandler claimed that works by Warhol and other Pop artists were "based on the abstractions of those younger artists who are exploring the expressive possibilities of pure color. . . . But . . . the New Realists have subverted their ends. . . . They are debased abstractions—a retrogressive realism in a new guise."[71] The following year, Donald Judd asserted that "at heart, [Warhol is] an Expressionist."[72] And comparing the "certain tenderness" of the *Jackie* series to the *Flowers*, Thomas Hess had written in 1965 that Warhol "had better keep these lapses into 18th-century impulse under control, or he might turn into a human artist."[73]

AUGUST Warhol is included in a pinup photo spread in *Esquire* themed after the "world's great directors," alongside auteurs such as Michelangelo Antonioni and Alfred Hitchcock.[74]

SEPTEMBER Warhol is included in the ninth São Paulo Bienal. This year he also has shows in Cologne, Hamburg, Paris, and Montreal, in addition to numerous exhibitions in the United States.

Warhol hires the actor Allen Midgette to impersonate him on a college lecture tour. Midgette visits campuses in upstate New York, Utah, Montana, and Oregon before he is found out.

DECEMBER Inspired by Truman Capote's Black and White Ball, *Esquire* runs a feature on the redefinition of the party from 1956 to 1966. "The Emergence of Andy Warhol" is identified as one of four "things that shook the party world" in this time period.[75]

JANUARY / FEBRUARY The Factory moves to its second incarnation, the sixth floor of 33 Union Square West.

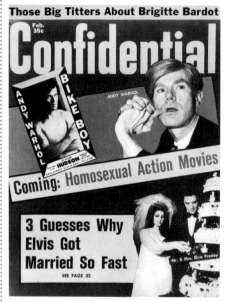

FEBRUARY Warhol's "Homosexual Action Movies" make the cover of the gossip rag *Confidential*. His films are as polarizing as ever. For the *Los Angeles Free Press* critic Gene Youngblood, *Nude Restaurant* is "a great and profoundly moving film, a distillation of everything that was ever valid and revolutionary and magical in Warhol's non-art," while the "strobecuts" of *I, a Man* are an invention "of major importance in film form."[76] Meanwhile, the *New York Times* bemoans *I, a Man*'s "dogged tone of waste and ennui" and labels *Bike Boy* "another of [Warhol's] super-bores."[77]

Warhol's first European retrospective opens at Stockholm's Moderna Museet. The catalogue features hundreds of Billy Name's and Stephen Shore's photographs of life at the Factory and beyond. The show travels to the Stedelijk Museum in Amsterdam, the Kunsthalle in Bern, and the Kunstnernes Hus in Oslo. Later in the year, Warhol is included in Documenta 4, in Kassel.

MARCH The Merce Cunningham dance piece *RainForest* debuts at the Buffalo Festival of the Arts; the set is designed by Warhol and features his *Silver Clouds* (p. 134).

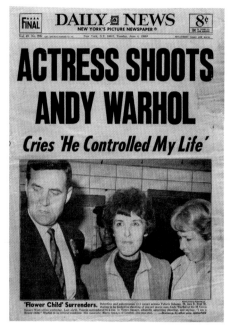

JUNE On June 4, the day after Valerie Solanas shoots Warhol in the chest, the *New York Times* and the New York tabloids *Daily News* and *New York Post* all feature the incident in front-page headlines. For the *Times*, he is "the artist who brought a bewildering new dimension to American pop culture." The *Daily News* describes him as a "Pop Art Movie Man" and the "darling of the avant-garde set."[78] (*New York Post*, June 4, 1968. Collection of The Andy Warhol Museum, Pittsburgh, TC1.131)

Some rush to blame Warhol, who nearly died, for his own shooting—and even for the assassination of Robert Kennedy the following day. *Time* says, "Americans who deplore crime and disorder might consider the case of Andy Warhol, who for years has celebrated every form of licentiousness. . . . He surrounded himself with freakily named people . . . playing games of lust, perversion, drug addiction and brutality before his crotchety cameras. Last week one of his grotesque bit players made the game quite real."[79] The managing editor of *Life*, shunting a planned Warhol cover story for the Kennedy story, reportedly blamed Warhol for "having injected so much craziness into American society that it was leading to the killing of the country's political heroes."[80] And an internal memo by *Time*'s art critic, Piri Halasz, claimed that Warhol's "art and life-style . . . helped to create the atmosphere that made the Kennedy shooting."[81]

Warhol's films are regularly advertised in the gay press. Here, *My Hustler* and *Blow Job* are part of a gay film festival advertised in the *Los Angeles Advocate*, July 1968.

SEPTEMBER Warhol's *Campbell's Soup Cans* (1961–62) adorn the cover of the Pasadena Art Museum's *Serial Imagery* exhibition catalogue. The show's curator, John Coplans, surmises: "Perhaps no single image in the second half of the Twentieth Century is so daring in concept and so beautiful in appearance as Warhol's helium-filled Series of floating aluminum pillows. . . . In their form they represent the most perfect visual analogy of a continuum the human mind has conceived: identical, manufactured objects remorselessly stamped out by a machine, which when filled with gas and clustered within a space, become more organic in their relationship than the interweaving strands of a Pollock painting."[82]

OCTOBER Warhol produces his first television ad, a sixty-second spot for the "Underground Sundae" at Schrafft's, a popular restaurant chain. Table cards at the restaurants read, "Did you see the Andy Warhol Sundae on TV? Try the Original at Schrafft's."

NOVEMBER 1 Undercover FBI agents attend a screening of *Lonesome Cowboys* at the San Francisco International Film Festival on the suspicion that Warhol is involved in the interstate transportation of obscene material. Prosecutors decline to charge Warhol with any crimes.

DECEMBER *a*, Warhol's "tape novel," is released. It is pilloried by critics. *Time* headlines its review "Zzzzzzzz," while the *New York Review of Books*, using it as an occasion to consider Warhol's oeuvre as a whole, claims that "a Warhol work reminds one of those plights in science fiction where an interplanetary germ or some amorphous plant life invades human consciousness and everything sloppy and slight takes over."[83]

ALSO THIS YEAR Warhol begins making appearances in contemporary philosophy. French theorist Gilles Deleuze praises Warhol's "'serial' series" as an important instance of what he calls "repetition"—the radical presentation of things as they are in and of themselves, rather than within preordained categories that constitute language and culture. For Deleuze, Warhol's repetitions—his decontextualizing use of quotidian subject matter, the irregularities in his supposedly mechanical reproductions, and his complication of the idea of the "original"—highlight the continued possibility of defying categories in a world increasingly "standardised, stereotyped and subject to an accelerated reproduction of objects of consumption."[84]

1969

JANUARY Warhol is named one of *Life*'s "Winners of '68" for surviving "after a kooky feminist tried to zap him with her .32."[85]

MAY *Esquire* features one of the earliest and most egregious examples of the phenomenon of Warhol as a stage-setting quantity. An article that otherwise has nothing to do with him, Elenore Lester's "The Final Decline and Total Collapse of the American Avant-Garde," is illustrated on the front cover by a photocollage of Warhol drowning in a soup can by the legendary art director George Lois. Her introductory text describes popular acceptance of avant-garde culture as being "hell for people trying to stay ahead, like Andy Warhol." The accompanying article is largely about avant-garde theater groups active in the late 1960s and does not make a single mention of Warhol—although a portfolio of his photographs of some of these groups runs alongside the article.

JULY *Blue Movie* premieres at the Andy Warhol Garrick Theatre, a rented space in Greenwich Village, which is promptly raided by city police, who seize the print. A criminal court rules it hard-core pornography and fines the theater manager $250.[86]

FALL Warhol launches *Interview* magazine.

OCTOBER "Raid the Icebox 1" opens in Houston. Warhol is invited to curate the show from the Rhode Island School of Design Museum of Art's permanent collection. He chooses many objects that the public never sees, such as an entire cabinet full of antique footwear, damaged paintings, and works undergoing restoration.

DECEMBER Warhol epitomizes the art of the 1960s, according to *Life*'s retrospective issue on the decade, with his "simultaneously mordant affirmations and biting parodies of the inane materialism of our age."[87] Barbara Rose later writes, "the images he leaves will be the permanent record of America in the sixties."[88]

ALSO THIS YEAR Alongside heavyweight boxer Sonny Liston, Warhol stars in his first ad campaign, for Braniff Airlines, which runs in both print and television formats. (Braniff Airlines ad, 1969. Collection of The Andy Warhol Museum, Pittsburgh, 2001.9a–b)

1970

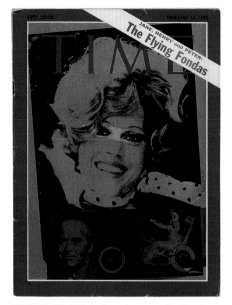

FEBRUARY Warhol designs the cover for *Time*'s feature on "The Flying Fondas," February 16, 1970. (*Time*, February 16, 1970. Collection of The Andy Warhol Museum, Pittsburgh, 1995.3.3)

MARCH As anticipation builds over Warhol's upcoming retrospective (which is shown in Pasadena, Chicago, Eindhoven, Paris, London, and finally in New York at the Whitney Museum of American Art in spring 1971), many writers seek to assess his legacy and standing. In a profile for *Vogue*, John Perreault notes that Warhol "is the most famous artist in America. For millions, [he] is the artist personified."[89]

Warhol's *Rain Machine* is installed at Expo '70, the world's fair in Osaka, Japan. The work was developed as part of the Los Angeles County Museum of Art's "Art and Technology" program, which was an experiment in pairing artists with high-tech corporations.

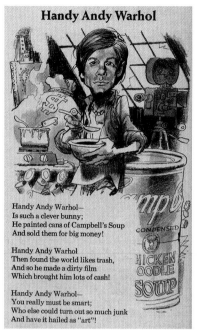

Handy Andy Warhol

Handy Andy Warhol—
Is such a clever bunny;
He painted cans of Campbell's Soup
And sold them for big money!

Handy Andy Warhol
Then found the world likes trash,
And so he made a dirty film
Which brought him lots of cash!

Handy Andy Warhol—
You really must be smart;
Who else could turn out so much junk
And have it hailed as "art"!

APRIL Warhol is parodied in *MAD* magazine, April 1970. The magazine taunts, "Who else could turn out so much junk and have it hailed as 'art'!"

MAY *Big Torn Campbell's Soup Can (Vegetable Beef)* (1962, Kunsthaus, Zurich) sells for $60,000 at the Parke-Bernet auction house in New York, setting the sales record for a living American artist and creating a boom in Warhol's prices.

John Perreault's cover story for *ARTnews*, "Andy Warhola, This Is Your Life," is a kind of companion piece to his profile of Warhol in the March issue of *Vogue*, pointing to the artist's bifurcated cultural status. Trenchantly, Warhol tells Perreault that "you could just quote your other article and correct the mistakes and nobody would know the difference because people who read *ARTnews* don't read *Vogue*."[90]

JULY The young German art historian Rainer Crone publishes the first major study of Warhol, *Andy Warhol*, which appraises the artist in neo-Marxist terms.[91] Later this year, a second monograph is published, John Coplans's *Andy Warhol*, which includes contributions by Jonas Mekas and Calvin Tomkins. In it, Tomkins suggests that in the 1960s Warhol "made visible what was happening in some part to us all."[92] Crone next publishes, with Wilfried Wiegand, *Die revolutionäre Ästhetik Andy Warhol in Kunst und Film*.[93]

OCTOBER *Trash* opens at the mainstream Cinema II in New York, going on to gross a reported $3 million worldwide.[94] *Rolling Stone* calls it "a masterpiece, and the 'Best Movie of the Year.'" Liz Smith, writing in *Cosmopolitan*, counsels her readers that the film "proves that Warhol is one of the most moral prophets of our time. . . . *Trash* is hard to take, but hold your nose and swallow. It is important — as meaningful to our moment as hell was to the Middle Ages."[95]

In the same year, *Flesh* opens in Germany, where it becomes one of the five highest-grossing films of the year.[96]

ALSO THIS YEAR French theorist Jean Baudrillard discusses Pop art at length in *The Consumer Society: Myths and Structures*. He concludes that Pop cannot be an "art of the commonplace," as it claims, since everyday elements cannot remain commonplace when they are decontextualized within the culturally elevated realm of art. For Baudrillard, Warhol's "approach is the most radical" of the Pop artists, yet he "is also the one who best epitomizes the theoretical contradictions" of Pop's ostensible "ordinariness."[97] Baudrillard continues this line of thought in 1972's *For a Critique of the Political Economy of the Sign*, arguing that claims for a radical break with the traditions of art in Warhol's use of everyday themes or serial repetition are "either very naïve or in very bad faith," since "art can neither be absorbed into the everyday. . . nor grasp the everyday as such" and "there is no greater affectation for art than for it to pose as mechanical."[98]

In the essay "Theatrum Philosophicum," Michel Foucault, following Gilles Deleuze (see 1968), also considers Warhol. For Foucault, Warhol's "canned foods, senseless accidents, and . . . advertising smiles" provide a liberating space of "stupidity" (an alternative to the stultifying "intelligence" of normative thought) through which we are able to escape the Deleuzian prison of linguistic and cultural categories. He writes, "In concentrating on [Warhol's] boundless monotony, we find the sudden illumination of multiplicity itself."[99]

1971

FEBRUARY Warhol's Pasadena retrospective opens at the Tate Gallery, London. Warhol attends with an entourage that includes Joe Dallesandro and Jane Forth; the group is welcomed with a reception at the House of Commons.[100] Warhol makes the covers of both art publications such as *Art and Artists* and popular magazines like *Time Out*. For Gregory Battcock in *Art and Artists*, Warhol "has revealed the hypocrisy of the social system and the absurdity of its culture."[101] (Cover of *Time Out* [London], March 7, 1971)

Trash premieres in Munich, going on to become Germany's second-highest-grossing film of the year.[102] The city's largest newspaper, *Abendzeitung*, presents Paul Morrissey and Joe Dallesandro with awards for best film and star of the year.[103] Star Joe Dallesandro is photographed by Annie Leibovitz for the April 15, 1971, cover of *Rolling Stone*.

Joe Dallesandro and his muscles on one of the German movie posters for *Trash*.

APRIL The Rolling Stones' *Sticky Fingers* is released, with its iconic zippered artwork by Warhol.

MAY Warhol's retrospective opens at the Whitney. A number of writers pan the show. In response, Harold Rosenberg writes an article in the *New Yorker* titled "Art's Other Self," arguing that Warhol represents art's "deformation and loss of identity." He states, "In demonstrating that art today is a commodity of the art market, comparable to the commodities of other specialized markets, Warhol has liquidated the century-old tension between the serious artist and the majority culture."[104]

For John Canaday in the *New York Times*, the show is evidence that "the products of [Warhol's] minor talent have been manipulated to create a major reputation. . . . Whatever Andy Warhol might have been under other circumstances, he . . . became a major figure during the nineteen-sixties . . . [and] one of the strongest influences across the land. . . . That it *could* happen legitimizes Andy Warhol under the premise that an artist is an expression of his time even if his time was only a decade, and even if he expressed the worst of it."[105]

With perhaps the greatest equanimity, Mary Josephson writes in *Art in America* that Warhol has been "ill-served" by a "dialectic of excessive acceptance and excessive rejection." Following Barbara Rose (see April 1964), she suggests Warhol himself as a medium, something "we can only know . . . through what is done with it. . . . Anything can be done through him, but nothing defines him."[106]

Similarly, John Perreault writes, "What most people don't know . . . is how much [Warhol] is respected by younger artists, often totally different in their outward styles. He is, like a cow, whatever you need. To minimal people, he is minimal. To publicity art people, he is publicity. . . . He is the smartest man I have ever met."[107]

With "Warhol as Illustrator: Early Manipulations of the Mundane," Joseph Masheck is one of the first writers to consider Warhol's pre-Pop art.[108] His article is precipitated by the exhibition "Andy Warhol: The Early Work, 1947–1959" at Gotham Book Mart.

Art in America uses a grainy blowup of the photograph run on the front page of the *New York Post* the day after Warhol's shooting as the cover of its May–June 1971 issue. The issue contains four major articles about Warhol, including a compilation of some of Warhol's most notable public moments to date, "A Catalogue Raisonné of Warhol's Gestures."

Simultaneously with the New York retrospectives of his art, Warhol's play *Pork* is presented in a two-week run at La MaMa Experimental Theater on the Lower East Side. The script was edited from transcriptions of Warhol's audio recordings of him and his superstars. In August, it moves to London's Roundhouse Theater.

DECEMBER David Bowie (who had seen the London production of *Pork*) releases the album *Hunky Dory*, which features the song "Andy Warhol," the chorus of which goes, "Andy Warhol looks a scream/ Hang him on my wall/ Andy Warhol, silver screen/ Can't tell them apart at all."

1972

JANUARY Ten years after "The New Realists" at Sidney Janis, Hilton Kramer is still incensed by the show. "Not since the Pyrrhic victories of the Pre-Raphaelites in Victorian England had the taste and standards of the professional art world been so radically debased [as by the New Realists]," he writes. "Although the Pop movement itself is moribund, it is worth recalling its enormous negative influence on the art scene. . . . We are still living with the consequences of that influence, which transformed a large part of the art scene into a branch of show business."[109]

Warhol returns to painting with the *Mao* series.

FEBRUARY For the exhibition "Art in Process V," Warhol exhibits a vacuum cleaner that he has used on the carpet in the Finch College Museum of Art in New York.

Women in Revolt, a parody of the women's liberation movement starring drag queens Candy Darling, Jackie Curtis, and Holly Woodlawn, is one of Warhol's most well-reviewed films to date. Vincent Canby writes that it is "a comparatively elaborate Warhol movie with limited intelligence, but unlike a lot of better movies, it uses almost all of the intelligence available to it. Thus, in a crazy way, it must be called a success."[110] According to Bob Colacello, the film was picketed by feminists; in his estimation, at this point "attacking any aspect of the revolution was taboo. The counterculture had become the Culture, and Andy, who had as much to do with that as any artist or activist of the time, was hated all the more for betraying his avant-garde roots."[111]

AUGUST Andrea Feldman, star of Warhol's next film, *Heat*, commits suicide. Her death casts a macabre shadow over the movie when it premieres. Peter Schjeldahl writes, "The pitiless exposure of [Feldman's] suicidal mood makes 'Heat' a repellent document."[112]

Lana Jokel's *Andy Warhol* is the first American documentary film on the artist.

1973

OCTOBER Stephen Koch's *Stargazer: Andy Warhol's World and His Films* is published. It is one of the earliest sustained considerations of Warhol's filmmaking.[113]

ALSO THIS YEAR The curator Henry Geldzahler, one of Warhol's early champions, says, "I suspect that Andy's going to feed a lot of artists for a long time."[114]

Pioneer enlists Warhol for a series of ads for high-fidelity sound systems. Another version reads, "Andy Warhol doesn't play second base for the Chicago Cubs. He doesn't even know who does. But he's a man of many talents and interests." The ad series inaugurates Warhol's role as a go-to figure to represent home-entertainment systems in advertising.

After the airing of the pioneering PBS documentary series *An American Family*, which focuses on his family, Lance Loud moves to New York. As the first openly gay person to appear on television, he has become an icon, and he is vocal about the inspiration he has drawn from Warhol. By December 1974, he and Warhol are socializing at the wedding of Sylvester Stallone.

1974

FEBRUARY The *Mao* series is exhibited in Paris at the Musée Galliera. A reviewer for the London *Times*, responding to a show of preparatory Mao drawings at the Mayor Gallery, writes that Warhol is "the most serious artist to have emerged anywhere since the war, and the most important American artist," and agrees with Rainer Crone that he is "a truly revolutionary artist whose work is an absolute condemnation of American capitalist society, made that much more subtle and effective because Warhol himself affects publicly a complete political innocence and naivety."[115]

MARCH Following the suicide of Andrea Feldman, the *Esquire* article "Andy's Children: They Die Young" explores the pervasive shadow of death that hangs over Warhol's entourage, casting Warhol as a spider who "listens and condones" as "America's kids run away and wander into [his] studio . . . and become unlike themselves to be like him."[116] Superstar Viva had suggested Warhol's vampiric and addictive influence six years earlier in *New York* magazine, musing, "Sometimes though when I think about Andy, I think he is just like Satan. He just gets you and you can't get away. . . . He has such a hold on all of us. But I love it when they talk about Andy and Viva."[117]

APRIL The circulation of *Interview* magazine (see Fall 1969), which is "creeping onto the lacquered coffee tables of international trend followers," is up to 74,000.[118]

MAY *Arts*, May 1974, features an installation of the *Mao* wallpaper on its cover. For Gregory Battcock, the *Mao* series furthers Warhol's ability to predict and shape new directions in contemporary art. In this case, Battcock writes, the new trends signaled by the *Mao* paintings are a return to Abstract Expressionist gesture and "functionalism" (as reflected by the wallpaper).[119]

JULY After two months playing in eight American cities, the critically reviled, X-rated 3-D film *Flesh for Frankenstein* by Warhol and Paul Morrissey has earned more than $1 million at the box office.[120]

1975

SUMMER Warhol moves his studio and offices north from 33 Union Square West to 860 Broadway. Concurrently, he begins his *Time Capsules*, which by the time of his death will consist of 612 containers holding tens of thousands of archival objects and hundreds of works of art.

OCTOBER Warhol travels to Japan for a retrospective of his 1960s paintings at the Daimaru department store in Tokyo—his first solo show in Japan. He also creates a suite of screenprints, many of which are based on Japanese ikebana floral arrangements.

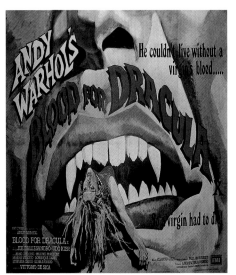

NOVEMBER *Blood for Dracula*, the "sequel" to *Flesh for Frankenstein*, is released in the United States. By 1977 the films had also been released in Germany, France, the Netherlands, Sweden, Norway, and Italy. (U.K. poster for *Blood for Dracula*, 1975)

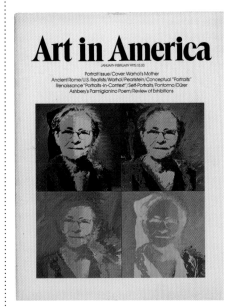

JANUARY–FEBRUARY Warhol's memorial portraits of his mother, Julia Warhola, appear on the cover of *Art in America*, January–February 1975. In this issue, David Bourdon is one of the first critics to write sympathetically about Warhol's 1970s portraits, calling them "society icons" and a body of work in which "Warhol's art and social life have meshed indissolubly."[121]

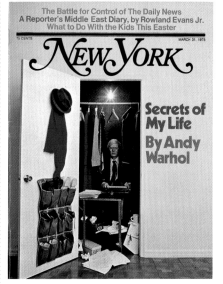

MARCH In advance of the publication of *The Philosophy of Andy Warhol (From A to B and Back Again), New York* magazine publishes an excerpt that promises to reveal "Secrets of My Life" in its March 31, 1975, issue.[122]

MAY Warhol receives an invitation to the White House, for a dinner in honor of the shah of Iran. The meeting eventually results in commissions to paint the shah and his wife, Empress Farah Pahlavi, and twin sister, Princess Ashraf Pahlavi. Warhol later records in his diary, "On TV I got a big mention when Barbara Walters interviewed the empress of Iran. In with the other art they did a big close up on my Mick print and Barbara said, 'And surprisingly they have a painting of rock star Mick Jagger by Andy Warhol', and the empress said, 'I like to keep modern.'"[123]

AUGUST A retrospective opens at the Baltimore Museum of Art. The critic Robert Hughes begins what will be a years-long jeremiad against Warhol with an essay in *Time* titled "King of the Banal." He disparages the artist's success with "café society portraits" and dismisses his reputation as a social critic as wishful thinking. "The alienation of the artist," he writes, "no longer exists for Warhol: his ideal society has crystallized round him and learned to love his entropy."[124]

SEPTEMBER *The Philosophy of Andy Warhol (From A to B and Back Again)* is released to generally favorable reviews. The *New York Times* calls it "fresh and illuminating" and posits Warhol's blankness as a Swiftian proposal in the face of an oversaturated media world.[125] Similarly, for Jack Kroll, Warhol is "a terror-stricken comic moralist, much like Nathanael West, and parts of his new book sounds like West's 'Miss Lonelyhearts.'"[126] It isn't the first time Warhol has been thus compared; at the time of his shooting, *Time* darkly compared him to "some Nathanael West hero . . . the blond guru of a nightmare world."[127]

OCTOBER *The Driver's Seat*, a truly bizarre Italian thriller in which Warhol guest stars as an English lord opposite Elizabeth Taylor, is released in the United States. The *New York Times* later reports that the movie "sank like a stone."[128]

1976

FEBRUARY Warhol, in a *National Lampoon* T-shirt, presides over the humor magazine's contents page, February 1976, as the patron saint of an issue containing the art-world spoof "ARTynews." In a nod to Pop art, the page's design exaggerates the Ben-Day dot pattern.

A retrospective of Warhol's drawings opens in Stuttgart and travels to six venues in Europe.

APRIL Warhol completes a five-panel series of portraits of Golda Meir at the suggestion of the Israel Museum in Jerusalem. The museum acquires two panels of the former Israeli prime minister, whom Warhol, in typical fashion, deems "great."[129]

Warhol arrives at work one day to find a masking-tape portrait of him by art students Chip Duyck, Jon Kasal, and Jody Elbaum on the street in front of Union Square.

MAY Annie Leibovitz includes Warhol in a group of seven master photographers in a photo-essay for *Rolling Stone*. He is in the company of Richard Avedon, Ansel Adams, and Henri Cartier-Bresson.[130]

AUGUST *New York Times Magazine* commissions Warhol for a cover portrait of Jimmy Carter, the Democratic presidential candidate. Warhol later agrees, at the request of the Democratic National Committee, to create an edition of 100 prints of the portrait to be sold to raise campaign funds. Fred Hughes, Warhol's business manager, is optimistic about the commission: "It'll get the art world intellectuals and the liberals in the press off our backs about this Iran thing."[131]

Warhol and Jimmy Carter, June 14, 1977.

SEPTEMBER A critic writes, seemingly without irony, "Warhol has a strong claim to being the leading portraitist of our era if only on the basis of the number of portraits executed, the notables included, and the development of an entirely new type of portraiture."[132]

1977

JANUARY Warhol shows his *Hammer and Sickle* series at the Leo Castelli Gallery, the first major display of new work in New York since the 1960s. The work receives generally favorable notices. The *New York Times*, though noting that the artist would turn fifty that year, also returns to the old motif of Warhol as little boy ("spreading the color as a schoolboy spreads jam on his first day at summer camp").[133]

APRIL Steve Rubell's Studio 54, where Warhol swiftly becomes a fixture along with celebrities such as Truman Capote, Bianca Jagger, and Liza Minnelli, opens. The Warhol-produced, Jed Johnson–directed *Bad* is released. Despite coverage in publications like *People*, the film is a failure. Warhol film historian Stephen Koch later writes that the film "marks the definitive end of Warhol's involvement in film-making."[134]

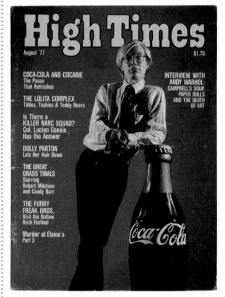

AUGUST *High Times* interviews Warhol, calling him "America's greatest artist." In the interview, Warhol demonstrates his continued familiarity with the art of the day: "I think Chris Burden is terrific. I really do. I went to the gallery, and he was up in the ceiling, so I didn't meet him, but I saw him." As his favorite women artists, he lists "Lynda Benglis, Alice Neel, Louise Nevelson."[135]

Hollywood continues to shut Warhol out. Though he reports in *High Times* that he has been hired to play the art teacher in the movie *Grease*, the role is quickly nixed. Coproducer Allan Carr later recounts, "One of the studio executives said, 'We'll give you everything you want, but I will not have that man in my movie.' It was some kind of personal vendetta."[136]

SEPTEMBER "Andy Warhol's Folk and Funk," presenting Warhol's personal collection of folk art, opens at the American Folk Art Museum, New York.

1978

MAY Kunsthaus Zürich opens a retrospective of Warhol's art; he creates new self-portrait wallpaper for the exhibition.

JUNE The experimental collective Squat Theatre presents an original production, *Andy Warhol's Last Love*, in its storefront theater at 256 West 23rd Street, on the same block as the Chelsea Hotel. The play concerns the accidental meeting between Warhol and the notorious Baader Meinhof Group cofounder Ulrike Meinhof.

AUGUST The fashion designer Halston throws Warhol a fiftieth birthday party at Studio 54, where he is feted with a silver garbage can filled with cash.

"Liza introduced us to white rum and soda at an Andy Warhol party."

ALSO THIS YEAR Warhol and Liza Minnelli are credited with introducing a social-climbing couple to the joys of rum and soda in an ad for Puerto Rican Rums.

1979

JANUARY Warhol displays his *Shadow* series at Heiner Friedrich Gallery in New York. The works are a commission by Friedrich's Lone Star Foundation (now Dia Art Foundation), which purchases 102 of them, keeping them together as a group. Soon after, the British collector Charles Saatchi begins putting together a collection of Warhols, catalyzing another rise in his prices.

MAY Warhol meets the legendary German artist Joseph Beuys at Hans Mayer's gallery in Düsseldorf. They remain in close contact, and Warhol executes a series of portraits of Beuys in 1980, as well as posters for the German Green political party. According to

Heiner Bastian, "Beuys admired Andy a lot. He thought he was a real revolutionary artist without probably understanding it in the correct way; he had this kind of intuitive feeling that he was saying more about society in a political sense than many other artists who made direct political statements. But Andy never understood what Beuys was doing."[137]

JUNE Warhol's hand-painted BMW art car, commissioned by the German automotive company, places sixth overall in a twenty-four-hour race at Le Mans.

NOVEMBER The Whitney opens "Andy Warhol: Portraits of the 70s." In his catalogue essay, Robert Rosenblum takes David Bourdon's assessment further (see January–February 1975), placing Warhol's society portraits in a "venerable international tradition" that includes Giovanni Boldini and John Singer Sargent. Rosenblum maintains that Warhol's connections to this grand tradition of portraiture "are not only social but aesthetic" and that in his portraits he has "captured an incredible range of psychological insights among his sitters." In the foreword, Whitney director Tom Armstrong writes, "It is difficult to know what will survive our times. However, my money is on Andy Warhol. He disgusts some, elates others, but is ignored by very few."[138]

Susan Anton, Sylvester Stallone, and Warhol at the Whitney's opening reception, November 20, 1979.

The critics are not kind to the show. In *Time*, Robert Hughes calls the portrait work "autistic cake icing . . . It can hardly be said to exist within the sphere of aesthetic debate."[139] In the *New York Times*, Hilton Kramer complains, "In that vast cultural space where the world of art and the world of the gossip columns meet, Mr. Warhol can do no wrong. And he has likewise swept the world of the academic art historians quite off their feet, too," despite "the debased and brutalized feeling that characterizes every element of this style."[140]

1980

FEBRUARY Mary Harron, who later directed the film *I Shot Andy Warhol*, argues in *Melody Maker*, "Andy Warhol is one of the great unacknowledged influences on pop music. He influenced it in a very specific way, by fostering the Velvet Underground. But his influence spreads beyond that—you see it everywhere, but it's hard to define. It's a matter of style and attitude. Not only did Warhol leave his mark on Roxy Music, David Bowie, the Ramones, Talking Heads and every other New York art rock group, but he helped make them possible."[141]

MARCH The book *POPism: The Warhol '60s,* by Warhol and Pat Hackett, is released but does not make a huge splash. The *Boston Globe* calls it "gossipy and alive, one of the best things you'll ever read about those crazy eight years—Warhol says the '60s ended in 1968. It's a Pop history in wraparound sunglasses and it reads like a dream." *Newsweek* calls it a "calculated narrative" with "little use for pathos or consequence."[142]

MAY Warhol's *Reversals* and *Retrospectives* are shown in Europe, at the Galerie Bischofberger in Zurich and later at the Galerie Daniel Templon in Paris and the Museum moderner Kunst in Vienna. They receive little attention in the United States but are hailed in Italy's *Flash Art* as "important new paintings . . . both old and new, epic and banal."[143]

Art investment adviser (and future gallerist and director of the Museum of Contemporary Art [MOCA] in Los Angeles) Jeffrey Deitch writes admiringly of the "Warhol Product" in *Art in America*. It is one of the first suggestions that capitalism is a medium for Warhol and inaugurates a decade—marked also by a boom in the art market—in which considerations of the relationship of the artist to money and power are brought to the forefront. Deitch observes, "Hans Haacke, Christo and Warhol are among the few [artists] who have been able to engage economic realities," and that Warhol is not only "totally in synch with the social and economic currents of Post-Eisenhower America; he has actually helped to create them."[144]

1981

In the same issue, reflecting on the overwhelmingly negative reviews of "Portraits of the 70s" at the Whitney, Peter Schjeldahl surmises that, although critics like Hughes and Kramer do not say so outright, they are motivated by resentment of the rich and of Warhol's untroubled acceptance of them as his patrons: "The complaining tone of Warhol's detractors in the great media organs of the middle class seems to me the tone of exactly this resentment." Schjeldahl is also one of the first to bring Warhol's working-class upbringing to bear on an interpretation of his art, arguing that it is by dint of his "enthusiastic worm's-eye view of the commodity and celebrity culture" that, unlike artists from tonier backgrounds, he is able to present consumer goods and social luminaries without being "distanced, even debilitated by middle-class irony."[145]

AUGUST Warhol's black-and-white photographs are exhibited at the Ludwig Museum, Cologne, and the Stedelijk Museum, Amsterdam.

ALSO THIS YEAR French theorist Roland Barthes considers Pop's relationship with art in a catalogue essay for the exhibition "Pop Art" at the Palazzo Grassi, Venice. Barthes, in agreement with Jean Baudrillard (see 1970), writes, "However much pop art has depersonalized the world, platitudinized objects, dehumanized images, replaced traditional craftsmanship of the canvas by machinery, some 'subject' remains." For Barthes, this means that Pop cannot escape art, because art is created the moment the viewer (who is the "subject") confronts something — with Pop, an image — that is neither a thing nor the meaning of the thing but rather its own fact. In the case of Warhol, Barthes notes, the viewer always brings to bear some perspective (desire, delight, boredom) on "Marilyn, Liz, Elvis" — whose repeated visages take on the facticity of "eternal identity."[146]

Warhol begins producing the interview program *Andy Warhol's TV* for Manhattan Cable, on which it airs until 1982. Underground heroes such as Debbie Harry and Jim Carroll, stars such as Steven Spielberg and Liza Minnelli, and unlikely personalities such as Senator Daniel Patrick Moynihan (father of Warhol's cohost Maura Moynihan) are among the many notable guests. It is Warhol's second extended foray into television programming after 1979's *Fashion*, a ten-part series that followed trends in clothing and makeup. *Andy Warhol's TV* runs for twenty-seven episodes, at times featuring up to thirty guests in a single episode.

JANUARY Warhol makes the January 1981 cover of *Forum*, the *Penthouse* magazine that bills itself as "The International Journal of Human Relations," alongside a model whose T-shirt proclaims, "Andy Warhol is a virgin."

APRIL Warhol signs with the Zoli modeling agency. (Zoli modeling agency headsheet, ca. 1980s. Collection of The Andy Warhol Museum, Pittsburgh, TC416.45)

SEPTEMBER Warhol appears in an ad for Sony Beta tapes, which uses a *Marilyn* print to demonstrate the tapes' ability to capture "brilliant color and delicate shading." He also designed an ad for the Sony Walkman that was never used — and had dutifully promoted the "really terrific" gadget in a March interview with BBC's Radio 4, saying that it allowed him to listen to opera while painting. In May, he touted its chic, telling the *Washington Post*, "We just got back from Paris and *everybody's* wearing them."[147] (Sony advertisement, 1981. Collection of The Andy Warhol Museum, Pittsburgh, 1998.3.5507.45)

OCTOBER Warhol appears in three episodes of *Saturday Night Live* in pretaped segments. In the October 18 episode hosted by Susan Saint James, he discusses makeup and death, presciently noting, "Death means a lot of money, honey. Death can really make you look like a star."

1982

FEBRUARY Robert Hughes savages the "supply-side aesthetics" of Warhol's work in the February 18, 1982, issue of *New York Review of Books*, writing, "It scarcely matters what Warhol paints; for his clientele, only the signature is fully visible. The factory runs, its stream of products is not interrupted, the market dictates its logic."[148] The cover and story feature a singularly unflattering caricature by David Levine that has Warhol outfitted as Dopey from Disney's *Snow White and the Seven Dwarfs*.

APRIL Thomas Lawson, writing in *Artforum*, echoes the sentiment. He argues that Warhol's *Dollar Signs* reach a craven new low, finally revealing the true vacuity of his art: "Warhol's work has always been empty but now it seems empty-headed. . . . [Its] nothingness has now developed into something banal, unfortunately proving right all those critics who always hated Pop Art."[149]

SEPTEMBER Warhol creates a poster for Rainer Werner Fassbinder's *Querelle* at the director's request.

Warhol designs the cover for Diana Ross's *Silk Electric* (RCA Records), released in September 1982. In the same time period, he also designs record covers for Billy Squier, John Cale, and Liza Minnelli, among others.

OCTOBER Federal agents seize forty cases of fake Château Mouton Rothschild and arrest three people in connection with the scheme. The enterprising criminals had been selling a fraudulent 1975 vintage, which bears a Warhol-designed label. They had forged their bottles by commissioning wallpaper made from Warhol's original label, which they selected out of nearly forty artist-designed labels—by heavyweights such as Pablo Picasso and Joan Miró—in the château's history. It is the latest in a rich history of Warhol forgeries.[150]

DECEMBER Warhol has a cameo as himself in the movie *Tootsie*. He is seen here with star Dustin Hoffman in a promotional shot.

By the end of the year, Warhol has traveled to Bonn, Berlin, Paris, Zurich, and China.

1983

APRIL The American Museum of Natural History in New York exhibits Warhol's editioned print portfolio *Endangered Species*. Warhol gifts many of the prints to charities concerned with the preservation of the natural environment.

JUNE *Andy Warhol's TV* moves to Madison Square Garden Cable in New York. *New York* magazine describes it as "evidence of how the sly, fey provocations of camp have become as tame and sweet as after-dinner mints."[151]

SEPTEMBER *Collaborations* by Warhol, Francesco Clemente, and Jean-Michel Basquiat are shown at Zurich's Bischofberger Gallery. The paintings and drawings on display are the result of a collaborative process whereby each individual artist began several works, which were then passed among the three, each responding freely to the others' successive contributions.

Warhol designs a cover featuring Princess Caroline of Monaco for the December 1983–January 1984 issue of *Vogue Paris*.

ALSO THIS YEAR Warhol appears in a 1983 Christian Dior ad that runs in publications such as *Vogue*. This was part of a popular serial ad campaign that featured "The Diors: Oliver, the Mouth, and the Wizard" and followed the luxe, fictional trio's globe-trotting and omnisexual adventures.

Carter Ratcliff asserts that Warhol is "one of the most influential artists of the last two decades. In America and Europe, his version of Pop has provided numerous younger artists with starting points for their own, often highly successful careers. . . . More than any other artist of the post-war period, Warhol has reinvented the premises of the artistic enterprise."[152]

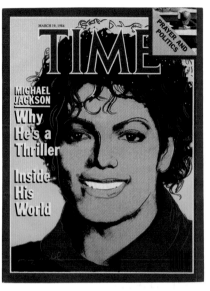

Warhol appears in an ad for TDK in Japan's *Studio Voice* magazine. (TDK advertisement, 1983. Collection of The Andy Warhol Museum, Pittsburgh, 1998.3.5508.10)

1984

FEBRUARY British musician Morrissey uses a cropped still of Joe Dallesandro in *Flesh* for the cover of the eponymous debut album by the Smiths. The band's April 1987 single "Sheila Take a Bow" features a still of Candy Darling in 1971's *Women in Revolt*.

MARCH Warhol creates a portrait of Michael Jackson for *Time*. Covers of Lee Iacocca (April 1, 1985) and John Gotti (September 29, 1986) follow. (*Time*, March 19, 1984. Collection of The Andy Warhol Museum, Pittsburgh, T588)

APRIL Artist Mike Bidlo (see p. 219) stages his full-floor re-creation of Warhol's silver Factory of the 1960s at P.S. 1 in Long Island City, New York. Bidlo is dressed as Warhol, and he signs his own name to the screenprints of Marilyn Monroe that visitors are encouraged to make.

MAY Warhol complains in his diary about MoMA: "And they have just *one* thing of mine, the little Marilyn. I just hate that. That bothers me."[153] However, after the artist's death in 1987, MoMA is the first museum to organize a major retrospective.

SUMMER Craig Owens, writing in *Art in America*, argues that the lately celebrated "bohemian" East Village art scene is "not an alternative to, but a miniature replica of, the contemporary art market." Owens contends that Warhol's Factory set a critical precedent for the "marketability of the alluring avant-garde pose," and that it marks the first moment when the role of the avant-garde "in the mechanisms of the cultural economy" became visible.[154]

NOVEMBER Though the popular press is intrigued by Warhol's friendship with Jean-Michel Basquiat, critics begin accusing Warhol of diluting the "nitty-gritty hip-hop and the jagged power" of the younger artist's work. Nicolas Moufarrege writes that his paintings now seem "fresh out of the Factory. . . . Warhol's formula is clear, but it doesn't work here."[155] Later, reviewing their collaborative works at the Tony Shafrazi Gallery in New York, the *New York Times* states that Basquiat has been reduced to "an art world mascot."[156]

DECEMBER Warhol's studio completes its final move, to an extensively renovated former Con Edison substation on Madison Avenue between East 32nd and 33rd Streets.

ALSO THIS YEAR The New Museum of Contemporary Art publishes the seminal anthology *Art After Modernism: Rethinking Representation*, which is billed as "a comprehensive survey of the most provocative directions taken by recent art and criticism." Underscoring Warhol's ill repute in the art world of the 1980s is his representation in the compendium by Robert Hughes's scathing essay, "The Rise of Andy Warhol" (see February 1982).[157]

1985

In 1985, perhaps the year of Warhol's most complete commercial saturation, he creates the *Absolut Vodka* paintings that were used in "Absolut Warhol" advertisements, the first in the famous artist-created series. Campbell's Soup asks Warhol to commemorate its new line of soup-in-a-box with a series of paintings. Warhol also appears in a television commercial for Diet Coke and as a guest star in the 200th episode of the television program *The Love Boat*, during which a character enthuses, "I just want to say how honored I am that you chose my wife to be the subject of your portrait."

Warhol in his guest appearance on *The Love Boat*, 1985.

Echoing Harold Rosenberg's 1962 assessment of Pop as "advertising art advertising itself as art that hates advertising," the abstract painter Jeremy Gilbert-Rolfe writes that Warhol's art would have the viewer "believe that it is in fact adopting a critical posture towards that to which it has actually surrendered."[158]

MARCH In a cover story for *Artforum*, Carter Ratcliff writes, "The aura of the '80s Warhol sheds a bright light on the barrier of privilege we hoped would always separate the art world from fashion, entertainment, and everything else art flirts with. . . . To trace Warhol's progress is to see along the way a future in which our culture won't contain sanctuaries for privileged images of the self or of art." Ratcliff suggests that, in this sense, the value of Warhol's work in the 1980s may be to make us "conscious of our own impoverishment . . . [and to] remember that we have a natural right to more."[159]

MAY *People* magazine exclaims, "Famous Artists Are the Top Draw at Area, New York's Super Nightclub." Warhol, along with artists such as Jean-Michel Basquiat, Larry Rivers, and Alex Katz, has been invited to take part in an artists' redecoration of the nightclub, "an art show many museum directors would hang themselves to have." Warhol contributes *Invisible Sculpture*, an empty white pedestal next to which he occasionally poses, to the show.[160]

AUGUST Warhol attends the wedding of Madonna and Sean Penn. He collaborates with fellow guest Keith Haring on tabloid-based works as wedding gifts.

ALSO THIS YEAR Warhol's hair (or rather, his wig) is the focus of an ad for Vidal Sassoon hairspray. (Vidal Sassoon advertisement, 1984–86. Collection of The Andy Warhol Museum, Pittsburgh, 1998.3.5509.32a)

The magazine-format show *Andy Warhol's Fifteen Minutes* debuts on MTV this year. The show features a mix of established and rising stars, including a young Courtney Love, who appears in episode 4 — the final episode to air before Warhol's untimely death (see February 1987).

1986

"I THOUGHT I WAS TOO SMALL FOR DREXEL BURNHAM."

In the investment world, it's not how big you are. It's how big you want to be. If your portfolio balances to grow, call 1-800-387-8000, Ext. 78

Warhol appears in a series of ads for the investment group Drexel Burnham Lambert, which run from 1985 to 1987. (Drexel Burnham Lambert advertisement, 1985–87. Collection of The Andy Warhol Museum, Pittsburgh, T185)

A portrait of Gérard Depardieu by Warhol appears on the cover of *Vogue Hommes* (France), November 1986.

DECEMBER In the introduction to the catalogue for the Los Angeles showing of the soup boxes commissioned by Campbell's, Martin S. Blinder asks, "Ironic? Perhaps. Historic? Most definitely: for this turnabout by one of America's largest corporations is indicative of the effect that contemporary art has had on western society over the past 25 years. And, it is also a testimonial to the power and the ability of one particular artist, Andy Warhol, to affect all our lives on a daily basis."[161] For others, however, the soup boxes represent yet another low in the artist's crass commercialism. Irving Blum, one of the artist's most important early supporters and the first person to exhibit— and own—*32 Campbell's Soup Cans* (1962), says the works have "hurt Warhol in the world of art."[162]

Interview's circulation is up to 180,000, with 1,177 ad pages.[163]

1987

JANUARY Warhol travels to Milan for an exhibition of his *Last Supper* paintings. Bob Colacello later quotes the Italian editor of *Interview* as saying the opening was "the biggest event that ever happened in Milano. They were expecting five or six hundred people, but there were five or six *thousand*. One paper said ten thousand."[164]

FEBRUARY Shortly after returning from Milan, Warhol grits his teeth through extreme pain to model clothes with Miles Davis at the Tunnel nightclub on Tuesday, February 17. By Saturday, he is at New York Hospital having his gallbladder removed. He dies unexpectedly at 5:30 AM on Sunday, February 22.

Warhol's death is reported around the world, making the front pages of the *New York Times*, the *New York Post*, and *Le Monde*, among other newspapers. He also appears on the covers of *Art in America*, *New York*, *Artforum*, *Flash Art*, *Studio International*, and the *Sunday Times Magazine* (London). At right, top to bottom: *Art in America*, May 1987; *New York*, March 9, 1987; *Artforum*, April 1987; and *New York Post*, February 23, 1987. (*New York Post*, Collection of The Andy Warhol Museum, Pittsburgh, 1996.16.3.1)

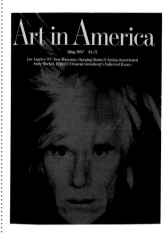

The *New York Times* writes that his "keenest talents were for attracting publicity, for uttering the unforgettable quote and for finding the single visual image that would most shock and endure. That his art could attract and maintain the public interest made him among the most influential and widely emulated artists of his time."[165] On the topic of influence, the *Los Angeles Times* reports that Warhol was "increasingly irrelevant in the art world until the recent rise of Post-Modernist art. As Marcel Duchamp acted as a guru to Warhol's generation, he himself came to be regarded as an archetypal role model by younger artists. . . . Recent art that sees a lack of originality as a virtue is often aesthetically traceable to Warhol."[166]

New York magazine runs a cover feature that praises the way "Warhol blurred the traditional distinctions and encouraged the young photographers and artists he hired to break boundaries, too. The result was a graphics explosion that helped revive New York as the world capital of hard-edged style."[167] The article also points out Warhol's influence in filmmaking, especially on young directors like Jim Jarmusch, and on music, crediting him with creating the milieu that spawned punk rock. The influential rock critic Ellen Willis writes that Warhol's example "helped to free me from rules about what to take seriously that I didn't even know I was obeying."[168] Arthur C. Danto describes Warhol's work as a "philosophical triumph. By transforming art, he transformed the entire relationship between reality and art, making reality an internal feature of art itself."[169] Peter Schjeldahl recalls of the sixties, "One was forever catching onto Warhol's genius at the instants when it shrugged and went elsewhere. *How can he be so right?!*"[170]

As the encomia mount, so do the condemnations. The critic Michael Welzenbach, writing in *New Art Examiner*, claims that Warhol "was one of those responsible for robbing art of its magic," and that "the Warhols of the late twentieth century are in some part responsible for the sheepish acceptance of a media image like Reagan instead of a real, flesh-and-blood, mind-and-matter-type Head of State."[171] Hilton Kramer, in the *New Criterion*, describes the "Warhol phenomenon" as a cynical marriage of art with fashion, which Warhol was able to create only "in an art world that no longer had the moral stamina to resist it. . . . [It is] a model that has proved to be so irresistible that it is now a permanent, and permanently disabling, component of cultural life."[172]

A New York City cab driver writes to the *Daily News*, "To cabbies, like me, Andy Warhol was a hero. Once, in my cab, he praised my Irish pug nose. I hold my head higher now so people can see my fine Celtic nostrils. . . . He was as visible on the New York streets as the traffic signals. May the lights always stay green for Andy."[173]

In Tokyo, the Watari Gallery puts together "Remembering Andy: Warhol's Recent Works." Dia Art Foundation shows "Skulls" in New York and "Andy Warhol: A Memorial" in Bridgehampton.

In his will, Warhol allocates most of his estate to establishing the Andy Warhol Foundation for the Visual Arts, dedicated to the "advancement of the visual arts." The Foundation's grant-making activity focuses on "the creation, presentation, and documentation of contemporary visual art."[174]

APRIL The *New Yorker* reports that Warhol's memorial Mass at St. Patrick's Cathedral in New York "had the character of a state funeral, with people coming from as far away as Los Angeles and Milan to attend. There were so many celebrities among the more than 2,000 mourners that traffic on Fifth Avenue was disrupted by spectators and photographers trying to get a glimpse of them. No other twentieth-century artist—not even Picasso—could have drawn this sort of crowd, and it is difficult to think of any other public personality who could have done so, either."[175]

MAY In *Art in America*, art historian Thomas Crow argues that careful attention to Warhol's subject matter, especially in his work through 1964, reveals an artist deeply interested in "the open sores of American political life." In Crow's view, the typical explanations of Warhol's artistic stance—exploitation or naïve regurgitation—gloss over the visual evidence of the early work, which hewed "to an all-but-buried tradition of truth-telling in American commercial culture" and inspired the countercultural experiments of "an international underground soon to be overground."[176]

1988

JANUARY D. Keith Mano writes that Warhol was "the most influential American artist of our time." Mano also claims that Warhol was "probably—who can say for sure?—the biggest joke ever played on New York liberals by a capitalist conservative."[177]

FEBRUARY With "The Metaphysical Nosejob: The Remaking of Warhola, 1960–1968," Bradford Collins is one of the first scholars to take a psychoanalytic approach to the interpretation of Warhol's work. He surmises that its deadpan quality stems from trauma, loneliness, and the "desire to be freed from the troublesome baggage of the human heart."[178] Similarly, but in a more censuring vein, Donald Kuspit had recently characterized the artist's portraits as "sado-masochistic," at once a "sadistic photographic overpowering of others" and "the opium he uses to anaesthetize himself against the fate of forever feeling inadequate, empty, meaningless, unlovable, even non-existent."[179]

"Andy's Empire," a *New York* cover story by John Taylor, delves into the controversy surrounding business manager Fred Hughes's handling of Warhol's estate. Taylor reports that Hughes's decision to auction off Warhol's personal collection has been met with resistance; Warhol's friend Paige Powell says she is desperately trying "to persuade a major American art collector to acquire the entire collection and keep it together." The collection is eventually sold at auction (see May 1988).[180]

APRIL Dia Art Foundation hosts a symposium, "The Work of Andy Warhol," which was organized in the wake of Warhol's death. The participants are scholars of modern art, including Rainer Crone, who wrote the first monograph on Warhol. Though he is unable to attend the symposium, Simon Watney contributes an essay, "The Warhol Effect," to the published proceedings. In it, Watney suggests that Warhol's work and life are inextricably linked, and that efforts to "indict . . . or reprieve" him based on one or the other are "restrictive attempts to measure him against the criteria of predetermined models of artistic value which his own work quietly invalidates."[181] This essay is an early model for approaching Warhol's work from the perspectives of queer and visual-culture studies, which treat his art and life as equally constitutive parts of the whole.

The exhibition "The Films of Andy Warhol" opens at the Whitney, publicly launching the Andy Warhol Film Project, a collaboration between the Whitney and MoMA that aims to catalogue, preserve, and re-release Warhol's entire film collection. The project was approved by Warhol himself, who gave all of his original films to MoMA in 1984.

MAY Margo Hornblower reports in *Time* magazine that Sotheby's ten-day auction of Warhol's collection of furniture, jewelry, art, and kitsch was called "the garage sale of the century," attracting more than 45,000 people in its first week.[182]

Other observers have subsequently noted the perspicacity of Warhol's eye, notably in his collections of Art Deco and Native American objects. The sale raises more than $25 million for the Andy Warhol Foundation.

DECEMBER Two movies, *Beaches* and *Working Girl* (above), feature antagonistic and/or self-involved characters who have Warhol-style portraits of themselves prominently on display in their homes. For Hollywood, this has become the go-to visual shorthand for a combination of worldly success and overinflated ego. (Still from *Working Girl*, 1988)

1989

JANUARY Jean Baudrillard has significantly changed his original thinking on Warhol and the effective "everydayness" of his images (see 1970). He says, "Warhol is art stripped bare by anti-art even . . . drawing its irony . . . from the banal extravaganza of the commodity. . . . It is useless to be inspired by Warhol. After him, the objects speak for themselves, like Duchamp's bride, once she is stripped."[183]

FEBRUARY MoMA opens a full-scale Warhol retrospective curated by Kynaston McShine. Opinions remain strongly divided, as Sanford Schwartz reports in the *Atlantic*: "[Warhol's] place in American art and culture is so enormous and fuzzy—there are so many claims for what he did, or failed to do, or symbolized—that he's like a din in your head."[184] Later in the year, *Art International* has Carter Ratcliff and Dore Ashton write "Pro and Contra" opinions, respectively, on the artist.[185] Bradley Bloch, writing in the *New Leader*, observes that although Warhol by and large created "enjoyable yet uninspired second-rate art . . . [his] influence has been so strong that Picasso and even Pollock today appear to be distant, chthonic gods."[186]

SPRING *October* publishes Thierry de Duve and Rosalind Krauss's "Andy Warhol, or The Machine Perfected." Though he has been regularly mentioned in passing as an influence on other artists since the esteemed art theory and criticism journal's founding in 1976, this is the publication's first sustained consideration of Warhol.[187]

MARCH "Success Is a Job in New York: The Early Art and Business of Andy Warhol," a survey of Warhol's pre-Pop art, is presented at the Grey Art Gallery at New York University. The nearly 200 works in the show travel to Pittsburgh, London, Philadelphia, Turin, and Jouy-en-Josas, France.

Simon Doonan gives the windows of Barneys New York department store a Warhol theme (the first of many to come in subsequent years).

APRIL Arthur C. Danto argues, "the greatest contribution to [twentieth-century art] history was made by Andy Warhol, to my mind the nearest thing to a philosophical genius the history of art has produced. It was Warhol himself who revealed as merely accidental most of the things his predecessors supposed essential to art, and who carried the discussion as far as it could go without passing over into pure philosophy."[188]

MAY *Shot Red Marilyn* (1964) sells at Christie's New York for $4.07 million, tripling the previous high paid for a Warhol.

JUNE *The Andy Warhol Diaries* is released to a mix of fascination and derision. The *New York Times* calls it "monumentally tedious" and "terrifying." It is also a national bestseller. *National Lampoon* publishes a spoof that purports to reveal unpublished portions of the manuscript ("Just then the phone rang and it was Truman Capote inviting me to Henry Kissinger's party for Carlos the Jackal. Who is Carlos the Jackal? He must be somebody. It sounded great.").[189]

DECEMBER The *Advocate* publishes an article criticizing the "de-gaying" of Warhol in criticism and culture, specifically calling out MoMA's retrospective (see February 1989). Robin Hardy argues, "The booming Warhol industry and the critical reassessment that places him in the first ranks of 20th-century art . . . succeed in stripping away Warhol's identity as a gay man. . . . In the retrospective catalog, a biographical videotape at MoMA, and sundry reviews and books, Warhol's Catholic upbringing is credited with profoundly influencing his aesthetic. A gay sensibility is never mentioned."[190]

1990

Three years after Warhol's death, British sketch comedians Dawn French and Jennifer Saunders lampoon the continued sycophancy of his Factory cohorts for their series on the BBC. Playing aging Superstars "Ultra" and "Viva," they squabble over who starred in *Sleep*, who had the soup idea first, and which one understood Andy best.

APRIL Lou Reed and John Cale release *Songs for Drella*, their concept album about Warhol, who was referred to as Drella in the Factory years. In "Smalltown," Reed sings, "When you're growing up in a small town / Bad skin, bad eyes—gay and fatty / People look at you funny." The music critic Robert Christgau writes that the album makes "an argument worth hearing: Andy Warhol was a hard-working genius—a great artist, if you will—betrayed by hangers-on who no matter what carping philistines say gave a lot less to him than he did to them."[191]

JUNE Warhol's MoMA retrospective opens at the Centre Pompidou in Paris. Critics say the exhibition is "one of those that should not be missed under any circumstances. It is an absolute success."[192] Warhol is featured on the covers of magazines throughout the city, from *L'Amateur d'Art* and *Libération* to a four-cover special edition of *Elle* (France), suggesting the level of anticipation that had been building in Paris.

1991

Warhol in France: cover of *Libération*, June 20, 1990; multiple-cover "Spécial Andy Warhol," *Elle*, June 18, 1990.

FEBRUARY The documentary *Superstar: The Life and Times of Andy Warhol* is released. This year, Warhol also appears for the first time as a character in a movie, the Italian film *Suffocating Heat*. He is played by Allen Midgette, who was his impersonator during the 1967 college tour (see September 1967). The same year, cult actor Crispin Glover plays Warhol in Oliver Stone's *The Doors* (March). Warhol is later portrayed by Jared Harris (*I Shot Andy Warhol*, 1996), David Bowie (*Basquiat*, 1996), and Guy Pearce (*Factory Girl*, 2006), among others.

MAY Acclaimed novelist Don DeLillo releases *Mao II*, which is titled after Warhol's *Mao* series. Michiko Kakutani finds it to be an apt choice, writing in the *New York Times*, "With his nihilistic repudiation of originality, his fascination with the bright shiny surfaces of contemporary consumer culture and his determined pursuit of publicity, Warhol himself seems like the embodiment of Mr. DeLillo's bleak vision of an America perched on the brink of apocalypse and self-destruction."[193]

"It is the shot from Valerie Solanas' gun," Annette Michelson claims in *October*, "that marks the boundary" between Warhol's "prelapsarian" period of 1960–68 and the "Business Art" that followed.[194] This concept of a bifurcated, early equals good/late equals bad Warhol has been advanced many times over the years. Peter Schjeldahl has maintained that Warhol was a great painter, but just for "a short while, roughly 1962–64," while Robert Hughes has nostalgically looked back to "1962 [to] 1966, when his soup cans and other baleful icons of American glut and repetition could be taken quite seriously as art."[195] This assessment — along with the notion that the attempt on Warhol's life was the decisive turning point in his career — continues its currency. In 2011, the *Economist* reported, "Most now agree . . . that the shooting marked the start of a steady decline in the quality of Warhol's work. . . . He slowly ground to an aesthetic halt."[196]

SPRING Gianni Versace's *Evening Dress* (spring/summer 1991), based on Warhol's print series *Marilyn Monroe* (1967) and *Rebel Without a Cause (James Dean)* (1985), is the latest high-fashion take on Warhol's work. It follows Warhol-based designs by Halston and Stephen Sprouse, as well as Warhol's own fashion experiments of the 1960s and 1970s. (The Metropolitan Museum of Art, New York, Gift of Gianni Versace, 1993. 1993.52.4)

SEPTEMBER John Warhola, Andy's brother, founds the Andy Warhol Family Museum of Modern Art (later Andy Warhol Museum of Modern Art) in Medzilaborce, Slovakia, near the village where their parents were born.

1992

JANUARY On the topic of the Persian Gulf War, John Shy, a professor of history at the University of Michigan, tells the *New York Times*, "This seems to be the Andy Warhol war. A quarter-hour of fame and maximum attention and, in retrospect, horrendous losses of life on the other side, but remarkably trivial in its consequences otherwise."[197]

A *New York* cover story continues to cover the disputes over Warhol's estate, reporting that some observers believe that many items of value have gone missing, "in particular, Warhol's favorite diamond ring . . . a piece known to have belonged to him when he died. It wasn't in the Sotheby's sale; it has never surfaced."[198]

AUGUST Reviewing a show of serial and sequential photography at New York's International Center of Photography, Vicki Goldberg in the *New York Times* claims Warhol originated this trend, "Like just about everything else in contemporary life."[199]

DECEMBER Carol Vogel reports on the ongoing financial struggles of the Andy Warhol Foundation for the Visual Arts, whose cash assets have declined by $5 million since the previous fiscal year, and on the fights between the foundation and Fred Hughes, executor of Warhol's estate, on one side, and Edward Hayes, the lawyer for the estate, on the other. Hayes predicts, "At the present rate, [the foundation] will be unable to continue within three years."[200]

Art historian Kenneth E. Silver publishes one of the first scholarly considerations of Warhol as a queer artist, "Modes of Disclosure: The Construction of Gay Identity and the Rise of Pop Art." This becomes an important aspect of Warhol studies over the decade, in works such as the anthology *Pop Out: Queer Warhol*.[201]

Artist Deborah Kass later says, "I find Andy so fascinating because he was the first queer artist—I mean queer in the political sense we mean queer. While some of his homosexual contemporaries were into coding and veiling and obscuring, Andy really made pictures about what it was like being a queer guy in the '50s."[202]

1993

JANUARY Thomas Armstrong, former director of the Whitney, is named director of the planned Andy Warhol Museum in Pittsburgh, a joint effort by the Andy Warhol Foundation, the Carnegie Institute, and Dia Center for the Arts.

MAY Fred Hughes puts ten Warhol paintings up for auction at Sotheby's New York; only two find buyers. *Old Telephone (1)* (1961) sells for $552,500, while *Portrait of Princess Diana* (1982) sells for $57,500. The next night at Christie's, none of the four Warhols up for auction sells. Carol Vogel reports that the disastrous auction results have "created a domino effect in the entire Warhol market," and quotes Irving Blum, who says Warhol has "always suffered fits and starts, but now he's been leveled in the most terrifying way."[203]

JULY The Andy Warhol Foundation values the Warhol estate at $220 million, notably less than the $600–700 million estimated by Edward Hayes, former lawyer for the estate. Christie's provides appraisal services to the foundation, later having to defend its appraisals in court during a lawsuit brought by Hayes.

AUGUST Warhol is noted for undermining traditionally masculine tropes: the Whitney includes one of his *Piss Paintings* in its show "Abject Art," as part of the section called "Unmaking Modernist Masculinity." Frank Rich had recently pointed out the conspicuous presence of *The Andy Warhol Diaries* on the shelf of the protagonist of the film *A Few Good Men*, there to signal his "anti-machismo" character.[204]

This aspect of Warhol seems to have had a liberating effect on some artists following in his high-society footsteps, who are able to be more open about their sexuality. The *New York Times* profiles the painter Ross Bleckner, remarking, "Not since Andy Warhol, it seems, has a painter been such a significant presence on the New York social scene," and noting that he has recently landed on *Newsweek*'s list of "gay power brokers."[205]

DECEMBER The video for Madonna's "Deeper and Deeper" is, in part, an homage to Warhol's films. It features a Joe Dallesandro look-alike dancing in his underwear, as well as a cameo by Udo Kier, star of *Flesh for Frankenstein* and *Blood for Dracula*.

1994

MARCH "The Films of Andy Warhol, Part II" opens at the Whitney, presenting fourteen films recently restored by MoMA as part of the Andy Warhol Film Project (see April 1988).

APRIL A Manhattan court rules that the Andy Warhol estate is worth more than four times what the foundation claims. Valued by Christie's at $95 million, the art in the estate was actually worth nearly $391 million when the foundation received it in 1991, according to the judge. The total estate is valued at nearly $510 million.[206]

MAY The Andy Warhol Museum opens in Pittsburgh. The largest single-artist museum in the United States, its collection includes more than 8,000 works in all media, from Warhol's earliest work in the 1940s to the latest in the 1980s. Visitors number 25,000 during its opening weekend. The art critic Roberta Smith praises the museum's "warts-and-all" approach, while the conservative writer Roger Kimball says, "A museum dedicated to Warhol is a monument to facetiousness."[207]

AUGUST The media theorist Douglas Rushkoff describes Generation X, the post-baby-boom generation: "Taking their cue from postmodern artists like Andy Warhol, GenXers examine and re-examine the images from the media that formed their own world-views and do so with humor."[208]

NOVEMBER The art world is relieved, after 1993's dismal sales, to see Warhol "again catapulted to the top of the art market." At Christie's New York, *Shot Red Marilyn* (1964)—which had established the previous sales record for the artist, selling for $4.07 million in 1989—sells for $3.6 million, well above its estimate. "It's the recognition we were waiting for," says Doris Ammann, the sister of Warhol collector Thomas Ammann.[209]

ALSO THIS YEAR Alternative rock group the Dandy Warhols is formed in Portland, Oregon.

A 1994 Gap ad romanticizes a bow-tie-wearing Warhol's early days in New York. The advertisement uses a 1949 photo of Warhol by his then-roommate, the artist Philip Pearlstein.

1995

JANUARY Jean Baudrillard continues his reappraisal of Warhol (see 1970 and January 1989). He takes Arthur C. Danto's argument about Warhol's exploration of the limits of art one step further, arguing that Warhol ended the avant-garde. According to Baudrillard, Warhol "liberates us from art" through his "annihilation of the artist and the creative act."[210]

APRIL : The Warhol Museum hosts a three-day conference, "Warhol's Worlds." Among the fifteen presenters are the cultural critic Christopher Hitchens; Richard Martin, curator of the Costume Institute of The Metropolitan Museum of Art; the art historian Hal Foster; and Warhol superstar Mary Woronov. In 1997 the British Film Institute publishes the papers as *Who Is Andy Warhol?*

MAY The Warhol Foundation establishes a separate corporation, the Andy Warhol Authentication Board, which is made up of Warhol associates and independent scholars.

OCTOBER The "Dionysian loft parties" thrown by Internet entrepreneur Josh Harris, the "Andy Warhol of Silicon Alley, New York's new-media mecca,"[211] are described as "the Warhol Factory of 1995." Says Harris, "Maybe our goal is to beat Andy Warhol, to be bigger or better than him."[212]

NOVEMBER The *New York Times* reports that Campbell's Soup is "taking a calculated risk" in trying to modernize its product line, "even daring to vary the look of the soup can made immortal by Andy Warhol."[213]

1996

APRIL "Andy Warhol 1956–1986: Mirror of His Time," the first major traveling exhibition organized by the Andy Warhol Museum, opens at the new Museum of Contemporary Art in Tokyo. More than 125,000 people visit the exhibition, with 7,000 attending on the last day alone. The exhibition also travels to the Fukuoka Art Museum in Fukuoka and the Hyogo Prefectural Museum of Modern Art in Kobe.

MAY The director of the Grey Art Gallery at New York University, Tom Sokolowski, is named director of The Andy Warhol Museum, succeeding Tom Armstrong.

Mary Harron's *I Shot Andy Warhol*, which focuses on Valerie Solanas and her relationship to Warhol, is released. Reviewing the film, Stephen Holden (who sat for a Warhol *Screen Test* in the 1960s) remarks, "It took 25 years for the rest of the world to catch on to what Warhol already understood about fame. . . . Nowadays, on any morning you can flip from channel to channel and find the descendants of Warhol's 'superstars' getting naked, going crazy and ripping open their lives for Jerry Springer . . . and any number of other talk-show ringmasters."[214]

AUGUST New York's Gershwin Hotel begins a tradition of throwing Warhol a birthday party every year. Former Warhol superstars regularly attend the fete.

Julian Schnabel's *Basquiat* is released, starring David Bowie as Warhol. Janet Maslin writes, "On the evidence of this and 'I Shot Andy Warhol' . . . Warhol becomes a tremendous scene-stealer in any downtown drama that is name-dropping enough to make him a character."[215]

OCTOBER MoMA acquires *32 Campbell's Soup Cans* (1962) from dealer Irving Blum for $15 million (see July 1962).

NOVEMBER In a *New York Times Magazine* article, Michiko Kakutani surveys the scope of Warhol's lasting influence, writing that he has been "picked up willy-nilly by successive generations of artists and artistes. [David] Letterman is a post-Warholian performer. So, obviously, is Madonna. 'Access Hollywood,' the Jacqueline Onassis auction, Dennis Rodman's book, Planet Hollywood, Calvin Klein ads and the new 'Brady Bunch' movies are all post-Warholian phenomena, just as Cindy Sherman's photographs and Damien Hirst's dead cows are post-Warholian art."[216]

The Warhol market continues to rebound. At Christie's New York, *Two Marilyns (Double Marilyn)*—which had gone unsold in its previous time at auction, in 1993—sells for $370,000, significantly above the auction house's high prediction of $300,000.

1997

MAY The art writer Philippe Trétiack argues, "There will always be a pre- and a post-Warhol and that post-Warhol period is having difficulty establishing itself."[217]

NOVEMBER "The fashion world is having a Warhol moment," reports the *Chicago Tribune*. "Ten years after the death of the artist, the ideas and images—and not least, the cult of celebrity—that he cultivated were all very much in evidence as New York's Spring 1998 fashion week got under way last weekend."[218]

The Whitney opens "The Warhol Look/Glamour Style Fashion," organized by the Warhol Museum. The fashion writer Suzy Menkes praises the show's celebration of Warhol's "role as Svengali and showman in 20th century fashion," while art critic Holland Cotter pans the show, writing that the "Warhol Lite" treatment does not adequately capture his importance, since he "remains one of the most provocative American artists of the postwar years" and "his influence on contemporary art and thinking has been immense and continues to grow."[219] Windows at several department stores throughout Manhattan are given a Warhol theme. The exhibition travels to Toronto, London, Marseille, Sydney, Perth, Auckland, and Pittsburgh.

The Warhol Foundation announces plans to divide its collection of Warhol's film, video, and television work among four institutions: The Andy Warhol Museum, MoMA, the Museum of Television and Radio, and the UCLA Film and Television Archive. A *New York Times* editorial responds that the gifts "will insure the steady re-estimation of a figure who needs no retrospective. The culture we live in is retrospective enough for Andy Warhol."[220]

ALSO THIS YEAR Chanel uses Warhol's *Chanel No. 5* from the 1985 *Ads* series in a Paris campaign for the perfume's seventy-fifth anniversary and the tenth anniversary of the artist's death.

1998

MAY *Shot Orange Marilyn* (1964) fetches $17.3 million at Sotheby's New York, quadrupling Warhol's previous record high (see May 1989). The selling price is nearly triple the high estimate of $6 million and is met with animated applause in the salesroom.

JUNE Warhol makes *Time* magazine's list of the 100 most influential people of the twentieth century. Steven Henry Madoff writes, "For the last quarter of the century, and in the 11 years since his death, Warhol has floated over the art world like a slightly sinister saint. Scads of artists have grown bold from his example. . . . The best-known of them . . . epitomize the Post-Warhol Effect: whole careers can now be spun from a clutch of industrial knock-offs and icons of calculated sensationalism."[221]

JULY To commemorate the Israel Museum's fiftieth anniversary, an international group of donors gives the museum Warhol's *Ten Portraits of Jews in the Twentieth Century* screenprint series.

AUGUST The magazine impresario Jason Binn says that his publishing role model is Warhol—and that he gives himself a curfew, "just like Andy did."[222]

Warhol's house at 57 East 66th Street is commemorated with a plaque by the Historic Landmarks Preservation Center.

SEPTEMBER The experimental theater director Anne Bogart presents *Culture of Desire*, in which Warhol must descend into hell to atone for the ills of the consumer society he helped to create.

ALSO THIS YEAR Liberia issues commemorative Warhol-style stamps after the death of Princess Diana of Wales.

1999

APRIL Warhol appears as a character on *The Simpsons* in an episode called "Mom and Pop Art."

MAY "Andy Warhol Photography" opens at the Hamburg Kunsthalle. The exhibition draws extensively on the artist's personal archive and demonstrates Warhol's reliance on photography to create his art and his persona. It is also shown in Pittsburgh and at the International Center of Photography, New York.

SUMMER Building on earlier work by Simon Watney (see April 1988), Douglas Crimp, in "Getting the Warhol We Deserve," mounts a defense of cultural studies. Responding to a 1996 issue of *October* in which numerous art historians defended the field against the expanded scope of "visual culture," Crimp points out that to consider an artist like Warhol solely from an art-historical perspective is to overlook key cultural elements that are integral to both the artist and the art, notably queer culture of the 1960s and 1970s.[223]

2000

JANUARY The United States Information Agency (a now-defunct agency dedicated to "promoting diplomacy") sponsors the exhibition tour of "Andy Warhol," a major retrospective, throughout Asia and Eastern Europe. Ninety works by the artist are seen in fourteen cities, from Almaty to Saint Petersburg to Prague, through May 2002.

MAY Peter Schjeldahl calls for a reconsideration of Warhol, writing that his works, "when you step right up and look at them, are nakedly beautiful, unstinting, and grand." Perhaps including himself, he notes, "The number of smart people who have outsmarted themselves while presuming to explain Warhol would overflow a stadium."[224]

SEPTEMBER Philip Leider, a founding editor of *Artforum*, says in an interview that there has been a lack of quality and content in art since 1973, when "all the good people walked away: the better critics, the better artists. The void got filled with Warholism. . . . About the only thing I get, in all this art that I don't get, is the sense that it all goes back to Warhol."[225]

2001

FEBRUARY Warhol is number eight on the first annual *Forbes* list of the highest-earning dead celebrities, with his estate earnings of $8 million in 2000. He outranks icons such as Marilyn Monroe, Frank Sinatra, and James Dean.[226] He drops off the list from 2002 to 2004.

SEPTEMBER The *Art Bulletin*, the journal of the College Art Association (the principal professional association for art historians in the United States), publishes its first article on Warhol, Blake Stimson's "Andy Warhol's Red Beard."[227]

OCTOBER The largest Warhol retrospective to date, curated by Heiner Bastian, opens at Berlin's Neue Nationalgalerie. Nearly 200,000 people visit the exhibition, which is named exhibition of the year by the German wing of the International Association of Art Critics.

2002

FEBRUARY The Berlin Warhol retrospective (see October 2001) opens at the Tate Modern in London. Jonathan Jones writes in the *Guardian Weekend*, "It now looks as though [Warhol] will be remembered as the most important artist of the second half of the 20th century," arguing that we are at the end of an "American era defined visually by Warhol and recorded by him more precisely than by any novelist or film-maker."[228]

MARCH Reviewing the retrospective at the Tate, Peter Schjeldahl dismisses the claims for Warhol as social critic: "[He] simply made use of his childhood as a working-class sissy who had been weaned on movie magazines and tabloids."[229]

The Andy Warhol Catalogue Raisonné of Paintings and Sculpture, Volume 1 is published, covering Warhol's output for the years 1961 to 1963. The second volume (1964–69) follows in July 2004, and the third (1970–74) in July 2010. Coverage of the remainder of Warhol's corpus is planned in further volumes.

SPRING The art historian T. J. Clark admits, "My militant hostility to Andy Warhol . . . has not stood the test of time."[230]

MAY The Berlin retrospective opens in Los Angeles at MOCA. The *Los Angeles Times* reports on the long-standing resentment of many of Warhol's actors and calls the retrospective a "bittersweet treat, like an old uncle you forgot you disliked — and then remembered why."[231]

Echoing the *Advocate*'s criticism of MoMA's 1989 retrospective (see December 1989), Holland Cotter, in the *New York Times*, says the show "misrepresents" Warhol by ignoring his sexuality and the way he "put gay identity . . . at the very center of his work." Cotter also makes this decisive pronouncement: "Andy Warhol was the most important artist of the second half of the 20th century. . . . His influence was profound. Gerhard Richter, among many other artists, would not exist without him. . . . Warhol's work gets more astonishing every time out: more prescient, beautiful, radical, expansive, incisive."[232]

AUGUST The United States Postal Service issues a stamp honoring Warhol. (Warhol postage stamp with custom First Day of Issue cancellation stamp, 2002. Collection of The Andy Warhol Museum, Pittsburgh)

OCTOBER In a *BusinessWeek* interview, Amy Cappellazzo, head of Christie's Contemporary Art Department in New York, argues that Warhol outranks Picasso as the twentieth century's most important artist, based on his enormous influence. "Every 18-year-old artist in art school right now is desperately trying to figure out how to get out of Warhol's shadow," she notes.[233]

2003

JULY "SuperWarhol" opens at the Grimaldi Forum, Monaco, with 130 works that include many of the enormous late paintings. In his preface to the catalogue Prince Rainier states, "Is Warhol topical? To be convinced you just need to read magazines, observe fashion, follow what we call trends."[234]

SEPTEMBER National Public Radio reports that Takashi Murakami is being "touted as Japan's Andy Warhol."[235]

"Andy Warhol's *Time Capsules*" opens at the Museum für Moderne Kunst in Frankfurt. It presents all of the approximately 4,000 individual objects held in just fifteen of Warhol's 612 *Time Capsules* (see Summer 1974). In selecting it as one of the best exhibitions of the year, *Artforum* critic Daniel Birnbaum states, "I couldn't stop poring over all the letters and postcards and stuff Warhol collected. For an artist who likened his mind to a tape recorder equipped only with an erase button, this is a strangely Proustian project."[236]

NOVEMBER The scholar Michael Rush writes that Warhol's 1965 portable-video-camera footage, which he showed at a party in a train tunnel beneath the Waldorf-Astoria Hotel (see September 1965), was likely "the first artist videotape to be shown in public . . . [and] one of the first examples of what has developed into video installation art, now ubiquitous in the art world."[237]

2004

APRIL *ELLEgirl* features a fashion guide to emulating the style of Warhol, the "Pop Icon" who predates MTV and *American Idol*.

JULY Ralph Rugoff, curator at London's Hayward Gallery, argues that the best-selling, critically reviled "Painter of Light" Thomas Kinkade is a direct heir to Warhol: "In very different ways, each artist has rejected that central Modernist myth that proclaims business and art to be unrelated pursuits. . . . If Warhol stands as the radical pioneer in this revolution, Kinkade's enterprise represents the fulfillment of several of Andy's dearest dreams."[238]

ALSO THIS YEAR Campbell's Soup produces limited-edition Warhol cans.

2005

OCTOBER Apple releases the iMac G5. The computer comes packaged with a photo-taking application called PhotoBooth, which features a "Warhol effect" filter. This option is an out-of-the-box version of an effect that has been a popular DIY technique among designers for years.

The first instance of a computer-generated approximation of the Warhol look may in fact have been by Warhol himself, when he used the graphics program ProPaint to create a portrait of Debbie Harry at the Commodore Amiga product-launch press conference at New York's Lincoln Center in July 1985. (*Debbie Harry* computer printout, Collection of The Andy Warhol Museum, Pittsburgh)

Warhol rockets back to number four on the *Forbes* list of the highest-earning dead celebrities, with $16 million in estate earnings for 2004.[239]

2006

FEBRUARY Levi Strauss & Co. releases its Warhol Factory X Levi's® collection of "ultrapremium" jeans.

APRIL The first volume of *The Films of Andy Warhol Catalogue Raisonné*, by the film scholar Callie Angell, is published. The volume, a product of the Andy Warhol Film Project (see April 1988 and March 1994), covers his *Screen Test* films. It is the first catalogue raisonné to be produced for a filmmaker.

JULY The Art Gallery of Ontario opens "Andy Warhol Supernova: Stars, Deaths and Disasters, 1962–64," organized by the Walker Art Center and guest-curated for the AGO by the film director David Cronenberg. A custom-painted hearse is driven around to advertise the exhibition.

SEPTEMBER A four-hour, two-part Ric Burns documentary about Warhol airs on PBS. Quotes from Warhol are narrated by Jeff Koons.

The artist Glenn Ligon (see p. 66) draws from the Warhol Museum's collection to curate "Have Another Piece: 'Just a little piece.......smaller....... smaller,'" which opens in Pittsburgh. The exhibition examines Warhol's identity and sexuality through dozens of artworks and hundreds of archival items; its title is borrowed from Warhol's book *The Philosophy of Andy Warhol*.

OCTOBER In an article titled "The Selling of St. Andy," the *New York Times* reports, "Warhol-inspired wares are being sold in stores like Macy's and Nordstrom and in youth-oriented chains like Urban Outfitters and high-end fashion boutiques like Fred Segal in Los Angeles. This month Barneys New York will roll out a holiday marketing campaign around the artist [called "Happy Andy War-Holidays"], including shopping bags with Warhol-like doodles, four store windows and a limited edition of Campbell's soup cans."[240]

A rendering of a Warholized Times Square illustrates the article.

NOVEMBER Hong Kong real-estate magnate Joseph Lau buys *Mao* (1972) at Christie's New York for $17.4 million, setting the new record for Warhol.

2007

JANUARY *New York* magazine's January 7, 2007, cover features a story on "Warhol's Children," the up-and-coming artists Ryan McGinley, Dash Snow, and Dan Colen, who are "trying to jump-start a Warholian moment."

FEBRUARY *New York* reports, "Twenty years after his death, Andy Warhol refuses to fade away . . . he just gets bigger and bigger. . . . Today, he still seems present at the mass party, half-there behind every new craze from Paris Hilton to reality TV."[241]

Bemoaning the venality and absurd permissiveness of the contemporary art world—which, he reports, is exemplified by the "clowns" profiled in *New York*'s January 7 issue—Jed Perl writes in the *New Republic* that Warhol "is the Moses who first saw the Promised Land of laissez-faire aesthetics . . . the evil prophet of the profit motive."[242]

MARCH Artprice reports that Warhol is 2006's "unquestioned star of the New York contemporary arts sales," with forty-three works having sold for more than $1 million each. He is number two on the list of top-selling artists for the third year in a row, with nearly $200 million in total sales worldwide.

MAY *Green Car Crash (Green Burning Car I)* (1963, Collection of Philip Niarchos) sells at Christie's New York for $71.7 million, by far the most ever paid for a Warhol. It is also the second-highest price ever paid for any postwar work after Mark Rothko's *White Center (Yellow, Pink and Lavender on Rose)* (1950, Al-Thani Family Collection, Qatar), which had sold for $72.8 million at Sotheby's the night before. Warhol's sales this evening total $136.7 million, the highest figure a contemporary artist has ever realized.

OCTOBER The Stedelijk Museum in Amsterdam opens "Andy Warhol: Other Voices, Other Rooms." Borrowing the title of Truman Capote's novel, the show is focused on Warhol's work outside the practice of painting: film, television, books, graphic design, publishing, and other forms of production.

DECEMBER "Andy Warhol" opens at the Gallery of Modern Art, Brisbane, Australia. With more than 300 works, it is the largest and most comprehensive Warhol exhibition ever seen in Australia and attracts more than 230,000 visitors.

2008

MARCH Artprice reports that Warhol has surpassed Picasso in total sales for 2007, taking the number one spot for the first time, with $420 million in global sales.

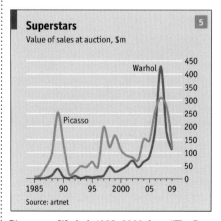

Picasso vs. Warhol, 1985–2009, from "The Pop Master's Highs and Lows: Andy Warhol Is the Bellwether," *Economist*, November 28, 2009.

AUGUST Martini & Rossi and *Interview* magazine throw Warhol an eightieth birthday party at New York's New Museum. The fete celebrates Martini & Rossi's new ad campaign, which features Warhol's 1950s illustrations for the brand.

SEPTEMBER The Montreal Museum of Fine Arts opens "Warhol Live: Music and Dance in Andy Warhol's Work." Nearly 600 works of art and archival objects present Warhol's creative and personal connections to modern dance, opera, Broadway shows, Hollywood musicals, rock and roll, and avant-garde music and dance.

OCTOBER *Eight Elvises* (1963) sells for more than $100 million in a private sale brokered by the art consultant Philippe Ségalot. Only four other artists—Picasso, Pollock, Willem de Kooning, and Gustav Klimt—have met this benchmark.

NOVEMBER The hotel heiress and socialite Paris Hilton (see p. 69) wears herself, Warhol style.

2009

MARCH As the largest Warhol exhibition to focus on Warhol's portraiture, "Le grand monde d'Andy Warhol," opens at the Grand Palais in Paris, the *Guardian*'s Jonathan Jones blames Warhol for "the shallowness of modern mass culture. . . . We're Warhol's ugly brood. . . . The Modern world has screwed itself and art led the way."[243] The show's visitors include Iran's Empress Farah Pahlavi (see May 1975).

APRIL An ad for Britain's *Daily Telegraph* positions Warhol as one of the great success stories of the later twentieth century, alongside John Lennon and Bill Clinton.

JUNE "Andy Warhol, Mr. America," the largest Warhol exhibition to tour South America, opens in Bogotá, Colombia. The 150 works in the show are also presented in Buenos Aires and São Paulo.

SEPTEMBER Madonna's third greatest-hits album, *Celebration*, styles the pop icon as Warhol's Marilyn Monroe. It is a design by Mr. Brainwash (see January 2010).

NOVEMBER The *Economist* reports, "The Warhol market is considered the bellwether of post-war and contemporary art. . . . Since 2002 Warhol has consistently been one of the three most traded artists."[244]

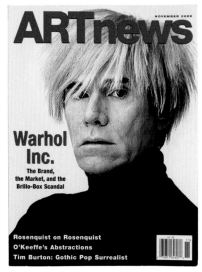

ARTnews runs the cover story "Warhol Inc.," which explores the steady growth in demand for the artist's work and the concurrent explosion of Warhol-branded merchandising. Warhol Museum director Tom Sokolowski observes, "If you're going to study Warhol, it is always about high and low."[245]

ALSO THIS YEAR Madelyn Roehrig, a resident of Upper St. Clair, Pennsylvania, begins a series of documentary shorts on the pilgrims to Warhol's grave, interviewing hundreds and documenting the Campbell's Soups, Coca-Colas, and other tributes regularly left by his tombstone.

2010

JANUARY Banksy's *Exit Through the Gift Shop* premieres at the Sundance Film Festival. It follows Thierry Guetta, a French immigrant in Los Angeles whose obsessive interest in graffiti art propels him to begin his own career as a street artist. Adopting the name Mr. Brainwash, Guetta espouses a Warholian aesthetic and workshoplike production style, going on to achieve enormous success.

SEPTEMBER "Andy Warhol: The Early Sixties, Paintings and Drawings 1961–1964" opens at the Kunstmuseum Basel, touting itself as the first exhibition ever to address the artist's transition from commercial to fine-art work.

In the *Financial Times*, David Pilling coins the term "Andy Warhol politics" to describe a situation in which Japan is facing the prospect of electing its third prime minister within the span of a year. In this political system, "everybody gets to spend 15 minutes as prime minister."[246]

Political poster for Japanese House of Representatives member Furukawa Motohisa, 2010.

OCTOBER Dom Pérignon releases a limited-edition Warhol-inspired bottle by the Design Laboratory at Central Saint Martins College of Art and Design in London. It is the first time the company has produced an alternate to its signature label. The marketing campaign touts Dom as the only thing Andy drank at Studio 54.

According to art market research firm ArtTactic Ltd., Warhol paintings account for 17 percent of all contemporary-art auction sales in 2010. By contrast, the combined sales of Jeff Koons and Damien Hirst make up 3.1 percent of the market.[247]

2011

FEBRUARY Kate Middleton is featured in a Warhol-style portrait on the cover of the UK's *Tatler* in advance of her April 2011 nuptials to Prince William.

MARCH The Public Art Fund unveils Rob Pruitt's sculpture of Warhol, *The Andy Monument*, down the street from the second Factory and in front of Warhol's third office, on New York's Union Square.

APRIL The value of Warhol's paintings has gone up by more than thirty times. Felix Salmon reports that his estate, "valued at some $220 million when he died, would be worth some $7 billion today."[248]

MAY A new record for a Warhol self-portrait is set at Christie's New York, where his 1963–64 *Self-Portrait* goes for $38.5 million.

JULY Following a 2009 run at the Yale Repertory Theatre, "Pop!"—a musical about Warhol and the Factory—premieres at the Studio Theatre in Washington, D.C.

SEPTEMBER Designer Tommy Hilfiger shows his spring 2012 collection, "Pop Prep," at New York Fashion Week. The collection is inspired by the Pop palette and includes fabrics that pay direct homage to Warhol's *Camouflage* series. Hilfiger says, "When I moved to New York in the 70s, I had the opportunity to meet Andy Warhol and become influenced by all of his talent, and I'm using that influence and that inspiration in my work today."[249]

OCTOBER After years of legal battles and controversy over its methods, the Warhol Foundation announces that it is dissolving the Art Authentication Board.

WINTER The *Economist*, surveying the astronomical appetite for Warhol in the contemporary-art market, sniffs, "In time . . . the idea that [Warhol] is a greater artist than Robert Rauschenberg or Jackson Pollock will be seen as the absurdity that it is."[250]

2012

FEBRUARY Twenty-five years to the minute after Warhol's death, Jim Sharman, the cowriter and director of the cult classic *The Rocky Horror Picture Show*, releases *Andy X*, an online musical conceived as a "cinematic séance" with the artist. In a payment scheme also inspired by the artist and his milieu, the more Facebook friends a person has, the less he or she pays for access.

MARCH "Andy Warhol: 15 Minutes Eternal" opens at the ArtScience Museum in Singapore, beginning an Asian tour that travels to Hong Kong, Beijing, Shanghai, and Tokyo. The exhibition includes more than 400 artworks and 300 archival objects.

NOTES

DIALOGUES WITH WARHOL

1. Rainer Crone, *Andy Warhol* (New York: Praeger Publishers, 1970), p. 9.
2. Henry Geldzahler, quoted in Tony Scherman and David Dalton, *Pop: The Genius of Andy Warhol* (New York: HarperCollins, 2009), p. 113. Two later writers who elaborated on Warhol's importance were Benjamin H. D. Buchloh, "The Andy Warhol Line," in *The Work of Andy Warhol*, edited by Gary Garrels, Dia Art Foundation Discussions in Contemporary Culture, 3 (Seattle: Bay Press, 1989), pp. 65–67; and Robert Rosenblum, "Warhol as Art History," in *Andy Warhol: A Retrospective*, by Kynaston McShine et al., exh. cat. (New York: The Museum of Modern Art, 1989), pp. 25–37.
3. Jason Rhoades, as told to Daniel Birnbaum, "My Pop," *Artforum* 43, no. 2 (October 2004), p. 90.
4. Gerhard Richter, *The Daily Practice of Painting: Writings and Interviews 1962–1993*, edited by Hans-Ulrich Obrist, translated by David Britt (London: Anthony d'Offay Gallery, 1995), p. 180.
5. Andy Warhol and Pat Hackett, *POPism: The Warhol '60s* (New York: Harcourt Brace Jovanovich, 1980), pp. 11–12. For a commentary on this story, see Kenneth E. Silver, "Modes of Disclosure: The Construction of Gay Identity and the Rise of Pop Art," in *Hand-Painted Pop: American Art in Transition, 1955–62*, by Donna De Salvo et al., exh. cat. (Los Angeles: Museum of Contemporary Art; New York: Rizzoli International, 1992), pp. 193–202.
6. Warhol and Hackett, *POPism*, pp. 5–6.
7. Stuart Klawans, "The Corpse in the Mirror: The Warhol Wake," *Grand Street* 8 (Winter 1989), pp. 176–87; reprinted in *The Critical Response To Andy Warhol*, edited by Alan R. Pratt, Critical Responses in Arts and Letters, 25 (Westport, Conn., and London: Greenwood Press, 1997), p. 228.

8. Warhol said, "I think John Cage has been really influential." Interviews by G[ene] R. Swenson, "What Is Pop Art?: Answers from 8 Painters, Part I," *ARTnews* 62, no. 7 (November 1963), p. 61. For more on the influence of Cage on Warhol, see Bradford R. Collins, "The Metaphysical Nosejob: The Remaking of Warhola, 1960–1968," *Arts Magazine* 62, no. 6 (February 1988), p. 49; and Peter Gay, *Modernism: The Lure of Heresy, from Baudelaire To Beckett and Beyond* (New York and London: W. W. Norton, 2008), p. 423.
9. Kenneth Baker draws a relationship between Frank Stella's ambitions and those of Warhol, with regard to a concentration of surface events, in *Minimalism: Art of Circumstance* (New York: Abbeville Press, 1988), pp. 38–39.
10. Scherman and Dalton, *Pop*, p. 259.
11. Rauschenberg said, "Painting relates to both art and life. Neither can be made. (I try to act in the gap between the two.)" Quoted in Dorothy Canning Miller, *Sixteen Americans*, exh. cat. (New York: The Museum of Modern Art, 1959), p. 58.
12. Cage's aesthetic breakthrough had other fascinating parallels in the visual arts, including the paintings of Frank Stella. In 1966 he famously explained about his work that viewers should not seek psychological or emotional depth beneath the surface of the painting. To those looking for "humanistic values," he said, "My painting is based on the fact that only what can be seen there *is* there." Cited in interview by Bruce Glaser, "Questions To Stella and Judd," edited by Lucy R. Lippard, *ARTnews* 65, no. 5 (September 1966), p. 58.
13. For a full consideration of Warhol's use of the newspaper, see Molly Donovan et al., *Warhol Headlines*, exh. cat. (Washington, D.C.: National Gallery of Art, 2011).
14. Swenson, "What Is Pop Art?," p. 61. Interpolation by the author.
15. Andy Warhol, *The Philosophy of Andy Warhol (From A To B and Back Again)* (New York and London: Harcourt Brace Jovanovich, 1975), p. 93.

16. Francesco Bonami, "Painting-slaughter: How Andy Warhol Did Not Murder Painting, But Master-minded the Killing of Content," in *Andy Warhol/Supernova: Stars, Deaths, and Disasters, 1962–1964*, by Douglas Fogle et al., exh. cat. (Minneapolis: Walker Art Center, 2005), p. 25.
17. See, for instance, John Coplans, *Andy Warhol*, exh. cat. (New York: Graphic Society; Eindhoven: Van Abbemuseum, 1978), p. 14.
18. Notably, Crone, *Andy Warhol*, pp. 9–11, 22–24. For a summary of the contradictory points of view, see Buchloh, "Warhol Line," pp. 55–69.
19. Michelle White, "Arresting Ambiguity: Vija Celmins in the 1960s," in *Vija Celmins: Television and Disaster, 1964–1966*, by Franklin Sirmans and Michelle White, exh. cat. (Houston: Menil Collection, 2010), p. 16. Celmins's work was imbued with generalized violence and doom at this period, as it was for Gerhard Richter in works of 1963–64.
20. Adrianna Valdés, ed., *Jaar SCL 2006/Alfredo Jaar, Santiago de Chile 2006*, exh. cat. (Santiago de Chile: Sala de Arte Fundación Telefónica Chile; Galería Gabriela Mistral; Barcelona: Actar, 2006), p. 88.
21. Described by the artist in Theodora Vischer et al., *Robert Gober: Sculptures and Installations, 1979–2007*, exh. cat. ([Basel]: Schaulager Basel, 2007), p. 334. Warhol, too, had manipulated, altered, and reconfigured his newspaper sources. See Molly Donovan, "Where's Warhol? Triangulating the Artist in the Headlines," in *Warhol Headlines*, pp. 3–4, 8–9.
22. Hannah Arendt, *Eichmann in Jerusalem: A Report on the Banality of Evil* (New York: Viking Press, [1963]). Helen Molesworth explores this subject matter in relation to another contemporary artist who has relevance to Warhol, in "Luc Tuymans: Painting the Banality of Evil," in *Luc Tuymans*, by Madeleine Grynsztejn et al., exh. cat. (San Francisco: San Francisco Museum of Modern Art, Wexner Center for the Arts, 2009), pp. 15–29.

23. Warhol said that he chose to make flower paintings in advance of his 1965 Paris exhibition at Sonnabend Gallery because he had the impression that "the French would probably like flowers because of Renoir and so on" (Crone, *Andy Warhol*, p. 30). The flower paintings were first exhibited at the Leo Castelli Gallery, New York, in late 1964.
24. For more on the relationship of Richter to Warhol, see Kaja Silverman, "Photography by Other Means," in *The Painting of Modern Life: 1960s To Now*, by Ralph Rugoff et al., exh. cat. (London: Hayward Publishing, 2007), p. 23.
25. Warhol, *Philosophy*, pp. 100–101. Regarding the spread of American exports and the "Made in U.S.A." label starting in the late 1950s, and this phenomenon in contemporary art, see Sidra Stich, *Made in U.S.A.: An Americanization in Modern Art, the '50s & '60s*, exh. cat. (Berkeley: University Art Museum; University of California Press, 1987), pp. 90–93.
26. Warhol and Hackett, *POPism*, pp. 39–40. Simon Watney notes, "Cans of soup are only 'banal' to those who didn't have to grow up on canned food." "Queer Andy," in *Popout: Queer Warhol*, edited by Jennifer Doyle, Jonathan Flatley, and José Esteban Muñoz (Durham, N.C., and London: Duke University Press, 1996), p. 30.
27. Warhol, *Philosophy*, p. 71.
28. Susan Sontag, "Notes on 'Camp,'" originally published in *Partisan Review* 31, no. 4 (Fall 1964), pp. 515–30; citations here are from the reprint of this essay in *Camp: Queer Aesthetics and the Performing Subject, a Reader*, edited by Fabio Cleto (1999; Ann Arbor: University of Michigan Press, 2002), p. 62.
29. Ibid., pp. 62–63.
30. Warhol and Hackett, *POPism*, p. 39.
31. Ibid., p. 40.
32. Fabio Cleto, "Section IV. . . . Introduction," in Cleto, ed., *Camp*, p. 303.
33. Warhol and Hackett, *POPism*, p. 194. Warhol was photographed as Robin, with his singer-friend Nico as Batman, in 1966.
34. Andrew Ross, "Uses of Camp," in Cleto, ed., *Camp*, p. 320.

35. Ibid. For more on Warhol with regard to camp, see Sasha Torres, "The Caped Crusader of Camp: Pop, Camp, And the *Batman* Television Series," in Cleto, ed., *Camp*, p. 336; and Matthew Tinkcom, "Warhol's Camp," in *Camp*, p. 344.
36. Milan Kundera, "Reflections; Die Weltliteratur: How We Read One Another," *New Yorker* 82, no. 44 (January 8, 2007), pp. 34–35.
37. Cady Noland, quoted in Rhea Anastas with Michael Brenson, eds., *Witness To Her Art: Art and Writings by Adrian Piper, Mona Hatoum, Cady Noland, Jenny Holzer, Kara Walker, Daniela Rossell and Eau de Cologne* (Annandale-on-Hudson, N.Y.: Center for Curatorial Studies, Bard College, 2006), p. 157.
38. Indeed, Sachs was prescient, for Chanel introduced a limited-edition gun-shaped makeup case in 2011. See *Finally Hip*, June 17, 2011, http://www.finallyhip.com/blog/2011/06/17/ted-noten-makeup-gun/.
39. Swenson, "What Is Pop Art?," p. 60. Just before mentioning his intended title "Death in America" for the Paris exhibition, Warhol described, in this interview, just having witnessed a gratuitous act of violence in Times Square. Then, immediately after, to the question, "Why did you start these 'Death' pictures," he responded: "I believe in it."
40. For a good introduction to this subject matter, see Neil Printz, "Painting Death in America," in *Andy Warhol: Death and Disasters*, by Neil Printz et al., exh. cat. (Houston: The Menil Collection; Houston Fine Art Press, 1988), pp. 11–23. Trevor Fairbrother interprets the *Flower* series to be concerned with death, too, in "Skulls," in Garrels, ed., *The Work of Andy Warhol*, p. 105.
41. The word "Silence" often appears in the *Electric Chair* series, repeating a sign in the execution chamber but also evoking the title of a famous book by Cage, *Silence: Lectures and Writings* (Middletown, Conn.: Wesleyan University Press, 1961).
42. Warhol, *Philosophy*, p. 48.
43. Ibid., p. 112.

44. Rosenblum, "Warhol as Art History," p. 36. Sontag explains that pathos and tragedy do not exist in camp aesthetics; "Notes on 'Camp,'" p. 62.

45. For a discussion of this work, see Nancy Spector, "Nowhere Man," in *Richard Prince*, by Nancy Spector [et al.], exh. cat. (New York: Solomon R. Guggenheim Museum, 2007), pp. 47–48.

46. See Gober's discussion of this work and its sources, in Vischer et al., *Robert Gober*, p. 204. With regard to Gober's series of leg sculptures, the artist confirmed to the author in a 2010 interview the point made in a *Village Voice* review, which was that these works were based on a *Car Crash* painting by Warhol. Jan Avgikos, "Everything Is Nothing: Andy Warhol, Presented with Spielbergian Intensity," *Village Voice*, July 13–19, 2005, p. C67.

47. Other artists who subsequently worked with the skull include Damien Hirst, Gabriele Orozco, Robert Lazzarini, and Richter, among others.

48. Norman Mailer, quoted in Andreas Killen, *1973 Nervous Breakdown: Watergate, Warhol, and the Birth of Post-Sixties America* (New York: Bloomsbury, 2006), p. 146.

49. Robert Rosenblum, "Andy Warhol: Court Painter To the 70s," in *Andy Warhol: Portraits of the 70s*, by David Whitney et al., exh. cat. (New York: Random House; Whitney Museum of American Art, 1979), p. 139.

50. See Georg Frei and Neil Printz, eds., *The Andy Warhol Catalogue Raisonné*, vol. 01, *Paintings and Sculpture, 1961–1963* (New York: Thomas Ammann Fine Art AG Zurich and The Andy Warhol Foundation for the Visual Arts; London and New York: Phaidon Press, 2002), pp. 231–32, 235, 247, 249.

51. Katz reports that Warhol saw these works in 1959 (conversations with the author, 2009 and 2011).

52. Andy Warhol, quoted in Collins, "The Metaphysical Nosejob," p. 53; from Andy Warhol, *A: A Novel* (New York: Grove Press, 1968), p. 68.

53. David McCarthy, "Andy Warhol's Silver Elvises: Meaning through Context at the Ferus Gallery in 1963," *Art Bulletin* 88, no. 2 (June 2006), pp. 354–72.

54. Coplans, *Andy Warhol*, p. 49.

55. Regarding the "Hyannis Port Jackies," see Frei and Printz, eds., *The Andy Warhol Catalogue Raisonné*, vol. 02A, *Paintings and Sculptures, 1964–1969* (2004), pp. 272, 279.

56. Warhol said, "I started those . . . when she was so sick and everybody said she was going to die." Swenson, "What Is Pop Art?," p. 60.

57. See Sara Doris, "Your Fifteen Minutes Are Up: Fame, Obsolescence, and Camp in Warhol's Star Portraits, 1962–1967," in *Reframing Andy Warhol: Constructing American Myths, Heroes, and Cultural Icons*, by Wendy Grossman et al., exh. cat. (College Park, Md.: The Art Gallery at the University of Maryland, 1998), pp. 32–34.

58. Andy Warhol, quoted in "Art; Products," *Newsweek* 60, no. 20 (November 12, 1962), p. 94.

59. Warhol, *Philosophy*, p. 61. In the context of *The Last Supper*, Danto described Warhol creating a "dark world of radiant beings, whose presence among us is redemptive." Arthur C. Danto, *Andy Warhol* (New Haven and London: Yale University Press, 2009), p. 60.

60. Discussed in Scherman and Dalton, *Pop*, p. 232.

61. See Michael Fried, "New York Letter," *Art International* 6, no. 10 (December 20, 1962), p. 57, for his emotional reaction to the sight of a Marilyn painting by Warhol.

62. Anastas with Brenson, eds., *Witness To Her Art*, pp. 127–29, 155.

63. Besides the series devoted to Jackie Kennedy, Warhol painted Nelson Rockefeller, 1967, and the 1972 *Vote McGovern* poster in which an image of Richard Nixon appeared.

64. See Bob Colacello, *Holy Terror: Andy Warhol Close Up* (New York: HarperCollins, 1990), p. 111.

65. For a full description of the iconographic details of *Taking Stock*, see Matthias Flügge and Robert Fleck, eds., *Hans Haacke For Real: Works 1959–2006*, exh. cat. (Düsseldorf: Richter Verlag; Berlin: Akademie der Kunste; Hamburg: Deichtorhallen, 2006), pp. 170–71.

66. See Scott Rothkopf et al., *Glenn Ligon: America*, exh. cat. (New York: Whitney Museum of American Art, 2011), p. 40, for a discussion of the source of the image in a children's coloring book.

67. For more on the history of the title, see Frei and Printz, eds., *The Andy Warhol Catalogue Raisonné*, vol. 02A, pp. 240–41.

68. The "Breck Girl" campaign helped to launch the careers of several sex symbols of the 1970s and 1980s, including Cheryl Tiegs, Cybill Shepherd, Kim Basinger, and Farrah Fawcett.

69. See Nate Freeman, "Nude Statue of Peter Brant's Wife Stephanie Seymour Graces Cover of Auction Catalogue," *New York Observer*, October 15, 2010, http://www.observer.com/2010/10/nude-statue.

70. Watney, "Queer Andy," p. 22.

71. One exception is the French photographer Claude Cahun (1894–1954).

72. On rare occasions, Warhol did show himself as desirable. See Richard Meyer, "Warhol's Clones," *Yale Journal of Criticism* 7, no. 1 (Spring 1994), p. 105.

73. Warhol, *Philosophy*, p. 10.

74. Warhol said, "If you want to know all about Andy Warhol, just look at the surface: of my paintings and films and me, and there I am. There's nothing behind it." Quoted in *Andy Warhol: A Retrospective*, p. 457.

75. Warhol, *Philosophy*, p. 10.

76. Warhol loved to hear other people talk about their sex lives but his own was off-limits, as was his town house, which very few, even close, intimates ever visited.

77. For another point of view, see Caroline A. Jones, *Machine in the Studio: Constructing the Postwar American Artist* (Chicago and London: The University of Chicago Press, 1996), pp. 244–47.

78. Warhol and Hackett, *POPism*, pp. 222–24.

79. Elsewhere, Warhol praised "drag queens" for being "living testimony to the way women used to want to be, the way some people still want them to be" (Warhol, *Philosophy*, p. 54), this through their costumes and makeup. Warhol made a series on drag queens titled *Ladies and Gentlemen*, 1975.

80. See Killen, *1973 Nervous Breakdown*, pp. 152, 155.

81. See Warhol and Hackett, *POPism*, p. 294, for Warhol's mention of pornography. For more on this subject, see Simon Goldhill, "The Anatomy of Desire," in *Andy Warhol, Eros and Desire: The Late Nudes*, exh. cat. (London and New York: Anthony D'Offay Gallery; Cheim & Reid Gallery, 2005), pp. 3–18.

82. For additional discussion of the *Most Wanted Men* series, see Meyer, "Warhol's Clones," pp. 79–92. Also of note are Marcel Duchamp's *Wanted $2000 Reward*, 1923, and Rauschenberg's *Hymnal*, 1955, which includes a "wanted" poster.

83. Vischer et al., *Robert Gober*, p. 278.

84. Lisa Phillips characterizes this look as perhaps having its source in pornographic movies. "Cindy Sherman's Cindy Shermans," in *Cindy Sherman*, exh. cat. (New York: Whitney Museum of American Art, 1987), p. 14.

85. Jean Baudrillard, *Simulations*, translated by Paul Foss, Paul Patton, and Philip Beitchman (New York: Semiotext[e], 1983), p. 148.

86. Ibid., pp. 136, 149.

87. Ibid., p. 152. Baudrillard aptly described how, regardless of the relative gravity of a subject, an air of "non-intentional parody hangs over everything" (p. 150).

88. Steven Kurtz, "Uneasy Flirtations: The Critical Reaction To Warhol's Concepts of the Celebrity and of Glamour," in Pratt, ed., *Critical Response To Andy Warhol*, p. 251.

89. Formerly it was thought that Warhol learned this technique from Rauschenberg but, in fact, the opposite development occurred. See Branden W. Joseph, "'A Duplication Containing Duplications': Robert Rauschenberg's Split Screens," *October*, no. 95 (Winter 2001), p. 7 n. 11.

90. For more on this subject, see Douglas Fogle [et al.], *The Last Picture Show: Artists Using Photography, 1960–1982*, exh. cat. (Minneapolis: Walker Art Center, 2003).

91. Richter, too, kept an extensive "image bank," which he titled *Atlas*, 1962–66; so did Baldessari and Prince.

92. See Walter Benjamin's discussion of the "aura" of the work of art: "The Work of Art in the Age of Mechanical Reproduction [1936]," in *Illuminations*, edited and introduced by Hannah Arendt, translated by Harry Zohn (New York: Schocken Books, 1969), pp. 217–51.

93. Baudrillard, *Simulations*, p. 144.

94. Crone, *Andy Warhol*, p. 24.

95. See Mark Rosenthal, *Critiques of Pure Abstraction*, exh. cat. (New York: Independent Curators, 1995), pp. 9–12.

96. Barry Blinderman, "Modern 'Myths': An Interview with Andy Warhol," *Arts Magazine* 56, no. 2 (October 1981), p. 145. For further discussion, see Keith Hartley, "Andy Warhol: Abstraction," in *Andy Warhol: The Last Decade*, by Joseph D. Ketner II et al., exh. cat. (Milwaukee: Milwaukee Art Museum; New York: DelMonico Books/Prestel, 2009), pp. 48–71.

97. Swenson, "What Is Pop Art?," pp. 60–61.

98. Discussed in Meyer, "Warhol's Clones," p. 79.

99. Warhol's use of the blank is repeated by Basquiat in his *Self-Portrait*, 1982, wherein, given the representational subject on one side of the diptych, the blank can assume all manner of personal implication.

100. Rosenblum calls "blanks" "found objects," in "Warhol as Art History," p. 33; see also Warhol's plays on Barnett Newman in the *Matchbook* series.

101. Donald Kuspit, *The Cult of the Avant-Garde Artist* (Cambridge and New York: Cambridge University Press, 1993), p. 66.

102. Tim Hunt and David Hockney, "The Interview," in *Andy Warhol Stitched Photographs*, exh. cat. (Milan: Galleria Lawrence Rubin; New York: Paul Kasmin Gallery, 1999), p. 6. There are numerous precedents for Warhol's practice, including the work of Monet and Stella. See John Coplans, *Serial Imagery*, exh. cat. (Pasadena, Calif.: Pasadena Art Museum, 1968), p. 16; Rosenblum, "Warhol as Art History," p. 29; and Neil Printz, "Andy Warhol's Flowers and the Modern Tradition," in *Georgia O'Keeffe and Andy Warhol: Flowers of Distinction*, by Barbara Buhler Lynes et al., exh. cat. (Santa Fe: Georgia O'Keeffe Museum, 2005), pp. 14–19.

103. Warhol, *Philosophy*, p. 150; see also Warhol and Hackett, *POPism*, p. 149. I thank Neil Printz for pointing out these passages, in an email of July 2011.

104. Cited in Margery King, comp., "Chronology," in *The Andy Warhol Museum* (Pittsburgh: The Andy Warhol Museum, 1994), p. 180.

105. Warhol and Hackett, *POPism*, p. 162.

106. Colacello, *Holy Terror*, pp. 373–74.

107. Carlo McCormick, quoted in Elizabeth Currid, *The Warhol Economy: How Fashion, Art, and Music Drive New York City* (Princeton, N.J.: Princeton University Press, 2007), p. 31.

108. Philip Larratt-Smith, "Interview with Guillermo Kuitca," in *Andy Warhol, Mr. America*, by Philip Larratt-Smith et al., exh. cat. (Bogotá, Colombia: Museo de Arte del Banco de la República, 2009), p. 277.

109. Swenson, "What Is Pop Art?," p. 26.

110. Rosenblum made this comparison in "Warhol as Art History," p. 30.

111. Designing for record albums had occupied Warhol since the late 1940s; see Paul Maréchal, *Andy Warhol: The Record Covers, 1949–1987; Catalogue Raisonné*, exh. cat. (Montreal: The Montreal Museum of Fine Arts; London: Prestel Publishing, 2008).

112. Killen, *1973 Nervous Breakdown*, p. 150.

113. See Anny Shaw, "Walls Come Tumbling Down," *The Art Newspaper, International Edition*, no. 226 (July–August 2011), p. 35.

114. Note Warhol's chandeliers in *Untitled*, 1976–86, illustrated in *Andy Warhol: A Retrospective*, p. 379. Add to these chandeliers by John Armleder, Banks Violette, Virgil Marti, Jorge Pardo, and Franz West, to name a very few.

115. Simon Doonan, quoted in Ruth La Ferla, "The Selling of St. Andy," *New York Times*, October 26, 2006, p. G5.

116. Warhol, *Philosophy*, p. 92.

117. Colacello's account of life with Warhol is rife with references to the pressure he felt to find new commissions.

118. In January 2012, some three hundred of Hirst's *Spot* paintings altogether went on view at the eleven branches of the Gagosian Gallery in the world.

119. See, for example, *Untitled (When I hear the word culture, I take out my checkbook)*, 1985. Kruger admired Warhol for his "coolness"; see Ann Goldstein et al., *Barbara Kruger*, exh. cat. (Los Angeles: The Museum of Contemporary Art; Cambridge, Mass.: The MIT Press, 1999), pp. 34–35. Her portrait of Warhol is titled *Not Cool Enough*.

120. See Jones, *Machine in the Studio*, pp. 189–207, 263–67.

121. See Jeff Wall in an online symposium distilled in Jack Bankowsky et al., "Pop after Pop: A Roundtable," *Artforum* 43, no. 2 (October 2004), p. 167.

122. Andy Warhol, quoted in *Andy Warhol: A Retrospective*, p. 460.

123. Who then are the successors to the Warhol form of branding and identity? According to the artist Rob Pruitt, an aficionado of Warhol, "I think the closest thing to Andy Warhol today is Larry Gagosian. . . . he is the figure of this moment that bridges worlds, like art and Hollywood or international jet-set. He's a real media-ready figure and a cipher. I don't know if Larry hangs out with drug addicts and drag queens" ("24 Questions for Artist Rob Pruitt," *Blouin Artinfo*, April 4, 2011, http://www.artinfo.com/news/story/37332/24-questions-for-artist-rob-pruitt/). It should be added that both Warhol and Gagosian, early in their careers, were scorned by the more reserved art world for their overtly materialistic approaches. Yet another individual who has a kind of Warholian career trajectory is Jeffrey Deitch. Having been an art dealer for decades, he recently became the director of the Museum of Contemporary Art in Los Angeles. One might argue that the museum board acted in a Warholian manner by making such a leap beyond the conventional museum world in order to create a hybrid director who had both art and business experience.

124. One exception to this characterization is Richard Prince, in "My Warhol: Guns and Poses," *Artforum* 43, no. 2 (October 2004), p. 143, reprinted in this volume on pp. 110–11.

125. Frederic Jameson puts Warhol on page one with regard to the phenomenon of Postmodernism, in *Postmodernism, or, The Cultural Logic of Late Capitalism* (Durham, N.C.: Duke University Press, 1991), p. 1.

126. Gustave Flaubert, quoted in Crone, *Andy Warhol*, p. 22.

127. Oscar Wilde, quoted in Jonathan Dollimore, "Post/Modern: On the Gay Sensibility, or the Pervert's Revenge on Authenticity," in Cleto, ed., *Camp*, p. 221. According to Sontag, "Notes on 'Camp,'" p. 63, the camp artist displays "detachment."

128. Kuspit, *Cult of the Avant-Garde Artist*, p. 66. This writer also describes Warhol as the "archetype postmodernist artist" (idem, p. 71).

129. Doonan, in La Ferla, "The Selling of St. Andy," op cit.

130. Watney, "Queer Andy," p. 22.

131. Bradley W. Bloc[h], "On Art; Where Warhol Failed [1989]," in Pratt, ed., *Critical Response To Andy Warhol*, p. 199; reprinted from *New Leader* 72, no. 6 (March 20, 1989), pp. 22–23.

132. Mark Stevens, "The Endless Fifteen Minutes," *New York* 40, no. 5 (February 12, 2007), pp. 65–66.

133. Roberta Smith, "Art Review; 'Ryan Trecartin': Like Living, Only More So," *New York Times*, June 23, 2011, pp. C25–C26.

134. Peter Schjeldahl, "The Art World; Party On: Ryan Trecartin at P.S. 1," *New Yorker* 87, no. 18 (June 27, 2011), p. 84.

135. See Ariel Levy, "Chasing Dash Snow," *New York* 40, no. 2 (January 15, 2007), p. 24. An article about Bob Dylan (A. O. Scott, "Another Side of Bob Dylan, and Another, and Another . . . ," *New York Times*, November 21, 2007, p. E1) starts: "From Andy Warhol to Lonelygirl15, modern media culture thrives on the traffic in counterfeit selves."

136. Currid, *The Warhol Economy*.

137. "How Art Killed Our Culture," *Jonathan Jones on Art Blog, Guardian*, March 6, 2009, http://www.guardian.co.uk/artanddesign/jonathanjonesblog/2009/mar/06/capitalism-culture-art-market.

PREVIOUSLY PUBLISHED ARTISTS' STATEMENTS

Page 21. Barbara Kruger, "Adoration," *Village Voice*, May 5, 1987, special section, pp. 10–11.

Page 25. Edward Ruscha, in *Andy Warhol: A Retrospective*, by Kynaston McShine et al., exh. cat. (New York: The Museum of Modern Art, 1989), p. 429.

Page 36. Tom Sachs, as told to David Rimanelli, "My Pop," *Artforum* 43, no. 2 (October 2004), p. 269.

Pages 39–40. Cady Noland, "My Warhol: Tin Foiled," *Artforum* 43, no. 2 (October 2004), p. 151.

Page 46. Jean-Michel Basquiat, in *Jean-Michel Basquiat: The Radiant Child*, Tamra Davis, Producer and Director, New York: Arthouse Films, Curiously Bright Entertainment & LM Media, 2010.

Page 81. Maurizio Cattelan, as told to Katy Siegel, "My Warhol: Army of One," *Artforum* 43, no. 2 (October 2004), p. 148.

Page 106. Richard Artschwager, in *Andy Warhol: A Retrospective*, by Kynaston McShine et al., exh. cat. (New York: The Museum of Modern Art, 1989), p. 432.

Pages 110–11. Richard Prince, "My Warhol: Guns and Poses," *Artforum* 43, no. 2 (October 2004), p. 143.

Page 117. Kelley Walker, as told to Bob Nickas, "My Pop," *Artforum* 43, no. 2 (October 2004), p. 173.

Page 138. Takashi Murakami, as told to Katy Siegel, "My Warhol: On the Level," *Artforum* 43, no. 2 (October 2004), p. 155.

INTERVIEW WITH POLLY APFELBAUM

1. Lane Relyea, "A Dozen Paragraphs Scattered Around the Topic of Stains," in *Polly Apfelbaum: What Does Love Have To Do With It*, exh. cat. (Boston: Stephen D. Paine Gallery, Massachusetts College of Art, 2003), p. 35.

2. Libby Lumpkin, "Vive la résistance: Polly Apfelbaum's Vanitas of Painting," in *Polly Apfelbaum*, exh. cat. (Helsinki: Kiasma, Museum of Contemporary Art, 1998), n.p.

INTERVIEW WITH CHUCK CLOSE

1. Roberta Bernstein is currently Emerita Professor of the Art Department at the State University of New York in Albany. Deborah Wye was formerly Chief Curator in the Department of Prints and Illustrated Books at the Museum of Modern Art in New York.

INTERVIEW WITH HANS HAACKE

1. Charles Saatchi, "The Hideousness of the Art World," *Guardian*, December 2, 2011, www.guardian.co.uk/commentisfree/2011/dec/02/saatchi-hideousness-art-world, accessed March 14, 2012.

2. Paul Overy, "The Different Shades of Mao," *Times* (London), March 12, 1974, p. 7.

3. Henry Geldzahler, quoted in Victor Bockris, *The Life and Death of Andy Warhol* (New York: Bantam Books, 1989), p. 266.

4. Kate Sennert, "Hans Haacke Biting the Hand That Feeds Him for Thirty-Five Years," *THEBLOWUP* 4 (Winter 2005), www.theblowup.com/springsummer2006/PASTPRINT/haacke.html, accessed July 19, 2011.

5. Hans Haacke, "Museums: Managers of Consciousness," in *Art Museums and Big Business*, edited by Ian North (Kingston: Art Museums Association of Australia, 1984), p. 33.

INTERVIEW WITH ALFREDO JAAR

1. Interview with Gretchen Berg, 1971. Enno Patalas, *Andy Warhol und seine Filme: Eine Dokumentation* (Munich: Heyne, 1971), p. 18, quoted in Peter-Klaus Schuster, "Warhol and Goya," in *Andy Warhol Retrospective*, by Heiner Bastian et al., exh. cat. (London: Tate Publishers, 2001), p. 55.

INTERVIEW WITH DEBORAH KASS

1. Terry Castle, *The Apparitional Lesbian: Female Homosexuality and Modern Culture* (New York: Columbia University Press, 1993).

INTERVIEW WITH ALEX KATZ

1. Hilton Kramer, "Art; Disciple of Pop School, or Victim: Fischbach Shows Work of the New Alex Katz," *New York Times*, November 27, 1965, p. 27.
2. Frank O'Hara, "Art Chronicle," *Kulchur* 2, no. 6 (Summer 1962), pp. 50–56.
3. Lita [R.] Hornick, *The Green Fuse: A Memoir* (New York: Giorno Poetry Systems, 1989), p. 31.
4. Tony Scherman and David Dalton, *Pop: The Genius of Andy Warhol* (New York: HarperCollins, 2009), p. 153.
5. Warhol met Ted Berrigan (1934–1983) in 1963 at a poetry reading by Frank O'Hara. Berrigan sat for a Warhol *Screen Test* in 1965. See Callie Angell, *Andy Warhol Screen Tests: The Films of Andy Warhol, Catalogue Raisonné*, vol. 1 (New York: Harry N. Abrams; Whitney Museum of American Art, 2006), pp. 37–38.
6. Frank O'Hara, "Alex Katz," *Art and Literature*, no. 9 (Summer 1966), p. 100.
7. Ibid., p. 101.

INTERVIEW WITH JULIAN SCHNABEL

1. According to Bischofberger, he introduced Basquiat to Warhol at the Factory in 1982. Bruno Bischofberger, "Collaborations: Reflections on My Experiences with Basquiat, Clemente, and Warhol," in *Andy Warhol: The Last Decade*, by Joseph D. Ketner II et al., exh. cat. (Milwaukee: Milwaukee Art Museum; New York: DelMonico Books/Prestel, 2009), p. 199.
2. Transcript by Caroline Jones. From "Andy Warhol and Roy Lichtenstein," produced by Lane Slate and Curtis W. David for *U.S.A.: Artists Series*, broadcast on WNET, New York, March 6, 1966.
3. Warhol's *Zeitgeist* series, 1982, was made for a group exhibition "Zeitgeist" at the Martin-Gropius-Bau, Berlin, 1982.
4. "Andy Warhol: Shadows," Heinrich Friedrich Gallery, New York, 1979. Dia acquired *Shadows* from this inaugural exhibition. The complete series was first shown at Dia's Chelsea space at 535 West 22nd Street (December 4, 1998–June 13, 1999). A portion of the series was included in "Warhol Shadows," 1987, The Menil Collection, Houston (Richmond Hall of the Menil Collection was a former Weingarten's grocery store).

INTERVIEW WITH RYAN TRECARTIN

1. Ryan Trecartin, interview with Whitney Ford, "The Q&A: Ryan Trecartin, Video Artist," *Economist: More Intelligent Life*, http://moreintelligentlife.com/blog/whitney-ford/qa-ryan-trecartin, accessed March 19, 2012.

2. Ryan Trecartin, interview with Katie Kitamura and Hari Kunzru, "Ryan Trecartin: In Conversation," *Frieze*, no. 142 (October 2011), http://www.frieze.com/issue/article/ryan-trecartin-in-conversation, accessed March 19, 2012.

INTERVIEW WITH LUC TUYMANS

1. On this maternal theme, see Alison Gass and Paulina Pobacha, "On 'The Reality of the Lowest Rank': Notes on an Exhibition, a Written Exchange," in *The Reality of the Lowest Rank, A Vision of Central Europe*, by Luc Tuymans (Tielt, Belgium: Lannoo, 2010), pp. 64, 74, 80.
2. "[Rice] is first and foremost Secretary of State, and a black female second; a public figure of intimidating flawlessness first, and an individual person second. . . . Through the 'Disney-fication' of American media, she almost becomes the Cinderella of American politics, prepared for the utmost restriction in the spectrum of identity. As we all know in a Walt Disney story, a woman can only be a virgin, a mother, or a villain." Gerrit Vermeiren, *Luc Tuymans: Proper*, exh. cat. (New York: David Zwirner, 2005), p. 19.
3. Dick Morris and Eileen McGann, *Condi vs. Hillary: The Next Great Presidential Race* (New York: ReganBooks, 2005).
4. "The dust cloud simultaneously becomes a veil and a projection screen, a chaotic but sublime mass of disinformation." Vermeiren, *Luc Tuymans*, p. 11.

THE WARHOL EFFECT: A VISUAL ARCHIVE

1. Simon Watney, "The Warhol Effect," in *The Work of Andy Warhol*, edited by Gary Garrels, Dia Art Foundation Discussions in Contemporary Culture, 3 (Seattle: Bay Press, 1989), pp. 115–23. Because of scheduling conflicts, Watney was unable to participate in the symposium in person, and his paper was not delivered there; Gary Garrels, however, included it in the published anthology. See Gary Garrels, "Introduction," in *The Work of Andy Warhol*, p. x.
2. Watney, "Warhol Effect," pp. 116–17.
3. John Russell, "The Season of Andy Warhol: The Artist as Persistent Presence," *New York Times*, April 11, 1988, p. C13; as quoted in Watney, "Warhol Effect," p. 117. As Watney insists, Warhol's posthumous auction is in itself one of Warhol's greatest works: it "makes art of collecting itself, by drawing attention to the institutions which attend collecting (the museum, the auction room, the private gallery, the library, the supermarket), and the effect of the discrete, originating Self which they materialize and perpetuate. . . . [Warhol] made an art of shopping." Watney, "Warhol Effect," p. 121.
4. Watney, "Warhol Effect," p. 121.
5. Douglas Crimp, "Getting the Warhol We Deserve: Cultural Studies and Queer Culture," *Invisible Culture: An Electronic Journal for Visual Studies*, no. 1 (Winter 1998), http://www.rochester.edu/in_visible_culture/issue1/crimp/crimp.html, accessed December 11, 2011.
6. See Richard Bolton, ed., *Culture Wars: Documents from the Recent Controversies in the Arts* (New York: New Press, 1992), for a survey of the various discourses surrounding art-making in the late 1980s and early 1990s.
7. Crimp, "Getting the Warhol We Deserve." Or, as Watney puts it, "Warhol simply cannot be reconciled to the type of the heroic originating Fine Artist required as the price of admission to the Fine Art tradition." Watney, "Warhol Effect," p. 118, quoted in Crimp.
8. Indeed, Warhol exhibited his *Cow* wallpaper for the first time in an otherwise empty room in his 1966 show at the Leo Castelli Gallery; in a way, it *substituted* for painting. See Mark Rosenthal's essay in this volume, p. 130.
9. Bruce Hainley, "Erase and Rewind: Elaine Sturtevant," *Frieze*, no. 53 (June–August 2000), p. 83.
10. "A Conversation with Liza Lou and Lawrence Weschler," in *Liza Lou* (New York: Skira Rizzoli International Publications, 2011), p. 102.
11. Artist's statement on *Medien Kunst Netz*, http://www.medienkunstnetz.de/works/empire24-7/, accessed November 15, 2011.
12. See Karen Rosenberg, "Reviews; Dust Memories, Swiss Institute, New York," *Frieze*, no. 78 (October 2003), p. 127.
13. Jean Wainwright, "Mirror Images: Douglas Gordon Interviewed," *Art Monthly*, no. 262 (December 2002–January 2003), p. 4. This work by Gordon and the Staehle on p. 226 were both installed along with Warhol's original in a small exhibition at the Hirshhorn Museum and Sculpture Garden, Washington, D.C. ("Directions: Empire³," November 10, 2011–February 26, 2012).
14. Ralph Blumenthal and Carol Vogel, "Museum Says Giuliani Knew of Show in July and Was Silent," *New York Times*, October 5, 1999, pp. B1, B8.
15. Sarah Lyall, "Art That Tweaks British Propriety," *New York Times*, September 20, 1997, pp. B7, B14.
16. Steven Heller, "Books in Brief; Snazi Nazis," *New York Times*, March 12, 2000, p. BR22.
17. R. C. Baker, "Girl with Curious Art: An Adventure Up the Hudson To See Rachel Harrison—Plus, Francis Bacon's Strange Scraps," *Village Voice*, July 8–14, 2009, p. 31.
18. Press release for "Rudolf Stingel," Paula Cooper Gallery, New York, February 12–March 12, 2005.
19. The exhibition, in 2006, was for the gallery Power House in Memphis. See his interview with Craig McDean, "15 for '09: Kelley Walker," *Interview* (December 2008–January 2009), pp. 158–59.

A TIMELINE

Note: For decades, scholars have been carefully researching and documenting Andy Warhol's life and art, particularly at The Andy Warhol Museum in Pittsburgh. For an example of the museum's scholarship, see the "About Andy" page on its website at http://www.warhol.org/collection/aboutandy.

1. Tony Scherman and David Dalton, *Pop: The Genius of Andy Warhol* (New York: HarperCollins, 2009), p. 57.
2. Ibid., p. 80.
3. "Art; The Slice-of-Cake School," *Time* 79, no. 19 (May 11, 1962), p. 52.
4. John Coplans, "The New Paintings of Common Objects," *Artforum* 1, no. 6 (November 1962), p. 28.
5. Postcard from Irving Blum to Andy Warhol, June 26, 1962, Andy Warhol Museum Archives, paraphrased in Scherman and Dalton, *Pop*, p. 118. Though Blum himself reports years later that he paid Warhol $1,000 in monthly installments of $100 for the full set of paintings, a postcard from the gallerist to the artist, dated July 23, 1962, Andy Warhol Museum Archives, states a payment of $3,000. I thank Matt Wrbican, archivist at the Warhol Museum, for this information and for his careful review of and contributions to this timeline.
6. Jack Smith, "Of Smith and Men; Soup Can Painter Uses His Noodle," *Los Angeles Times*, July 23, 1962, p. C1.
7. Henry J. Seldis, "In the Galleries; Canadian Impressive in Debut," *Los Angeles Times*, July 13, 1962, p. D6.
8. H[enry] T. H[opkins], "Reviews; Andy Warhol, Ferus Gallery," *Artforum* 1, no. 4 (September 1962), p. 15.
9. Harold Rosenberg, "The Art Galleries; The Game of Illusion," *New Yorker* 38, no. 40 (November 24, 1962), p. 167.
10. T[homas] B. H[ess], "Reviews and Previews; New Realists [Janis]," *ARTnews* 61, no. 8 (December 1962), p. 12.
11. Irving Hershel Sandler, "New York Letter," *Quadrum*, no. 14 (1963), p. 118.

12. Brian O'Doherty, "Art: Avant-Garde Revolt; 'New Realists' Mock U.S. Mass Culture in Exhibition at Sidney Janis Gallery," *New York Times*, October 31, 1962, p. 41; and O'Doherty, "'Pop' Goes the New Art," *New York Times*, November 4, 1962, p. X23.
13. Stuart Preston, "On Display: All-Out Series of Pop Art," *New York Times*, March 21, 1963, p. 8.
14. G[ene]. R. S[wenson], "Reviews and Previews; Andy Warhol [Stable]," *ARTnews* 61, no. 7 (November 1962), p. 15.
15. Dore Ashton, "New York Report," *Das Kunstwerk* 16, no. 5–6 (November–December 1962), pp. 68–73.
16. Michael Fried, "New York Letter," *Art International* 6, no. 10 (December 20, 1962), p. 57.
17. Donald Judd, "In the Galleries; Andy Warhol," *Arts Magazine* 37, no. 4 (January 1963), p. 49.
18. Aline B. Saarinen, "Explosion of Pop Art: A New Kind of Fine Art Imposing Poetic Order on the Mass-Produced World," *Vogue* 141, no. 8 (April 15, 1963), pp. 86–87, 134, 136, 142.
19. "Art; Pop Art—Cult of the Commonplace," *Time* 81, no. 18 (May 3, 1963), p. 72.
20. "New Faces, New Forces, New Names in the Arts," *Harper's Bazaar*, no. 3019 (June 1963), pp. 64–67.
21. Andy Warhol and Pat Hackett, *POPism: The Warhol '60s* (New York: Harcourt Brace Jovanovich, 1980), pp. 35–45.
22. Statement written by Larry Bell, September 1963, in Philip Leider, "Saint Andy: Some Notes on an Artist Who, for a Large Section of a Younger Generation, Can Do No Wrong," *Artforum* 3, no. 5 (February 1965), p. 28.
23. Reva Wolf, *Andy Warhol, Poetry, and Gossip in the 1960s* (Chicago: University of Chicago Press, 1997), pp. 15–33.
24. S[wenson], "Reviews and Previews; Andy Warhol [Stable]," p. 15.
25. Alain Jouffroy in *Warhol: Janvier–février 1964, Ileana Sonnabend*, by Jean-Jacques Lebel et al., exh. cat. (Paris: Ileana Sonnabend, 1964). Translation by the author.

26. Film-Makers' Cinematheque balance book, Andy Warhol Museum Archives, Pittsburgh. Cited in Scherman and Dalton, *Pop*, p. 230.
27. Scherman and Dalton, *Pop*, p. 221.
28. Arthur C. Danto, "The Artworld," *Journal of Philosophy* 61, no. 19 (October 15, 1964), pp. 571–84.
29. Sidney Tillim, "In the Galleries; Andy Warhol [Stable]," *Arts Magazine* 38, no. 10 (September 1964), p. 62.
30. Marcel Duchamp, quoted in Rosalind Constable, "New York's Avant Garde, And How It Got There," *New York Herald Tribune*, May 17, 1964, *New York* [Sunday magazine], p. 10.
31. Barbara Rose, "New York Letter," *Art International* 8, no. 5–6 (Summer 1964), p. 80.
32. William P. MacFarland, Campbell Soup Company, letter to Andy Warhol, May 19, 1964, collection of Billy Name, reproduced in warholstars.org, http://www.warholstars.org/warhol1/13stable.html.
33. Scherman and Dalton, *Pop*, p. 234.
34. Calvin Tomkins, "You think this is a supermarket? No. Hold your hats . . . it's an art gallery; Art or Not, It's Food for Thought," *Life* 57, no. 21 (November 20, 1964), p. 144.
35. "Art; Saint Andrew," *Newsweek* 64, no. 23 (December 7, 1964), pp. 100–103A.
36. T[homas] B. H[ess], "Reviews and Previews; Andy Warhol [Castelli]," *ARTnews* 63, no. 9 (January 1965), p. 11.
37. Tom Wolfe, "The Girl of the Year," *New York Herald Tribune*, December 6, 1964, *New York* [Sunday magazine], pp. 8–11, 67; Kurt Von Meier, "Los Angeles Letter," *Art International* 10, no. 8 (October 20, 1966), p. 44.
38. Shana Alexander, "The Feminine Eye; Report from the Underground," *Life* 58, no. 4 (January 29, 1965), p. 23.
39. Leider, "Saint Andy," pp. 26–28.
40. John S. Waters Jr., letter to the editor, *Life* 58, no. 7 (February 19, 1965), p. 23.
41. Peter Schjeldahl, "The Art World; Warhol in Bloom," *New Yorker* 78, no. 3 (March 11, 2002), pp. 82–84.

42. John Ashbery, "Andy Warhol Causes Fuss in Paris," *International Herald Tribune*, May 18, 1965.
43. John Rublowsky, *Pop Art* (New York: Basic Books, 1965), p. 5.
44. Eliot Fremont-Smith, "Books of the Times; Behind the Maid, a Tire and a Toothpaste Grin," *New York Times*, July 15, 1965, p. 27.
45. Sidney Tillim, "Further Observations on the Pop Phenomenon: 'All revolutions have their ugly aspects . . . ,'" *Artforum* 4, no. 3 (November 1965), pp. 17–19.
46. Roger Vaughan, "Superpop or A Night at the Factory," *New York Herald Tribune*, August 8, 1965, *New York* [Sunday magazine], pp. 6–9.
47. "Society; Edie & Andy," *Time* 86, no. 9 (August 27, 1965), p. 65.
48. The date of the Warhol event has been identified elsewhere as October 29, 1965, but an article in the *New York Herald Tribune* confirms the date as September 29 ("On Videotape . . . From New York . . . The Underground Party That Was," *New York Herald Tribune*, October 3, 1965, section 2, p. 28). Paik's later video display was accompanied by a statement by the artist, "Electronic Video Recorder," that described his Rockefeller Foundation–funded "combination of electronic television and video tape recorder" as the culmination of a years-long dream. The statement is reprinted in *Nam June Paik: Videa 'N' Videology, 1959–1973*, exh. cat. (Syracuse: Everson Museum of Art, 1974), n.p.
49. Archer Winsten, "Reviewing Stand; Andy Warhol at Cinematheque," *New York Post*, February 9, 1966, p. 55.
50. Andy Warhol, ad in "Village Bulletin Board," *Village Voice*, February 10, 1966, p. 2.
51. Victor Bockris, *Warhol: The Biography*, 2nd ed. (1989; Cambridge, Mass.: Da Capo Press, 2003), p. 188.
52. Robert Pincus-Witten, "New York; Andy Warhol, Leo Castelli Gallery," *Artforum* 4, no. 10 (June 1966), p. 52.
53. Shana Alexander, "The Feminine Eye; A Reluctant Pilgrim To Paris," *Life* 61, no. 8 (August 19, 1966), p. 18.

54. David Newman and Robert Benton, "Remember the Sixties?," *Esquire* 66, no. 2 (August 1966), p. 109. Photograph by Frank Bez.
55. Alan Solomon, "Introduction," in *Andy Warhol*, exh. cat. (Boston: Institute of Contemporary Art, 1966), n.p.
56. Von Meier, "Los Angeles Letter," p. 43.
57. Vincent Canby, "'Chelsea Girls' in Midtown Test," *New York Times*, December 1, 1966, p. 56.
58. Dan Sullivan, "Andy Warhol's 'Chelsea Girls' at the Cinema Rendezvous," *New York Times*, December 2, 1966, p. 46; Rosalyn Regelson, "Where Are 'The Chelsea Girls' Taking Us?," *New York Times*, September 24, 1967, p. D15.
59. "Cinema; Nuts from Underground: The Chelsea Girls," *Time* 88, no. 27 (December 30, 1966), p. 37; Jack Kroll, "Movies; Underground in Hell," *Newsweek* 68, no. 20 (November 14, 1966), p. 109.
60. Grace Glueck, "Warhol's World: Life Imitates Art—Sometimes Violently," *New York Times*, June 9, 1968, p. E6.
61. Bosley Crowther, "The Underground Overflows," *New York Times*, December 11, 1966, p. D3.
62. "Cinema; Nuts from the Underground," p. 37.
63. Robert Taylor, "The Roving Eye; Andy Warhol: Derivative Art," October 31, 1966, unidentified newspaper, quoted in Christoph Grunenberg, "The Politics of Ecstasy: Art for the Mind and Body," in *Summer of Love: Art of the Psychedelic Era*, exh. cat. (London: Tate, 2005), p. 32.
64. "Time Essay; What Is Art Today?," *Time* 89, no. 4 (January 27, 1967), pp. 24–25.
65. [Peter Benchley], "Special Report; The Story of Pop: What It Is and How It Came To Be," *Newsweek* 67, no. 17 (April 25, 1966), pp. 56–61.
66. For *Batman*'s deliberate mining of Pop sources, see Sasha Torres, "The Caped Crusader of Camp: Pop, Camp, and the *Batman* Television Series," in *Pop Out: Queer Warhol*, edited by Jennifer Doyle, Jonathan Flatley, and José Esteban Muñoz (Durham, N.C., and London: Duke University Press, 1996), pp. 238–56.
67. Bockris, *Warhol: The Biography*, p. 204.

68. Clement Greenberg, "Where Is the Avant-Garde?," *Vogue* 149, no. 10 (June 1967), p. 113.

69. Paul Bergin, "Andy Warhol: The Artist as Machine," *Art Journal* 26, no. 4 (Summer 1967), p. 363; "Time Essay; What Is Art Today?," pp. 24–25.

70. John Sandberg, "Some Traditional Aspects of Pop Art," *Art Journal* 26, no. 3 (Spring 1967), p. 245.

71. Sandler, "New York Letter," p. 121.

72. Donald Judd, "Black, White and Gray," *Arts Magazine* 38, no. 6 (March 1964), p. 38.

73. H[ess], "Reviews and Previews; Andy Warhol [Castelli]," p. 11.

74. "Helping Barbara Parkins," *Esquire* 68, no. 2 (August 1967), p. 103.

75. "Great Moments of a Decade; The Emergence of Andy Warhol," *Esquire* 68, no. 6 (December 1967), p. 158.

76. Gene Youngblood, "Expanded Cinema," *Los Angeles Free Press*, October 25, 1968, pp. 40–42; Youngblood, "New Warhol at Cinémathèque," *Los Angeles Free Press*, February 16, 1968, p. 12.

77. Howard Thompson, "The Screen; Andy Warhol's 'I, a Man' at the Hudson," *New York Times*, August 25, 1967, p. 28; and Thompson, "Screen; More Warhol: 'Bike Boy' Opens at the Hudson Theater," *New York Times*, October 6, 1967, p. 31.

78. Richard F. Shepard, "Warhol Gravely Wounded In Studio; Actress Is Held," *New York Times*, June 4, 1968, pp. A1, A36; "Actress Shoots Andy Warhol . . . ," *Daily News* (New York), June 4, 1968 (final edition), pp. 1, 3.

79. "New York: Felled by Scum," *Time* 91, no. 24 (June 14, 1968), p. 25.

80. David Bourdon, *Warhol* (New York: Harry N. Abrams, 1989), p. 288.

81. *Time* magazine memo, June 14, 1968. David Bourdon Papers, Archives of American Art, Smithsonian Institution, Washington, D.C., quoted in Scherman and Dalton, *Pop*, p. 426.

82. John Coplans, *Serial Imagery*, exh. cat. (Pasadena, Calif.: Pasadena Art Museum, 1968), pp. 16–17.

83. Robert Mazzocco, "a a a a a a . . . ," *New York Review of Books* 12, no. 8 (April 24, 1969), pp. 34–37.

84. Gilles Deleuze, *Difference and Repetition*, translated by Paul Patton (1968; New York: Columbia University Press, 1994), p. 293.

85. "Winners and Losers, And a Few Suspended Judgments '68," *Life* 66, no. 1 (January 10, 1969), p. 99.

86. John Baxter, *Carnal Knowledge: Baxter's Concise Encyclopedia of Modern Sex* (New York: Harper Perennial, 2009), p. 123. The dialogue and images from *Blue Movie* were published in Andy Warhol, *Blue Movie: A Film* (New York: Grove Press, 1970).

87. "The Sweep of the '60s," *Life* 67, no. 26 (December 26, 1969), p. 27.

88. Barbara Rose, "In Andy Warhol's Aluminum Foil, We All Have Been Reflected," *New York* 4, no. 22 (May 31, 1971), p. 56.

89. John Perreault, "Andy Warhol Disguised Here as Andy Warhol," *Vogue* 155, no. 5 (March 1, 1970), p. 165.

90. John Perreault, "Andy Warhola, This Is Your Life," *ARTnews* 69, no. 3 (May 1970), p. 80.

91. Rainer Crone, *Andy Warhol* (Stuttgart: Hatje Verlag, 1970).

92. John Coplans, with Jonas Mekas and Calvin Tomkins, *Andy Warhol* ([Greenwich, Conn.]: New York Graphic Society, [1970]).

93. Rainer Crone and Wilfried Wiegand, *Die revolutionäre Ästhetik Andy Warhols in Kunst und Film* (Darmstadt: Melzer Verlag, 1972).

94. Michael Ferguson, *Little Joe, Superstar: The Films of Joe Dallesandro* (Laguna Hills, Calif.: Companion Press, 1998), p. 103.

95. Both quoted in ibid., p. 101.

96. Ibid., p. 87.

97. Jean Baudrillard, *The Consumer Society: Myths and Structures*, translated by Chris Turner (1970; Thousand Oaks, Calif.: Sage Publications, 1998). **98.** Jean Baudrillard, *For a Critique of the Political Economy of the Sign*, translated by Charles Levin (1972; St. Louis: Telos Press, 1981), p. 109.

99. Michel Foucault, "Theatrum Philosophicum," in *Language, Counter-Memory, Practice: Selected Essays and Interviews*, translated by Donald F. Bouchard and Sherry Simon (Ithaca, N.Y.: Cornell University Press, 1977), pp. 165–96, originally appeared in *Critique*, no. 282 (November 1970), pp. 885–908.

100. Robert Colacello, "King Andy's German Conquest," *Village Voice*, March 11, 1971, p. 6.

101. Gregory Battcock, "'An Art Your Mother Could Understand,'" *Art and Artists* 5, no. 11 (February 1971), pp. 12–13.

102. Ferguson, *Little Joe, Superstar*, p. 102.

103. Colaciello, "King Andy's German Conquest," p. 6.

104. Harold Rosenberg, "The Art World; Art's Other Self," *New Yorker* 47, no. 17 (June 12, 1971), pp. 101–5.

105. John Canaday, "Brillo Boxes, Red Cows and the Great Soup Can Manipulation . . . ," *New York Times*, May 9, 1971, p. D23.

106. Mary Josephson, "Warhol: The Medium as Cultural Artifact," *Art in America* 59, no. 3 (May–June 1971), pp. 40–46.

107. John Perreault, "Art; Expensive Wallpaper," *Village Voice*, May 13, 1971, p. 27.

108. Joseph Masheck, "Warhol as Illustrator: Early Manipulations of the Mundane," *Art in America* 59, no. 3 (May–June 1971), pp. 54–59.

109. Hilton Kramer, "And Now . . . Pop Art: Phase II," *New York Times*, January 16, 1972, p. D19.

110. Vincent Canby, "Warhol's 'Women in Revolt,' Madcap Soap Opera," *New York Times*, February 17, 1972, p. 30.

111. Bob Colacello, *Holy Terror: Andy Warhol Close Up* (1990; New York: HarperPerennial, 1991), p. 77.

112. Peter Schjeldahl, "What's So Hot About 'Heat'?," *New York Times*, November 26, 1972, p. D12.

113. Stephen Koch, *Stargazer: Andy Warhol's World and His Films* (New York and Washington, D.C.: Praeger Publishers, 1973).

114. Unpublished interview with Jean Stein, 1973. Geldzahler Papers, Beinecke Library, Yale University, New Haven, Connecticut, quoted in Scherman and Dalton, *Pop*, p. 113.

115. Paul Overy, "The Different Shades of Mao," *Times* (London), March 12, 1974, p. 7.

116. Dotson Rader, "Andy's Children: They Die Young," *Esquire* 81, no. 3 (March 1974), p. 168.

117. Viva, quoted in Barbara L. Goldsmith, "La Dolce Viva," *New York* 1, no. 4 (April 29, 1968), p. 40. This important article features photographs by Diane Arbus.

118. Linda Francke, "The Media; The Warhol Tapes," *Newsweek* 83, no. 16 (April 22, 1974), p. 73.

119. Gregory Battcock, "Andy Warhol: New Predictions for Art," *Arts Magazine* 48, no. 8 (May 1974), pp. 34–37.

120. Paul Gardner, "Warhol—From Kinky Sex To Creepy Gothic," *New York Times*, July 14, 1974, p. D11.

121. David Bourdon, "Andy Warhol and the Society Icon," *Art in America* 63, no. 1 (January–February 1975), pp. 42–45.

122. Andy Warhol, "Everything Is Nothing: My Life and Philosophy," *New York* 8, no. 13 (March 31, 1975), pp. 36–42, 47–49.

123. Andy Warhol, *The Andy Warhol Diaries*, edited by Pat Hackett (1989; New York and Boston: Grand Central Publishing, 1991), p. 40.

124. Robert Hughes, "Art; King of the Banal," *Time* 106, no. 5 (August 4, 1975), pp. 65–66.

125. Barbara Goldsmith, "Affectless but Effective: The Philosophy of Andy Warhol," *New York Times*, September 14, 1975, pp. BR4–BR5.

126. Jack Kroll, "Art; Raggedy Andy," *Newsweek* 86, no. 11 (September 15, 1975), p. 69.

127. "New York: Felled by Scum," p. 25.

128. Janet Maslin, "Screen: 'Divine Nymph,' with Laura Antonelli," *New York Times*, October 12, 1979, p. C8.

129. Grace Glueck, "Art People; The Name's Only SoSo, But Loft-Rich TriBeCa Is Getting the Action," *New York Times*, April 30, 1976, p. C15.

130. Annie Leibovitz, "Capturing the Soul: Seven Master Photographers and the Tools of Their Magic Trade," *Rolling Stone*, no. 212 (May 6, 1976), pp. 41–56.

131. Fred Hughes, quoted in Colacello, *Holy Terror*, p. 362.

132. Noel Frackman, "Arts Reviews; Andy Warhol & Jamie Wyeth [Coe Kerr]," *Arts Magazine* 51, no. 1 (September 1976), p. 15.

133. John Russell, "Art: Warhol's Hammer and Sickle," *New York Times*, January 21, 1977, p. C14.

134. Stephen Koch, *Stargazer: The Life, World, and Films of Andy Warhol*, 3rd ed. (1973; New York and London: Marion Boyars, 1991), p. 150.

135. Glenn O'Brien, "Interview: Andy Warhol," *High Times*, August 1977, pp. 20–22, 34, 36, 38, 40, 42.

136. Rebecca Ascher-Walsh, "'Grease' Lightning Strikes Twice," *Entertainment Weekly*, March 20, 1998, pp. 46–49.

137. Heiner Bastian, quoted in Bockris, *Warhol: The Biography*, p. 436.

138. Robert Rosenblum, "Andy Warhol: Court Painter To the 70s," in *Andy Warhol: Portraits of the 70s*, by David Whitney et al., exh. cat. (New York: Random House; Whitney Museum of American Art, 1979), pp. 8–20; Tom Armstrong, "Foreword," in idem, p. 5.

139. Robert Hughes, "Art; Mirror, Mirror on the Wall," *Time* 114, no. 23 (December 3, 1979), p. 73.

140. Hilton Kramer, "Art; Whitney Shows Warhol Works," *New York Times*, November 23, 1979, p. C19.

141. Mary Harron, "Pop Art/Art Pop: The Warhol Connection," *Melody Maker*, February 16, 1980, reprinted in *The Sound and the Fury: A Rock's Backpages Reader, 40 Years of Classic Rock Journalism*, edited by Barney Hoskyns (London: Bloomsbury, 2003), pp. 354–76.

142. Warhol and Hackett, *POPism*; Thomas Sabulis, "Andy Warhol's Pop People," *Boston Globe*, May 8, 1980, Living section, p. 1; Jean Strouse, "Books; The Guru of Gaga: *POPism: The Warhol '60s*," *Newsweek* 95, no. 12 (March 24, 1980), p. 82.

143. Charles F. Stuckey, "Warhol: Backwards and Forwards," *Flash Art*, no. 101 (January–February 1981), p. 10.

144. Jeffrey Deitch, "The Warhol Product," *Art in America* 68, no. 5 (May 1980), p. 9.

145. Peter Schjeldahl, "Warhol and Class Content," *Art in America* 68, no. 5 (May 1980), pp. 112–19.

146. Roland Barthes, "That Old Thing, Art . . . " in *The Responsibility of Forms*, translated by Richard Howard (New York: Hill and Wang, 1985), pp. 204–5. Originally published in *Pop Art: Evoluzione di una generazione* (Venice: Electa Editrice, 1980), pp. 165–70.

147. Edward Lucie-Smith, interview with Andy Warhol, *BBC Radio 4*, March 17, 1981; Tom Zito, "Stepping To the Stereo Strut: On the Run with the Sony Walkman," *Washington Post*, May 12, 1981, pp. B1–B2.

148. Robert Hughes, "The Rise of Andy Warhol," *New York Review of Books* 29, no. 2 (February 18, 1982), pp. 6–10.

149. Thomas Lawson, "Reviews; New York; Andy Warhol," *Artforum* 20, no. 8 (April 1982), p. 75.

150. "Agents Seize Bogus Chateau Mouton Rothschild," *Palm Beach Post*, October 16, 1982, p. B8.

151. James Wolcott, "Buffalo Bill, Won't You Go Out Tonight?," *New York* 17, no. 26 (June 27, 1983), p. 75.

152. Carter Ratcliff, *Andy Warhol*, Modern Masters Series (New York: Abbeville Press, 1983), pp. 103–4.

153. Warhol, *Andy Warhol Diaries*, p. 576.

154. Craig Owens, "East Village '84; Commentary; The Problem with Puerilism," *Art in America* 72, no. 6 (Summer 1984), pp. 162–63.

155. Nicolas A. Moufarrege, "Reviews; New York; Jean-Michel Basquiat, Boone/Werner," *Flash Art*, no. 119 (November 1984), p. 41.

156. Vivien Raynor, "Art: Basquiat, Warhol," *New York Times*, September 20, 1985, p. C22.

157. Robert Hughes, "The Rise of Andy Warhol," in *Art After Modernism: Rethinking Representation*, edited by Brian Wallis (New York: The New Museum of Contemporary Art; Boston: David R. Godine, 1984), pp. 44–57.

158. Rosenberg, "The Art Galleries; The Game of Illusion," p. 167; Jeremy Gilbert-Rolfe, "Popular Imagery," in *Theories of Contemporary Art*, edited by Richard Hertz (Englewood Cliffs, N.J.: Prentice Hall, 1985), p. 130.

159. Carter Ratcliff, "Andy Warhol: Inflation Artist," *Artforum* 23, no. 7 (March 1985), p. 75.

160. Michael Small, "The Beat Goes On, but Famous Artists Are the Top Draw at Area, New York's Super Nightclub," *People* 23, no. 21 (May 27, 1985), pp. 108–10.

161. Martin S. Blinder, "Introduction," in *Warhol: Campbell's Soup Boxes*, exh. cat. (Van Nuys, Calif.: Martin Lawrence Limited Editions, 1986), p. 11.

162. Irving Blum, quoted in Dick Polman, "But Is It Art?," *Philadelphia Inquirer*, November 2, 1985, p. D1.

163. John Taylor, "Andy's Empire: Big Money and Big Questions," *New York* 21, no. 8 (February 22, 1988), p. 39.

164. Daniela Morera, quoted in Colacello, *Holy Terror*, p. 486.

165. Douglas C. McGill, "Andy Warhol, Pop Artist, Dies," *New York Times*, February 23, 1987, pp. A1, A16.

166. William Wilson, "Andy Warhol, Pioneer of '60s Pop Art, Dies," *Los Angeles Times*, February 23, 1987, p. 1.

167. Jesse Kornbluth, "Andy: The World of Warhol," *New York* 20, no. 10 (March 9, 1987), p. 41.

168. Ellen Willis, "The Artist, the Artist, and the Pop Star," *Village Voice*, March 3, 1987, p. 14.

169. Arthur C. Danto, "Who Was Andy Warhol?," *ARTnews* 86, no. 5 (May 1987), p. 131.

170. Peter Schjeldahl in Peter Schjeldahl et al., "Andy Warhol 1928–87," *Art in America* 75, no. 5 (May 1987), p. 137.

171. Michael Welzenbach, "Speakeasy," *New Art Examiner* 14, no. 8 (April 1987), pp. 11–12.

172. Hilton Kramer, "The Death of Andy Warhol," *New Criterion* 5, no. 9 (May 1987), pp. 1–3.

173. Patrick Cayne, "Voice of the People; Green Light for Andy," *Daily News*, March 4, 1987, p. 24.

174. See http://www.warholfoundation.org/foundation/index.html.

175. "The Talk of the Town," *New Yorker* 63, no. 10 (April 27, 1987), p. 27.

176. Thomas Crow, "Saturday Disasters: Trace and Reference in Early Warhol," *Art in America* 75, no. 5 (May 1987), pp. 128–36.

177. D. Keith Mano, "The Gimlet Eye; Warhol," *National Review* 40, no. 1 (January 22, 1988), p. 67.

178. Bradford R. Collins, "The Metaphysical Nosejob: The Remaking of Warhola, 1960–1968," *Arts Magazine* 62, no. 6 (February 1988), pp. 47–55.

179. Donald Kuspit, "Andy's Feelings," *Artscribe International*, no. 64 (Summer 1987), pp. 32–35.

180. Taylor, "Andy's Empire: Big Money and Big Questions," p. 39.

181. Simon Watney, "The Warhol Effect," in *The Work of Andy Warhol*, edited by Gary Garrels, Dia Art Foundation Discussions in Contemporary Culture, 3 (Seattle: Bay Press, 1989), p. 122.

182. Margo Hornblower, "Living; Garage Sale of the Century," *Time* 131, no. 19 (May 9, 1988), p. 90.

183. John Johnston, "Jean Baudrillard Interview," *Art Papers* 13, no. 1 (January–February 1989), pp. 4–5, reprinted as "The End of the End: Interview with John Johnston," in *Baudrillard Live: Selected Interviews*, edited by Mike Gane (London and New York: Routledge, 1993), p. 157.

184. Sanford Schwartz, "Andy Warhol the Painter," *Atlantic Monthly* 264, no. 2 (August 1989), pp. 73–77.

185. Dore Ashton, "Andy Warhol: Pro and Contra — Blinding with Gold Dust," *Art International*, no. 7 (Summer 1989), pp. 67–73; Carter Ratcliff, "Master of Modern Paradox," *Art International*, no. 7 (Summer 1989), pp. 74–83.

186. Bradley W. Bloch, "On Art; Where Warhol Failed," *New Leader* 72, no. 6 (March 20, 1989), pp. 22–23.

187. Thierry de Duve, translated by Rosalind Krauss, "Andy Warhol, or The Machine Perfected," *October*, no. 48 (Spring 1989), pp. 3–14.

188. Arthur C. Danto, "Art; Andy Warhol," *Nation* 248, no. 13 (April 3, 1989), pp. 458–61.

189. "Books of The Times; Warhol on Warhol, as Dictated by Warhol," *New York Times*, June 14, 1989, p. C25; "The Andy Warhol Party Diaries," *National Lampoon* (December 1989), p. 105.

190. Robin Hardy, "Andy Warhol Goes Straight: How the Life of an Artist Who 'Liked the Swish' Is Being Whitewashed," *Advocate*, no. 539 (December 5, 1989), p. 59.

191. Robert Christgau, *Christgau's Consumer Guide: Albums of the '90s* (New York: St. Martin's Press, 2000), p. 264.

192. Michel Nuridsany, "Warhol superstar," *Le Figaro*, June 19, 1990; translation by the author.

193. Michiko Kakutani, "Fighting Against Envelopment by the Mass Mind," *New York Times*, May 28, 1991, p. C15.

194. Annette Michelson, "'Where Is Your Rupture?': Mass Culture and the Gesamtkunstwerk," *October*, no. 56 (Spring 1991), pp. 42–63.

195. Peter Schjeldahl, "Andy Warhol," in *Art of Our Time*, by Alistair Hicks et al., exh. cat. (Edinburgh: Royal Scottish Academy, [1987]), p. 71; Hughes, "Art: Mirror, Mirror on the Wall," p. 73.

196. Bryan Appleyard, "A One-Man Market," *Intelligent Life* (Winter 2011) supplement to *Economist* 400, no. 8757 (October 29, 2011), pp. 18–19.

197. Peter Applebome, "A Year After the War in the Persian Gulf, Joy Is But a Ghost," *New York Times*, January 16, 1992, pp. A1, A20.

198. Paul Alexander, "What Happened To Andy's Treasures?," *New York* 25, no. 4 (January 27, 1992), p. 30.

199. Vicki Goldberg, "Seven Thousand Pictures Are Better Than One," *New York Times*, August 23, 1992, pp. H25, H30.

200. Carol Vogel, "The Art Market; A Financial Hand Joins the Warhol Foundation," *New York Times*, December 11, 1992, p. C6.

201. Kenneth E. Silver, "Modes of Disclosure: The Construction of Gay Identity and the Rise of Pop Art," in *Hand-Painted Pop: American Art in Transition, 1955–62*, by Donna De Salvo et al., exh. cat. (Los Angeles: Museum of Contemporary Art; New York: Rizzoli International, 1992), pp. 193–202; Doyle, Flatley, and Muñoz, eds., *Pop Out: Queer Warhol*.

202. Deborah Kass, interviewed by Holland Cotter, "Art After Stonewall: 12 Artists Interviewed," *Art in America* 82, no. 6 (June 1994), p. 57.

203. Carol Vogel, "The Art Market; Warhol's Slump Leaves Doubts . . . ," *New York Times*, May 21, 1993, p. C24.

204. Frank Rich, "Endpaper; Public Stages: Clintonian Cinema," *New York Times*, March 21, 1993, p. SM76.

205. Dan Shaw, "Bachelor of Arts: Ross Bleckner, Gay Power Broker . . . ," *New York Times*, August 29, 1993, p. V7.

206. Carol Vogel, "Warhol Estate Was Undervalued, Judge Rules," *New York Times*, April 15, 1994, p. B1.

207. Roberta Smith, "The New Warhol Museum: A Shrine for an Iconoclast," *New York Times*, May 26, 1994, pp. C13, C18; Roger Kimball, quoted in Grace Glueck, "A Little Late, Warhol Goes Home To Pittsburgh," *New York Times*, May 1, 1994, pp. H1, H39.

208. Douglas Rushkoff, *Media Virus! Hidden Agendas in Popular Culture* (New York: Ballantine Books, 1994), p. 32.

209. Doris Ammann, quoted in Carol Vogel, "At $3.6 Million, Warhol's 'Marilyn' Is a Star Again," *New York Times*, November 3, 1994, p. C19.

210. Jean Baudrillard, *The Perfect Crime*, translated by Chris Turner (1995; London and New York: Verso, 2008), p. 79.

211. David Kushner, "Listen Up, Talk Radio, This Is the Internet Speaking," *New York Times*, April 13, 1997, pp. 39, 40.

212. Trip Gabriel, "Where Silicon Alley Artists Go To Download," *New York Times*, October 8, 1995, pp. 49, 52.

213. Glenn Collins, "Updating an Icon, Carefully: Campbell Is Adding Some Spice . . . ," *New York Times*, November 17, 1995, pp. D1, D4.

214. Stephen Holden, "Adrift, Fleetingly, in Warhol's World," *New York Times*, April 28, 1996, pp. H17, H39.

215. Janet Maslin, "Film Review; A Postcard Picture of a Graffiti Artist," *New York Times*, August 9, 1996, p. C5.

216. Michiko Kakutani, "The United States of Andy," *New York Times*, November 17, 1996, p. SM34.

217. Philippe Trétiack, *Andy Warhol* (New York: Universe Publishing; Vendome Press, 1997), p. 5.

218. Lisbeth Levine, "Warhol's Influence Still Being Felt In Exhibit, On Runways," *Chicago Tribune*, November 6, 1997.

219. Suzy Menkes, "New York Goes Pop! With Tributes to the World of Warhol," *International Herald Tribune*, November 4, 1997, p. 10; Holland Cotter, "Fluffing Up Warhol: Where Art and Fashion Intersect," *New York Times*, November 7, 1997, pp. E33, E36.

220. "Andy Warhol's Durability," *New York Times*, November 24, 1997, p. A22.

221. Steven Henry Madoff, "Publicist, Prankster, Parvenu, Andy Warhol Was the Pan of Modern Art," *Time* 151, no. 22 (June 8, 1998), p. 77.

222. Monique P. Yazigi, "A Night Out With; Jason Binn, Night Owl With A Curfew," *New York Times*, August 2, 1998, p. ST6.

223. Douglas Crimp, "Getting the Warhol We Deserve," *Social Text*, no. 59 (Summer 1999), pp. 49–66.

224. Peter Schjeldahl, "The Art World; Barbarians at the Gate," *New Yorker* 76, no. 11 (May 15, 2000), p. 104.

225. Philip Leider, interviewed by Amy Newman, "Art/Architecture; An Art World Figure Re-emerges, Unrepentant," *New York Times*, September 3, 2000, pp. AR31–AR32.

226. Mei Fong and Debra Lau, "Earnings From the Crypt," in *Forbes.com*, February 28, 2001, http://www.forbes.com/2001/02/28/crypt.html.

227. Blake Stimson, "Andy Warhol's Red Beard," *Art Bulletin* 83, no. 3 (September 2001), pp. 527–47.

228. Jonathan Jones, "American Beauty," *Guardian*, Weekend section, January 19, 2002, p. 16.

229. Schjeldahl, "The Art World: Warhol in Bloom," pp. 82–84.

230. T. J. Clark, "Modernism, Postmodernism, and Steam," *October*, no. 100 (Spring 2002), pp. 154–74.

231. Tulsa Kinney, "Via Warhol, Lingering Fame—But No Lasting Fortune," *Los Angeles Times*, August 8, 2002, p. E1.

232. Holland Cotter, "Everything About Warhol But the Sex," *New York Times*, July 14, 2002, pp. A1, A32.

233. Amy Cappellazzo, quoted in Thane Peterson, "Are Warhol's 15 Minutes Up?," *Businessweek.com*, October 30, 2002, www.businessweek.com/bwdaily/dnflash/oct2002/nf20021030_8627.htm, accessed November 8, 2010.

234. H.S.H. The Sovereign Prince Rainer III, foreword to *SuperWarhol*, edited by Germano Celant (London: Thames & Hudson, 2003), n.p.

235. Madeleine Brand, "Takashi Murakami, Japan's Andy Warhol," *Day To Day*, NPR Radio, September 15, 2003, http://www.npr.org/templates/story/story.php?storyId=1431797.

236. Daniel Birnbaum, in "Best of 2003: 11 Top Tens," *Artforum* 42, no. 4 (December 2003), p. 124.

237. Michael Rush, *Video Art* (London: Thames & Hudson, 2003), p. 52.

238. Ralph Rugoff, "Kinkade, Warhol, Vallance," in *Thomas Kinkade: Heaven on Earth*, edited by Jeffrey Vallance (San Francisco: Last Gasp, 2004), pp. 13–14.

239. Leah Hoffmann, "Top-Earning Dead Celebrities; Andy Warhol," in *Forbes.com*, October 27, 2005, http://www.forbes.com/2005/10/26/dead-celebrities-earnings_cx_pk_lh_deadceleb05_1027list_4.html.

240. Ruth La Ferla, "The Selling of St. Andy," *New York Times*, October 26, 2006, p. G5.

241. Mark Stevens, "The Endless Fifteen Minutes," *New York* 40, no. 5 (February 12, 2007), pp. 65–66.

242. Jed Perl, "Laissez-Faire Aesthetics: What Money Is Doing To Art, or How the Art World Lost Its Mind," *New Republic* 236 (February 5, 2007), pp. 21–27.

243. "How Art Killed Our Culture," *Jonathan Jones on Art Blog, Guardian*, March 6, 2009, http://www.guardian.co.uk/artanddesign/jonathanjonesblog/2009/mar/06/capitalism-culture-art-market.

244. "The Pop Master's Highs and Lows: Andy Warhol Is the Bellwether," *Economist* 393 (November 28, 2009), p. 9.

245. Eileen Kinsella, "Warhol Inc.," *ARTnews* 108, no. 10 (November 2009), p. 88.

246. David Pilling, "The Perils of Japan's Andy Warhol Politics," *Financial Times*, *FT.com*, September 1, 2010, http://www.ft.com/cms/s/0/1347ab18-b5ff-11df-a048-00144feabdc0.html#axzz1nsO3hjFK.

247. Anders Petterson, "Is the Warhol Market a Proxy for the Art Market?," paper presented at symposium, Artelligence: Understanding Art as an Asset, New York, April 13, 2011.

248. Felix Salmon, "Andy Warhol Datapoints of the Day," *Reuters*, Edition U.S., April 14, 2011, http://blogs.reuters.com/felix-salmon/2011/04/14/andy-warhol-datapoints-of-the-day/.

249. Tommy Hilfiger, speaking on NY1, September 14, 2011. http://www.ny1.com/content/special_reports/fashion_week_2011/147153/diane-von-furstenberg-modernizes-print--tommy-hilfiger-updates-warhol.

250. Appleyard, "A One-Man Market," p. 19.

CHECKLIST OF THE EXHIBITION

Unless otherwise noted, works are on view at both the New York and Pittsburgh venues.

WORKS BY ANDY WARHOL

1. *Before and After [1]*, 1961
Casein on canvas
68 × 54 in. (172.7 × 137.2 cm)
The Metropolitan Museum of Art,
New York
Gift of Halston, 1981 (1981.536.1)
p. 84

2. *Dr. Scholl's Corns*, 1961
Casein and wax crayon on canvas
48 × 40 in. (121.9 × 101.6 cm)
The Metropolitan Museum of Art,
New York
Gift of Halston, 1982 (1982.505)
p. 15

3. *Icebox*, 1961
Oil, ink, and graphite on canvas
67 × 53⅛ in. (170.2 × 134.9 cm)
The Menil Collection, Houston
p. 22

4. *Baseball*, 1962
Silkscreen on canvas
91½ × 82 in. (232.4 × 208.3 cm)
The Nelson-Atkins Museum of Art,
Kansas City, Missouri
Gift of the Guild of the Friends of
Art and other friends of the Museum
(F63-16)
p. 104

5. *Big Campbell's Soup Can, 19¢
(Beef Noodle)*, 1962
Acrylic and graphite on canvas
72 × 54 ½ in. (182.9 × 138.4 cm)
The Menil Collection, Houston
p. 32

6. *A Boy for Meg [2]*, 1962
Casein and graphite on linen
72 × 52 in. (182.9 × 132.1 cm)
National Gallery of Art,
Washington, D.C.
Gift of the International Art
Foundation, through the generosity
of Mr. and Mrs. Burton Tremaine
(1971.87.11)
Pittsburgh only
p. 14

7. *Cagney*, 1962
Screenprint
30 × 40 in. (76.2 × 101.6 cm)
The Museum of Modern Art,
New York
Partial and promised gift of UBS,
2002 (127.2002)
p. 119

8. *Green Coca-Cola Bottles*, 1962
Silkscreen, acrylic, and graphite
on canvas
82⅜ × 57 in. (209.2 × 144.8 cm)
Whitney Museum of American Art,
New York
Purchase, with funds from the
Friends of the Whitney Museum of
American Art (68.25)
p. 30

9. *Marilyn Monroe's Lips*, 1962
Synthetic polymer, silkscreen,
and graphite on canvas
82¾ × 80¾ in. (210.2 × 205.1 cm)
left panel
82¾ × 82⅜ in. (210.2 × 209.2 cm)
right panel
Hirshhorn Museum and Sculpture
Garden, Smithsonian Institution,
Washington, D.C.
Gift of Joseph H. Hirshhorn, 1972
(72.313.A–B)
p. 124–25

10. *Twenty Marilyns*, 1962
Acrylic, silkscreen, and graphite
on canvas
76⅞ × 44⅝ in. (195.3 × 113.3 cm)
Mugrabi Collection
New York only
p. 76

11. *Mona Lisa*, 1963
Acrylic and silkscreen on canvas
44 × 29 in. (111.8 × 73.7 cm)
The Metropolitan Museum of Art,
New York
Gift of Henry Geldzahler, 1965
(65.273)
p. 108

12. *Orange Disaster #5*, 1963
Acrylic, silkscreen, and graphite
on canvas
106 × 81¾ in. (269.2 × 207.6 cm)
Solomon R. Guggenheim Museum,
New York
Purchased with funds contributed by
the Photography Committee, 2005
(2005.68)
p. 42

13. *Silver Liz*, 1963
Spray paint and silkscreen on canvas
40 × 40 in. (101.6 × 101.6 cm)
Dr. George and Vivian Dean
p. 53

14. *Triple Elvis*, 1963
Aluminum paint and silkscreen
on canvas
84 × 72 in. (213.4 × 182.9 cm)
Courtesy Gagosian Gallery
p. 52

15. *Triple Silver Disaster*, 1963
Silver paint and silkscreen on canvas
63⅝ × 83⅛ in. (161.6 × 211.1 cm)
Wadsworth Atheneum Museum of
Art, Hartford, Connecticut
The Ella Gallup Sumner and Mary
Catlin Sumner Collection Fund
New York only
p. 118

16. *Ambulance Disaster*, 1963–64
Silkscreen on canvas
119 × 80⅛ in. (302.3 × 203.5 cm)
The Andy Warhol Museum,
Pittsburgh (1997.1.5)
p. 16

17. *The American Man (Portrait of
Watson Powell)*, 1964
Acrylic and silkscreen on canvas
32¼ × 32 in. (81.9 × 81.3 cm) overall
Des Moines Art Center Permanent
Collections
Gift of Watson Powell (1971.11)
p. 70

18. *Brillo Soap Pads Boxes*, 1964
Silkscreen and enamel on plywood
17 × 17 × 14 in. (43.2 × 43.2 ×
35.6 cm) each of four boxes
The Andy Warhol Museum,
Pittsburgh (1998.1.606, 708, 709,
710)
[not illustrated]

19. *Brillo Soap Pads Box*, 1964
Silkscreen and enamel on plywood
17 × 17 × 14 in. (43.2 × 43.2 ×
35.6 cm)
Gilbert B. and Lila Silverman, Detroit
p. 32

20. *Empire*, 1964
16mm film transferred to DVD in
black-and-white with sound, 8 hr.
5 min.
The Andy Warhol Museum,
Pittsburgh
p. 26

21. *Flowers*, 1964
Acrylic and silkscreen on canvas
24 × 24 in. (61 × 61 cm)
Mugrabi Collection
p. 141

22. *Flowers*, 1964
Acrylic and silkscreen on canvas
24 × 24 in. (61 × 61 cm)
Mugrabi Collection
p. 141

23. *Most Wanted Men No. 2,
John Victor G.*, 1964
Silkscreen on linen
48½ × 37⅛ in. (123.2 × 94.3 cm)
full face
48⅝ × 38½ in. (123.5 × 97.8 cm)
profile
The Andy Warhol Museum,
Pittsburgh
Founding Collection, Contribution
Dia Center for the Arts (2002.4.4a,b)
p. 92

24. *Nine Jackies*, 1964
Acrylic and silkscreen on canvas
65 × 53 × 2 in. (165.1 × 134.6 ×
5.1 cm) overall
The Metropolitan Museum of Art,
New York
Gift of Halston, 1983
(1983.606.14–.22)
p. 55

25. *Red Jackie*, 1964
Acrylic and silkscreen on canvas
40 × 40 in. (101.6 × 101.6 cm)
The Andy Warhol Museum,
Pittsburgh (1998.1.54)
p. 54

26. *Turquoise Marilyn*, 1964
Acrylic and silkscreen on canvas
40 × 40 in. (101.6 × 101.6 cm)
Private collection
New York only
p. 51

27. *Cow Wallpaper*, 1966
Silkscreen on wallpaper
Each sheet: 46 × 28 in.
(116.8 × 71.1 cm)
The Andy Warhol Museum,
Pittsburgh
p. 29

28. *Marlon*, 1966
Silkscreen on canvas
81 × 49½ in. (205.7 × 125.7 cm)
The Andy Warhol Museum,
Pittsburgh (1992.2)
p. 50

29. *Screen Test: Lou Reed*, 1966
16mm film transferred to DVD in
black-and-white, 4 min. 18 sec.
The Andy Warhol Museum,
Pittsburgh
p. 57

30. *Screen Test: Nico*, 1966
16mm film transferred to DVD in
black-and-white, 4 min. 30 sec.
The Andy Warhol Museum,
Pittsburgh
p. 57

31. *Silver Clouds*, 1966
Metalized polyester film with helium
39 × 59 × 15 in. (99.1 × 149.9 ×
38.1 cm) each
The Andy Warhol Museum,
Pittsburgh (1994.13)
p. 134

32. *Self-Portrait*, 1967
Acrylic and silkscreen on canvas
72 × 72 in. (182.9 × 182.9 cm)
Detroit Institute of Arts
Founders Society Purchase,
Friends of Modern Art Fund
p. 85

33. *Self-Portrait*, 1967
Acrylic and silkscreen on canvas
72 × 72 in. (182.9 × 182.9 cm)
Detroit Institute of Arts
Founders Society Purchase,
Friends of Modern Art Fund
p. 85

34. *Flowers*, 1967–68
Acrylic and silkscreen on canvas
115⅛ × 115¾ in. (292.4 × 294 cm)
The Metropolitan Museum of Art,
New York
Gift of Irving Blum, 1985 (1985.426)
p. 141

35. *Flowers*, 1967–68
115¼ × 115⅜ in. (292.7 × 293.1 cm)
Acrylic and silkscreen on canvas
The Metropolitan Museum of Art,
New York
Gift of Mr. and Mrs. Peter M. Brant,
1979 (1979.549)
p. 141

36. *Lonesome Cowboys*, 1968
35mm film transferred to DVD in color with sound, 1 hr. 49 min.
The Andy Warhol Museum, Pittsburgh
p. 101

37. *Mao*, 1973
Synthetic polymer paint and silkscreen on canvas
50⅛ × 42⅜ in. (127.3 × 107.6 cm)
Corcoran Gallery of Art, Washington, D.C.
Gift of the FRIENDS of the Corcoran Gallery of Art
p. 64

38. *Nan Kempner*, 1973
Acrylic and silkscreen on canvas
40 × 40 in. (101.6 × 101.6 cm)
The Andy Warhol Museum, Pittsburgh (1998.1.594)
p. 71

39. *Torso from Behind*, 1977
Acrylic and silkscreen on linen
50 × 42 in. (127 × 106.7 cm)
The Andy Warhol Museum, Pittsburgh (1998.1.442)
p. 93

40. *Oxidation Painting*, 1978
Urine and metallic pigment in acrylic on canvas
76 × 52 in. (193 × 132.1 cm)
The Baltimore Museum of Art
Purchase with funds provided by Esther and Richard Pearlstone through the Pearlstone Family Fund; and partial gift of The Andy Warhol Foundation for the Visual Arts, Inc. (1994.30)
p. 121

41. *Shadows*, 1978
Acrylic on linen
78 × 138 in. (198.1 × 350.5 cm)
The Andy Warhol Museum, Pittsburgh
Founding Collection, Contribution The Andy Warhol Foundation for the Visual Arts, Inc. (1998.1.229)
Pittsburgh only
p. 118

42. *Diamond Dust Joseph Beuys*, 1980
Silkscreen, diamond dust, and synthetic paint on canvas
40 × 40 in. (101.6 × 101.6 cm)
The Hermes Trust, UK, courtesy Francesco Pellizzi
p. 77

43. *Dollar Sign*, 1981
Acrylic and silkscreen on canvas
20 × 16 in. (50.8 × 40.6 cm)
The Andy Warhol Museum, Pittsburgh (1998.1.246)
p. 142

44. *Dollar Sign*, 1981
Acrylic and silkscreen on canvas
20 × 16 in. (50.8 × 40.6 cm)
The Andy Warhol Museum, Pittsburgh (1998.1.251)
p. 142

45. *Dollar Sign*, 1981
Acrylic and silkscreen on canvas
20 × 16 in. (50.8 × 40.6 cm)
The Andy Warhol Museum, Pittsburgh (1998.1.253)
p. 142

46. *Dollar Sign*, 1981
Acrylic and silkscreen on canvas
20 × 16 in. (50.8 × 40.6 cm)
The Andy Warhol Museum, Pittsburgh (1998.1.254)
p. 142

47. *Dollar Sign*, 1981
Acrylic and silkscreen on canvas
20 × 16 in. (50.8 × 40.6 cm)
The Andy Warhol Museum, Pittsburgh (1998.1.255)
p. 142

48. *Dollar Sign*, 1981
Acrylic and silkscreen on canvas
20 × 16 in. (50.8 × 40.6 cm)
The Andy Warhol Museum, Pittsburgh (1998.1.256)
p. 142

49. *Jean-Michel Basquiat*, 1984
Acrylic and silkscreen on canvas
90 × 70 in. (228.6 × 177.8 cm)
The Andy Warhol Museum, Pittsburgh (1998.1.498)
p. 94

50. *Self-Portrait*, 1986
Acrylic and silkscreen on canvas
80 × 80 in. (203.2 × 203.2 cm)
The Metropolitan Museum of Art, New York
Purchase, Mrs. Vera G. List Gift, 1987 (1987.88)
p. 87

WORKS BY OTHER ARTISTS

51. Ai Weiwei
Neolithic Vase with Coca-Cola Logo, 2010
Paint on Neolithic vase (5000–3000 BC)
9¾ × 9¾ × 9¾ in. (24.8 × 24.8 × 24.8 cm)
Mary Boone, New York
New York only
p. 37

52. Polly Apfelbaum
Pink Crush, 2007
Dye on synthetic velvet
Dimensions variable
Collection of the artist, courtesy Lucien Terras Inc., New York
p. 140

53. Cory Arcangel
Super Mario Clouds v2k3, 2003
Hacked Super Mario game cartridge, Nintendo gaming system, projector
Dimensions variable
Whitney Museum of American Art, New York
Purchase, with funds from the Paintings and Sculpture Committee (2005.10)
p. 135

54. Richard Artschwager
Rockefeller Center IV, 1974
Acrylic on Celotex with artist's frame
63⅝ × 52⁹⁄₁₆ in. (161.6 × 133.5 cm)
The Honorable Ann Brown and Mr. Donald Brown
p. 107

55. Richard Avedon
Andy Warhol and members of the Factory: Paul Morrissey, director; Joe Dallesandro, actor; Candy Darling, actor; Eric Emerson, actor; Jay Johnson, actor; Tom Hompertz, actor; Gerard Malanga, poet; Viva, actress; Paul Morrissey; Taylor Mead, actor; Brigid Polk, actress; Joe Dallesandro; Andy Warhol, artist, New York, October 30, 1969, 1969
Printed September 1975
Gelatin silver print
8 × 30 in. (20.3 × 76.2 cm)
The Metropolitan Museum of Art, New York
Gilman Collection, Purchase, Ann Tenenbaum and Thomas H. Lee Gift, 2005 (2005.100.447)
pp. 132–33

56. Richard Avedon
Truman Capote, Writer, New York, December 18, 1974, 1974
Gelatin silver print
41¾ × 32¾ in. (106 × 83.2 cm)
The Metropolitan Museum of Art, New York
Gift of the artist, 2002 (2002.379.67)
New York only
[not illustrated]

57. Richard Avedon
Truman Capote, Writer, New York, December 18, 1974, 1974
Gelatin silver print
10 × 8 in. (25.4 × 20.3 cm)
The Richard Avedon Foundation, New York
Pittsburgh only
[not illustrated]

58. Richard Avedon
John Martin, Les Ballets Trockadero de Monte Carlo, New York, March 15, 1975, 1975
Gelatin silver print
45¾ × 37¼ in. (116.2 × 94.6 cm)
The Metropolitan Museum of Art, New York
Gift of the artist, 2002 (2002.379.78)
New York only
p. 89

59. John Baldessari
Econ-O-Wash, 14th and Highland, National City, Calif., 1966–68
Acrylic and photo emulsion on canvas
59 × 45 in. (149.9 × 114.3 cm)
Courtesy the artist and Marian Goodman Gallery, New York and Paris
p. 34

60. John Baldessari
A Two-Dimensional Surface . . ., 1967
Acrylic on canvas
58 × 67 in. (147.3 × 170.2 cm)
Courtesy the artist and Marian Goodman Gallery, New York and Paris
p. 119

61. John Baldessari
Man and Woman with Bridge, 1984
Gelatin silver prints
14½ × 48 in. (36.8 × 121.9 cm) overall
Ealan and Melinda Wingate
p. 108

62. Matthew Barney
Cremaster 2: The Drone's Cell, 1999
Chromogenic print in artist's acrylic frame
54 × 43 in. (137.2 × 109.2 cm)
Courtesy the artist
p. 44

63. Matthew Barney
Cremaster 3: 1967 Chrysler Imperial, 2002
Chromogenic print in artist's acrylic frame
44 × 54 in. (111.8 × 137.2 cm)
Courtesy the artist
p. 35

64. Jean-Michel Basquiat
Untitled (Head), 1981
Acrylic and oil stick on canvas
81½ × 69¼ in. (207 × 175.9 cm)
The Broad Art Foundation, Santa Monica, California
p. 47

65. Maurizio Cattelan
Stephanie, 2003
Colored pigment, wax, synthetic hair, glass, metal
43⁵⁄₁₆ × 25⁹⁄₁₆ × 16 ⅝ in. (110 × 65 × 42.2 cm)
Mugrabi Collection
p. 80

66. Vija Celmins
Time Magazine Cover, 1965
Oil on canvas
22 × 16 in. (55.9 × 40.6 cm)
Private collection, courtesy Hauser & Wirth
p. 18

67. Chuck Close
Phil, 1969
Synthetic polymer on canvas
108¼ × 84 × 2¾ in. (275 × 213.4 × 7 cm)
Whitney Museum of American Art, New York
Purchase, with funds from Mrs. Robert M. Benjamin (69.102)
New York only
p. 79

68. John Currin
Kissers, 2006
Oil on canvas
23 × 25 in. (58.4 × 63.5 cm)
Private collection
p. 98

100. Barbara Kruger
Esquire, May 1992
Magazine cover
10¾ × 9⅛ in. (27.3 × 23.2 cm)
Private collection
p. 20

101. Barbara Kruger
Newsweek, June 8, 1992
Magazine cover
10¾ × 8 in. (27.3 × 20.3 cm)
Private collection
p. 20

102. Louise Lawler
Pollock and Tureen, Arranged by Mr. and Mrs. Burton Tremaine, Connecticut, 1984
Silver dye bleach print
28 × 39 in. (71.1 × 99.1 cm)
The Metropolitan Museum of Art, New York
Purchase, The Horace W. Goldsmith Foundation Gift, through Joyce and Robert Menschel, and Jennifer and Joseph Duke Gift, 2000 (2000.434)
p. 114

103. Glenn Ligon
Malcolm X (small version 1) #1, 2001
Paint, silkscreen, and gesso on canvas
48 × 36 in. (121.9 × 91.4 cm)
San Francisco Museum of Modern Art
Gift of Anthony and Celeste Meier (2002.127)
p. 66

104. Kalup Linzy
Conversations wit de Churun V: As da Art World Might Turn, 2006
Digital video in color with sound, 12 min. 10 sec.
The Metropolitan Museum of Art, New York
Funds from various donors, 2012
p. 98

105. Sarah Lucas
Hunk of the Year, 1990–92
Four gelatin silver prints
31¾ × 24 in. (80.6 × 61 cm)
Rubell Family Collection, Miami
p. 17

106. Christopher Makos
Lady Warhol, 1981, printed 2012
Gelatin silver print
24 × 20 in. (61 × 50.8 cm)
Courtesy the artist
p. 87

107. Robert Mapplethorpe
Bill Joulis, 1977
Gelatin silver print
20 × 16 in. (50.8 × 40.6 cm)
Robert Mapplethorpe Foundation
p. 96

108. Robert Mapplethorpe
Self Portrait, 1980
Gelatin silver print
20 × 16 in. (50.8 × 40.6 cm)
Robert Mapplethorpe Foundation
p. 92

109. Robert Mapplethorpe
Edythe Broad, 1987
Gelatin silver print
30 × 29 in. (76.2 × 73.7 cm)
The Broad Art Foundation, Santa Monica, California
p. 74

110. Robert Mapplethorpe
Eli Broad, 1987
Gelatin silver print
30 × 29 in. (76.2 × 73.7 cm)
The Broad Art Foundation, Santa Monica, California
p. 74

111. Allan McCollum
Ten Plaster Surrogates #13, 1982–90
Enamel on hydrostone
Dimensions variable
Detroit Institute of Arts
Founders Society Purchase, Friends of Modern Art Fund
p. 130

112. Vik Muniz
Memory Rendering of the Man on the Moon, 1988–90
Gelatin silver print
15⁷⁄₁₆ × 10¹¹⁄₁₆ in. (39.2 × 27.2 cm)
The Metropolitan Museum of Art, New York
Purchase, Anonymous Gift, 1995 (1995.323.1)
p. 18

113. Vik Muniz
Action Photo II (after Hans Namuth), from the series *Pictures of Chocolate*, 1997
Silver dye bleach print
60 × 47½ in. (152.4 × 120.7 cm)
Collection of David and Marlene Persky, Worcester, Massachusetts
p. 115

114. Takashi Murakami
Kaikai Kiki, 2001
Acrylic on canvas over panel
39⅜ × 39⅜ in. (100 × 100 cm)
Collection of Marianne Boesky and Liam Culman, New York
p. 139

115. Takashi Murakami
Cosmos, 2003
Silkscreen on wallpaper
Each sheet: 45½ × 60¼ in. (114.9 × 153 cm)
Courtesy Marianne Boesky Gallery, New York
[not illustrated]

116. Bruce Nauman
Eat/Death, 1972
Neon tubing, clear glass suspension frame
7½ × 25¼ × 2⅛ in. (19.1 × 64.1 × 5.4 cm)
Collection of Angela Westwater, courtesy Sperone Westwater, New York
p. 44

117. Bruce Nauman
OFFICE EDIT I (Fat Chance John Cage), 2001
Single-channel video installation transferred to DVD with color and sound, 51 min. 44 sec.
Courtesy Sperone Westwater, New York
p. 26

118. Cady Noland
Bluewald, 1989–90
Silkscreen on aluminum with flag
72 × 48 × 7 in. (182.9 × 121.9 × 17.8 cm)
Wadsworth Atheneum Museum of Art, Hartford, Connecticut
The Ella Gallup Sumner and Mary Catlin Sumner Collection Fund
p. 60

119. Cady Noland
Untitled (Bin with Octane Boost), 1992–93
Aluminum basket with Octane Boost, Quick Clip, plastic tape, and metal fittings
11 × 12¾ × 12¾ in. (27.9 × 32.4 × 32.4 cm)
Collection of Nancy and Stanley Singer
p. 38

120. Catherine Opie
Dyke, 1992
Silver dye bleach print
40 × 30 in. (101.6 × 76.2 cm)
Private collection
p. 100

121. Nam June Paik
Zen for TV, 1963–75
Altered television set
22¹³⁄₁₆ × 16¹⁵⁄₁₆ × 14³⁄₁₆ in. (57.9 × 43 × 36 cm)
The Museum of Modern Art, New York
The Gilbert and Lila Silverman Fluxus Collection Gift, 2008 (2625.2008)
New York only
p. 122

122. Nam June Paik
Zen for TV, 1963–78
Altered television set
21 × 15½ × 12¼ in. (53.3 × 39.3 × 31.1 cm)
The Hood Museum of Art, Dartmouth College, Hanover, New Hampshire
Gift of the artist in honor of George Maciunas (GM.978.211)
Pittsburgh only
p. 122

123. Elizabeth Peyton
Blue Kurt, 1995
Oil on canvas
20 × 16 in. (50.8 × 40.6 cm)
Private collection, New York
p. 58

124. Sigmar Polke
Porträt Heinz Kluncker (Portrait of Heinz Kluncker), 1964
Dispersion and graphite on canvas
55⅛ × 39⅜ in. (140 × 100 cm)
Constance R. Caplan
New York only
p. 70

125. Sigmar Polke
Plastik-Wannen (Plastic Tubs), 1964
Oil on canvas
37⅜ × 47¼ in. (94.9 × 120 cm)
Private collection, New York
New York only
p. 23

126. Sigmar Polke
Bavarian, 1965
Oil and dispersion on canvas
62¹³⁄₁₆ × 49 in. (159.5 × 124.5 cm)
Private collection
p. 17

127. Sigmar Polke
Hochsitz II (Watchtower II), 1984–85
Silver, silver oxide, and resin on canvas
119¹¹⁄₁₆ × 88⁹⁄₁₆ in. (304 × 225 cm)
Carnegie Museum of Art, Pittsburgh
William R. Scott, Jr. Fund, 1985
Pittsburgh only
p. 48

128. Sigmar Polke
Hochsitz mit Gänsen (Watchtower with Geese), 1987–88
Artificial resin and acrylic on various fabrics
114½ × 114½ in. (290.8 × 290.8 cm)
The Art Institute of Chicago
Restricted gift in memory of Marshall Frankel; Wilson L. Mead Fund (1990.81)
New York only
p. 48

129. Richard Prince
Drink Canada Dry, 1989
Acrylic and silkscreen on canvas
75¼ × 58 in. (191.1 × 147.3 cm)
Collection of Mandy and Cliff Einstein
p. 122

130. Richard Prince
Untitled (Cowboy), 1989
Chromogenic print
50 × 70 in. (127 × 177.8 cm)
The Metropolitan Museum of Art, New York
Purchase, The Horace W. Goldsmith Foundation Gift, through Joyce and Robert Menschel, and Jennifer and Joseph Duke Gift, 2000 (2000.272)
New York only
p. 112

131. Richard Prince
Untitled (Cowboy), 1989
Chromogenic print, exhibition copy
50 × 70 in. (127 × 177.8 cm)
Courtesy of the artist
Pittsburgh only
[not illustrated]

132. Richard Prince and Cindy Sherman
Untitled (Richard Prince and Cindy Sherman), 1980
Two chromogenic prints
20 × 24 in. (50.8 × 61 cm) each
Courtesy Skarstedt Gallery, New York
p. 100

ACKNOWLEDGMENTS

We knew that the success of a complex exhibition such as this one depended on our securing the best examples by Warhol and other artists, and our pursuit of those loans from public collections was helped enormously by the generosity and support of our many colleagues at museums close and far. At the Detroit Institute of Arts, where the exhibition was first conceived, we extend special thanks to Graham Beal, Rebecca Hart, and Michelle Smith, who also assisted with early conversations about the show; and in New York we are in deep obligation to our local colleagues Richard Armstrong, Nancy Spector, and Jodi Myers at the Solomon R. Guggenheim Museum; Glenn D. Lowry, Ann Temkin, Ramona Bannayan, Christophe Cherix, Cora Rosevear, Gretchen Wagner, Lanka Tattersall, and Katherine Alcauskas at the Museum of Modern Art; and Adam Weinberg, Donna de Salvo, Chrissie Iles, Barbi Spieler, Matt Heffernan, and Jane Panetta at the Whitney Museum of American Art.

Farther afield many other professionals assisted us with great kindness and generosity, including Matthew Teitelbaum, Elizabeth Smith, and Alison Beckett at the Art Gallery of Ontario, Toronto; Douglas Druick, James Rondeau, Therese Peskowits, Darrell Green, and Nora Riccio at the Art Institute of Chicago; Doreen Bolger, Jay M. Fisher, Kristen Hileman, and Mandy Bartram at the Baltimore Museum of Art; Fred Bollerer, Philip Brookman, Andrea Romeo Jain, Sarah Newman, and Pam Steel at the Corcoran Gallery of Art, Washington, D.C.; Jeff Fleming and Rose Wood at the Des Moines Art Center; Silvia Wolf and July Sourakli at the Henry Art Gallery, University of Washington, Seattle; Richard Koshalek, Kerry Brougher, and Rebecca Withers at the Hirshhorn Museum and Sculpture Garden, Washington, D.C.; Michael Taylor and Juliette M. Bianco at the Hood Museum of Art, Dartmouth College, Hanover, New Hampshire; Josef Helfenstein and Judy Kwon at The Menil Collection, Houston; Sjarel Ex and Margreet Wafelbakker at the Museum Boijmans Van Beuningen, Rotterdam; Walter Smerling and Marie-Louise Hirschmüller at the Museum Küppersmühle für Moderne Kunst, Duisburg, Germany; Madeleine Grynsztejn and Jude Palmese at the Museum of Contemporary Art, Chicago; Hugh M. Davies and Cameron Yahr at the Museum of Contemporary Art, San Diego; Jeremy Strick, Jed Morse, and Catherine Craft at the Nasher Sculpture Center, Dallas; Julián Zugazagoitia, Jan Schall, Julie Mattson, former director Marc F. Wilson, and former chief curator Deborah Emont Scott at the Nelson-Atkins Museum of Art, Kansas City; Timothy Rub, Peter Barberie, and Carlos Basualdo at the Philadelphia Museum of Art; Neal Benezra, Gary Garrels, Alison Gass, Kelly Parady, Jill Sterrett, Rose Candelaria, and Maria Naula at the San Francisco Museum of Modern Art; Lawrence Rinder, Lucinda Barnes, and Lisa Calden at the University of California, Berkeley Art Museum & Pacific Film Archive; and Susan L. Talbott, Patricia Hickson, and Mary Busick at the Wadsworth Atheneum Museum of Art, Hartford.

As with any project involving a great number of contemporary artists, we are deeply indebted to the special guidance and research assistance we received from galleries around the world, whose distinctive and close relationships with their artists and collectors were a pleasure to see. In particular, we would like to acknowledge those abroad: Ivor Braka of Ivor Braka Ltd., London; Marta Cesteros and Cristina Yagüe at Galería Javier López, Madrid; Franco Noero and Pierpaolo Falone of Galleria Franco Noero, Turin; Iwan Wirth, Angelika Felder, and Laura Bechter at Hauser &

Wirth, Zurich; Timothy Taylor, Cassie Vaughan, and Saskia Goodway of Timothy Taylor Gallery, London — and those in California: Jenny Baie at Rena Bransten Gallery, San Francisco; Anthony Meier and Megan Spencer McConnell at Anthony Meier Fine Arts, San Francisco; and Jennifer Loh at Regen Projects, Los Angeles — as well as the many closer to home in New York, where Warhol's legacy is clearly alive and well: Marianne Boesky, Serra Pradhan, and Adrian Turner at Marianne Boesky Gallery; Mary Boone and Ron Warren at Mary Boone Gallery; Gavin Brown and Lisa Williams at Gavin Brown's Enterprise; James Cohan at James Cohan Gallery; Paula Cooper, Steven Henry, and Kristoffer Haynes at Paula Cooper Gallery; Glenn McMillan at CRG Gallery; Elizabeth Dee at Elizabeth Dee Gallery; Larry Gagosian, Bob Monk, Ealan Wingate, Andy Avisi, Rysia Murphy, Tiffany Stover Tummala, and Michael Cary at Gagosian Gallery; Mary Sabbatino and Bianca Cabrera at Galerie Lelong; Barbara Gladstone, Rosalie Benitez, Lauren Murphy, and Caroline Luce at Gladstone Gallery; Marian Goodman, Lissa McClure, and Catherine Belloy at Marian Goodman Gallery; Cristopher Canizares at Hauser & Wirth; Paul Kasmin, Mark Markin, and P. Hayden Dunbar at Paul Kasmin Gallery; Sean Kelly and Cecile Panzieri at Sean Kelly Gallery; Sukanya Rajaratnam at L&M Arts; Lawrence Luhring, Roland Augustine, Vanessa Critchell, Natalia Sacasa, Tiffany Edwards, and Alexandra Ferrari at Luhring Augustine; Matthew Marks, Jeffrey Peabody, and Ryan Hart at Matthew Marks Gallery; Helene Winer, Janelle Reiring, and Tom Heman at Metro Pictures; Andrea Rosen, Branwen Jones, and Samantha Sheiness at Andrea Rosen Gallery; Per Skarstedt at Skarstedt Gallery; Antonio Homem and Queenie Wong at Sonnabend Gallery; Angela Westwater, Eileen Jeng, Jennifer Burbank, and Jennifer Nichols at Sperone Westwater; Lucien Terras at Lucien Terras, Inc.; Lisa Spellman and Kathryn Erdman at 303 Gallery; and David Zwirner, Angela Choon, and Silva Skenderi at David Zwirner Gallery. We are also enormously grateful to our colleagues at the auction houses, including Amy Cappellazzo — to whom we owe particular thanks for her great expertise — as well as Robert Manley and Dina Amin at Christie's, and Zach Miner and Philae Knight at Phillips & de Pury. Their informed advice on locating lenders for many objects in the show was invaluable.

Countless individuals at other organizations assisted us with myriad requests relating to the exhibition, and it is with deep gratitude that we acknowledge the help of art consultants Sandy Heller and Chloe Geary at the Heller Group, Nancy Rosen and Amy Lehrburger at Nancy Rosen Inc., and Suzanne Modica at Thea Westreich Art Advisory Services; of artist studio managers and assistants Phil Curtis (Baldessari studio), Michael Bellon (Barney studio), Naro Taruishi (Celmins studio), Beth Zopf (Close studio), Claudia Carson (Gober studio), Gary McCraw (Koons studio), Peter Wise (Makos Archive), Eric Brown (Prince studio), Jason Kotara (Sachs studio), Bianca Turetsky (Schnabel studio), and Tommy Simoens (Tuymans studio); of foundations and private-collection support from James Martin and Michelle Franco at the Richard Avedon Foundation; Joanne Heyler, Vicki Gambill, and Maria J. Coltharp of the Broad Art Foundation; Lori Zippay at Electronic Arts Intermix; Laura Satersmoen of the Fisher Family Collection; Elizabeth Gerard and Esty Neuman; Casey Kenyon and Maureen Procureur at LVMH; Joree Adilman and Eugene at the Robert Mapplethorpe Foundation; Anita Sharma and Juan Roselione-Valdez of the Rubell Family Collection; and Georgina Hepburne-Scott, Caroline Hession, Vincent Katz, Alisa Ochoa, George Pineda, Josh Shaddock, Tim Stevens, and Ilene Waterstone.

We are most grateful to the many artists and colleagues whose conversations about the show were invaluable to the forging of our specific approach. For their intellectual support and insight in this context, we thank Arthur Danto, Jeffrey Deitch, John Hanhardt, John Ravenal, Peter Schjeldahl, Allan Schwartzman, Tom Sokolowski, Nancy Spector, Charles Stuckey, and Joel Wachs. A very special thank you is due to Neil Printz, whose deep, unparalleled knowledge of Warhol's work was the greatest boon.

At the Met, many colleagues supported our project tirelessly. We are in special debt to colleagues Malcolm Daniel, Jeff Rosenheim, Douglas Eklund, Meredith Friedman, and Anna Wall in the Department of Photographs, who graciously agreed to lend many examples from their holdings for this show. Jennifer Russell gave wise counsel, as did Martha Deese. Conservation was provided by Isabelle Duvernois and Shawn Digney-Peer for paintings, Kendra Roth for sculpture, Rachel Mustalish and Rebecca Capua for drawings, and Nora Kennedy and her team for photographs. Meryl Cohen and Allison Bosch oversaw the complicated shipping arrangements with grace and good humor, while Mary McNamara assisted her with a successful application for government indemnity. Michael Lapthorn and Connie Norkin provided the dynamic exhibition design and graphics, while Linda Sylling and Patricia Gilkison administered the complicated budget, schedule, and design matters with their usual elegance and unflappability. Our digital media team, including Robin Schwalb, Jessica Glass, and Paul Caro, were invaluable in their assistance with the intricacies of the new media and video that appeared in the show. And in the Department of Modern and Contemporary Art, Christina Rosenberger provided important research while colleagues Kay Bearman, Catherine Brodsky, and Rebecca Tilghman were always available to lend a kind hand at a moment's notice.

Mark Polizzotti, Publisher and Editor in Chief, oversaw the catalogue with enthusiasm along with Michael Sittenfeld, Managing Editor. We were thrilled to have the expert, always professional, and extremely organized Elisa Urbanelli as our editor; she improved so many aspects of this catalogue in her elegant and precise way. Transcriber Denise Rohlfs has a remarkable way with words. Penny Jones was our skillful bibliographer, while Peter Antony and Jennifer Van Dalsen supervised production, corrected the color proofs, and sent the book off to the presses with élan. There would not be a picture in this colorful book were it not for the exhaustive efforts of Jane Tai and her colleagues Crystal Dombrow, Ling Hu, Amelia Kutschbach, and Mary Jo Mace in tracking them all down. The catalogue's outstanding design is due to the talented Roy Brooks of Fold Four, Inc.

Gary Tinterow, formerly Englhard Chairman of the Department of Nineteenth-Century, Modern, and Contemporary Art, was key in shepherding this exhibition through the doors of the Met and, as ever, provided invaluable support and advice on many aspects of the project; and we are grateful to his successor, Sheena Wagstaff, Chairman of Modern and Contemporary Art, for her sage counsel on the final stages of our preparation. We were overjoyed to discover in director Thomas P. Campbell a sincere engagement with contemporary art and send many thanks for his unflagging support of this complicated project from the very beginning.

Our dear colleagues at The Andy Warhol Museum in Pittsburgh, our only other venue for the show and largest lender, were integral to this project from its inception at the Met, and we extend our warmest thanks to director Eric C. Shiner, whose enthusiasm for the project never tired. He was aided in numerable ways by Heather Kowalski, Greg Burchard, Christine Daulton, Geralyn Huxley, Patrick Moore, and Matt Wrbican, who have shown for us in New York great generosity of time and spirit.

Mark Rosenthal, *Guest Curator*
Marla Prather, *Curator*
Ian Alteveer, *Assistant Curator*
Rebecca Lowery, *Research Assistant*
    Department of Modern and Contemporary Art
    The Metropolitan Museum of Art, New York

INDEX

PHOTOGRAPH CREDITS

Front cover, back cover, frontispiece, pages 12 top, bottom, 14 (image courtesy the National Gallery of Art, Washington), 15, 16, 22 (photograph by George Hixon, Houston), 29 top, right, 30 (photograph by Sheldon C. Collins), 32 top, right (photograph by Paul Hester), 32 bottom right (photograph by Robert Hensleigh), 41, 42, 50, 51, 52 (photo courtesy of Gagosian Gallery, New York), 53, 54, 55, 56 (digital image © The Museum of Modern Art / Licensed by SCALA / Art Resource, NY), 64, 70, 71 top, 76, 77, 84, 85 (photographs courtesy The Bridgeman Art Library), 87 top left, top and bottom right, 92 top, 93 top, 94, 101 top, 104 (photograph by Jamison Miller), 108 bottom, right, 113 (photograph courtesy Skarstedt Gallery), 118, 119 bottom (digital image ©The Museum of Modern Art / Licensed by SCALA / Art Resource, NY), 120, 121 (photograph by Mitro Hood), 124, 125, 134, 136 bottom (photograph by Shunk-Kender courtesy the Roy Lichtenstein Foundation), 141, 142, 169 top, 172 top, 175: © 2012 The Andy Warhol Foundation for the Visual Arts, Inc. / Artists Rights Society (ARS), New York

Pages 17 left, 23, 48 top left (photograph © The Art Institute of Chicago) and right, 70 bottom: © 2012 The Estate of Sigmar Polke, Cologne / ARS, New York / VG Bild-Kunst, Bonn

Page 17: © Sarah Lucas

Page 18 left: Courtesy the Artist and Hauser & Wirth, Zurich

Pages 18 right, 115 (image courtesy Rena Bransten Gallery, San Francisco): © Vik Muniz/Licensed by VAGA, New York, NY

Pages 19, 173 top: Courtesy of the Artist

Pages 20 top left and right, 173: © Barbara Kruger

Pages 20 bottom, 32 left, 43, 90 left, 93 bottom: Courtesy of the Artist

Pages 24: © Ed Ruscha

Pages 26, 57 top and middle, 101 top left and right (film stills courtesy of the Andy Warhol Museum, Pittsburgh): © The Andy Warhol Museum, Pittsburgh, a museum of Carnegie Institute. All rights reserved

Pages 26 bottom, 44 (photographs courtesy Sperone Westwater, New York): © 2012 Bruce Nauman / Artists Rights Society (ARS), New York

Pages 27, 29 top left, 31, 59, 68 left, 140: © Jeff Koons

Pages 29 bottom (photograph by Olaf Bergmann, Witten, Germany), 48 bottom, 61, 62, 105: © Gerhard Richter

Pages 33, 65, 72, 172: © 2012 Hans Haacke / Artists Rights Society (ARS), New York / VG Bild-Kunst, Bonn, courtesy Paula Cooper Gallery

Pages 34 top, 108 top, 119, 170: Courtesy of the artist and Marian Goodman Gallery, New York / Paris

Pages 34 bottom, 35 bottom, 44 left (photographs by Chris Winget): © 1999 Matthew Barney / Courtesy Gladstone Gallery, New York and Brussels

Pages 37 top, 220 bottom: © Tom Sachs courtesy Tom Sachs Studio

Page 37 bottom: Courtesy Mary Boone Gallery, New York

Page 38: Courtesy the Artist

Page 45: Photograph © The Art Institute of Chicago

Page 47 (photograph by Douglas M. Parker Studio, Los Angeles): © 2012 The Estate of Jean-Michel Basquiat / ADAGP, Paris / ARS, New York

Pages 49, 73, 78, 174 top: © Alex Katz / Licensed by VAGA, New York, NY

Pages 57 bottom, 68, 100, 109: Courtesy of the Artist and Metro Pictures

Page 58 left: © The Artist courtesy Gavin Brown's enterprise

Page 58 right, top: © 2012 Artists Rights Society (ARS), New York / SIAE, Rome

Page 58 bottom: © Keith Haring Foundation, photograph by Pablo Mason

Page 69 top: Courtesy 303 Gallery, New York

Page 69 bottom: © Luc Tuymans

Pages 74, 75, 92 bottom, 96 bottom: © The Robert Mapplethorpe Foundation, used by permission

Pages 75, 176: © 2012 Julian Schnabel / Artists Rights Society (ARS), New York

Pages 79 (photograph by Sheldon Collins), 171: © Chuck Close, courtesy The Pace Gallery

Page 82: © Wolfgang Tillmans

Pages 89, 132–33: © The Richard Avedon Foundation

Pages 90 right, 96: © Nan Goldin, courtesy Matthew Marks Gallery, New York

Pages 91 top, 227, 238: © 2012 Studio lost but found courtesy Gagosian Gallery

Page 91 bottom: © The Estate of Peter Hujar / Courtesy Matthew Marks Gallery, New York

Page 95: © The Artist; courtesy Timothy Taylor Gallery, London

Pages 97, 136 middle, 139: © Takashi Murakami / Kaikai Kiki Co., Ltd. All rights reserved

Page 98 (photograph by Robert McKeever): © John Currin, courtesy Gagosian Gallery

Page 98: © Kalup Linzy Studio

Page 100 top: © Catherine Opie

Page 100 bottom: Courtesy Richard Prince Studio

Page 101 bottom: © 2012 Artists Rights Society (ARS), New York / ADAGP, Paris

Pages 102, 173: © 2012 Deborah Kass / Artists Rights Society (ARS), New York

Page 103: © Ryan Trecartin

Page 107: © 2012 Richard Artschwager / Artists Rights Society (ARS), New York

Page 112: © Betye Saar, courtesy Michael Rosenfeld Gallery, LLC, New York

Pages 116, 147: © Kelley Walker Courtesy Paula Cooper Gallery, New York

Pages 122 top left (digital image © The Museum of Modern Art / Licensed by SCALA / Art Resource, NY), 122 bottom left: © 2012 Estate of Nam June Paik

Page 122 top right: © Richard Prince, Courtesy Gladstone Gallery, New York and Brussels

Page 123: Courtesy of the artist and Luhring Augustine, New York

Page 128: © 2012 Damien Hirst and Science Ltd. / Artists Rights Society All rights reserved

Page 129: © 2012 Andreas Gursky / Artists Rights Society (ARS), New York / VG Bild-Kunst, Bonn

Page 136 top (photograph by Robert McKeever): © The Artist, courtesy Gagosian Gallery

Page 136 middle: © 1986 Muna Tseng Dance Projects, Inc., New York

Page 140: Courtesy of the artist and Lucien Terras, Inc., New York

Page 169: Courtesy the artist and McKee Gallery, New York

Page 215: © Elaine Sturtevant, courtesy of Sotheby's Picture Library

Page 217: © 2012 Artists Rights Society (ARS), New York / VG Bild-Kunst, Bonn, courtesy Galerie Barbara Weiss

Page 218: © Roy Arden, courtesy Richard Telles Fine Art, Los Angeles

Page 220: Copyright the Artist, courtesy Gavin Brown's enterprise

Page 222: Courtesy the Artist, Pace Gallery, Beijing

Page 224: Courtesy the Artist and Cheim & Read, New York

Page 225: Courtesy the Artist and Blum & Poe, Los Angeles

Page 226: Courtesy Wolfgang Staehle

Page 228: Courtesy Dong-Yoo Kim and Gallery Hyundai, Seoul

Page 229: © 2012 Mickalene Thomas / Artists Rights Society (ARS), New York, courtesy Lehmann Maupin, New York

Page 230: Tom Powell Imaging, Inc., courtesy of Richard Phillips

Page 232: © The Artist, courtesy White Cube, photograph by Stephen White

Page 233: © Piotr Uklański, courtesy Gagosian Gallery

Page 234: © The Artist / courtesy James Cohan Gallery, New York/ Shanghai

Page 235: © Richard Misrach, courtesy Fraenkel Gallery, San Francisco, Marc Selwyn Fine Art, Los Angeles and Pace/MacGill Gallery, New York

Page 236 top: Courtesy the Artist and Sperone Westwater, New York

Page 236 bottom: © Gavin Turk, courtesy Riflemaker London

Page 239: Courtesy the Artist and David Zwirner Gallery, New York

Page 240: Courtesy the Artist and Greene Naftali Gallery, New York

Page 241: © Gillian Wearing courtesy Tanya Bonakdar Gallery

Page 242: © Jim Hodges, courtesy the Artist and Gladstone Gallery

Page 243: Tom Powell Imaging, Inc., courtesy the Artist

Page 248: © Cary Leibowitz

Page 249: © Shepard Fairey/Obey Giant.com

Page 250: Photograph by Alfred Statler

Page 251 top left: Frank Interlandi, courtesy the Los Angeles Times

Page 253: © Artforum, December 1964 [cover]

Page 254 middle bottom: © Burt Glinn, Magnum Photos

Page 255: Courtesy Frank Bez

Page 261 middle bottom (photograph by Carl Fischer): Courtesy New York Magazine

Page 262: Courtesy the Jimmy Carter Library

Page 263: Photograph by Ron Galella

Page 267 middle: Courtesy Jeff Jackson

Page 267 right: © Peter Serling 2012

Page 268 right: © Artforum, April 1987 [cover]

Page 277 left (photograph by Cass Bird): Courtesy New York Magazine

Page 277 middle: © The Economist Newspaper Limited, London 2009

Page 277 right (photograph by Jenny Buhl): Courtesy Pacific Coast News

Page 279 middle (photograph by Peter Michael Dills): Courtesy Getty Images